The New Science of Skin and Scuba Diving

A Project of the Council
for National Cooperation in Aquatics

THE NEW SCIENCE OF SKIN AND SCUBA DIVING

Fourth Revised Edition

Illustrations by JAMES E. YOUNG

ASSOCIATION PRESS • NEW YORK

The New Science of Skin and Scuba Diving

•

•

Association Press, 291 Broadway, New York, N.Y. 10007

•

Fourth Revised Edition

Second Printing—1975

Library of Congress Catalog Card Number: 73-18139

Library of Congress Cataloging in Publication Data

Council for National Cooperation in Aquatics.
The new science of skin and scuba diving.

Published in 1957 and 1959 by Conference for National Cooperation in Aquatics under title: The science of skin and scuba diving; in 1962 by Conference for National Cooperation in Aquatics under title: The new science of skin and scuba diving.

1. Skin diving. 2. Aqualung. I. Conference for National Cooperation in Aquatics. The science of skin and scuba diving. II. Title.

GV840.S78C64 1974 797.2'3 73-18139

International Standard Book Number
Hardbound: 0-8096-1876-1
Paperback: 0-8096-0472-8

Printed in the United States of America

CONTENTS

LIST OF ILLUSTRATIONS

LIST OF TABLES

TEN COMMANDMENTS FOR SAFE DIVING

1. *Be fit.* Have a medical checkup. Be a good swimmer. Exercise regularly. Don't dive if you feel below par.
2. *Get good training.* Reading a book is not enough; enroll in a good course. Learn the facts and procedures of safe diving.
3. *Have good equipment*. Be careful about bargains and don't build it yourself. Keep your equipment in top condition; check it before every dive. Use only tested and approved equipment. Refrain from alteration or untrained adjustment of equipment.
4. *Never dive alone.* Always have a buddy with you under water. Have a tender at the surface whenever possible.
5. *Know the diving area.* Avoid dangerous places and poor conditions. Take whatever special precautions the area requires.
6. *Use a boat, float, or both.* Fly the diver flag. Be able to reach safety fast. If motorboats are in the area, surface only close to your diver flag and with caution. Wear an inflatable vest suitable for the diving activity.
7. *Plan your dive.* Solve the problems in advance. Know decompression rules. Keep track of depth and time. Stick to your plans.
8. *Be ready for emergencies.* Have plans of action ready. Know lifesaving, first aid, and rescue breathing. Have first-aid equipment. Have a diver's I.D. card. Know the location of the nearest recompression chamber.
9. *Beware of breath-holding.* WITH SCUBA: breathe continuously throughout the dive; exhale all the way up on an emergency ascent. WITHOUT SCUBA: avoid excessive "overbreathing" before skin dives; don't overexert; don't push your limit on breath-holding.
10. *Get medical attention* if any abnormality develops during or after a dive. Don't waste time; don't try to "drown the problem." Wear your I.D. card after any dive that might cause bends.

E. H. LANPHIER, M.D.

ABOUT THE CNCA

Purpose

The purpose of the Council for National Cooperation in Aquatics (CNCA) is to provide a setting in which official respresentatives from *national organizations* conducting and/or promoting aquatic activities can come together to:

(1) report on individual agency programs, plans, and projects,
(2) share and discuss common problems,
(3) plan ways of working together on agreed-upon projects,
(4) help advance the broad field of aquatics.

It is the hope that this planning and working together on appropriate and well-defined tasks will bring about a greater understanding among agencies and make it possible to serve a larger number of people more effectively. Such co-operative efforts, added to the independent work carried on continuously by the various agencies, should creatively advance the entire field of aquatics.

Membership

Participation on the CNCA Board of Directors is of two types:

Agency members: Representatives from national organizations that have an interest in aquatics.

Selected consultants: Persons who have particular abilities or interest in aquatics or closely related fields.

Participating National Groups

Amateur Athletic Union of the United States (AAU)
American Academy of Pediatrics (AAP)

American Association for Health, Physical Education, and Recreation (AAHPER)
General representation (AAHPER—staff)
Division for Girls' and Women's Sports (DGWS)
American Camping Association (ACA)
American National Red Cross (ARC)
American Public Health Association (APHA)
American Swimming Coaches Association (ASCA)
Athletic Institute, Inc. (AI)
Boy Scouts of America (BSA)
Boys' Clubs of America (BCA)
Camp Fire Girls, Inc. (CFG)
National Association of Intercollegiate Athletics (NAIA)
National Association of Underwater Instructors (NAUI)
National Board of the Young Women's Christian Association (YWCA)
National Collegiate Athletic Association (NCAA)
National Council of Young Men's Christian Associations (YMCA)
—General representation (YMCA—staff)
—National YMCA Operating Council on Aquatics (NYOCA)
National Federation of State High School Athletic Associations (NFSHSAA)
National Jewish Welfare Board (JWB)
National Recreation and Park Association (NRPA)
National Safety Council (NSC)
National Surf Lifesaving Association of America (NSLSA)
National Swimming Pool Institute (NSPI)
President's Council on Physical Fitness and Sports (PCPFS)
Underwater Society of America (USA)
United States Office of Education (USOE)
United States Power Squadrons (USPS)
United States Public Health Service (USPHS)
Women's National Aquatic Forum (WNAF)

Additional information concerning the CNCA can be obtained by writing to the national offices of the member organizations or to CNCA national headquarters at 51 Clifford Avenue, Pelham, N.Y. 10803.

FOREWORD

The lure of the sea continues to draw divers from many walks of life. The sport diver, the scientist, the commercial diver, the military diver—all require the same basic knowledge.

Man and his ways are pervasive. A scientist in recent months diving under the polar cap reported visibility of 1,000 feet in that pellucid water. Yet ubiquitously, there he found an aluminum beer can and a flashlight battery washed from what distant region, who can say.

If the collected space of the shallow continental shelves of earth represents an area equal to the size of North America, we are reminded nevertheless of the paradox that, often, more is less. As our space tends to shrink in terms of aggravated use and abuse we learn that even the boundless sea has its limits. The precious watery portion of earth has its own special mortality. Lacking an ecological balance we must all perish.

Thus, while the instruments of science take us deeper into the seas and provide far-ranging capabilities for the recreational diver we discern an ever-increasing responsibility for all to share the common requirement of preserving this treasure that is the sea.

Since 1954 the Council for National Cooperation in Aquatics (CNCA) has, with the aid of interested experts from the United States and abroad, continued to conduct workshops and seminars and to revise and publish *The New Science of Skin and Scuba Diving*. Indeed, over the period since 1954 this text has become the recognized authority for sports divers in the United States. As new developments have emerged and been tested they have found their way into the text.

The Council for National Cooperation in Aquatics acknowledges with appreciation the work of the editorial committee and the many interested divers and manufacturers who continue to support and assist in the improvement of this work.

Of the many persons who through the years have begun their diving via this book there are many who have become scientists, along with archaeologists, teachers, students, adventurers, salvage experts, explorers, photographers and just plain diving enthusiasts. CNCA salutes these who have found their place in life via this road.

This book is dedicated to great adventure, to concern for the water environment, and to progress through education and cooperation.

John Fleming
Chairman
Council for National Cooperation in Aquatics

INTRODUCTION

Nineteen years have sped by since the idea for this book first took form. This is the fourth revision. Over a million copies have found their way into the hands of diving students all over this country and in many other parts of the world. Each fresh revision has been based upon changes in both instruction and technology. A whole new generation of divers has come along since the fall of 1954 when the fourth annual meeting of the Council for National Cooperation in Aquatics (CNCA) first considered the need for an authoritative work on diving.

Literally thousands of diving clubs existed in the United States in 1954. Diving was being carried on in lakes, rivers, quarries, mudholes and oceans. The spirit was for adventure. There were few restrictions. Invention was rife. The great scientific thrust into the sea was yet to come. "Inner space" was a term then unborn.

Now in the 1970's we find a greatly expanded emphasis on scientific exploration to abyssal depths. The shallow continental shelves have become known to thousands of divers. Trips to the islands of the Pacific, to South America, the Caribbean, to the Greek isles, to Australia's Great Barrier reef, and to most other remote places of the earth are commonplace. The age of the jet plane has changed our mode of travel as well as most of our ideas concerning distance.

There have been great changes in the technology also. Much is still imperfect but substantial progress has been made. Changeless and immutable, however, are the laws by which man dives. The laws of depth and pressure are the same as they were in 1954. The need for rules of safety and standards for teaching, for air purity, and equipment performance is the same as in 1954. If anything, the years have taught us how important it is to continue to pool our best thinking in the interests of the diving community.

The YMCA developed the first nationally accredited diving course in 1959. It was based on the CNCA standards which the Y had had a large share in developing. In 1960 the National Association of Underwater Instructors (NAUI) followed the example of the YMCA. The Boy Scouts of America adopted the YMCA course early and later added the NAUI course as well.

West Point, Annapolis, the Coast Guard Academy and the Merchant Marine Academy all taught the YMCA standard diving course. Throughout the years this text, *The New Science of Skin and Scuba Diving,* has been used everywhere in the United States as the standard civilian text for diving instruction. An independent survey in 1972 showed it to far surpass in use any other similar text. The success of this effort lies in the willingness of divers to pool their resources, to give time and energy to improve the product, to help keep pace with the changing technology and evolving science of instruction.

While it is impossible to fully acknowledge the contributions of all who in some small way helped, we have tried to record the significant contributions. The small team which makes this revision possible is comprised of Dr. Edward H. Lanphier, M.D., State University of New York at Buffalo, Mr. Loyal G. Goff, National Aeronautics and Space Administration, Wash. D.C., Mr. James E. Young (retired), former White House Police Training Division. These men have labored mightily to make this fourth revision a success. The changes have been substantial, and many months of hard digging are represented here.

Others of the original crew whose trail is still clear are: Captain James T. Wren, formerly of the Panel on Underwater Swimmers of the Committee on Undersea Warfare, National Academy of Science; Wallace Hagerhorst of Wash. D.C.; E. R. Cross, Master Diver; Gilbert Abbe (retired), Medical Gas Division of Southern Oxygen Co., Wash. D.C.; Richard Morris, water safety director for the Red Cross, West Palm Beach, Fla.; William T. Burns, M.D., Long Beach, Cal.; Fred Schwankovsky (deceased), former director of lifesaving and water safety, Long Beach, Cal.; John Moloney, chairman, National YMCA Aquatic Council.

Those who have given a great deal of helpful service this edition include: Jon Hardy, of NAUI, Grand Terrace, Cal.; George Knode, M.D., Williamsport; Joseph Kimber, Silver Spring, Md.; Alan Corey, HM2, USN School U/W Swimmers, Key West, Fla.; William Kessen, West Carollton, Ohio; Robert Geeslin, Tallahassee, Fla.; Juergen Mueller, Wakefield, Mass.; Dustin Leer, Mill Valley, Cal.; Admiral Charles Cundiff, USN (retired), Albuquerque, New Mex.; John Zumbado, Gaithersburg, Md.; James Gregory, Apia, West Samoa; Lowell Collier, Plantation, Fla.; Robert E. Lenhard, Compressed Gas Assn., New York City; Diane Christian, YMCA, New York City; John McAniff, University of Rhode Island.

Acknowledgment is given for permission to reprint the NU-WAY to use the 1970 U.S. Navy Repetitive Dive Tables by Ralph Maruscak of Arora,

CPR

IN BASIC LIFE SUPPORT

FOR UNWITNESSED CARDIAC ARREST

Now that you have completed the training course in cardiopulmonary resuscitation (CPR), you will want to keep this leaflet as a review of what you have learned until you take your next refresher course.

Each year, more than 650,000 Americans die suddenly. There are many causes: poisoning, drowning, suffocation, choking, electrocution and smoke inhalation. But the most common cause of sudden death is heart attack. In some cases of sudden death caused by heart attack, the victim might have been saved. If he had known the usual early warnings of heart attack, if he had gotten to a hospital quickly or if someone near him could have performed CPR, his chances of surviving would have been increased greatly.

The most common signal of a heart attack is:

•• uncomfortable pressure, squeezing, fullness or pain in the center of the chest behind the breastbone.

Other signals may be:

- sweating
- nausea
- shortness of breath, or
- a feeling of weakness

Sometimes these signals subside and return.

Basic CPR, an emergency first aid procedure, may save the life of a victim of cardiac arrest. From your training course, you know it is a simple procedure, as simple as A-B-C, Airway, Breathing and Circulation.

American Heart Association

EMERGENCY MEDICAL SYSTEM

Any victim whom you may resuscitate must be considered to need advanced life support. They will have the best chance of surviving if your community has a total emergency medical system. This includes an efficient communications alert system, such as 911, with public awareness of how or where to call; well trained rescue personnel who can respond rapidly; vehicles that are properly equipped; an emergency facility that is open 24 hours a day to provide advanced life support; and an intensive care section in the hospital for the victims. You should work with all interested agencies to achieve such a system.

Prepared by the Committee on Emergency Cardiac Care.

American Heart Association
7320 Greenville Avenue
Dallas, Texas 75231

Printed by the American Heart Association Communications Division
70-023-A
74-76-1.85MM
6-76-200M

Penna. Acknowledgment is also given the American National Standards Institute for permission to reprint the Z-86 standards which appear in this text. The Z-86 project on Underwater Safety is a further CNCA/ANSI endeavor to provide safe-diving standards for the sport-diving world. We acknowledge with appreciation permission to reprint the U.S. Navy Dive Tables.

The following manufacturers have given of their equipment and help from the beginning: U.S. Divers; Northill Garrett Corporation, The Southern Oxygen Company of Washington D.C.; and Adolf Kiefer of Chicago, Ill.

Dr. Lanphier has again carefully revised his chapter on the medical aspects of diving. As a research scientist of world renown in the field, his work adds a very special dimension to this book. Loyal Goff has enlisted and utilized the help of a dozen experts to improve the physics section. A distinguished scientist, Loyal has striven to clarify and simplify what, for many, may be difficult. James Young has accomplished a herculean task in redrawing many figures and modifying a half dozen sections. A teacher for many years, Jim has brought his great breadth of interest and knowledge to the job and, in the process, has consolidated the suggestions of many other fine teachers.

So, here once more, seventeen years later, this fourth revised edition comes as the testimony of a small team backed by the concern of dozens of interested and competent divers across the world. To all who make this possible, sincere thanks.

The time and energies of all contributors have been given freely in the public interest.

Bernard E. Empleton
Chairman
Editorial Committee

1

BASIC REQUIREMENTS FOR SKIN AND SCUBA DIVING

With or without scuba, diving and underwater swimming make unusual demands on the participant both physically and psychologically. A person will run more than ordinary risks in this kind of activity if he has certain physical defects, if he is not in good general physical condition and "fitness," or if he tends toward emotional instability. If he does not mind accepting the risk, this might be considered his own business. However, he should not expect an organization which sponsors training or other activities in the sports to welcome him with open arms. Sponsorship involves concern (and sometimes some actual responsibility) for an individual's own safety, and instructors and fellow participants also deserve consideration. Both physical condition and swimming ability are important.

Swimming Ability and Watermanship

1. Tread water, feet only, 3 minutes.
2. Swim 300 yards without fins.
3. Tow an inert swimmer 40 yards without fins.
4. Stay afloat 15 minutes without accessories.
5. Swim under water 15 yards without fins—without pushoff.

These requirements are not difficult, but they do indicate a degree of watermanship which would enable an individual in difficulty to help himself without the aid of specialized gear.

Physical Status

A person who gets into trouble in water always endangers his companions to some degree, sometimes very seriously. For the candidate's own good as well as for this reason, most organizations concerned with underwater activities set up some kind of physical standards and insist that each prospective participant be examined by a doctor. Many of them also make an effort to size up whether the candidate is "in shape" or not, either through special fitness tests or in the course of checking his swimming ability. They also remain alert for evidence of psychological difficulties in the course of both testing and training.

From the doctor's standpoint, evaluating a person's fitness for diving, and deciding just where to draw the line on minor or questionable defects, is not an entirely simple matter. Most physicians have had little direct experience with diving problems, and even the best set of "specs" is bound to leave much to the doctor's judgment. There are also important matters which he may have a hard time evaluating unless he has known the candidate for a long time. Episodes in a prospective diver's medical history and factors like psychiatric problems can easily remain undisclosed in a routine examination, and a doctor should not be blamed when such things slip by. The candidate himself, if he is willing to be honest, can help the doctor very much and may be able to do a good part of the "sizing up" job himself. (In the process, he may even spontaneously come to the conclusion that diving is not for him.)

Partly with such possibilities in mind, as well as to save the doctor's time, the suggested medical history and examination forms included in this chapter have a "do it yourself" section and include useful notes for the candidate as well as for the doctor.

Medical History and Examination Forms

TO THE APPLICANT:

You have requested training in an activity which makes considerable demands on your physical condition. Diving with certain defects amounts to asking for trouble—not only for you but for anybody who has to come to your aid if you get into difficulties in the water. For these reasons, the CNCA insists that you have a doctor's OK on your fitness for diving.

You are asked to fill out the Medical History form mainly to save the doctor's time. Not all the questions have a direct bearing on your fitness for diving. Some have to do with medical problems which should be looked into whether they concern diving or not. All are questions the doctor would ask you if he had time.

In many instances, your answers to the questions are more important in determining your fitness than what the doctor can see, hear, or feel when he examines you. Obviously, you must give accurate information, or the whole process becomes a waste of time. The forms will be kept in confidence. However, if you feel that any question amounts to an invasion of your privacy, you may omit the answer *provided that you discuss the matter with the doctor* and that he indicates that you have done so.

If the doctor concludes that diving would involve undue risk for you, remember that he is concerned only with your well-being and safety. Respect his advice.

MEDICAL HISTORY

Name:______________________________ Age:________ yrs. Sex:________

Address:______________________________ Telephone:________________

Height:____________inches Weight:____________pounds

(If answers to the following questions require explanation, use the space labeled "Remarks," giving the number of the question.)

1. Have you had previous experience in diving? Yes___ No___ Have you done any flying? Yes___ No___ If so, did you often have trouble equalizing pressure in your ears or sinuses? Yes___ No___ Can you go to the bottom of a swimming pool without having discomfort in ears or sinuses? Yes___ No___
2. Do you participate regularly in active sports? Yes___ No___ If so, specify what sport(s). If not, indicate what exercise you normally obtain.________________

   ____
3. Have you ever been rejected for service or employment for medical reasons? Yes___ No___ *(If "Yes," explain in Remarks or discuss with doctor.)*
4. When was your last physical examination? Month____________ Year________
5. When was your last chest X ray? Month____________ Year________
6. Have you ever had an electrocardiogram? Yes___ No___ An electroencephalogram (brain wave study)? Yes___ No___

(Check the blank if you have, or ever have had, any of the following. Explain under "Remarks," giving dates and other pertinent information; or discuss with the doctor.)

7. Frequent colds or sore throat ___
8. Hay fever or sinus trouble ___
9. Trouble breathing through nose (other than during colds) ___
10. Painful or running ear, mastoid trouble, broken eardrum ___
11. Asthma or shortness of breath after moderate exercise ___
12. Chest pain or persistent cough ___
13. Spells of fast, irregular, or pounding heartbeat ___
14. High or low blood pressure ___
15. Any kind of "heart trouble" ___
16. Frequent upset stomach, heartburn, or indigestion; peptic ulcer ___
17. Frequent diarrhea. Blood in stools ___
18. Belly or back ache lasting more than a day or two ___
19. Kidney or bladder disease; blood, sugar, or albumin in urine ___
20. Syphilis or gonorrhea ___
21. Broken bone, serious sprain or strain, dislocated joint ___
22. Rheumatism, arthritis, or other joint trouble ___
23. Severe or frequent headaches ___
24. Head injury causing unconsciousness ___
25. Dizzy spells, fainting spells, or fits ___
26. Trouble sleeping, frequent nightmares, or sleepwalking ___
27. Nervous breakdown or periods of marked depression ___
28. Dislike for closed-in spaces, large open places, or high places ___
29. Any neurological condition ___
30. Train, sea, or air sickness ___
31. Alcoholism, or any drug or narcotic habit (including regular use of sleeping pills, stimulants, etc.) ___
32. Recent gain or loss of weight or appetite ___
33. Jaundice or hepatitis ___
34. Tuberculosis ___
35. Diabetes ___
36. Rheumatic fever ___
37. Any serious accident, injury, or illness not mentioned above (*Describe under "Remarks," giving dates.*) ___

REMARKS

____

____

____

____

____

____

____

I certify that I have not withheld any information and that the above is accurate to the best of my knowledge.

Signature: ______________________________

NOTE: A report form (FM-104) of this kind is available from Association Press, 291 Broadway, New York, N.Y. 10007. It is sold only in quantities of 25 copies for $2.50.

Medical Examination of Divers

TO THE PHYSICIAN:

The bearer requests evaluation of his fitness for *diving with breathing apparatus.* He has completed a medical history form (1) that should assist you. Besides assessment of his history, he requires a good general physical examination. Attention to psychiatric status is also indicated. Other procedures are at your discretion *(see below).*

Please bear in mind that diving involves a number of unusual medical considerations (2, 3). The main ones can be summarized as follows:

1. Diving involves *heavy exertion.* (A diver must be in good general health, be free of cardiovascular and respiratory disease, and have good exercise tolerance.)
2. All body air spaces must *equalize pressure* readily. (*Ear* and *sinus* pathology may impair equalization or be aggravated by pressure. Obstructive *lung* disease may cause catastrophic accidents on ascent.)
3. Even momentary *impairment of consciousness* underwater may result in death. (A diver must not be subject to syncope, epileptic episodes, diabetic problems, or the like.)
4. Lack of *emotional stability* seriously endangers not only the diver but also his companions. (Evidence of neurotic trends, recklessness, accident-proneness, panicky behavior, or questionable motivation for diving should be evaluated.)

SUGGESTED ADDITIONAL PROCEDURES: (at physician's discretion)

Routine: Chest film (if none within one year), urinalysis, wbc, hematocrit.
Divers over 40: Electrocardiogram with step test.
Questionable respiratory status: Lung volumes, timed vital capacity.

INOCULATIONS:

Divers often enter polluted water and are subject to injuries requiring anti-tetanus treatment. It is strongly advised that all routine immunizations be kept up to date: tetanus, typhoid, diphtheria, smallpox, poliomyelitis.

- -

(Please detach and return to examinee)

Impression

I have examined ________________________________ and reached the following conclusion concerning his fitness for diving:

_____ *Approval.* (I find no defects that I consider incompatible with diving.)

_____ *Conditional approval.* (I do not consider diving in examinee's best interests but find no defects that present marked risk.)

_____ *Disapproval.* (Examinee has defects that I believe constitute unacceptable hazards to his health and safety in diving.)

The following conditions should be made known to any physician who treats this person for a diving accident (include medical conditions, drug allergies, etc.):

____

____

Signature: ________________________________ M.D.

Address: ________________________________

Date: ________________________________

The following paragraphs, extracted from an article by Dr. E. H. Lanphier ("Medical Progress: Diving Medicine," *N. Eng. J. Med.,* Jan. 17, 1957), may assist you in evaluating the applicant:

"One of the primary considerations is that diving involves *heavy exertion.* Even if a man does not intend to engage in spearfishing or other activities which are obviously demanding, he will sooner or later find himself in situations which tax his strength and endurance. Even the best breathing apparatus increases the work of breathing, and this adds to the problem of exertion under water. Lifting and carrying the heavy equipment on dry land is also hard work. The necessity for *freedom from cardiovascular and respiratory disease* is evident. Individuals who are sound but sedentary should be encouraged to improve their *exercise tolerance* gradually by other means before taking up diving. The influence of exertion on conditions such as diabetes should be considered carefully. It is not reasonable to apply a fixed age limit to sport divers, but *men over 40 deserve special scrutiny.*

"An absolute physical requirement for diving is the *ability of the middle ear and sinuses to equalize pressure changes.* The Navy applies a standard 'pressure test' in a recompression chamber to assess this ability since usual methods of examination have insufficient predictive value unless obvious pathology is present. However, even going to the bottom of a swimming pool will generally tell a man whether his Eustachian tubes and sinus ostia will transmit air readily or not. In the case of middle ear equalization, part of the problem is learning the technique of 'popping your ears.' Presence of *otitis* or *sinusitis* is a definite contraindication for diving, even in a man who can normally equalize pressure. A history of disorders of this sort suggests that diving is unwise; but as in the case of frequent colds or allergic rhinitis, prohibition of diving is not invariably justified. Here, much depends on the individual's common sense and ability to forego diving if he has trouble. A *perforated tympanic membrane* should rule out diving because of the near-certainty of water entering the middle ear. The use of ear plugs presents no solution to any of these problems and is, in fact, strongly contraindicated.

"Any organic *neurological disorder,* or a history of *epileptic episodes* or *losses of consciousness* from any cause, makes diving highly inadvisable. A more difficult problem for the physician to evaluate and handle adroitly arises in the *psychiatric* area. The *motivation* and *general attitude* of some aspirants make safe diving unlikely from the outset; and those individuals who tend to panic in emergencies may well find occasion for doing so in diving. *Recklessness* or *emotional instability* in a diver is a serious liability for his companions as well as for himself."

REFERENCES:

(1) *The New Science of Skin and Scuba Diving.* New York: Association Press, 1974.

(2) Lanphier, E. H. "Medical Progress: Diving Medicine," *New Eng. J. Med.,* 256 (Jan. 17, 1957), 120–30.

(3) Duffner, G. J. "Scuba Diving Injuries, Predisposing Causes and Prevention," *J. Am. Med. Assn.,* 175 (Feb. 4, 1961), 375–78.

2

PHYSICS AS RELATED TO DIVING

Physics is that field of science dealing with matter and energy and their interactions. In this chapter we will explore physical laws and principles only in relationship to the diving environment and the influence of that environment on the diver. No rigorous treatment of the subject will be undertaken. Our objective is to define the diving environment and to learn to cope with it successfully. The extent to which these objectives are achieved and ultimately applied to the practice of diving will be controlling factors in the student's success or failure as a diver.

The subject matter covered includes pressure and the gas laws, temperature, density and viscosity, energy, and optics. Detailed definitions of the terms used are contained in the glossary. Therefore, only general definitions or explanations are used in the text.

The student should become thoroughly familiar with the equations, tables, and charts used in diving calculations. The calculations are not always simple, and practice is required to be able to use them efficiently and effectively. However, speed is not enough. A correct equation properly solved is of no value if it is not the one appropriate to the question being asked.

In carrying out diving calculations, the concept of significant figures will be used. This concept assumes that the last digit of a number is doubtful. Therefore, any answer arrived at is not meaningful beyond the least number of digits contained in one of the factors entering the calculation. For example, if 2.68 is multiplied by 1.9, the product must be 5.1. The 8 in 2.68 indicates the value of that number to be between 2.675 and 2.685, while 1.9 represents a value between 1.85 and 1.95. The product 5.092 must therefore be rounded to 5.1 since the 5 in the product is the only digit whose value is not influenced by at least one doubtful digit.

Gas, Pressure, and the Gas Laws

If a column of air with a cross section of 1 square inch and extending from sea level to the top of the atmosphere could be isolated and weighed, the observed weight would be 14.7 pounds. Since the base of the column is 1 square inch we say that air exerts a pressure of 14.7 pounds per square inch (psi) at sea level. This is also called a standard atmosphere of pressure. Note that the weight in pounds represents mass while pounds per square inch (psi) represents pressure or force per unit area.

If this air column could be separated into two parts, one extending from sea level to 18,000 feet in altitude and the other from 18,000 feet to the top of the atmosphere, and the parts weighed separately, they would weigh the same (7.35 pounds). Since the upper part of the column would be many times longer than the lower part, the obvious and correct assumption is that, due to gravity, one half of the earth's atmosphere is compressed into the first 18,000 feet above sea level. This is shown graphically in Figure 1*a*.

Repeating this type of experiment with a one-square-inch column of water would reveal that the weight of water varies directly with the length of the column. Thus, while air is found to be compressible, water is not, at least for the range of pressures important in diving. From this experiment it will be found that fresh water exerts a pressure of 0.432 pounds per square inch for each foot of depth, while for sea water the corresponding pressure increase is 0.445 psi for each foot of depth.

Since one atmosphere of pressure is 14.7 psi, if we divide that number by the above pressure changes per foot of water we find that there is a pressure change of one atmosphere for each 33 feet of depth in sea water or for each 34 feet in fresh water. The surface of the water supports the weight of the atmosphere above it and transmits the force of this weight directly, so the actual (or absolute) pressure at depth is the pressure calculated from the weight of the water plus the weight of the air. Thus at 33 feet (in sea water) the absolute pressure will be 2 atmospheres, or 29.4 psi. These relationships are shown graphically in Figures 1*b* and 1*c*.

In summary we can state that the pressure exerted by a mass of air is a function of the volume it occupies (a direct consequence of its compressibility), while the pressure exerted by water is a function of the depth at which the pressure measurement is made (the weight of the water above that point plus any pressure exerted on its surface).

In 1610 Robert Boyle reported that, if a given quantity of gas is held at constant temperature, and the volume varied over a wide range, the absolute pressure also varies in such a way that the product of the two variables remains a constant. This relationship, known as Boyle's Law, is expressed mathematically as

$$PV = \text{a constant } (k)$$

If two measurements are made at $P_1 V_1$ and $P_2 V_2$ we can write,

$$P_1 V_1 = k = P_2 V_2$$

or

$$P_1 V_1 = P_2 V_2.$$

This law was taken advantage of in the design of the diver's depth gauge which employs an air bubble in a capillary tube which is open to the water at one end. As the diver descends, the air bubble is compressed by the increased

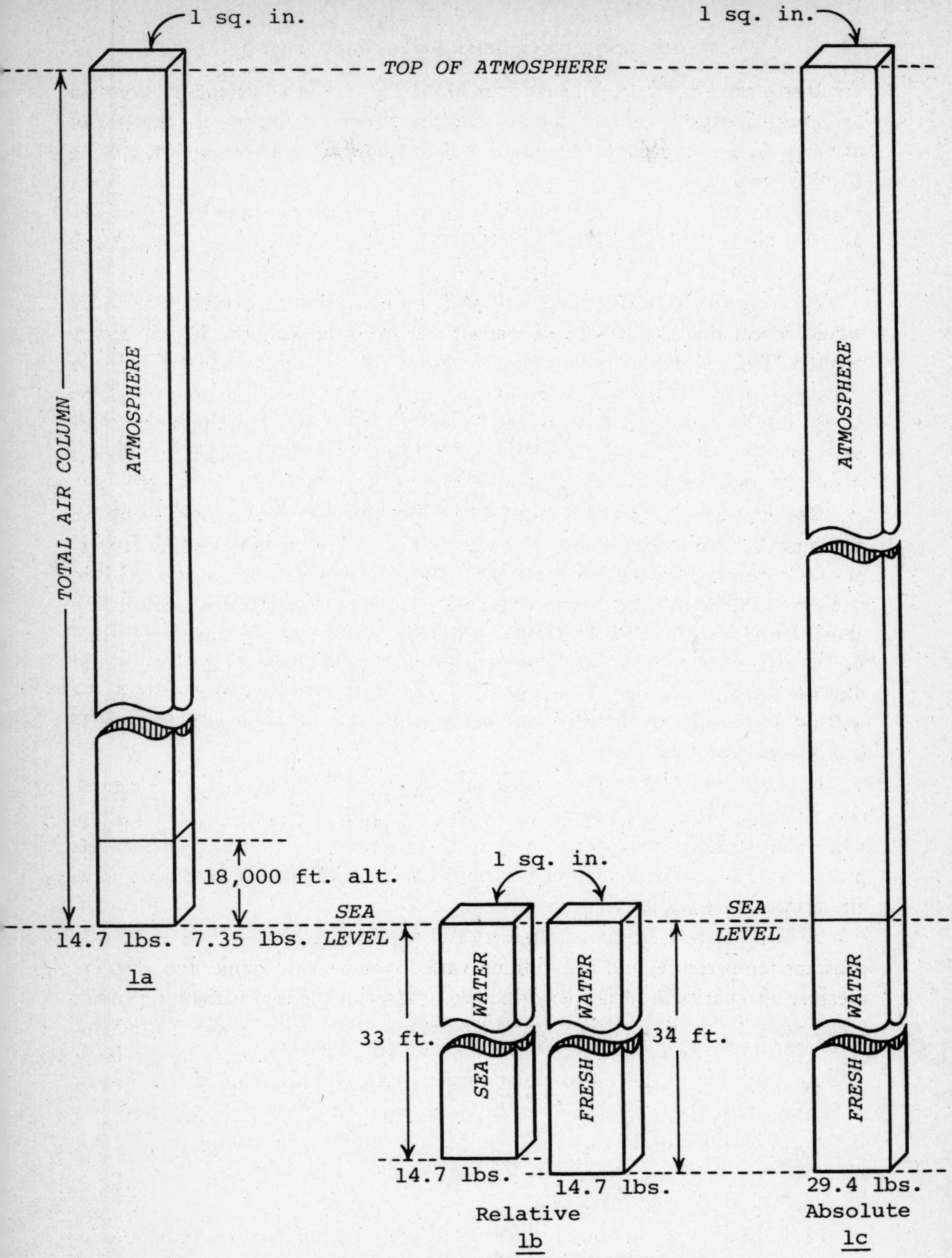

FIGURE 1. WEIGHT OF AIR AND WATER

1*a.* A column of air one inch square extending from sea level to the top of the atmosphere (approximately 60 miles) weighs 14.7 pounds. One half of the weight is contained in the first 18,000 feet of the column. 1*b.* One-inch-square columns of sea and fresh water 33 and 34 feet long respectively weigh 14.7 pounds. 1*c.* At depth, the weight includes both the weight of the air and the water.

pressure at depth. The depth markings along the capillary become progressively closer together at greater depths since the volume V_2 varies as the ratio of P_1 to P_2. This fact is shown by dividing both sides of the above equation by P_2 to give,

$$\frac{P_1}{P_2} V_1 = V_2$$

At the surface both P_1 and P_2 are 1 atmosphere and the bubble is fully extended in the capillary. At a depth of 33 feet (sea water) or 34 feet (fresh water), the pressure P_2 is 2 atmospheres absolute and the ratio $P_1 P_2$ becomes ½. The bubble is therefore compressed to one half of its original volume. At three times this depth, i.e., 99 feet (sea water) or 102 feet (fresh water), the value of P_2 is four atmospheres absolute. The ratio $P_1 P_2$ is now ¼ and the bubble is again reduced in length by one half and is now one quarter of its original length. If a depth gauge of this type is not available, the effect can be demonstrated in a swimming pool with a clear drinking straw. Only a limited pressure change is available but it is enough to demonstrate the principle.

In studying the pressure-volume relationship, it was noted by Boyle that the value of the constant increased with increasing temperature. Not until the end of the nineteenth century, however, did Joseph Gay-Lussac publish his observation that if a given mass of gas is maintained at a constant pressure, the volume varies directly with the absolute temperature. In 1787 Jacques Charles had showed this relationship to be

$$V/T = \text{a constant}$$
$$\text{or } V = kT.$$

If this expression, known as Charles's Law, is combined with Boyle's Law, the resulting expression

$$PV = kT$$

gives the relationship between pressure, volume, and temperature when P and T are expressed in absolute units. The equation has general application only when the amount of gas is defined. If a factor (n) is added to the equation for the amount of gas, and a combined constant (R) for the appropriate factors in the equation, the total expression can be written as,

$$PV = nRT.$$

This is called the Ideal Gas Law.

In using the gas laws, the terms may be expressed in any appropriate units such as psi or atmospheres for pressure, degrees Kelvin or Rankine for temperature, liters or cubic feet for volume, and pounds, mols or grams for amount of gas. The value of R will depend upon the units used for the other terms in the equation. In diving problems, most of the questions involve only pressure and volume (or its time equivalent) changes so that the other factors cancel out and are not used. Except where otherwise indicated, pressures are always expressed in absolute value.

In the range of pressures usually encountered in diving, air can be considered to obey the Ideal Gas Law. Carbon dioxide (CO_2) is more compressible than air and thus does not obey that law. We will consider CO_2 in more detail in the discussion of flotation devices.

The value of 14.7 psi found for air pressure in the experiment described earlier was absolute pressure. The pressure of 14.7 psi at the depth of 33 feet in sea water or 34 feet in fresh water is relative, since the surface of the water is supporting the weight of the air column above it. To convert depth pressure due to the weight of water to the absolute value, 14.7 psi or 1 atmosphere (depending upon the units being used) must be added to it. (See Figure 1*b* and 1*c*.) Pressure gauges used in diving also measure relative pressure, since they are set to read "0" on an empty tank or when exposed directly to the atmosphere. Thus, if a pressure gauge reads 1,500 pounds when attached to a tank it is noted as 1,500 psig. The "g" is added to the notation to indicate gauge pressure. The absolute pressure would be 1,514.7 psia (1500+14.7).

In calculating pressures at depth in water we will use atmospheres (atm) instead of psi. You will recall that there is one atm of pressure change for a change in depth of 33 feet in salt water or 34 feet in fresh water. The fraction of an atmosphere due to depth is thus the number of feet down divided by the depth equivalent to one atmosphere of pressure change. Convert this to absolute by adding 1 for the air pressure above the water. For sea water the expression is

$$P_{(abs)} = 1 + \frac{D}{33}$$

and for fresh water

$$P_{(abs)} = 1 + \frac{D}{34}$$

How much air does a diver carry? This is determined by the volume of the air tank (compressed air cylinder) and the pressure to which it is filled. Diving tanks and their characteristics are discussed in Chapter 4, so we will draw on that information for an example. The tank we will use is marked DOT 3AA 2250 7-67 +. This means that the tank was manufactured* in July 1967 (7-67) according to approved specifications for breathing air cylinders and has a working pressure of 2,250 psig. The "plus" sign means that the tank can be filled to 10% above the rated pressure. If there is no + after the date, no overload filling is permitted.

* Date may be inspection date or manufacture date.

The internal volume of the tank is 0.423 cubic feet (c.f.) which may be determined by either calculating the volume from the internal dimensions or from measuring the volume of water it will hold. How many cubic feet of air will this tank deliver at 1 atmosphere of pressure when it is filled to 2,250 psig? From Boyle's Law we have the relationship $P_1 V_1 = P_2 V_2$.

The "empty" tank contains 0.423 c.f. of air at 14.7 psi. When fully charged it still contains 0.423 c.f. of air but at 2,264.7 psi absolute (2,250 psig + 14.7 psi). Thus P_1 is 2,264.7, P_2 is 14.7, and V_2 is to be determined. Substituting these values in the equation we have

$$2{,}264.7 \times 0.423 = 14.7 \times V_2$$

Divide each side of the equation by 14.7 and solve.

$$\frac{2{,}264.7 \times 0.423}{14.7} = 65.1687\ldots$$

Since the "empty" tank still contains 0.423 c.f. at 14.7 psi we must subtract that amount from the contained volume to determine the delivered volume.

$$\begin{array}{l} 65.169 \text{ (rounded off)} \\ -0.423 \\ \hline 64.746 \end{array}$$

Thus the tank will deliver (to three significant figures) 64.7 c.f. of air which is the rated volume of the example tank chosen. At 10% overpressure (2,250 + 225) of 2,475 psig, the deliverable volume is 71.2 c.f. In the jargon of divers, this tank is frequently referred to as a 72-foot tank although it will not deliver that volume even with the 10% overfill.

If we repeat the calculation of deliverable volumes at a variety of pressures between 0 psig and 2,250 psig and plot the values, we find they will fall on a straight line. In other words a constant volume of gas is delivered for each pound of pressure drop in the tank. Therefore, a simple line graph can be constructed (as in Figure 2) which indicates the available volume of air at any given gauge pressure.

How long will a fully charged tank support a diver? This depends upon the diver, the type of dive, and the depth at which the dive is carried out. Let us look at the diver first.

Divers come in all sizes, shapes and ages, as well as in varying degrees of physical fitness and diving experience, and may be of either sex. All these factors contribute to controlling the metabolic rate, which in turn controls the rate of pulmonary ventilation (amount of air required per unit of time). Persons in good physical condition are generally more efficient in energy utilization, and those with a reasonable amount of subcutaneous fat are better insulated against heat loss in the water, and so on. A beginning diver uses more air than is required, and cold water tends to cause many people to hyperventilate or overbreathe. Thus the "average diver" is more a statistical figure than a real person. The real diver may vary in his breathing requirements depending upon such things as amount (if any) of smoking, rest, anxiety, etc. These factors are discussed in detail in Chapter 3.

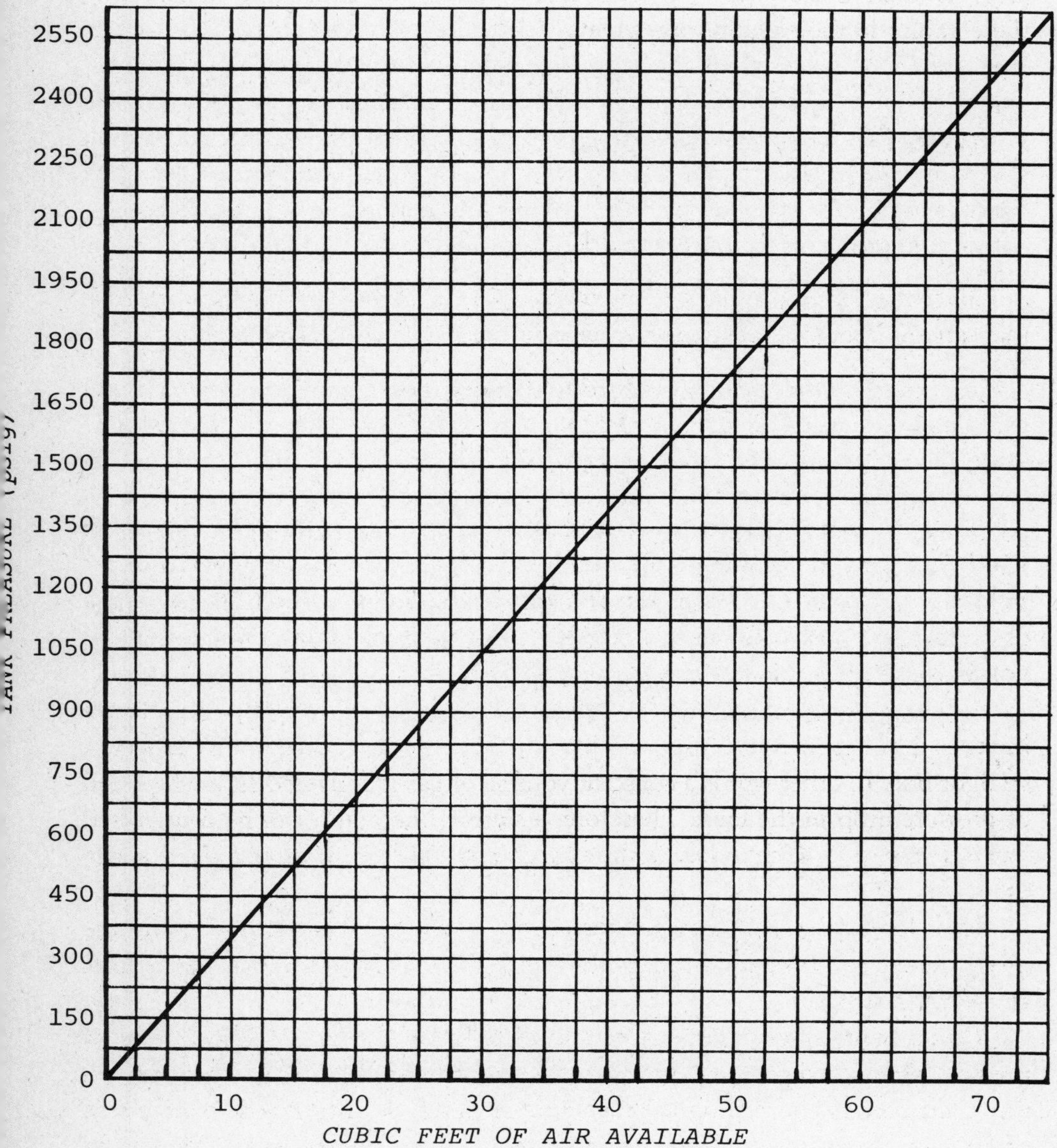

FIGURE 2. AVAILABLE VOLUME OF AIR
Deliverable air volume at sea level from a 71.2-cubic-foot tank @ 2475 psig (10% overpressure).

By type of dive we mean whether or not it is an easy recreational dive or one involving hard work and whether it is in warm or cold water.

The effect of the depth of a dive or available diving time, with a given tank pressure, is a direct consequence of the gas laws. A diver will breathe at the same volume per minute at depth as at the surface. Since the *volume* will be the same, it will take a *larger amount* (mass) of gas to fill that volume at the higher pressures encountered at depth. (There is, in fact, a slight reduction in the volume used at depth, but the difference is small enough that we can ignore it.)

If a diver uses air at a constant rate, then the volumes can be expressed in terms of time. In observing the breathing volumes of a large number of divers the National Association of Underwater Instructors found ranges from about ¼ c.f./min. to 3.0 c.f./min. In another group of observations on experienced male divers in good physical condition and swimming at a moderate rate, the average air consumption was about 1 c.f./min. Thus any reasonable figure can be used for sample problems as long as it is kept in mind that the figure used does not necessarily represent a particular individual. In practice, each diver should know and use the value for his or her breathing requirements for the type of dive planned.

A further consideration is that a dive should never be planned which will completely exhaust a tank. There are two reasons for this: First, the diver should always have a margin of safety. Second, an "empty" tank is more likely to become contaminated than one with a small amount of residual pressure in it. A good practice is to always plan to have about 300 psi remaining in reserve at the end of a dive.

How long can a diver swim at surface pressure on a fully charged tank (71.2 c.f. at 2,475 psig) with 300 psi reserve at the end of the swim? From the graph (Figure 2) we can determine that at 300 psig the deliverable volume is about 8.2 c.f. Therefore, the diver has available,

$$\frac{71.2 - 8.2 \text{ c.f.}}{1 \text{ c.f./min.}} = \frac{63 \text{ c.f.}}{1 \text{ c.f./min.}} = 63 \text{ min.}$$

How long could he dive at a depth of 33 feet in sea water? Since the rate of air consumption is constant, we can safely rewrite Boyle's Law as,

$$P_1 T_1 = P_2 T_2$$

where

$P_1 = 1$ atmosphere
$T_1 =$ time available at the surface
$P_2 =$ depth pressure, and
$T_2 =$ time at depth.

Calculate P_2 substituting

$$1 + \frac{33}{33} = 2 \text{ atm.}$$

we have

$$1x63 = 2 \times T_2$$

or

$$\frac{1x63}{2} = T_2 = 31.5 \text{ min.}$$

Rounding off,

$$T_2 = 31 \text{ min.}$$

(If the decimal had been .6 we would have rounded off to 32 minutes.)

When calculating dive times involving decompression stops, dive time (bottom time) is measured from the beginning of the dive rather than from the time of reaching the desired depth. That practice is followed here for all dives, whether or not decompression stops are required.

How long a dive can be planned at a depth of 40 feet in fresh water using our reference tank with a starting pressure of 1,575 psig? Referring to Figure 2 the tank can deliver about 45 c.f. of air. Subtracting the 300 psig reserve volume of 8.2 c.f. there remains 45 – 8.2 or 36.8 c.f. of air available. At the assumed use rate of 1 c.f./min. the surface time is 36.8 minutes and the dive time is

$$\frac{1}{1+\frac{40}{34}} \times 36.8 = \frac{1}{2.2} \times 36.8 = 16.7 \quad \text{or 17 minutes.}$$

For individual divers, or for the type of dive planned, air consumption may be different from the 1.0 c.f. value we have assumed. In that event, surface time (T) is determined by dividing the volume of air available by the use rate. For example, if a diver will use 0.9 c.f./min., what is his surface time on the example tank with an initial reading of 2,100 psig? Again referring to Figure 2 we have 60 c.f. – 8.2 or 51.8 c.f. available. Time is determined by dividing this volume by the use rate, or

$$T_1 = \frac{51.8 \text{ c.f.}}{0.9 \text{ c.f./min.}} = 57.5 \text{ min.}$$

How long a dive could be planned for a 60-foot depth in fresh water? Since we have already corrected for the reserve,

$$\frac{1}{1+\frac{60}{34}} \times 57.5 = \text{time at depth}$$

or

$$T_2 = \frac{1}{2.76} \times 57.5 = 20.8 = 21 \text{ minutes.}$$

In all these calculations we assume a constant air use rate for a diver and a given type of dive. To determine the surface time for an available air supply we divide the air available by that constant. Thus,

$$T_S = \frac{V}{K}$$

where

T_S = surface time

V = available air supply

and K = use rate.

If we now substitute this into our modified Boyle's Law we have,

$$\frac{P_1 V}{K} = T_2 P_2$$

where

P_1 = 1 atmosphere

V/K = surface time as calculated above

P_2 = depth pressure

and T_2 = time at depth

Divide both sides of the equation by P_2 to give

$$\frac{P_1 V}{P_2 K} = T_2$$

P_1 = surface pressure (1 atmosphere)

P_2 = depth pressure defined by

$$1 + \frac{D \text{ (depth of dive)}}{D' \text{ (depth equivalent to 1 atmosphere)}}$$

V = the volume of air available

K = the diver's use rate

and T_2 = the time at depth

Using these values we can again substitute and rearrange to derive a general equation which fits all cases for a simple dive.

$$T_d = \frac{V}{K\,(1 + D/D')}$$

where

T_d = dive time

V = volume of air available at the surface

K = use rate

D = depth of the dive

and D′ = depth equivalent to 1 atm. pressure change.

For a given depth of water the factor $\frac{1}{1+\frac{D}{D'}}$ is a constant depending upon the value of D′, i.e., fresh or sea water. Therefore, we can calculate factors for ready reference to simplify diving-time calculations. Table I gives the values for 10-foot intervals down to 120 feet. Interpolation of this table for intermediate 5-foot depths introduces an error of about 1% at 15 feet. The error decreases to 0.7% at 45 feet and to 0 at 120 feet. This error is not significant for simple single dives. In more complex dives involving decompression or multiple dive schedules, actual clocked dive time is used. Thus, for dive planning the small error is of no consequence.

TABLE I

PRESSURE RATIO FACTORS FOR CORRECTING SURFACE TIME TO DEPTH TIME

Depth (feet)	*Sea Water* P_D (D/33)	PA (1+D/33)	F (1/1+D/33)	*Fresh Water* P_D (P/34)	PA (1+D/34)	F (1/1+D/34)
0	0	1	1	0	1	1
10	.303	1.30	.768	.294	1.20	.775
20	.606	1.61	.622	588	1.59	.628
30	.909	1.91	.524	.882	1.88	.532
40	1.21	2.21	.453	1.18	2.18	.458
50	1.51	2.51	.398	1.47	2.47	.405
60	1.82	2.82	.355	1.76	2.76	.362
70	2.12	3.12	.320	2.06	3.06	.326
80	2.42	3.42	.292	2.35	3.35	.298
90	2.72	3.72	.269	2.64	3.64	.274
100	3.03	4.03	.248	2.94	3.94	.254
110	3.34	4.34	.230	3.24	4.24	.236
120	3.64	4.64	.216	3.53	4.53	.221

To calculate the time at depth which can be safely planned, multiply the expected (calculated) time at the surface for the available air supply by the appropriate depth factor (F). P_D = calculated water pressure at depth; PA = absolute pressure at depth; and F = factor to calculate time at depth.

Inspection of Table I shows that the factor changes by decreasing amounts as depth increases. In other words, if these values were plotted against depth, the result would not be a straight line. However, since the factor is constant for a given depth, the time available at that depth is a direct function of tank pressure. Thus, time can be plotted as a straight line against pressure for any given depth and for a known air use rate from a tank of known volume. Examples of such a plot are shown in Figure 3 for ocean dives using the tank given in previous examples, and with an assumed air use rate of 1 c.f./min. The figure is based on the deliverable volume between 300 psig and 2,250 psig so that there is 0 time remaining at 300 psig tank pressure. In doing this, the built-in reserve, or safety factor, is already in the value for available time that is read from the curves.

A similar set of lines (or curves) based upon the air capacity of your dive equipment and your air use rate will simplify your dive-time calculations at the dive site. Remember that the slope of the lines may vary with the type of dive, i.e., they will be steeper for a hard-working situation than for an easy dive.

To construct such a figure, determine the time available (at the surface) on your equipment based upon its air volume when fully charged and whatever reserve pressure you wish to retain. In this case, the time is 56.5 minutes with a reserve of 300 psi, and this is shown as point 1 on the surface line. Place the point at the intersection of the full-pressure and available-time lines and draw a straight line from that point to the lower left-hand corner of the graph. Next select the appropriate factor for the depth for any other line you wish to add to the figure, and multiply it by your value at point 1 to get the depth time available with a full tank. Spot that point as for point 1 and draw the new line. In Figure 3, points 2 and 3 were obtained by multiplying point 1 by 0.768 and 0.622 respectively, which are the sea-water factors for 10 and 20 feet respectively as given in Table I. Be sure to note on each line, the depth for which it was drawn. To use the curves, first determine the pressure in the tank; then follow across the graph from that pressure value on the left side to the line for the depth to which you plan to dive, and read the time available on the scale at the bottom of the graph directly below the intersection of the pressure reading and the depth line. Figure 3 will be used for some examples.

Example 1. If the example tank is gauged at 1,750 psig, how long a dive could be made at a depth of 20 feet? Find the point where the 1,750 psig pressure line (between 17 and 18 on the left-hand margin) intersects the 20-feet-depth line (point 4) and read the time on the bottom of the graph directly below this point. The time is 26 minutes.

Such a family of lines is useful in calculating multilevel dive times.

Example 2. With an initial charge of 2,200 psig can the diver make a dive to 80 feet (point 5) for 10 minutes and then spend 20 minutes at 10 feet before surfacing? The time below point 5 indicates 16 minutes are available at 80 feet. After 10 minutes there are thus 6 minutes remaining at that depth.

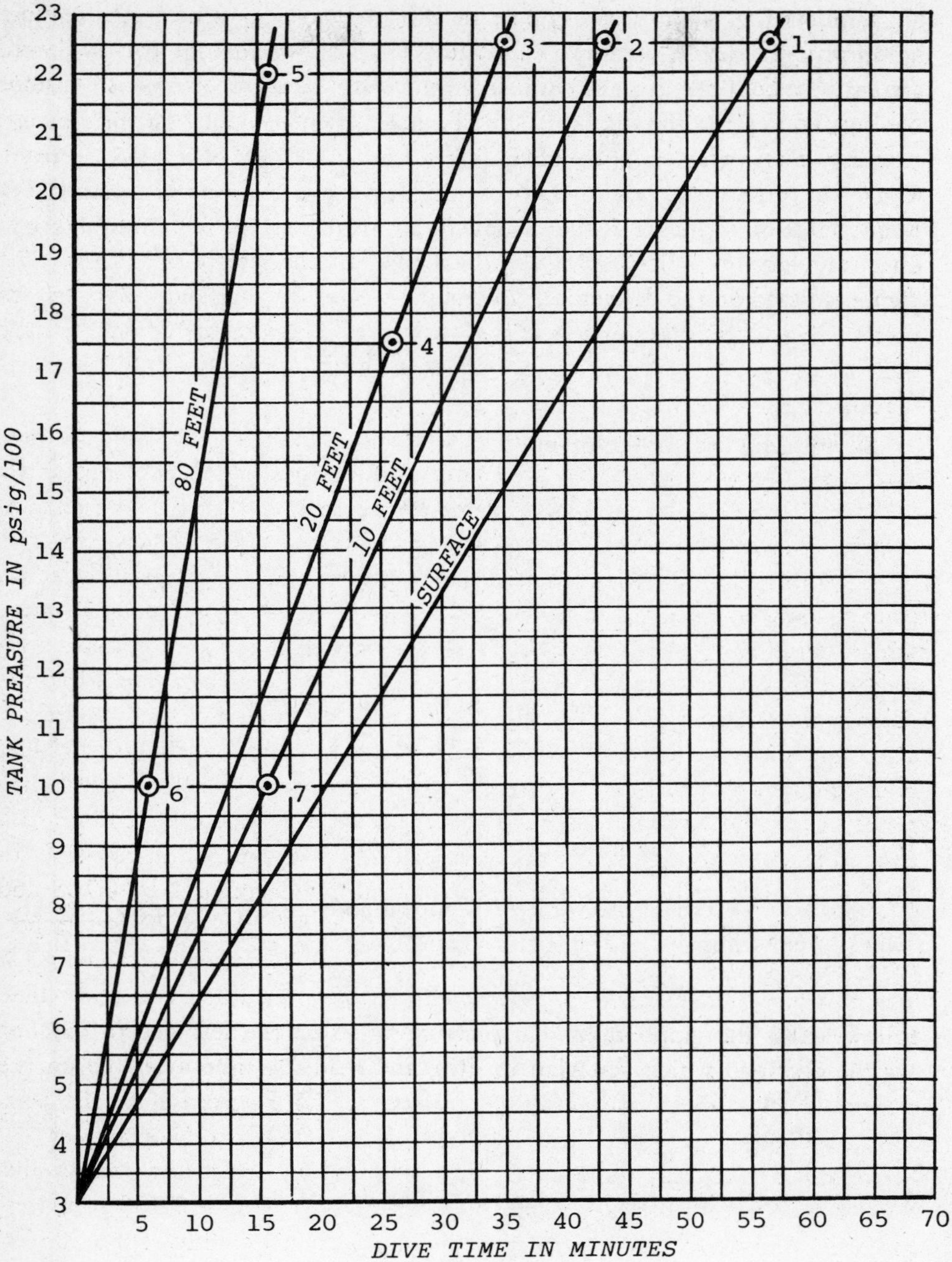

FIGURE 3. PLOTTED TIMES FOR OCEAN DIVES

Diving times in sea water based on a "standard 72" c.f. tank used in the examples in the text. Such a tank delivers 56.5 c.f. of air between the gauge pressures of 300 and 2250 psi. A use rate of 1 c.f./min. is used for this figure. See text for an explanation of the numbered points.

Now follow the 6-minute line up to the 80-feet line and note that there are 1,000 psig pressure remaining in the tank. Reading the time below the intersection of the 1,000 psig and 10-feet lines (point 7) we find only 15.5 minutes available. Thus the dive could not be made without depleting the reserve.

Example 3. How long could the diver stay at a depth of 23 feet in fresh water with an air use rate of 0.80 c.f./min. and a starting pressure of 1,300 psig? Referring to Figure 2, the volume of air available is 37 c.f. Use the equation:

$$T_D = \frac{V}{K \times \left[1 + \left(\frac{D}{D'}\right)\right]}$$

Substituting the correct numbers,

$$T_D = \frac{37}{0.80 \times \left[1 + \frac{23}{34}\right]}$$

$$= \frac{37}{0.80 \times 1.675}$$

$$= \frac{37}{1.34}$$

$$= 27.6$$

or 28 minutes

Now let us estimate the value of K in the above equation for a diver who makes three swims just at the surface for 10, 15, and 30 minutes respectively. Observed pressure drops for the tanks are as follows:

Time of swim	*Start psig*	*Finish*	*Change*	*Change/Min.*
10 min.	2,250	1,775	475	47.5
15 min.	1,775	1,060	715	47.6
20 min.	2,100	1,140	960	48.0

Averaging the three pressure changes we find,

$$\frac{47.5 + 47.6 + 48.0}{3} = 47.7 \text{ psi/min.}$$

Since the tank can deliver 71.2 c.f. when filled to 2,475 psig, the volume delivered for each pound of pressure drop is

$$\frac{71.2 \text{ c.f.}}{2{,}475 \text{ psig}} = 0.0288 \text{ c.f./psig.}$$

Now multiply this by the average rate determined above to get,

$$0.0288 \text{ c.f./psig} \times 47.7 \text{ psig./min.} = 1.37 \text{ c.f./min.}$$

The above figures, table, and examples provide the necessary background. Make up your own problems and work with them using both the basic formulas and the table-figure combinations until you are confident of your ability to use them properly.

In determining your air requirements always make several measurements and take an average. Remember that your air requirements will probably decrease as you become more skilled in diving. It is of interest to note your progress by making such determinations two or three times during the learning period.

If you dive with a poorly fitted mask: remember that you may use more than the calculated amount of air if excessive mask clearing is required. Normal mask clearing should not require extra air since it can be done with a part of the normal exhalation.

Dalton's Law and Gas Mixtures

If one could count the number of molecules in a cubic foot of helium and in a cubic foot of nitrogen at the same temperature and pressure, the numbers would be the same. This result is a consequence of the Ideal Gas Law which can be written,

$$n = \frac{RT}{PV}$$

To state that for a given constant temperature, pressure, and volume, the number of mols (or molecules) is the same for any gas that obeys the gas law at those temperatures and pressures. Stated another way, gas molecules at the same temperature contain the same kinetic energy. Since nitrogen molecules are four times as heavy as helium molecules, it follows that the helium moleclues must travel at a higher rate of speed to produce the same pressure as does nitrogen.

If the above volumes are combined to produce a two-cubic-foot volume containing the same amounts of the two gases at the same temperature, the pressure would not change. Each gas would exert only half the pressure that it did in the original volume since it now has twice the space in which to move about.

This is an example of Dalton's Law which states: "In a mixture of gases, each gas exerts a pressure proportional to the percentage of the total gas which it represents." In air there are approximately 21 molecules of oxygen in each 100 molecules of total gas. About 1/5 of the total number of molecular collisions therefore involve an oxygen molecule. Thus oxygen exerts about 1/5 of the total pressure. These fractions are called the partial pressures of the various gases. This is an important factor in diving, since the body functions are more directly influenced by the individual, or partial, pressures of metabolically active gases (such as oxygen or carbon dioxide) than by total pressure.

"Breathing air" as defined by the Compressed Gas Association may be either compressed pure air or it may be artificially produced by combining pure oxygen and pure nitrogen in the proper proportions. Figure 4 is a graphic representation of Dalton's Law assuming an 80% nitrogen (N_2), 20% oxygen (O_2) mixture.

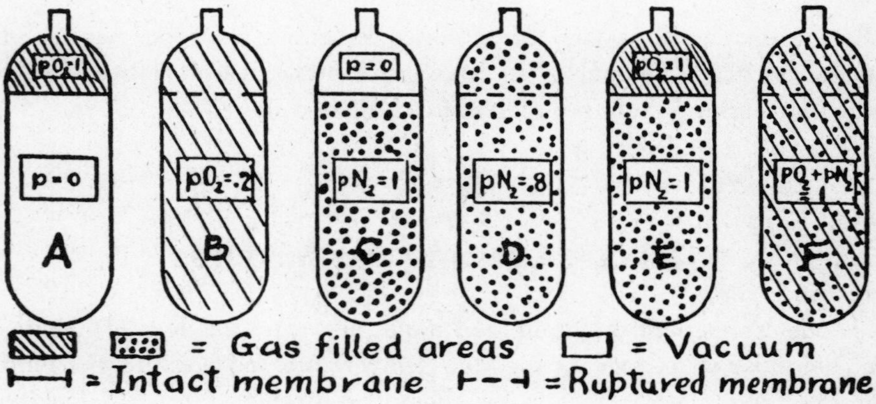

FIGURE 4. DALTON'S LAW OF PARTIAL PRESSURES

P = Pressure. O_2 = Oxygen. N_2 = Nitrogen.
A. Oxygen at one atmosphere occupies 1/5 of volume.
B. Oxygen now occupies total volume; P = .2 atmosphere.
C. Nitrogen at one atmosphere occupies 4/5 of volume.
D. Nitrogen occupies total volume; P = .8 atmosphere.
E. Oxygen 1/5, Nitrogen 4/5, both at one atmosphere.
F. Oxygen and Nitrogen mixed; total P = 1 atmosphere.
E and F combine A, B, C, D to show gases exert pressure directly proportional to percentage in a mixture.

The application of Dalton's Law, the handling of compressed air and its container, additional information on air and gas mixtures is taken up in Chapter 4.

Air is a mixture of the gases (or vapors) of oxygen (about 21%), nitrogen (78%), and small amounts of carbon dioxide and other, less common substances. The composition of "air" is generally quite constant everywhere, and precise values are given in Table II. It should be recognized that these values may vary in certain special cases and that the exact composition is also dependent upon the amount of water vapor (humidity). Air analysis is usually expressed in percentages of "dry" air unless otherwise stated.

TABLE II

AIR COMPOSITION

Gas	Per Cent	Partial mm Hg	Pressure psi	Atmospheres	Feet of Salt Water
Nitrogen (N_2)	78.00	592.8	11.5	.780	25.74
Oxygen (O_2)	21.00	159.6	3.09	.21	6.93
Carbon Dioxide (CO_2)	.03	.23	.004	.0003	.01
Others	.97	7.37	.106	.0097	.32
TOTAL	100.00	760.00	14.700	1.0000	33.00

Temperature

Temperature may be defined as the thermal condition of a body which determines the transfer of heat to or from other bodies. Thus temperature tells you only whether a body is relatively hot or cold but nothing about its absolute heat content. Temperature is expressed in degrees (°) and may be measured or "scaled" by any of several scales. The scales most commonly used are Fahrenheit (F.) and Centigrade (C.). By convention (or definition), water under 1 atmosphere of pressure freezes at 32° F. or 0° C. and boils at 212° F. or 100° C. Therefore, the temperature range over which water is in a liquid form is from 212° to 32° (180 degrees) on the Fahrenheit scale and 100° to 0° (100 degrees) on the Centigrade scale. The relationship of a one-degree change in temperature on one scale to a like change on the other is shown by the ratio of 180/100. Thus,

$$1°\text{C.} \times \frac{180}{100} = 1.8\,°\text{F.}$$

Since 0° C. = 32 ° F. we can write,

$$°\text{F.} = (1.8 \times °\text{C.}) + 32. = (9/5\ \text{C.}) + 32$$

$$\text{and } \frac{°\text{F.} - 32\,°}{1.8}\ \text{C.} = 5/9\ (\text{F.} - 32).$$

All materials contain energy at any temperature above absolute zero. Therefore, as mentioned earlier, absolute temperatures rather than relative temperatures must be used in gas-law equations. The absolute temperature scales corresponding to Fahrenheit and Centigrade are Rankine and Kelvin respectively. On the Rankine scale, the freezing point of water is 491.69° and on the Kelvin scale it is 273.16°. The relationships between these four scales is shown in Table III.

TABLE III

COMPARISON OF TEMPERATURE READINGS IN DEGREES ON DIFFERENT SCALES AT SELECTED REFERENCE POINTS

Scale	*Absolute Zero*	*Melting Ice*	*Comfort Zone*	*Boiling Water*
Centigrade	—273.16	0	20–25	100
Fahrenheit	—459.61	32	68–77	212
Kelvin	0	273.16	293.16–298.16	373.16
Rankine	0	491.69	527.69–536.69	671.69

A quick inspection of Table III shows that it would require about 3° C. or 5.3° F. change to cause a 1% change in any result based on the ratio T_1/T_2 in the range of temperatures at which water is liquid. Since the volume of air breathed is measured by the lungs and the lungs must be assumed to always remain at constant temperature, we can safely ignore that factor. However, temperature can play a significant role in determining tank pressure during filling. This is discussed in detail in Chapter 4.

Temperature affects diving time in other ways than breathing requirements and apparent air supply. For example, certain practical knowledge is derived from a temperature measurement; for example, all temperatures may become uncomfortable above about 90° F. and below 60° F. unless protective measures are taken. However, man may tolerate air temperatures considerably higher and lower for considerable periods of time without any serious or permanent effects. Tolerable water temperatures are confined to a much narrower range. In general, water colder than 70° F. cannot be endured indefinitely by the unprotected swimmer, and from 60° F. downward good protective suits are required. Water above 80° F. becomes uncomfortable if much activity is carried on. The degree of comfort or discomfort experienced in water at any given temperature will vary among individuals, depending upon personal differences, state of nutrition, health, age, etc., but the general values given above will be valid for most persons. The difference in tolerable temperatures between a gaseous and liquid environment depends upon heat capacity rather than upon temperature.

Heat is energy and is usually measured in calories or in British thermal units (Btu); for most of our discussion we will use the calorie, which is that amount of heat required to raise the temperature of 1 gram of water by 1 degree Centigrade (453 grams equal 1 pound). It therefore requires about 100 calories to raise the temperature of 1 gram of water from the freezing to the boiling point. Energy is required for melting and for vaporization as well as for raising temperature. Ice at a temperature of 0° C. requires about

80 calories per gram to convert it to water, and water at 100° C. requires about 540 calories per gram to convert it to steam. Ice at 0° C. and steam at 100° C. therefore differ in heat content by 80 + 100 + 540, or 720 calories per gram, while water at these temperatures differs by only 100 calories. While water varies in heat content by about 1 calorie per gram per degree, ice varies by about 1/2 calorie per gram per degree. The amount of heat required to change the temperature of a material by one degree Centigrade is called the *specific heat* of that material.

TABLE IV

Specific Heat for Several Common Substances

Material	*Specific Heat Calories/Gram**
Air	0.25
Water	1.00
Iron	0.11
Copper	0.10
Aluminum	0.22
Lead	0.03

* Values from the *Handbook of Chemistry and Physics*, 29th ed. (Cleveland: Chemical Rubber Publishing Co.)

If we compare the cooling capacities of air and water it is evident from Table IV that, pound for pound, water will absorb four times as much heat as that required by air for the same temperature change. On a volume basis, water is about 900 times as heavy as air at sea level; therefore, on a volume basis, water absorbs 900 × 4 or about 3,600 times as much heat as air to bring about a comparable temperature change. It should also be pointed out that water is better than air as a conductor of heat and will therefore remove heat from the body more rapidly. The high heat capacity and heat conductivity of water make it necessary to use some type of protection for any extended period in the water except in the warmest climates.

The rate at which heat is transferred to the water is given by

$$Q = KA\ (T_B - T_W) \text{ in Btu* per hr.}$$

where A is the surface area of the body and $(T_B - T_W)$ is the temperature difference between the body and the water.

Table V lists values of K for several materials. In the case of a diver protected by a foam neoprene suit (called "wet suit"), K will also vary with pres-

* A British thermal unit (Btu) is the amount of heat required to raise the temperature of one avoirdupois pound of water one degree Fahrenheit. A Btu equals about 252 calories.

sure since the suit will compress with depth. In Figure 5 the value of K for several types of wet-suit material is shown versus depth. Small differences may be observed between manufactures and suit construction (nylon-lined one side or two sides, textured, skin two sides, etc.) The biggest difference in K for moderate depths (less than 5 atm) is noticeable in the three standard thicknesses of suits: 3/16″, 1/4″, and 3/8″. Comfort is important in selecting a suit and, since the stiffness of the suit increases with thickness, the thinnest suit that will afford adequate protection for the water temperatures expected should be chosen.

TABLE V

VALUES FOR HEAT CONDUCTIVITY OF SOME SUIT TYPES

Material	*K = Conductivity* coefficient*
Bare skin	65.00
1/8″ natural rubber	9.60
1/4″ wool underwear (stillwater)	13.40
1/4″ underwear (dry) under 1/8″ rubber suit	0.68

* Expressed in British thermal units per hour per square foot of material per degree Fahrenheit temperature difference across the material.

The importance of a wet suit is obvious when considering that the conductivity coefficient of bare skin is 65. (Table V.) Thus, at one atmosphere in water the bare-skin diver would lose heat approximately 30 times faster than a diver in a 1/4″ wet suit. (K=2, Figure 5.)

Even in a wet suit, however, the rate of heat lost by the body can be appreciable. For example, consider a diver in a 1/4″ wet suit at 66 feet (3 atmosphere) in 50° F. water (K = 4). The approximate surface area of the body for an average adult six feet tall and weighing 170 pounds is 19 square feet. For adults 5′ 10″ tall, weighing 160 pounds to adults 6′ tall and weighing 190 pounds the surface area varies from 18 to 20 square feet.

The skin temperature will rapidly approach 90° F. Since the body-core temperatures remain 98.6° F., heat is transferred from the core to the skin surface and from the skin to the water.

The rate of heat loss from the skin through the suit to the water is:

$$Q = 4 \times 19 \times (90 - 50) = 3{,}040 \text{ Btu/hr.}$$

Expressing this loss in the calorie used to rate food value (1000 × calorie defined previously)

$$Q = 768 \text{ food calories/hr.}$$

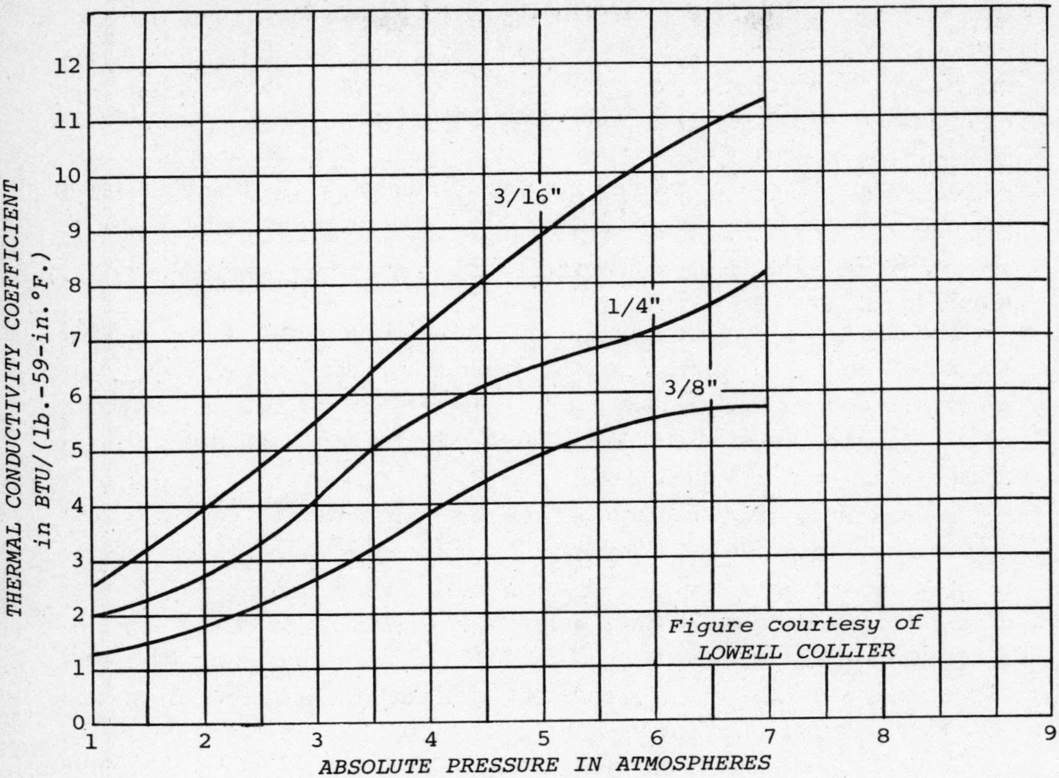

FIGURE 5. VALUE OF K FOR SEVERAL TYPES OF WET-SUIT MATERIAL

Effect of pressure on conductivity coefficient of three different thicknesses of nylon-lined neoprene foam material.

If long exposure is anticipated, more protection than the 1/4″ suit would be needed.

The greatest thermal protection can be obtained from a dry suit. In this type of suit thermal or wool underwear is worn under the dry suit and, as the name implies, the diver stays dry. The disadvantage of this type of suit is that it can be difficult to seal and may be easily torn. Because the underwear will absorb water, a marked change in the buoyancy of the diver will result if water leaks into the suit.

Maximum protection and minimum danger can be obtained, of course, with a dry suit worn over a wet suit. This type of suit has been used for some of the most extreme diving conditions.

Freedom of limb movement within a suit is important. Extreme suit thickness can cause discomfort leading to tension. Tension, in turn, can induce increased air consumption and so reduce one's efficiency. The ideal that is well worth seeking is a happy combination of comfort and warmth that encourages optimum efficiency.

Density, Buoyancy, and Viscosity

If one lifts a 2-oz. fishing sinker he refers to it as "heavy," but a large block of balsa wood or similar material is called "light," even though it may weigh twice as much. The term *density* reconciles this discrepancy, since it is an expression of mass (or weight) per unit volume. A small "heavy" object is one that has a high density and is heavy by virtue of comparison with some less dense material. Relative density is also expressed in terms of specific gravity.

The densities of various materials are compared by means of their specific gravities. The specific gravity of pure water is arbitrarily set at 1.0. If the weight per unit volume (density) of another material is twice that of water, it has a specific gravity of 2.0. If the specific gravity of a substance is 0.5, its density is half that of water.

In determining the depth equivalent to one atmosphere of pressure it was found to be 33 feet for sea water and 34 feet for fresh water. This is a direct result of the salts dissolved in the oceans, making the water heavier, or more dense, by a factor of 34/33. Since pure water is assigned the density value of 1, sea water has a density of 1.03 ($1 \times 34/33$). Certain bodies of water such as the Great Salt Lake, Red Sea, etc., contain higher concentrations of salt and have considerably higher densities.

The average density of the human body, considering the air spaces in the lungs and sinuses, is slightly less than 1. As a result of this, most people find it comparatively easy to learn to float and can spend long periods in the water safely with little effort. This, again, is a generality and there are a few individuals with a comparatively high density who find that they must scull or tread water to stay afloat.

Whether a body will sink or float in a liquid is defined by *Archimedes' principle* which states: "A solid body immersed in a liquid is buoyed upward by a force equal to the weight of the liquid it displaces." If the body floats, it is said to have positive buoyancy; i.e., the liquid it displaces weighs more than the body. If the body sinks, it is heavier than the liquid it displaces and is said to have negative buoyancy. A body which is neutrally buoyant neither sinks nor floats, but will remain at the depth in the liquid at which it is placed.

The density of the human body is very nearly equal to that of water, and a diver may normally ascend or descend at will. Small changes in buoyancy usually are not a serious problem; large changes may be quite significant. Small changes are encountered in scuba diving as a result of emptying the air cylinders. A charge of air may weigh between 3 and 10 pounds depending on the size and type of air cylinder used. Most open-circuit breathing devices are near neutral in sea water when the tanks are empty, but they readily sink when tanks are filled.

Since the fluid and solid tissues of the body are incompressible and the volume of the gas spaces is maintained by the use of scuba, no buoyancy change results from the increased pressure on the body. Excessive air trapped in a rubber suit can be hazardous if carried to depths or if lost even in comparatively shallow water.

For a long swim under water, buoyancy should be adjusted to as near neutral as possible to avoid unnecessary energy expenditure to maintain the desired depth against the force of either positive or negative buoyancy. The average diver, equipped with a face mask, snorkle and other gear, and wearing a bathing suit, may need up to 8 or 10 pounds on a weight-belt to achieve neutral buoyancy. In a heavy-duty wet suit he may need 20 pounds or more.

Archimedes' principle is also the basis upon which flotation devices such as vests, hoists, etc., operate. Most vests are inflatable by operating a mechanical device that punctures the seal of a small CO_2 cylinder. These devices should be examined frequently to make certain that they have not become corroded or fouled so that they are inoperable and that the CO_2 cylinder has not lost its charge. Standard vests may be equipped to take CO_2 cylinders charged with 12, 16 or 25 grams of CO_2. The flotation offered per gram of CO_2 is about 1.1 pounds at the surface. Thus a 12-gram cylinder would provide about 13 pounds of buoyancy at the surface, a 16-gram cylinder would provide about 18 pounds, and a 25-gram cylinder about 28 pounds. This rough guide can be used in choosing the appropriate vest for individual needs.

Carbon dioxide (CO_2) volumes are affected to a greater degree by temperature and pressure than is indicated by the Ideal Gas Law. Thus the amount of buoyancy afforded by a given CO_2 cylinder size will be less at depth than at the surface. A good vest will also be equipped with a tube such that you can inflate it by blowing into the tube. It will also have an overpressure valve so that if it is fully inflated at depth, gas will vent off during ascent so that the vest will not rupture and leave you without any additional buoyancy. This overpressure valve should also be inspected frequently.

The density and viscosity of a medium are important factors in controlling the amount of energy required to move bodies through it. For our purposes here we can consider viscosity as a measure of the resistance of a medium to flow, and thus water is more viscous than air. An average swimmer equipped with scuba will offer about 9 pounds of drag resistance when towed through the water at about 0.8 miles per hour. In water, drag resistance increases roughly as the square of the velocity, which means that doubling the speed would quadruple the drag resistance and therefore the energy needed to tow the swimmer. In swimming, the effort expended goes in part to the vertical and sideways displacement of water as well as for the direct propulsion of the swimmer so that, in fact, the energy requirement increases more nearly as the cube of the velocity.

A good average underwater swimming rate is about 0.8 or 0.9 miles per hour. Very few experienced divers in good physical condition can swim more than 1.2 miles per hour for more than a few minutes. Thus a diver should be aware of current conditions in any anticipated diving area and know his limitations in order to avoid getting into trouble.

In reference to the flotation vests discussed above, a positive buoyancy of 3 pounds will give an upright diver a maximum ascent velocity of about 100 feet per minute. Spreading the feet apart by about two feet will reduce this maximum to 50 or 60 feet per minute. Since drag resistance increases roughly as the square of the velocity, a buoyancy of 12 pounds would approximately double the maximum free ascent rate.

Humidity

Vapor tension, or the pressure exerted by "escaped" or gaseous particles of a substance, is determined by the temperature and is, for our purposes, independent of the total pressure. Therefore, there is not more water vapor in a cylinder of 1-cubic-foot capacity when charged to 2,100 pounds than when it is empty. This is true at ordinary swimming temperature even with liquid water in the cylinder. It may be assumed, then, that breathing air will always be "dry." Continued breathing of this dry air may produce an uncomfortable dryness in the mouth and throat. Such dryness is alleviated by removing the mouthpiece (or admitting water in the mask, as with full-face masks) and taking a drink or at least rinsing out the mouth.

Exhaled air is saturated with water vapor at body temperature. This exhaled moisture condenses in the breathing tubes and/or mask. If the water is cold, enough moisture may collect in the breathing tubes after a time to suggest a leak. The water is easily blown out through the exhaust valve and presents no problem.

Moisture from the breath used to equalize pressure in the face plate may also condense on the glass and result in fogging. Evaporation from the skin and eyes will also contribute to this problem. Moistening the glass with saliva or applying a commercial anti-fog compound will usually prevent any difficulty of this nature. In some cases it is advantageous to keep a small amount of water in the face plate to rinse the glass occasionally.

Illumination and Vision

Vision under the surface of the water is modified by two physical properties which are markedly different between air and water: refractive index and light penetration.

The index of refraction of a substance is the ratio of the speed of light in a vacuum to its speed in the substance. Light travels in water at about three fourths of its speed in air. This difference in velocity causes light rays to be "bent," when they pass from air into water or from water into air.

Because of the difference in refractive index between air and water, there is some visual displacement of images even under ideal conditions. Under conditions where the eye is in direct contact with the water, it loses its normal lens characteristics. Since it is unable to correct for this difference, considerable distortion results. When an air layer is interposed by using a face mask, this difficulty is eliminated. However, the difference in refractive index now comes into play. The distortion ratio is 3 to 4. Objects appear to be closer than the actual distance and correspondingly larger; angles are distorted. This phenomenon poses problems in spearing fish and in photography. For these activities it is best to calibrate photographic equipment individually and learn to accommodate one's self to the distortion.

Particles in water that are extremely small also diffract light and cause a fuzzy image. Fuzzy or blurred pictures may be taken quite easily by simply neglecting to include a packet of silica gel or other moisture-control compound in the camera case. If the camera case is closed when in moist air (as it usually is aboard a boat or on the beach) this moisture may condense on the face of the case or on the camera lens when taken into cold water.

The problem of vision is further complicated by the limited penetration of light into water. Where visibility is usually good (little or no turbidity or plankton) and the water is deep, photography still becomes difficult beyond 100 feet in depth without artificial light. When the sun is not directly overhead or when the surface is riffled, light is further reduced.

Color photography is a still more serious problem, since colors are differentially absorbed. Warm colors are absorbed first, with reds being removed in the first few feet, followed by orange at about 15 feet, and yellow at around 30 feet. Beyond 60 feet blues predominate and gradually deepen into darkness. The best underwater color photograph can be taken with artificial light either at night or at depths where sunlight is a negligible factor.

Underwater photography is an entire specialty by itself and cannot be treated adequately in the limited space available here. Only a few points are mentioned here to indicate that a student diver who plans to pursue this activity should first consult some of the numerous articles and books devoted to this subject.

Acoustics

In 1953, Capt. J. Y. Cousteau published his well-known book *The Silent World* depicting the pleasures of self-contained diving (and a few of its hazards). Despite the impression left by this book, the submarine environment is not a "silent world." In some areas it is in fact extremely noisy. The sounds heard beneath the surface arise from waves, surf, rocks, and gravel moving with water, boats, and even the marine life such as fish, shrimps, and crabs. According to reports, great pains must be taken to find and maintain waters sufficiently silent for the testing and calibrating of sonar and other underwater sound equipment.

Sound travels more rapidly in water (about 4,800 ft/sec) than in air (about 1,090 ft/sec) and certain noises may be heard for greater distances. In spite of this, it is difficult to use the voice for satisfactory communications under water. The difference in inertia, viscosity, and so on, between air and water is such that only about 1 part in 10,000 of the sound energy actually enters the water when speaking into an ordinary mask. In compressed-air scuba this is further complicated by the noise produced from escaping air during exhalation and speaking. Speaking diaphragms of metal or plastic may help considerably when properly located in a mask, but at best permit conversation only over a comparatively short distance. Even under optimum conditions it is difficult to attract the attention of a buddy some distance away by voice alone.

Banging on the air tanks with the butt of a knife handle or a stone produces a sharp loud noise which can be readily picked up for quite a distance. This is a satisfactory way of passing information when a standard set of signals has been worked out. Hitting stones together or cavitating the water by sharp claps of the hands also produces clear signals, but such signals can be heard for only a short distance.

In air we locate the source of a sound by the slight difference in elapsed time between the arrival of the sound at each of our ears and by the differences in intensity. The high rate of propagation of sound in water defeats this natural ability to a large extent, and most divers simply recognize sounds as alerts, attention-getters, or as evidence of what is going on in their immediate area.

Hydrophones and swimmers' telephones are available for application to special diving situations, but are not normally a part of the sport diver's equipment.

The foregoing pages by no means present a complete picture of all of the problems encountered in diving, even from a point of view of physics. While the major points are covered, much is left for discussion between the student and instructor, and much more will be learned from serious conversation with other divers and by experience.

FOR FURTHER READING

Frey, Hank, and Paul Tzimoulis. *Camera Below—The Complete Guide to the Art and Science of Underwater Photography.* New York: Association Press, 1968.

3

MEDICAL ASPECTS OF DIVING: UNDERWATER PHYSIOLOGY

Edward H. Lanphier, M.D.

When you first thought about taking up scuba diving you probably didn't expect to spend much time learning about medical matters. The truth is that there is no way to avoid this subject if you want to be reasonably safe and effective under water.

It is very unlikely that a doctor is going to be with you when the most crucial decisions affecting your well-being in the water will have to be made. It is extremely important that you realize very few non-diving physicians—no matter how expert they are in other respects—have a useful understanding of the most serious medical problems that divers can get into, and for which they may urgently need medical help on dry land. You, as a diver, must therefore have the essentials of this knowledge in your own mind.

The preceding chapter described the main physical forces that confront a diver. Now, we must consider the way certain parts of the body are constructed (our *anatomy*, that is), plus more about the way the body functions (*physiology*), and most of all, the underwater phase of *environmental physiology.* In the latter we look at the action on the body of factors encountered in the watery surroundings of depth and at the way the body reacts to them.

Anatomy and physiology are two of the basic sciences of medicine, and we must be able to apply them to actual *medical* problems that can result from diving. From the preventive standpoint, we must also take up medically important matters like the use of decompression tables. Equally important matters like physical qualifications, first aid, marine-life injuries, and the problem of cold are taken up elsewhere in this book.

For purposes of this chapter, we will define a diver as an individual who is: 1) underwater and fully exposed to the *increased surrounding pressure* of depth; 2) staying down longer than he can hold his breath and thus is obliged to provide himself with *something to breathe.* These two criteria also define the essential "Facts of Life" that set diving apart from life on dry land.

Direct Effects of Pressure

You will recall that pressure increases rather rapidly as you descend in the water. As a rough rule of thumb, it increases about 1 pound per square inch (psi) with each 2 feet of descent. (A more exact figure is 0.445 psi per foot of depth.)

Another way of looking at the pressure changes of descent is to consider that we are already under pressure at the surface—14.7 psi, 760 millimeters of mercury, 29.9 inches of mercury, or *1 atmosphere.* Each 33* feet of descent will add another atmosphere to the total, or absolute, pressure. The pressure at 33 feet of depth is two atmospheres, absolute, and so on. The atmosphere system is the easiest to use in considering many aspects of pressure. These relationships are worth remembering:

TABLE VI

INCREASE OF PRESSURE WITH INCREASE OF DEPTH

Pressure (atmospheres, absolute)	*Depth (feet)*
1	surface
2	33
3	66
4	99
5	132
6	165
10	297
	and so on

The term *absolute* indicates that the pressure already existing at the surface has been taken into account—as it must be in order to consider pressure-volume relationships, partial pressures, and the like. Since talking in atmospheres usually implies absolute pressures, it is not always specified as such. (Incidentally, all the figures given here are for sea water, assuming a specific gravity of 1.025.)

The effects of pressure can be classified into two categories: "direct" (or primary) and "indirect" (or secondary).

The direct effects are largely mechanical and fairly obvious. The indirect effects are more subtle, and understanding them requires digging a little deeper into physiology. They come about mainly through the partial pressures of the gases which the diver breathes. For this reason, they will be easier to handle after we've talked about that second big factor in diving: "something to breathe."

* These figures are for sea water. Corresponding figures for fresh water are 0.432 psi per foot and 34 feet.

The direct effects of pressure are produced either (1) by way of a pressure difference built up across some structure of the body, or (2) by way of a change in gas volume. In most cases, these two are actually very closely related, but the first is the more basic idea.

Unless a pressure difference, or "differential," exists, pressure does not have perceptible direct, mechanical effects—at least at common diving depths. Later, possible hydrostatic effects will be discussed in connection with dives to greater depths; but for practical purposes, we can assume that living tissue behaves like the water of which it is largely composed: it transmits pressure throughout itself without differentials or evident volume change and without noticeable change in structure or function.

The same is true of the body parts which are "solid tissues." For example, taking one of your legs from one depth to another produces no more change than it would in a leg-shaped bag of water. But the body is not *all* a mass of solids and solutions like a leg. It contains certain *air spaces*, and others may be hitched onto its surface in the form of goggles, mask, and what not. The following are all potential trouble spots:

1. Spaces associated with the ears.
2. The sinuses.
3. The lungs and airways.
4. Air pockets in the stomach and intestines.
5. Any air space applied to the surface of the body.

The body will transmit pressure freely through all its "fluid" portions directly to, but not necessarily into, these air spaces. If the space has a soft, movable wall, this pressure will simply cause the space to collapse until the air inside is compressed to the appropriate volume for that pressure (remember Boyle's Law). Once this volume is reached, nothing more will happen.

If the space has a semirigid wall and will not compress freely, the end result will be compromise—some compression of the gas, and some pressure difference across the wall. If the space is walled by bone, for example, the pressure inside will remain what it was to start with, while the outside pressure goes up. Here, the whole surrounding pressure (above one atmosphere) can act as a differential. But if a rigid or semirigid space is connected to a source of air at ambient (surrounding) pressure, the developing differential will simply force air into the space until the difference in pressure is *equalized.* The amount of air required to equalize also follows the Boyle's Law relationship: if a rigid space is equalized at 33 feet, it will contain twice as many air molecules as it did at the surface, and so forth.

When the ambient pressure is reduced, these processes simply go into reverse. A "soft" space will just re-expand, and nothing will happen unless the expanding gas overfills it. An equalized rigid space will simply vent the extra gas if the connection remains open. If there is overfilling or blockage, of course a differential will develop—higher pressure inside the space than outside.

All injuries resulting from pressure differences can be lumped under the term *barotrauma* (injury due to pressure), but the "up" and "down" troubles are best discussed separately.

SQUEEZE

For a long time, divers' jargon has included the word *squeeze.* It is so descriptive that it has come to be applied to virtually all the troubles that pressure can cause during *descent,* as a result of pressure differentials between two structures or spaces.

Actually, the type of accident which gave rise to the word happened to suit-and-helmet divers when their air hose broke near the surface and vented the helmet to lower pressure or when they *fell* to a greater depth or otherwise descended "ahead" of their air supply. Either mishap caused the pressure in the helmet to be lower than the pressure outside. Then the helmet formed a rigid space with one "soft" wall—namely the diver himself. You can fill in the rest

FIGURE 6. SQUEEZE

of the picture yourself. The tales about divers being buried in their helmets are not just sea stories. Similar but less drastic accidents have also happened with hose-supplied face-mask diving rigs. This kind of squeeze is rarer now that air hoses are usually equipped with non-return valves; but the danger involved in falling remains, and it can show up even in scuba.

Although scuba divers do not have to worry about this exact form of squeeze very often, there are still plenty of situations in which the same mechanism of local differences in pressure can operate.

Middle ear. What can happen to the middle ear serves as a good example. Figure 7 will help illustrate this. Consider the space marked "middle ear." When you leave the surface, this contains air at surface pressure. As you descend, the ambient pressure increases, but the internal pressure does not. This clearly produces a differential across the drum. In addition, the body is transmitting the pressure to the walls of the space as well: the blood pressure is going up along with the ambient pressure, and this means that the same differential is operating across the walls of every blood vessel in the membrane lining.

Normally, before any of the differentials get very high, you can get air at ambient pressure from the throat to go through the Eustachian tube and equalize the pressure. But the tube doesn't always pass air very readily. You may have to do some yawning, swallowing, jaw moving, or other maneuvers to get

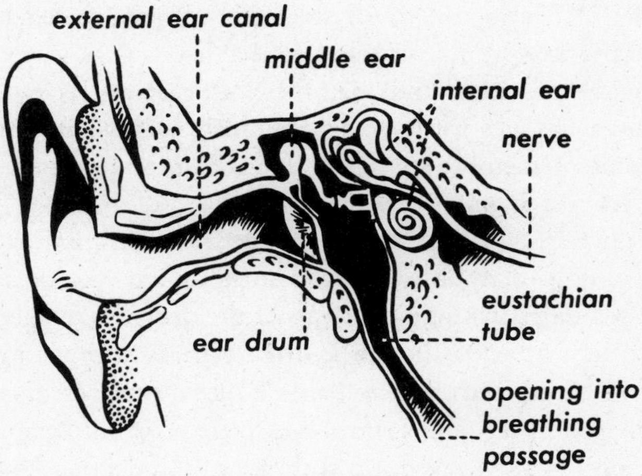

FIGURE 7. MECHANISM OF THE EAR

the tube to open. A few people have voluntary control over certain muscles and can open it at will, but most aren't so lucky. It may even be necessary to grab your nose and blow to get air started through; but if you blow too hard, the "trap door" may just shut tighter.

A few people never can "pop their ears" because of some structural difficulty. Almost anyone will have trouble if a cold, infection, or hay fever causes the membranes around the opening to swell. In these cases, using nose drops, spray, or an inhaler may shrink the membranes enough to make equalization possible. But remember that it never pays to push yourself when you have trouble.

If equalization gets too far behind as you descend, the trap-door effect may make it impossible to catch up without first coming up a few feet.

If it is impossible to equalize by getting air in through the tube, and you keep going down, what happens then? Those blood vessels are usually the first to get into trouble; and since the membrane lining continues over the inner surface of the drum, blood-vessel troubles appear in the drum also. In fact, the results can be seen by the doctor looking at the drum through his otoscope. The vessels are not designed to take much pressure, and the differential will squeeze a lot of blood into them. So they go through a definite series of stages. Just how far they go depends on how bad the squeeze is and how long it lasts. (1) The vessels dilate—become much larger than usual. (2) They start leaking—the fluid part of the blood oozes out and causes swelling of the membrane. (3) They burst—causing actual bleeding into the tissue.

If the swelling and bleeding process goes very far, the membrane is "blown up" and starts to peel off the bony wall. Before this has gone very far, the surface of the lining will break and let blood flow directly into the middle ear space. The drum itself will become a bloody mess during this process, and eventually it will break (rupture) if the squeeze is bad enough. Sometimes, however, there will be enough hemorrhage into the space to reduce the air volume and equalize pressure in that way before the drum gives way.

This squeeze process sounds painful, and it generally is. That is good because pain usually gives warning before much damage is done. A few people have ear drums or membranes so delicate that they can have damage without much pain, but this is quite a disadvantage.

It takes only a few feet of descent without equalization to cause discomfort and the beginning of trouble. Even as little as ten feet of such descent may cause serious damage, including rupture of the drum. Damage is not something you can take lightly, even though it *usually* heals without much trouble. For one thing, free blood in the space makes a nice culture medium for germs, and with the damaged membrane in no shape to fight off infection, the resulting infection can delay healing and form scar tissue, and deafness can result.

Without infection even a ruptured drum will usually heal up in a couple of weeks. Lesser damage may require only a few days. Normally, the only treatment is "hands off"—which means keeping *everything* which might carry infection (including medicine, fingers and all implements, and especially water) strictly *out* of the ear. It is always advisable to see a doctor and let him keep track of anything but a very slight ear injury. If there is an increase of pain after the injury, or if drainage appears, you should see a doctor at once. You may have some blood in your nasal secretions (or spit up traces) for a few hours after injury because blood from the middle ear will drain down the tube. In case of rupture, you *must not* dive again until the doctor says the drum has healed and until you are sure you can equalize without trouble.

Rupturing the ear drum in cold water can have very impressive effects. Cold water getting into the middle ear will cause a violent upset in the sense of balance resulting in marked dizziness and nausea. Although this will usually pass off as soon as the water warms up—a minute or so—things can be pretty tense in the meantime. You just have to hang on. Don't try to surface unless your dive-buddy can take charge. You literally won't know which way is up until the effect subsides.

The *external ear canal* is also subject to squeeze if it gets closed up for any reason. This possibility will be discussed under *External Air Spaces* later in this chapter.

Sinus. There are four pairs of paranasal sinuses: 1) maxillaries—in the cheek bones, below the eyes; 2) frontals—in the forehead, above the bridge of the nose; 3) ethmoid—between the eyes; 4) sphenoid—back under the brain.

These sinuses are cavities in the bones of the face and head. They are lined with a membrane which is continuous with that of the nose, running through the bony canals which connect the sinuses to the nose. If this membrane swells up where it goes through, it may shut off the sinus completely. This is not unusual during a bad cold, and makes it impossible for the sinus to equalize.

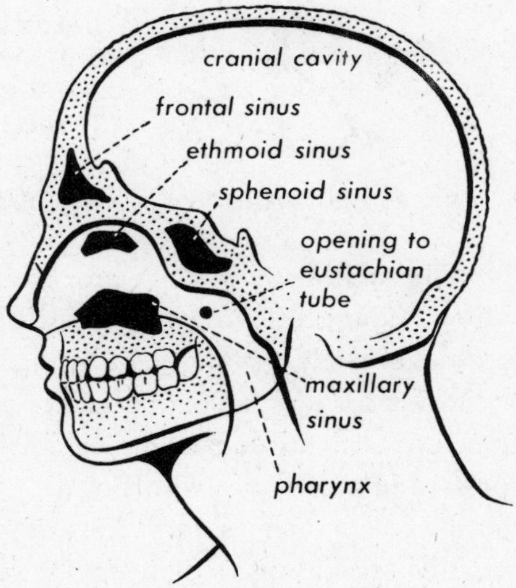

FIGURE 8. AIR SINUSES IN THE HEAD

Allowing for the obvious differences, almost everything said about the middle ear during squeeze will also apply to the sinuses, so you can fill in the details for yourself. Trying to take pressure when your sinuses won't equalize readily is asking for a good case of sinusitis. Sometimes nose drops and the like will help. There is, however, the unfortunate possibility that the effect will have worn off by the time you need it most. Sometimes, a rebound effect—even more congestion than before—occurs. Vasoconstrictor products for oral use (tablets or capsules) are effective for ear and sinus problems in many people. Take note, however, that many such decongestants, especially those that may be purchased without a prescription, are combined with antihistamine compounds that can cause drowsiness.

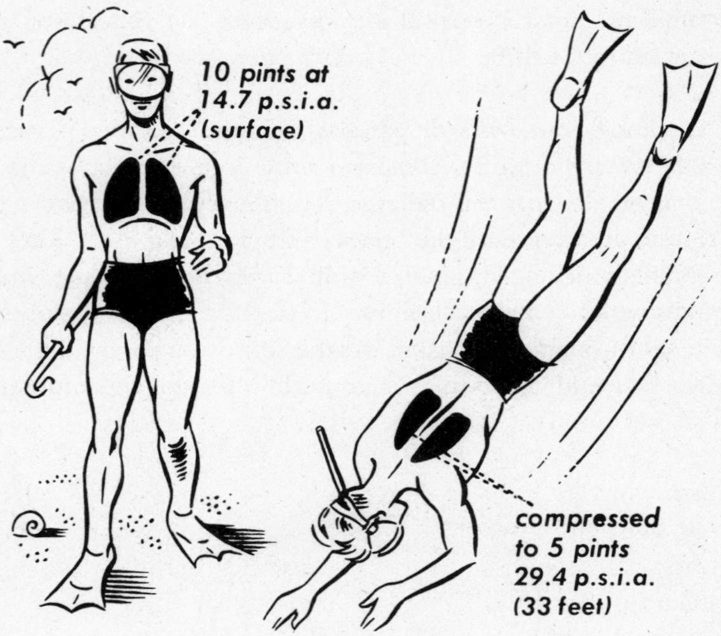

FIGURE 9. PRESSURE EFFECTS ON LUNG VOLUME

Thoracic (lungs). The lungs and airways won't give trouble during descent so long as you keep breathing and are able to get a plentiful supply of air from your scuba. But if you are deliberately making a breath-hold dive, or if your air is cut off on the way down, a form of squeeze becomes possible.

During descent without extra air for equalizing the lungs and airways, the existing lung gas is compressed in accordance with Boyle's Law. In this process, the lungs and thorax simply get smaller as they do during expiration—to a certain point, which is usually (not always) close to the lung volume at the end of a maximal expiratory effort. Beyond this point, the structures start to resist further reduction of volume, and pressure within the lungs falls below the surrounding pressure. The diaphragm rises more than usual, and the pulmonary blood vessels become distended with blood "pulled" into the thorax by the difference in pressure. By virtue of such changes, further descent is possible; but if it continues too far, blood vessels in the lungs will burst. Bleeding into the lungs from this cause is what is meant by *thoracic squeeze*, fortunately an uncommon accident. A very similar situation can develop if you try to breathe through a snorkel from more than a foot or two of depth.

The maximum depth of descent on a "full breath" is a highly individual matter and depends upon too many factors to be predicted with any accuracy. Current records, in the neighborhood of 250 feet, have been set by individuals with unusual lung capacities.

"Gut" squeeze. Don't memorize this one! It doesn't happen. The structures in the gastrointestinal tract all have supple walls, so any air pockets are simply compressed with no local differences in pressure and no strain. The only possible trouble comes on ascent.

External Air Spaces. You have probably noticed that your face mask can pull quite a suction on your face as you descend and that you have to let air into it through your nose to keep the sensation from becoming severe. The mask is just trying to give you a *face squeeze.* Of course, a very flexible mask could take care of some of the pressure-difference just by flattening out on your face.

The most easily damaged tissues within a mask are the membranes which cover the surface of the eyeball and which line the lids and spaces around the eyeball. Hemorrhage can also occur behind the eyeball, in the socket. None of these possibilities is very pleasant. You can see why goggles, normally having no method of equalization, are bad business for anything but very shallow diving.

One reason why the foam "wet suit" almost totally replaced the older "dry suit" is that it does not cause local squeeze. However, the wet suit has its own disadvantages, especially at greater depths; and new forms of dry suit are very likely to be introduced.

Within a dry suit there are bound to be several more or less incompressible air spaces, particularly in folds of the material and at anatomical points such as the external ear canal. As a result, the pressure within the suit can fall below ambient pressure on descent. This encourages water to leak in; and pinches, blisters, even bleeding, can develop in susceptible areas.

The cure for *suit squeeze* is to introduce just enough air into the suit to return the spaces to their normal volume and pressure—to equalize them. This is much easier said than done, and the problem is compounded by the fact that external pressure is naturally greater about the deeper parts of the body. A standing diver always has a mild sort of suit squeeze in his legs. If the diver is inverted, any excess air will promptly go to his feet and legs. Unless relief valves are provided there, he may find himself in an uncontrollable feet-first ascent. Another possibility is to make the legs of a suit out of nonstretchable material and to fit them carefully to each diver. Leg-lacings were provided in "hard-hat" suits for similar reasons.

One of the best of the scuba dry suits was Cousteau's "constant volume" suit. As the name suggests, this suit made it easy to equalize the air spaces within the suit, and exhaust ports at the ankles prevented air from accumulating in the legs when the diver was inverted.

As was mentioned above, closing off the external ear canal can cause an *external ear squeeze,* which is very much like middle-ear squeeze. For this reason, ear plugs are bad business. Suits made of smooth rubber, however, can occasionally seal over the external ear; but more often external ear squeeze is just a part of the general suit squeeze described above. Not only is there a big-

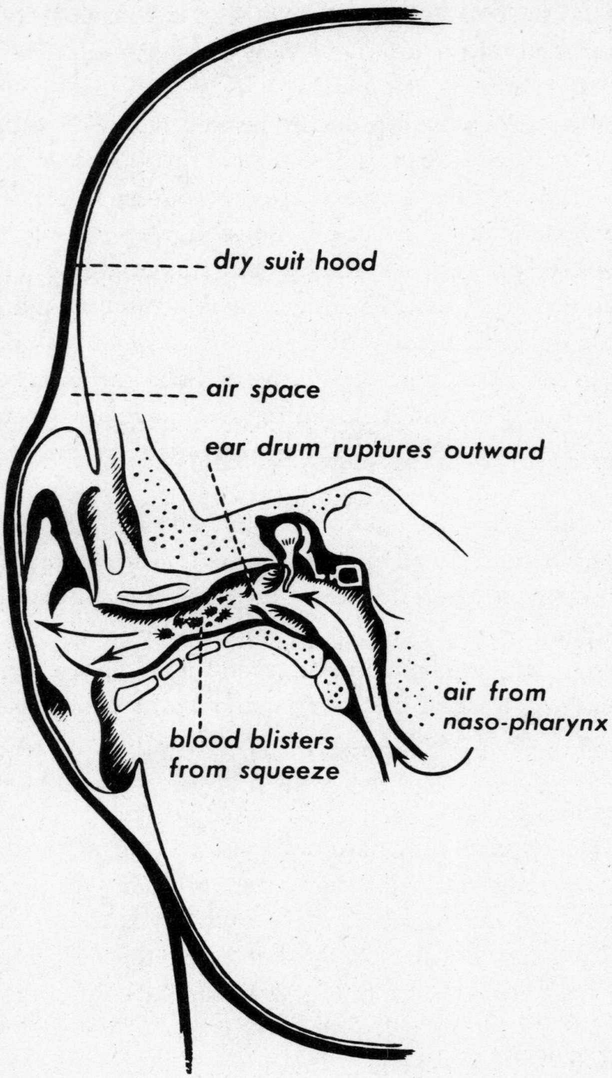

FIGURE 10. SUIT-SQUEEZE EFFECTS OF DRY SUIT HOOD ON EAR

ger irreducible air space at that point, but the ear is a lot more delicate than the skin; so a suit squeeze can show up there even if it doesn't appear very noticeable elsewhere. The cure and cautions are the same.

This form of ear squeeze can damage either the canal lining or the ear drum or both. The usual result looks like a bunch of blood blisters; and if one of the blisters has burst, there will be bleeding from the external ear. In this case bleeding to the outside *does not necessarily* mean that the drum is ruptured, as it does in the middle-ear squeeze. However, the drum *can* rupture under this circumstance.

Miscellaneous. Squeeze due to external air spaces may show up occasionally in unusual forms. For instance, the concave undersides of snap fasteners on one type of scuba harness proved capable of producing extra nipples on manly chests. And then there was the case of transient marital incapacitation which resulted from a misadventure with a "Convenience" provided on one type of rubber suit.

GAS DENSITY EFFECTS

Another direct effect of pressure which ought to be mentioned happens to have nothing to do with the squeeze mechanism, but, instead, concerns the way air behaves once it is compressed.

If you have noticed that breathing is more difficult at depth, this is not just your imagination at work. The number of molecules packed into a volume of gas is directly proportional to the absolute pressure, but the volume you breathe remains about the same. The air you breathe at 100 feet is about four times as dense (heavy) as air at the surface. If you are using open-circuit gear, each breath thus involves dragging four times as many molecules through your demand valve. Unless the scuba is very well designed, the extra effort required will be quite noticeable. In a homemade job you may just not get the air you need. Even moving the air through your own "pipes" is about twice as much work as it was at the surface. If you are free from asthma and other pulmonary conditions this doesn't involve much effort to start with; but trying to work very hard at depth may stop you.

DIRECT EFFECTS OF PRESSURE ON ASCENT

Most of the air spaces mentioned rarely give trouble when you come up. Even an ear or a sinus which gave you a bad time going down will usually behave. Air in suits, face masks, and the like just expands and escapes. (Of course, if you have an excess of air in your suit and no way for it to get out, it may give you unwanted buoyancy.)

Once in a great while, air pockets in the gut will give a bit of trouble. This might happen if a man swallowed air while he was on the bottom or if he had eaten some exceptionally potent baked beans or something similar. If the resulting gas were too far from either end of the alimentary canal to escape readily, it might overfill the gut and cause pain. It would probably work its way out one way or the other without harm, but ascent should certainly be slowed down if abdominal pain develops.

Air embolism and lung damage. Unfortunately, the troubles which can result from gas expansion in the lungs are serious enough to make up for the rosy situation elsewhere—and then some.

Recalling Boyle's Law again: If a man is at 99 feet and ascends, the air in his lungs will undergo a fourfold expansion by the time he surfaces. The volume will double between 99 feet and 33 feet, and it will double again between 33 feet and surface. The actual rate of expansion becomes more and more rapid as he approaches the surface. Thus, if the diver has much air in his lungs when he starts ascent, this expansion can fill the lungs completely, and any excess must be exhaled—or else.

The "or else" is quite sad. Failure to exhale promptly and adequately will cause the pressure in the lungs to rise above that in the rest of the body and on the outside. Once the lungs are fully expanded, the resulting differential will increase directly with the distance of further ascent. Since the lungs are very delicate, it does not take much of a differential like this to cause serious damage. The crucial amount of pressure is equivalent to about four feet of water. In other words, once the lungs have reached maximal expansion, *coming up only four feet more* can put you in real danger.

This is something to think about. For one thing, taking a really full breath on the bottom puts your lungs close to maximum expansion when you start. If you are practicing "ditching" a scuba and let the demand valve get much below your mouth while you are still breathing on it, you may be in some danger almost before you start. It is not surprising that cases of air embolism have been reported in ascents of ten feet or less, as in one case from the bottom of a swimming pool.

Consider what can happen if you are coming up rather fast and something causes you to hold your breath momentarily. Especially if you are close to the surface, your lungs could fill up very rapidly; and that deadly additional four feet of ascent wouldn't take long.

What, exactly, can happen? The most obvious thing is simply to *burst a lung*—an accident which is about as ugly as it sounds, but which isn't necessarily fatal in itself. The most serious possibility is *air embolism.* With or without an obvious "burst," a pressure of around four feet of water can force air from the air sacs into the blood vessels which surround them. Once the air is in the vessels, it is carried rapidly to the heart. From there, it is pumped out into the arteries which supply the whole body. And these are so arranged that some of the air is almost bound to go up the arteries which supply the brain.

Arteries look like the branches of a tree splitting and resplitting into finer and finer branches and twigs. Therefore, a bubble of any size much larger than a red corpuscle is bound to get stuck eventually. It will then form a plug (embolus) which will keep blood from flowing any farther in that particular branch. The brain tissue beyond the plug will be deprived of its blood supply and can survive such deprivation for only a few minutes without permanent damage.

A person who has suffered this kind of accident may be unconscious even before he reaches the surface, or he may climb out and appear normal for as long as a minute or two. It is possible to have a very small embolism with only limited symptoms, but this is rare. Usually, the victim collapses, loses conscious-

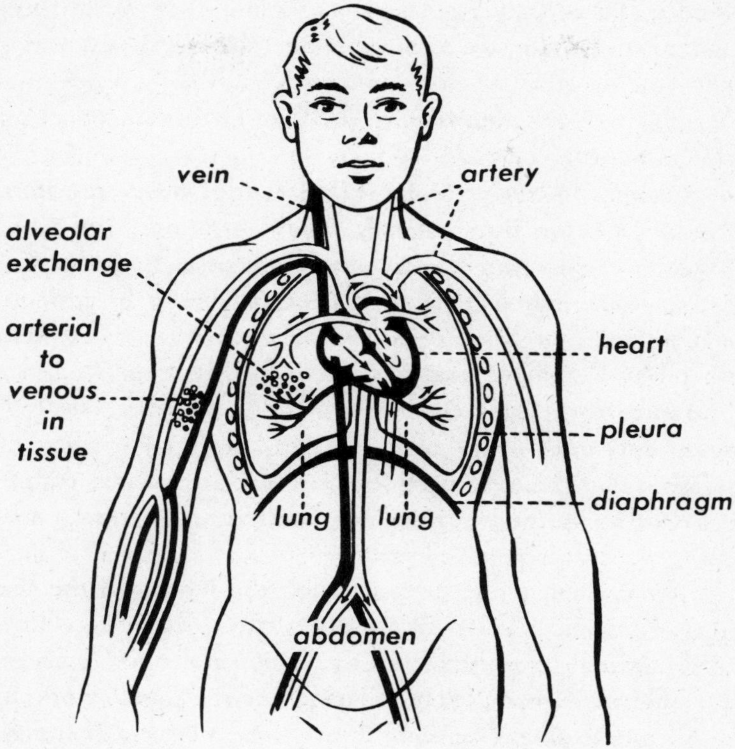

FIGURE 11. THE BODY'S CIRCULATORY SYSTEM

ness, and may go into convulsions. Other signs, such as showing bloody froth at the mouth, respiratory difficulty, and turning blue, will depend mainly on the extent of lung damage and the presence or absence of other consequences of overpressurization of the lungs. Sometimes the respiratory center will be involved in the embolism, and breathing will cease.

The only treatment with any real hope of success is *prompt recompression,* and even this carries no absolute guarantee. The principle is to reduce the size of the bubble-plugs to the point where substantial blood flow can resume. This phase may be rapid, but considerable time is required to ensure that the bubbles are absorbed and will not simply re-expand when the pressure is returned to normal.

Even if the nearest recompression chamber is at relatively great distance, attempting treatment in the water cannot be justified. During transportation, keep the victim turned slightly to his left, and tilted with his head somewhat lower than his feet to minimize the possibility that any remaining air will reach the brain. Keep him on oxygen.

Transportation by air can be justified if it will make a very great difference in time, but exposure to the low pressure of altitude should be kept to a minimum.

It should go without saying that divers should always know the location of the nearest manned-and-ready recompression chamber, how to reach it most rapidly, and who to call upon for authoritative advice in a questionable situation. (The subject of recompression is discussed further in connection with decompression sickness.)

Other possible consequences of overinflation of the lungs are usually far less serious than air embolism, but they deserve mention:

Mediastinal emphysema—air forced into the tissue-spaces in the middle of the chest. Symptoms may include chest pain, trouble in breathing, trouble in swallowing, shock.

TREATMENT: Recompression if of serious degree. Otherwise, rest and general medical care.

Subcutaneous emphysema—air under the skin, usually around the base of the neck. This is not serious in itself, but it is often associated with mediastinal emphysema. Air in the neck region may interfere with talking, breathing, or swallowing.

Pneumothorax—air in the space between the lungs and the lining of the chest wall on either side. This will cause the affected lung to collapse at least partially and may interfere with breathing. If pressure builds up in the pneumothorax, the lung will be completely collapsed and the contents of the chest will be pushed over to the other side. Both breathing and heart action may be affected in this case.

TREATMENT: Recompression will give temporary relief, but often the pneumothorax will have to be relieved by insertion of a needle in the chest before the man can be brought up. This is definitely a job for the doctor.

PREVENTION is the key word in lung accidents. As a cause of death in scuba diving, these probably run drowning a very close second. Many of the cases are probably not recognized as such even on the autopsy table.

In normal ascent with scuba, all you need to do is *breathe normally* throughout ascent. This keeps your "pipes" open.

Most of the accidents occur during emergency ascents where the scuba is either out of commission or has had to be left behind. Here, the big rule is to *exhale continuously* and exhale even more if any sensation of pressure in the chest is noticed. If you are wearing fins, don't worry about exhaling to the point of losing buoyancy; you can always keep yourself coming up. Don't rush; come up about as fast as your bubbles.

Most emergency ascents are likely to occur in panic-type circumstances, and it is contrary to all instinct to exhale when you've lost your air supply under water. This is where a cool head and good training really pay off. Specific training in "free ascent" is very valuable, but the procedure should not be prac-

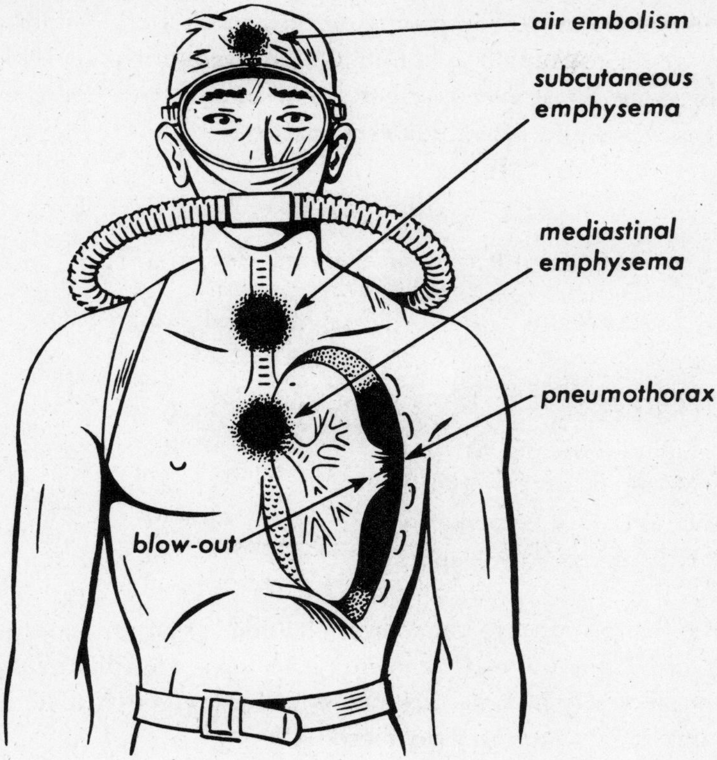

FIGURE 12. POSSIBLE CONSEQUENCES OF OVERINFLATION OF THE LUNGS

ticed from any depth unless a chamber is at hand and someone is in the water watching you.

The mechanics of starting ascent in an emergency are worth talking about. If you are wearing any kind of weights, they should be fastened in such a way that you can get rid of them almost instantaneously. Whether you should also ditch your scuba is debatable. Unless it is fouled or could otherwise hold you down, it seems better to leave it on even though it is useless. You will be in a much better position to get it off when you reach the surface. Even if it tends to hold you under, you can tread water enough to keep your head out and breathe.

Something to Breathe

"Why breathe?" That sounds like a silly question, but we don't often stop to think about it. Actually, the answer is quite a story. But in a word, we breathe because the body consumes oxygen and produces carbon dioxide in the process of living and working. Oxygen has to be taken in from what we breathe, and carbon dioxide has to be dumped out.

Oxygen consumption. The amount of air which has to be moved in and out of the lungs depends on the amounts of oxygen and carbon dioxide to be transferred. These amounts depend mainly on how much work we are doing. The rate of oxygen consumption is one of the best indications of the amount of work being done. Some average figures may interest you. They are in liters, but a liter is almost the same thing as a quart.

TABLE VII

AVERAGE RATES OF OXYGEN CONSUMPTION

Activity	*Average Consumption*
Basal—just staying alive	0.25 liters/min.
Quiet sitting	0.4
Light work—up to	1.0
Moderate work—up to	2.0
Heavy work—up to	3.0
Exhausting work—up to	4.0

The last figure applies to a man in good athletic shape; a lot of us wouldn't be able to hit 3.0 without really knowing it. A top-grade athlete may get up to 5.0 for a while. Every man has his top—his blood won't circulate fast enough beyond a certain point to carry any more.

The body does not have any real reserve of oxygen; but it does have a mechanism by means of which it can build up an oxygen debt. This lets us work beyond our maximum rate for short periods in emergencies and consume the necessary oxygen later.

Where does swimming under water fit into the oxygen consumption picture? The Experimental Diving Unit did a study on the subject and got these average values in experienced swimmers:

TABLE VIII

AVERAGE OXYGEN CONSUMPTION OF EXPERIENCED SWIMMERS

Swimming Activity	*Average Consumption*
Resting under water (just sitting quietly)	0.33 liters/min.
0.5–knot swimming (painfully slow)	0.8
0.85–knot swimming (about average)	1.4
1.2–knot swimming (too fast)	2.5

Carbon dioxide production. This is closely related to oxygen consumption, being generally just slightly less.

Respiratory minute volume (RMV). This refers to the total amount of air taken in and blown out in the course of a minute in order to supply oxygen and get rid of carbon dioxide. As a rough rule of thumb, it amounts to about 20 times the oxygen consumption. So, in round numbers, the amount of air you need under water would range somewhere between 7 liters a minute at rest and 50 liters a minute for fairly hard swimming. Average comfortable swimming would require about 28 liters per minute. This is a handy figure for rough calculations, since 28 liters is about the same thing as 1 cubic foot. Using such figures can be helpful in estimating the duration of your air supply and the like. However, individuals can vary quite a bit from these averages, so don't push the figures too far.

Rate of breathing and tidal volume. Respiratory rate (the number of breaths per minute) varies a great deal among individuals. Experimental Diving Unit (EDU) studies have shown rates between 5 and 30 during average swimming and between 2 and 20 during rest under water.

Tidal volume (the size of a single breath) can be determined by dividing the RMV by the rate. The maximum tidal volume would be equal to the man's vital capacity—the greatest amount of air that he can blow out after a maximal inspiration. The average vital capacity is around 5 liters, but this also varies quite a bit from man to man.

Regulation. The body's mechanisms for the control of breathing are interesting. There are special analyzers which sense the oxygen and carbon dioxide levels and can cause increases or decreases in breathing when the levels get out of line. When at rest, the carbon dioxide sensing system is the main controller. The oxygen mechanism serves mainly as an emergency standby most of the time. There are also special reflexes which increase breathing during work. The whole regulatory story is complex, and much of it is still incompletely understood. Diving complicates it further.

Overexertion. One of the things that stop people when they start to exceed their work capacity is "getting out of breath." There is enough lag in this reaction that you may go well beyond comfortable limits before you realize what you've done. Your limits in this sense are almost directly related to your state of cardiovascular-respiratory fitness.

Marked breathlessness is unpleasant even when on the surface with free access to air. Underwater, even with a good scuba, it can be very severe and unpleasant indeed. Especially for a beginner, it can be downright terrifying. In fact, it may be one of the most frequent causes of panic and death in diving. It can arise from something as simple as trying to keep up with a better swimmer who believes in the "same ocean" buddy system. (If you and he are diving in the same ocean at the same time, you're buddies—enough to satisfy him.)

Hyperventilation. Large increases in breathing are not always the result of purposeful exertion. A nervous novice may have such an unnecessary struggle with his gear that he is working hard and breathing to match even before he starts a dive. Anxiety and similar reactions can cause hyperventilation in the true sense of breathing more than is necessary or appropriate. This is not just an inconvenient waste of air. It can blow off CO_2 to the extent that the diver experiences lightheadedness, tingling, trembling, and perhaps other symptoms that heighten his anxiety. In such ways, a vicious circle can develop involving panic, collapse, and perhaps a fatal outcome.

Sometimes, what looks like *hyperpnea* (exaggerated breathing movements) may actually represent *tachypnea* (unusually rapid breathing) with shallow breaths that do not provide even normal ventilation of the alveoli. The end result may thus be *hypoventilation* instead of *hyperventilation.* The actual situation may be confusing enough, and confusing terminology does not help.

Depth versus air and oxygen requirements. At a given work rate, the body will consume the *same number of molecules of oxygen* per minute regardless of depth. In a scuba that supplied only the actual mass of oxygen consumed, the same supply cylinder would therefore last the same length of time at any depth. The total pulmonary ventilation per minute (RMV, expired volume, etc.) also remains, for practical purposes, the same at a given work rate. But here we are referring to volumes as measured at the diver's actual depth. This is not only over twenty times the oxygen consumption even at the surface, but the actual mass of gas increases in proportion to the absolute pressure of depth.

Nothing to Breathe

Before carrying the "Something to Breathe" subject any farther, it will be a good idea to consider some of the aspects of being underwater without anything to breathe. This may be intentional, as in breath-hold diving, or quite unintentional, as in running out of air or failure of the scuba.

When there isn't anything to breathe, you have two alternatives: 1) hold your breath, 2) drown. This isn't just an attempt to be funny. Both possibilities are quite important!

BREATH-HOLDING IN SKIN DIVING

The pitfalls of holding your breath during ascent in scuba diving have been covered. What about the sort of gambit where you take a breath at the surface, go down, stay as long as you can, and come up again? Of course, you can't get air embolism or lung damage from that. The air just re-expands and refills the lungs. It can't very well overfill them unless you've had access to extra air somewhere below the surface. So we can leave that dismal angle behind.

Among the devotees of the "no scuba" branch of the sport, ability to hold your breath for a long time is quite an asset; and how to hold it longer is a hot topic.

The most popular method is *hyperventilation:* breathing more than you need for a while before submerging. This can extend the time considerably, and until recently it was considered a fairly safe procedure. If not carried to excess (more than a few extra breaths), it is probably all right unless you "push your limits" by trying to stay down beyond the point when a real desire to resume breathing develops. Excessive hyperventilation, however, is now regarded as a means of achieving *permanent* breath-holding.

Hyperventilation has little effect on the body's oxygen supply but "blows off" carbon dioxide from the normal stores. Breath-holding time is lengthened because CO_2 now takes longer to build up to its "breakpoint" level. During the longer breath-hold, the diver's oxygen level can fall to a low value before he realizes that he must return to the surface and resume breathing. The oxygen level reached in this way would probably seldom be low enough to cause serious trouble were it not for two factors that have been spotlighted by recent research:

1. Exertion (like underwater swimming during the dive) not only causes oxygen to be used up faster but decreases the sensitivity of the CO_2 breakpoint mechanism. This permits the O_2 level to go even lower than it would otherwise.

2. When the diver finally starts up from depth and the pressure around him decreases, the drop in partial pressure of oxygen in his lungs may be sufficient to stop further uptake of oxygen completely. At the same time, the partial pressure of CO_2 in the lungs also drops, and this gives a false sense of relief from the need to breathe.

It is not at all surprising that divers who try to push their limits, especially after hyperventilation, sometimes lose consciousness from lack of oxygen (anoxia) and drown before regaining the surface. This has become recognized as a fairly common cause of death in skin diving. Underwater distance swimming events and spear-fishing competition thus seem very poor ideas, since they encourage divers to run this risk.

Breathing oxygen before a dive is an even more effective means of extending breath-holding time. If oxygen-breathing is combined with hyperventilation, spectacular durations are possible (close to fifteen minutes at rest, for example). Unfortunately, it appears that oxygen-breathing also upsets the normal breakpoint mechanisms and can be hazardous. Carbon dioxide poisoning, which can also cause unconsciousness under water, becomes possible. Like excessive hyperventilation, oxygen-breathing should be avoided.

Depth itself will prolong breath-holding time, probably because of the increased oxygen pressure involved.

DROWNING

This is without doubt by far the most frequent cause of death in scuba diving. The scuba diver gets himself into much riskier spots than either an ordinary swimmer or the suit-and-helmet diver. He is all right as long as his apparatus functions and nothing else goes wrong; but drowning can be the end result of a big assortment of mishaps, including a lot of seemingly trivial ones.

Getting panicky in a rough spot is probably involved in most scuba drownings. There are ways out of almost every conceivable emergency if you have been *trained* in what to do and can keep your head. But the man who just puts the gear on and shoves off is asking for trouble; and diving all by yourself without a buddy is another way of courting disaster.

Anybody who swims or dives should see to it that he knows how to give artificial respiration by the mouth-to-mouth (or mouth-to-nose) method. This provides much better lung ventilation than the older procedures, can be used anywhere (even in the water), and requires no equipment. There is nothing complex about it, but getting the head and jaw into proper position is essential and requires a little practice.

ANOXIA

Not getting enough oxygen is one of the results of having "Nothing to Breathe," but it isn't quite the same thing. *Anoxia* can be defined as a *lack of sufficient oxygen in the tissues.* And when the tissues don't have enough oxygen, they stop functioning normally and will eventually die. The brain is the most sensitive part of the body so far as lack of oxygen is concerned. Unconsciousness can occur very rapidly, and the brain cells will die if a severe lack of oxygen goes on for more than a very few minutes.

Anoxia can come about in many ways, since getting oxygen from the air around us all the way into the tissues is quite a process. Anoxia will be the major difficulty in any disease or mishap that can block the uptake, transport, or utilization of oxygen at any stage. Anoxia is the final cause in almost all deaths. Note that the term *hypoxia* is being used increasingly in place of *anoxia.* In ordinary usage, however, there is no difference in meaning.

How can hypoxia come about in diving? Fortunately, lack of oxygen is uncommon and unlikely in diving, short of major accidents like drowning or air embolism. The most likely cause is either (1) not having enough to breathe, or (2) not having enough oxygen in what you breathe.

Not getting enough to breathe can certainly produce hypoxia, but the basic problem here will usually be obvious before lack of oxygen can become serious. At least, this cause of hypoxia isn't likely to sneak up on you.

Not having enough oxygen in what you breathe is an entirely different matter, and its lack of clearcut warning is the main reason for being concerned about it. You may be helpless before you know that anything is wrong. There are, luckily, only a few ways in which lack of oxygen in the breathing medium can come about in diving. It cannot happen in open-circuit gear that is charged with decent air (but having scuba cylinders charged inadvertently with pure nitrogen or some other inappropriate gas is not entirely unheard of). Any time a gas mixture is deliberately used, the possibility of inaccurate mixing or faulty analysis arises.

Perhaps surprisingly, *closed-circuit oxygen-rebreathing equipment* is hazardous from the standpoint of hypoxia. It is very fortunate for several reasons that this type of equipment never became popular among sport divers and is not widely available. Nevertheless, some of its features continue to interest many divers and experimenters, and the potential hazards are too important and too seldom understood to be passed over.

A simple closed-circuit rig includes a breathing bag, a CO_2 absorption canister, an oxygen supply cylinder, and the necessary mask or mouthpiece, valves, tubing, etc. Ideally, the system contains essentially nothing but oxygen. As the diver consumes oxygen, the gas in the system is still almost-pure oxygen; but at some point, the volume remaining no longer suffices for comfortable inspiration. So then the diver (or a demand-type mechanism) cracks a valve to admit more oxygen into the system.

This sounds very fine and uncomplicated, but consider what could happen if a few liters of nitrogen or other inert gas had been left in the system at the start or had entered it from any supply gas other than pure oxygen. The diver's uptake of oxygen could drop the oxygen percentage in the system almost to zero while the volume of inert gas might be sufficient to permit perfectly comfortable inspiration. The diver would have no effective warning of impending hypoxia and would probably lose consciousness without realizing that anything was amiss.

This is a very hazardous situation indeed, and thus hypoxia is one of the predominant perils of any breathing apparatus in which gas is rebreathed. Before discussing such systems in any detail, however, we will have a closer look at hypoxia itself and the two other major hazards: CO_2 toxicity and oxygen poisoning.

What is "enough" oxygen? The *partial pressure* of oxygen is what counts. At the surface, with one atmosphere of absolute pressure and almost 21 per cent oxygen in air, we have over 0.2 atm partial pressure of oxygen in the inspired gas. This, of course, is ample. You would also have 0.2 atm oxygen pressure if you were breathing 5% oxygen at 99 feet or 1% oxygen at 20 atm.

What happens in hypoxia? The effects of low inspired-gas oxygen pressure depend on just how low the oxygen pressure actually is. It can drop to 0.17 atm with few obvious effects; but below that, a number of difficulties begin to appear.

The troubles we are most concerned about are so much like getting drunk that it is hardly necessary to go into details. They represent progressive depression of the brain and include such things as loss of ability to concentrate, inability to think clearly, loss of coordination, slowing of reflexes, and the like. Along with this, there is usually a good bit of euphoria—the medical word for feeling as if everything is wonderful when it isn't. All in all, anoxia is usually far from unpleasant. You lose not only your ability to recognize that anything is wrong but also your ability to get concerned about anything—or to do anything constructive about it. And before very long, you are just plain unconscious.

You will become almost completely helpless at about 0.12 atm., and unconsciousness occurs if you are down to 0.10 atm. (10 per cent at surface) for any length of time. Below that, death isn't far off unless you're rescued.

But aren't there any warning signs—things you can recognize before it is too late? Frankly, unless you can recognize the "drunk" sensation before it gets too marked, there aren't any other reactions that will help much underwater. Pulse and blood pressure will increase, but who takes his pulse during a dive? Breathing picks up a little, but usually not enough to notice until it is too late. You may get cyanotic (blue); but that is a poor warning even at surface, and who would see it underwater?

Treatment? If a victim of anoxia is fished out, treatment ordinarily is not very hard to figure out; if he's breathing, just getting fresh air will usually bring him around. If he's not breathing, you'd naturally use artificial respiration. Oxygen is good if it's available; but it isn't essential; various medications likewise are useful but not essential.

Short of death itself, permanent brain damage is the main concern. Most victims who can be brought around fairly readily haven't much to worry about. Even with some brain damage, a surprising amount of functional recovery may occur in time.

CARBON DIOXIDE EXCESS

How can it occur? Carbon dioxide intoxication is quite unlikely in *open-circuit scuba.* It might happen if the cylinders were charged with air containing carbon dioxide—rare, but worth keeping in mind. Another possibility is that the diver is simply not washing enough carbon dioxide out of his lungs because of insufficient breathing. For reasons unknown, some men tend to breathe inadequately when they are working at depth. This tendency can be aggravated by misguided efforts to "save air"—a process which appears to be potentially dangerous for this reason. Such problems also can be made worse by an excess of dead space in the breathing apparatus. (Dead space is defined as any part of a breathing system which catches expired air and gives it back on inspiration. Dead space apparently has to be fairly large to make much difference under ordinary conditions, but it should be kept as small as possible.)

Carbon dioxide buildup is much more likely to occur in rebreathing rigs than anywhere else. In addition to peculiarities on the part of the diver, and

Depth in feet	Atmospheres, absolute	Total Pressure in lbs. per sq. in	Partial Pressures (in atmospheres) assuming N₂ = 80%	O₂ = 20%	GAS VOLUME
0	1	14.7	0.8	0.2	1
33	2	29.4	1.6	0.4	1/2
66	3	44.1	2.4	0.6	1/3
132	5	73.5	4.0	1.0	1/5
165	6	88.2	4.8	1.2	1/6
297	10	147.0	8.0	2.0	1/10

FIGURE 13. EFFECT OF DEPTH ON PRESSURES AND VOLUMES

greatly complicating such problems, is the possibility that the CO_2 absorbent may become exhausted from unusually severe CO_2 loads, be inactivated by getting wet, or "channel" because of poor canister design. In one tragic and well-publicized case, the absorbent was apparently not put in when the rig was prepared for an extraordinarily important dive.

How much is too much? Here, again, it is partial pressure that counts. For example, breathing 5 per cent carbon dioxide at 33 feet gives the same effects as breathing 10 per cent at the surface—0.1 atm. in either case.

TABLE IX

Effects of Breathing Carbon Dioxide

Up to 2%	Not much happens.
Around 2%	Increase in breathing normally starts.
At 5%	There is considerable increase in breathing; normally noticeable and uncomfortable.
Up to 10%	Progressive increase in breathing is noticeable, *plus* mental effects not unlike those of *anoxia.*
At 10% and above	There are marked mental effects, eventual unconsciousness.
Higher percentages —20 to 30% or so	Can cause a form of *convulsion* as well as unconsciousness.

NOTE: A few miscellaneous symptoms may show up in the milder exposures. These include: headache, a general "unwell" feeling, fatigue, weakness, mild twitches. (Most headaches come on *after* exposure.)

Death from carbon dioxide itself is a very rare thing; but losing consciousness from it underwater is certainly dangerous. Note that "10%" is a crucial level in both carbon dioxide excess and anoxia.

To have a very uncomfortable increase in breathing before carbon dioxide levels become high enough to cause harm is the normal state of affairs. But not everybody will have this kind of response. A few can get into serious mental depression without knowing that anything is wrong—which makes carbon dioxide excess as dangerous for them as anoxia is for most people.

"Shallow water blackout." Occasionally, a diver will lose consciousness underwater without apparent warning or without sufficient warning to permit him to take effective action. This happened with alarming frequency during World War II among British frogmen and divers using oxygen-rebreathing equipment in underwater swimming or other exertion. When the cause was still unknown,

the term *shallow water blackout* was applied. Investigation and research eventually indicated that CO_2 buildup was most often responsible. It was also shown that many individuals, especially during exertion, could reach unconsciousness from CO_2 without the expected warning of breathlessness.

The blackout problem became much less frequent in the Royal Navy after the canisters were improved. All similar cases that the author has seen in the use of closed-circuit scuba have been associated with flooded canisters or other CO_2 absorption problems. It seems definite that the phenomenon can be produced by CO_2, but this does not mean that it is the only explanation. As already discussed, loss of consciousness from lack of oxygen follows a similar pattern. Under some conditions, hyperventilation could do the same. A condition dubbed *oxygen syncope* has also been described. This suggests that divers breathing oxygen have an unusual susceptibility to fainting.

In recent years, the term *shallow water blackout* has been applied to entirely different situations such as loss of consciousness from hypoxia during breath-hold diving. It seems better to keep the term for things resembling its original context more closely.

Many divers complain of *dizziness on starting ascent,* and in some this is accompanied by a feeling of impending blackout. This phenomenon has no proven explanation although several theories have been advanced. *Alternobaric vertigo* is the term applied to one of these theories. This theory attributes the problem to an increase of pressure in the middle ear and presumes that the expanding gas in that space is not venting freely. A survey showed that dizziness on ascent was more common in divers who had experienced some difficulty in equalizing pressure on descent. In most divers, the phenomenon appears to be more worrisome than dangerous.

CARBON MONOXIDE POISONING

This can result from contamination of the air used for charging scuba. Such contamination can be caused by (1) engine exhaust gas getting into compressor air intake—a real possibility with gasoline-driven compressors; (2) "flashing" of lubricating oil in the cylinders of oil-lubricated compressors, causing incomplete combustion of the oil.

For this reason, and because of the possibility of getting air which is loaded with oil vapor, it pays to be sure where your air comes from. Air from anything but a sure source should be checked for both carbon monoxide and oil vapor. A small pocket-sized carbon monoxide tester can be a big help in cases where you can't be sure.

The effects of carbon monoxide on the body are very similar to those of anoxia. It is basically an anoxic condition since carbon monoxide combines with hemoglobin and keeps it from transporting oxygen. Symptoms like headache and feeling sick sometimes occur, but they are not reliable warnings.

Present standards for allowable levels of CO and other contaminants in divers' air are discussed in Chapter 4.

Indirect Effects of Pressure

Pressure effects classified as "indirect" or "secondary" are those in which the partial pressure of a gas plays the main role, as has already been seen in the case of low-oxygen and high-CO_2 effects.

NITROGEN

Air contains about 79% nitrogen, taken to include a small fraction of argon and other inert gases. The high partial pressures of nitrogen encountered at depth have two principal effects: narcosis and decompression problems.

Nitrogen narcosis was identified and named in the early 1930's. When Captain Cousteau and his associates "discovered" it much later, they called it "Rapture of the Depths." The original French word is translated more accurately but less poetically as "drunkenness" instead of "rapture." The mechanism is still incompletely understood, but it probably is the same as that of gases used for anesthesia—whatever their mechanism may be. In other words, nitrogen is probably an anesthetic gas like nitrous oxide (laughing gas), only much weaker. *NOTE: Playing around with gases like nitrous oxide has caused death in a number of instances, presumably due to hypoxia but possibly involving other factors.* The effects can also be compared to something a lot more familiar: alcoholic intoxication. There are differences; but being drunk, being anoxic, and having nitrogen narcosis have much in common. The relationship to alcohol has been expressed in what might be called Martini's Law: The mental effects of each additional 50 feet of depth, breathing air, are approximately equivalent to those of one dry Martini, assuming the stomach to be empty.

Just as in the case of nitrous oxide and Martinis, individual susceptibility varies considerably. There are some who continue to carry on fairly nobly even after most of the others have slid under the table. There are a few who are pretty obviously "looped" as shallow as 100 feet. And, of course, there are also some who can be quite far gone without knowing it—"I've only had tee Martoonies," etc.

Incidentally, "tee Martoonies" equals 100 feet according to the above law. At that depth, you may not notice any impairment unless you try to do something which requires quick thinking or accuracy of thought or motion, like trying to read a depth gauge, figure decompression, or handle an emergency. In such cases, narcosis will be pretty apparent in most people. It is very important to realize that you are likely to be half shot in spite of feeling just dandy.

Experienced divers realize that they can barely be trusted to come in out of

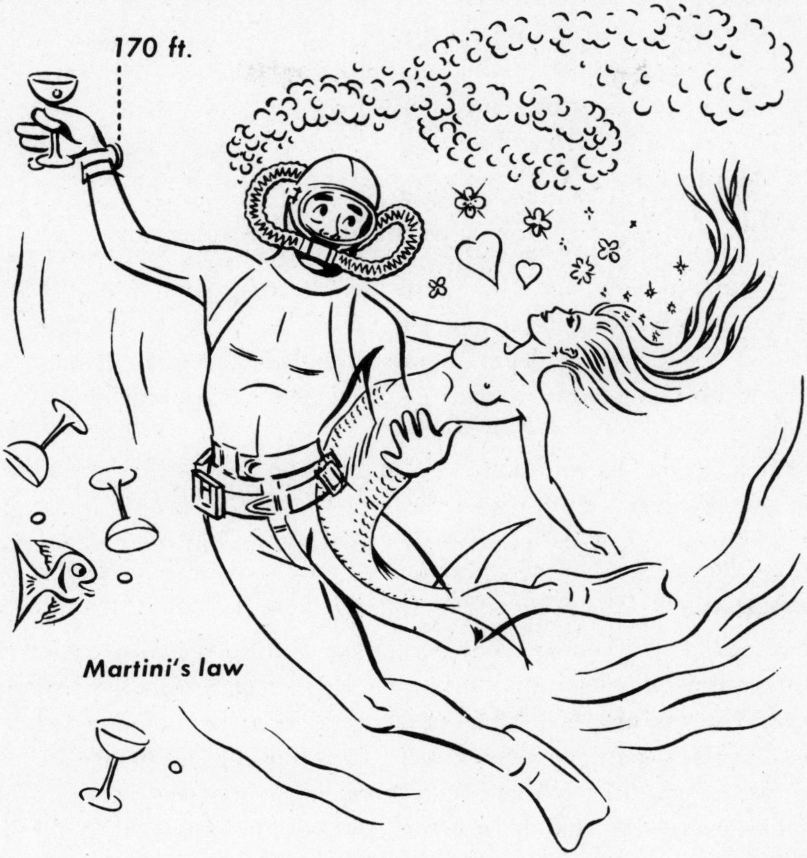

FIGURE 14. A CASE OF NITROGEN NARCOSIS

the rain once they get much below 200 feet—scarcely remembering what job they went down to do, caring less, and actually being a menace to themselves.

One of the best stories illustrating this fact, and quite possibly true, is about a diver who was at 250 feet or so and obviously accomplishing nothing in spite of the blue stream of profanity which issued from the topside phone. When his tender finally got a word in edgewise and asked what he was doing and what was the matter, the drunken voice replied that his air hose was getting in the way something awful but not to worry because he had about gotten the damned thing cut off. The diver was hauled up.

Whether it really is true or not, this story has several morals. One of these has to do with the difference between air-hose and scuba diving: the scuba diver doesn't have anybody on the other end of a telephone cable at the surface to keep track of him, keep him in contact with reality, and bring him up if worse comes to worst. And he doesn't have the protection of that clumsy, but sometimes very welcome, suit and helmet. If he feels like handing his mouthpiece to a passing fish—an impulse Cousteau mentions—he can. And if he drops his mouthpiece he may or may not have the wit to get it back in and cleared.

All this brings up a question: If a conventional diver doesn't generally trust himself at much over 200 feet, how deep should a scuba diver go? Perhaps you can form some conclusions of your own. No matter what record somebody finally sets for air diving with scuba, the deeper stuff remains largely useless.

Retention of CO_2 is not the cause of narcosis, but it can greatly accentuate the narcotic effects of inert gas.

Helium has no apparent narcotic action at any pressure reached to date by man or experimental animals. Absence of this effect is the principal reason for the use of helium-oxygen mixtures in place of air for deep diving. Neuromuscular effects encountered at depths approaching 1,000 feet were once called "helium tremors." It now seems more likely that these are attributable to hydrostatic pressure effects.

At greater depths, the duration of gas supply and the cost become so important that helium-oxygen mixtures can be used practically in only the more sophisticated types of mixed-gas scuba or in hose-supplied rigs with recirculation.

Decompression

"Why decompress?" When the body is exposed to an increased partial pressure of any gas, considerable amounts of that gas will go into solution in the blood and tissues. The gas gets in by diffusion across the lung membrane that separates the alveolar gas from the blood that flows through the lungs. This blood becomes charged with the gas and then transports it to the tissues. When the body remains exposed to the elevated ambient pressure, gases taken up in this way will remain in solution.

When the pressure is reduced, the gases will start leaving the same way they got in: through the circulating blood and the lungs. But for all the dissolved gas to get out in this way takes a long time; and if the surrounding pressure is reduced too rapidly, the unloading process will get seriously behind. The partial pressure of the tissue gas can then be quite far above the total (external, ambient) pressure, and a state called *supersaturation* will exist. A small degree of supersaturation can probably develop with little or no formation of bubbles, and some degree of bubble formation can apparently be tolerated. However, symptoms will appear if the process goes beyond a certain point.

Because it is constantly being consumed, oxygen seldom attains very high pressures in the tissues, and tissue oxygen pressure alone seldom initiates bubble formation. But "inert" gases like nitrogen or helium—which the body does not utilize—can cause grave difficulties. Opening a bottle of carbonated beverage provides a good demonstration of the principle. Before the cap comes off, the liquid holds the gas quietly in solution. But removing the cap drops the pressure. The liquid becomes supersaturated and starts to bubble.

In bringing a diver up, the objective is to keep the degree of supersaturation from becoming great enough to cause consequential formation of bubbles. The guide for managing such safe ascent is called a *decompression table.* Figure 15 is an example, taken from the *U.S. Navy Diving Manual.* The ascent rate of 60 ft./min. and the specified stops are *intended* to allow enough gas to depart quietly through the lungs to prevent trouble in almost all instances.

No stops at all are required for relatively short or shallow dives, as a look at the table shows. The "no decompression" limits, as specified by the standard air decompression table, are of greatest interest to most scuba divers and are presented in Table X. As will probably become very clear, scuba divers are extremely well-advised to stay within these depth-time limits and avoid entirely the necessity of making decompression stops. Even so, it remains necessary to consider the prescribed rate of ascent and to be fully cognizant of the implications of *repetitive dives* (see below).

TABLE X

"No Decompression" Limits

Depth (ft.)	*Bottom Time (min.)*
(less than 33)	(no limit)
35	310
40	200
50	100
60	60
70	50
80	40
90	30
100	25
110	20
120	15
130	10
140	10
150 to 190	5

Bottom time is the total elapsed time between leaving the surface and starting ascent—not just time spent at the maximum depth. Note that it would rarely be possible to make a dive to 150 feet or more, accomplish any useful work there, and be ready to start up—all within five minutes; so attempting to make such deep dives on a "no decompression" basis is seldom advisable.

Be sure to understand these important points about use of the decompression table and "no decompression" limits:

Depth (feet)	Bottom time (min)	Time to first stop (min:sec)	Decompression stops (feet) 50	40	30	20	10	Total ascent (min:sec)	Repetitive group
40	200						0	0:40	(*)
	210	0:30					2	2:40	N
	230	0:30					7	7:40	N
	250	0:30					11	11:40	O
	270	0:30					15	15:40	O
	300	0:30					19	19:40	Z
50	100						0	0:50	(*)
	110	0:40					3	3:50	L
	120	0:40					5	5:50	M
	140	0:40					10	10:50	M
	160	0:40					21	21:50	N
	180	0:40					29	29:50	O
	200	0:40					35	35:50	O
	220	0:40					40	40:50	Z
	240	0:40					47	47:50	Z
60	60						0	1:00	(*)
	70	0:50					2	3:00	K
	80	0:50					7	8:00	L
	100	0:50					14	15:00	M
	120	0:50					26	27:00	N
	140	0:50					39	40:00	O
	160	0:50					48	49:00	Z
	180	0:50					56	57:00	Z
	200	0:40				1	69	71:00	Z
70	50						0	1:10	(*)
	60	1:00					8	9:10	K
	70	1:00					14	15:10	L
	80	1:00					18	19:10	M
	90	1:00					23	24:10	N
	100	1:00					33	34:10	N
	110	0:50				2	41	44:10	O
	120	0:50				4	47	52:10	O
	130	0:50				6	52	59:10	O
	140	0:50				8	56	65:10	Z
	150	0:50				9	61	71:10	Z
	160	0:50				13	72	86:10	Z
	170	0:50				19	79	99:10	Z
80	40						0	1:20	(*)
	50	1:10					10	11:20	K
	60	1:10					17	18:20	L
	70	1:10					23	24:20	M
	80	1:00				2	31	34:20	N
	90	1:00				7	39	47:20	N
	100	1:00				11	46	58:20	O
	110	1:00				13	53	67:20	O
	120	1:00				17	56	74:20	Z
	130	1:00				19	63	83:20	Z
	140	1:00				26	69	96:20	Z
	150	1:00				32	77	110:20	Z
90	30						0	1:30	(*)
	40	1:20					7	8:30	J
	50	1:20					18	19:30	L
	60	1:20					25	26:30	M
	70	1:10				7	30	38:30	N
	80	1:10				13	40	54:30	N
	90	1:10				18	48	67:30	O
	100	1:10				21	54	76:30	Z
	110	1:10				24	61	86:30	Z
	120	1:10				32	68	101:30	Z
	130	1:00			5	36	74	116:30	Z
100	25						0	1:40	(*)
	30	1:30					3	4:40	I
	40	1:30					15	16:40	K
	50	1:20				2	24	27:40	L
	60	1:20				9	28	38:40	N
	70	1:20				17	39	57:40	O
	80	1:20				23	48	72:40	O
	90	1:10			3	23	57	84:40	Z
	100	1:10			7	23	66	97:40	Z
	110	1:10			10	34	72	117:40	Z
	120	1:10			12	41	78	132:40	Z
110	20						0	1:50	(*)
	25	1:40					3	4:50	H
	30	1:40					7	8:50	J
	40	1:30				2	21	24:50	L
	50	1:30				8	26	35:50	M
	60	1:30				18	36	55:50	N
	70	1:20			1	23	48	73:50	O
	80	1:20			7	23	57	88:50	Z
	90	1:20			12	30	64	107:50	Z
	100	1:20			15	37	72	125:50	Z

*See Table 1–11 on page 259 for repetitive groups in no-decompression dives.

FIGURE 15. STANDARD AIR DECOMPRESSION TABLE

This example is reproduced from the 1970 *U. S. Navy Diving Manual.*
See pages 256–258 in the Appendix of this book for the complete table.

1. *Depth* is tabulated in 10-foot steps. Unless your depth corresponds exactly to one of these tabulated depths (and you must be sure of this), use the *next greater* depth in selecting your decompression schedule. Example: a dive to 91 feet requires decompression according to a 100-foot schedule.

2. Remember that *bottom time* means the number of minutes that elapse from the moment you leave the surface to the moment you start your ascent—not just the time actually spent on the bottom. Times are tabulated in 5- or 10-minute steps, and unless your time is exactly equal to one of the tabulated times, you must use the next greater one. *Example:* a 26-minute dive to 102 feet requires use of the schedule for 30 minutes at 110 feet.

NOTE: If a dive involves exceptional cold or hard work, add a safety factor by using the schedule for the depth or time (or both) beyond that which would normally be used.

3. *Rate of ascent.* The table was calculated and tested for an ascent rate of 60 feet per minute (one foot per second), and this should be followed. If you come up faster, you are omitting some of the decompression that ascent at the specified rate provides. If you come up slower, this amounts to spending more time at depth (and thus taking up more nitrogen) than was expected. If your dive was at all close to the stated depth and time of the schedule you are using, either mistake might result in decompression sickness.

4. *Repetitive dives* are defined as successive dives made within a twelve-hour period. Every dive, whether it requires decompression stops or not, leaves some excess of nitrogen in the body. This leaves gradually while you are at the surface, but it is not completely cleared out in less than twelve hours. Therefore, if you make another dive within a twelve-hour period, your body will contain more nitrogen when you start up from that dive than it would have if the previous dive(s) had not been made. As a result, you will need more decompression—or will be able to spend less time at depth on a "no decompression" basis.

The Diving Manual provides a system for safe and sensible determination of limits and decompression schedules for repetitive dives, giving credit for nitrogen lost during the time at surface between dives. The old rule of adding the bottom times of all dives made during the past twelve hours and using the depth of the last dive usually yielded much more decompression or much more restrictive limits than were necessary; but in some cases it was not even safe.

Having to make decompression stops on ascent obviously makes scuba diving a lot more complicated, especially when there is a chance of running out of air during the stops, as is often the case. So, unless there is a very good reason for doing otherwise, the scuba diver is very much better off to stay within the "no decompression" limits and make sure that he does not unwittingly go beyond those limits by making repetitive dives.

When it comes to diving in the decompression range, the suit-and-helmet

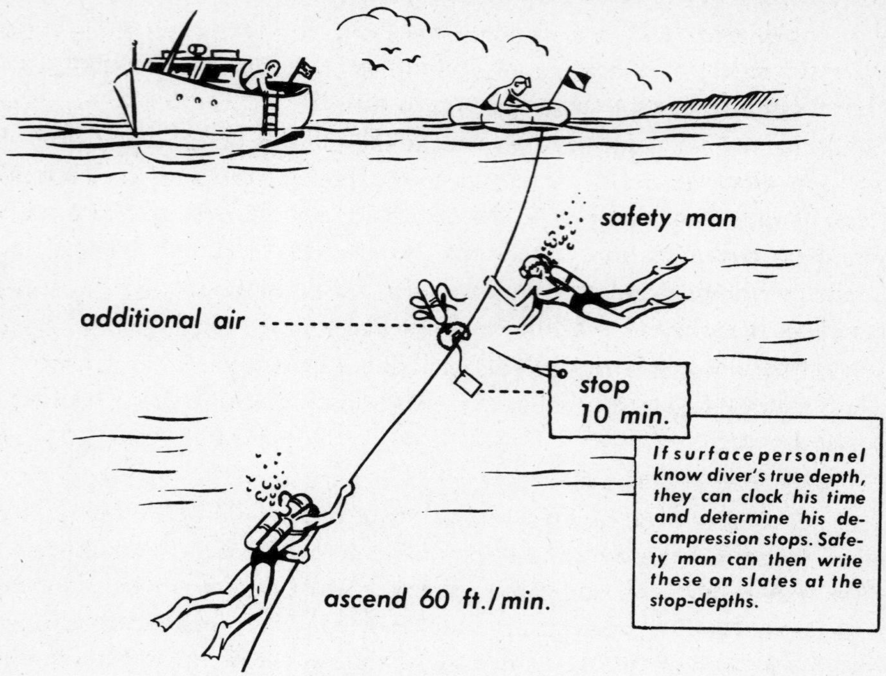

FIGURE 16. DECOMPRESSION STOPS

diver has a lot of advantages: unlimited air supply; tenders who keep track of his time, depth, and stops. Proper decompression can be accomplished with scuba, but it entails more planning and preparation and more attention to details than most scuba divers are willing to put into it. Mistakes are easier to make and more likely to be serious. For any dive requiring decompression, an added margin of safety can be provided by a five-minute stop at the first decompression stage below that recommended by the tables for that particular set of circumstances.

A lot of people have either or both of two serious misconceptions about decompression in scuba diving. One misconception is that you will always run out of air before you can get into decompression trouble. This is not true even with ordinary single-cylinder rigs; and it is quite untrue with larger models and with unusually high charging pressures. If a successful "liquid-air" scuba ever becomes available, its duration will invite grave decompression problems.

Misunderstandings about air supply duration and decompression limits stem in part from unwarranted use of round numbers on air-use rates. It is substantially true that an average man doing moderate work near the surface will use about one cubic foot of air per minute. This provides a very useful illustration and example. But the same man can use either a lot more or a lot less air if his work rate changes, while another man may use considerably more or less air even at the same work rate.

Safety margins. The second misconception is that the U.S. Navy decompression tables include a large margin of safety and are so unnecessarily conservative that you can violate them with reckless abandon. This impression has probably arisen from the fact that outrageous violations are on occasion committed with apparent impunity. The real truth comes out in a broader view: There is no great safety factor built into the tables at all. Any team that does a lot of diving will see its share of decompression sickness, including some serious cases, even if it follows the tables very closely.

Another myth concerns the *"un-bendable" diver*, who is under the impression that his extraordinary qualities of shape or spirit are a sure defense against bubble formation. It is true that susceptibility to decompression sickness can differ considerably between and among individuals. It can apparently vary also in the same individual from one time to another. Old "Bubble-proof" may one day push his luck too far.

It may come as a surprise to some divers that the U.S. Navy tables were never intended to be "100% safe." In Navy diving, with good recompression facilities always at hand, it is much better to accept a small percentage of "bends" cases than to use tables that are long enough to be perfectly safe. Experience with the standard air table since it was put forth in 1958 has, in fact, shown that some schedules have a much greater tendency to produce trouble than was ever intended. Unofficially, our own experience and that of communicating laboratories indicates that these are among the inadequate ones (the list is surely not complete): 140 ft./30 min.; 140/40; 150/30; 170/30; and 50/100. The problem that such schedules present is not extraordinarily serious for a Navy ship or station or a well-equipped high-pressure laboratory with good treatment capability, but a scuba diver with no such backup at hand could be in serious trouble. In fact, experienced divers have largely learned to avoid such troublesome schedules—which is one of the main reasons why more has not been said or done about this problem.

Exceptional exposures. Unusually deep or prolonged air dives present difficult problems in decompression. The U.S. Navy table provided for such dives admittedly has a rather high incidence of bad results and should be avoided whenever possible.

Diving above sea level. The U.S. Navy tables are understandably designed for diving in the ocean. Anywhere above sea level, "surfacing" puts the diver at a lower ambient pressure and under greater risk of bubble formation than was contemplated when the tables were calculated and tested. Diving in mountain lakes, for example, involves considerable risk if the tables are applied literally. Various rules, systems, and tables have been put forward for dealing with this problem, but none of these have yet had adequate experimental validation to this author's knowledge.

There is some evidence that even small elevations, such as the 600- to 800-

ft altitudes found around the Great Lakes, may affect the outcome with some schedules.

Flying after diving. Even after an uneventful "no decompression" dive, a man will have significantly more nitrogen in his tissues than he had before. Acute exposures to altitude might precipitate symptomatic bubble formation. Again, fully conclusive evidence is lacking, but a simple rule that is generally adequate is to put a 12-hour interval between surfacing from a dive and flying.

Decompression meters. There are many good reasons for wanting a device that will automatically take account of a diver's actual exposure and then furnish correct guidelines for decompression. This would be useful for all kinds of diving, but it would be especially valuable for the many real-life situations where tables cannot be applied realistically. Such an instrument has been produced by the Canadian Armed Forces, but it remains somewhat bulky and is not generally available.

One device that is available commercially has been used by several notable diving organizations. Tests in my laboratory indicated that in a relatively limited range of depths and times one of these meters called for decompression very close to that specified by the U.S. Navy tables. Shorter and shallower dives were given unnecessarily conservative decompression according to that standard, while longer and deeper dives appeared to be handled inadequately. Such an instrument, if it performed reproducibly, might be very useful in some situations and with adequate precautions.

Limits for scuba divers. The foregoing discussion must have made it clear that decompression problems can complicate scuba diving greatly. Staying within no-decompression limits simplifies the process materially, and observing the U.S. Navy scuba limit of 130 feet would also eliminate a number of problems. It does not seem sensible to urge divers to observe such limits without first giving them a reasonably complete view of the whole picture.

Saturation diving. The need for prolonged decompression is one of the most serious limiting factors in diving to greater depths and in tackling time-consuming jobs at any depth. Decompression time lengthens markedly as time increases at any given depth, but eventually (probably within 36 hours) the body becomes saturated with nitrogen (or helium) at the pressure of depth. By this is meant that the pressures of dissolved gas in all of the tissues have come to equilibrium with the external pressure of the gas, and no more gas will be taken up. Beyond this point of time, the decompression time needed on ascent will no longer increase. It will be very long—in the order of a day per 100 feet of depth—but a diver who has reached saturation would require no greater decompression time if he remained for a week or a month.

The saturation principle is the basis of the "undersea habitation" idea put into practice in U.S. Navy Sealab projects, the French Conshelf stations, and similar enterprises. The same principle is equally important in systems that keep the divers under pressure in a comfortable chamber on a surface ship and send them to depth in a connecting submersible chamber. At the moment, the latter approach is more prevalent; but improvements in equipment may make sea-floor living more attractive in the future.

For a great number of time-consuming jobs at depth, the long final decompression of a saturation dive will be vastly shorter than the combined decompression times of many short dives to the same depth.

The potential of saturation diving is augmented by the fact that *excursion dives* of reasonable duration can be made safely to depths greater than the actual saturation level.

Decompression Sickness

Symptoms. The most frequent manifestation of decompression sickness is *pain.* This dominates the picture in about 90% of the cases. (Strictly speaking, "the bends" refers only to the painful form of decompression sickness, but the term is very commonly used to refer to any manifestation and will be so used here.) Pain may occur anywhere, but it is usually confined to one well-localized part of the body, with joints in the limbs being most commonly affected.

A very frequent but less consequential aftermath of decompression is *itching.* Occasionally, this is accompanied by a *rash.* The rash may be scarcely noticeable or it may be very severe, and skin manifestations can progress as far as a corpse-like mottling. Regional *swelling* in the subcutaneous tissue can also occasionally occur. Unusual *fatigue* is a frequent aftereffect of diving; it is usually attributed to bubbles of unknown location. Itch, rash, and fatigue may occur singly, in various combinations, or with pain or other major signs and symptoms. Sometimes, they may precede a more serious development, so a diver with any of these manifestations deserves watching. Itch and rash are particularly common after dives in which the skin was warm during exposure and cold during decompression. In this case, there is reason to believe that the manifestation is only a local phenomenon of gas-trapping in the skin. Itch, rash, and fatigue are not usually treated by recompression; but severe instances and cases with local swelling may deserve such treatment.

A diver who has a real bends pain isn't likely to call it a mild symptom. However, there are some symptoms—fortunately less frequent than pain—which are really serious. These are produced by bubbles in the central nervous system (brain and spinal cord) or in the lung. The lung symptoms are called "chokes." They may involve such things as shortness of breath, pain on deep breathing, coughing and the like, and should be given prompt treatment.

The central nervous system symptoms can include a great variety of disorders. The following list will give some idea of the possibilities:

Dizziness.
Weakness or paralysis anywhere in the body.

Numbness—loss of sensation anywhere.
Collapse and loss of consciousness.
Blindness or other disorders of vision.
Ringing of the ears or other defects of hearing.
Convulsions.

Any one of these developments indicates that some part of the nervous system has been deprived of its blood supply or disrupted by pressure from a bubble in the tissue itself. Nerve tissue usually can't survive such insults for very long, so treatment must be both prompt and sufficient to relieve the symptoms.

Serious symptoms do not necessarily follow only deeper, longer dives or more outrageous violation of tables. They can occur after relatively mild exposures with decompression that would ordinarily have been fully adequate.

The possible variety of symptoms of decompression sickness is so great that almost any abnormality which shows up after a dive has to be considered a possible "bend" unless it is obviously caused by something else. The "obviously due to something else" idea can be misleading. For instance, a diver who develops a sore knee after a dive may know that he hit it on a rock during the dive—but such injuries may favor development of a bend in the affected location. The fact that a dive was within the "zero decompression" limits or that proper decompression was given doesn't mean very much, either.

Even an experience diving medical officer may have a tough time deciding whether a certain symptom is due to decompression sickness or not. Frequently, a "test of pressure" has to be given; and, if this is inconclusive, the patient may have to be treated just to be safe.

Almost every bend, if untreated, will produce permanent injury of some degree. Whether this will be negligible or serious depends on the location and severity of the case. The disability may not show up at once either.

Late manifestations of decompression sickness include the residual effects of untreated cases or of cases treated with incomplete success. *Paralysis* of the lower part of the body from a spinal cord "hit" may be the most common example. *Aseptic bone necrosis* is the term applied to death of bone tissue in localized areas. It is a long-recognized aftereffect of exposure to pressure in tunnel work. It is rare but not unheard-of in divers. When the death of bone takes place close to the bearing surface of a hip or shoulder joint, great pain and disability may follow. Association of the condition with prolonged exposures makes it of particular concern in saturation diving. It is also difficult to rule out the possibility that bone necrosis can result from repeated inadequacy of decompression or from failure to treat mild or questionable cases of bends.

Two commandments about decompression sickness are worth thinking about: *1*) remember that almost anything can happen, and *2*) when in doubt, treat—and treat adequately. Prompt treatment of a seemingly improbable case, or a doubtful or minor one—usually on a short table—will often avoid having to give long-table treatment and possibly a bad result later.

Treatment. Copies of the U.S. Navy treatment tables are included here as Tables XI and XII, and "Notes on Recompression" from the *U.S. Navy Diving Manual* are included with the decompression tables.

TABLE XI

Treatment of Decompression Sickness and Air Embolism*

Stops	Bends—Pain only		Serious Symptoms	
Rate of descent—25 ft. per min. Rate of ascent—1 minute between stops.	Pain relieved at depths less than 66 ft. Use table 1—A if O_2 is not available.	Pain relieved at depths greater than 66 ft. Use table 2—A if O_2 is not available. If pain does not improve within 30 min. at 165 ft. the case is probably not bends. Decompress on table 2 or 2—A.	Serious symptoms include any one of the following: 1. Unconsciousness. 2. Convulsions. 3. Weakness or inability to use arms or legs. 4. Air embolism. 5. Any visual disturbances. 6. Dizziness. 7. Loss of speech or hearing. 8. Severe shortness of breath or chokes. 9. Bends occurring while still under pressure.	
			Symptoms relieved within 30 minutes at 165 ft. Use table 3	Symptoms not relieved within 30 minutes at 165 ft. Use table 4

Pounds	Feet	Table 1	Table 1-A	Table 2	Table 2-A	Table 3	Table 4
73.4	165	----------	----------	30 (air)	30 (air)	30 (air)	30 to 120 (air)
62.3	140	----------	----------	12 (air)	12 (air)	12 (air)	30 (air)
53.4	120	----------	----------	12 (air)	12 (air)	12 (air)	30 (air)
44.5	100	30 (air)	30 (air)	12 (air)	12 (air)	12 (air)	30 (air)
35.6	80	12 (air)	12 (air)	12 (air)	12 (air)	12 (air)	30 (air)
26.7	60	30 (O_2)	30 (air)	30 (O_2)	30 (air)	30 (O_2) or (air)	6 hrs. (air)
22.3	50	30 (O_2)	30 (air)	30 (O_2)	30 (air)	30 (O_2) or (air)	6 hrs. (air)
17.8	40	30 (O_2)	30 (air)	30 (O_2)	30 (air)	30 (O_2) or (air)	6 hrs. (air)
13.4	30	↓	60 (air)	60 (O_2)	2 hrs. (air)	12 hrs. (air)	First 11 hrs. (air) Then 1 hr. (O_2) or (air)
8.9	20	5 (O_2)	60 (air)	↓	2 hrs. (air)	2 hrs. (air)	First 1 hr. (air) Then 1 hr. (O_2) or (air)
4.5	10	↓	2 hrs. (air)	5 (O_2)	4 hrs. (air)	2 hrs. (air)	First 1 hr. (air) Then 1 hr. (O_2) or (air)
Surface		↓	1 min. (air)	↓	1 min. (air)	1 min. (air)	1 min. (O_2)

Time at all stops in minutes unless otherwise indicated.

* From *U.S. Navy Diving Manual.*

TABLE XII

TABLE 1–31.—*Minimal recompression, oxygen breathing method for treatment of decompression sickness and air embolism* *

Stops	Bends—pain only						Serious symptoms and air embolism					
([a])	Pain relieved within 10 minutes at 60 feet. If any pain persists after 10 minutes at 60 feet, use table 6.			Pain relieved after 10 minutes at 60 feet. Serious symptoms include any one of the following: 1. Unconsciousness. 2. Nervous system symptoms. 3. Bends under pressure.			Treatment of air embolism. Rate of descent is as fast as possible. Use this table if all symptoms are gone within 15 minutes and proceed to 60 feet when relief is complete.			Treatment of air embolism if symptoms moderate to a major extent within 30 minutes at 165 feet. If symptoms persist, use table 4.		
	Table 5 [b]			Table 6 [b]			Table 5A [c]			Table 6A [c]		
Depth (feet)	Time (minutes)	Breathing media	Total elapsed time (minutes)	Time (minutes)	Breathing media	Total elapsed time (minutes)	Time (minutes)	Breathing media	Total elapsed time (minutes)	Time (minutes)	Breathing media	Total elapsed time (minutes)
165							[d] 15	Air	15	30	Air	30
165 to 60							4	Air	19	4	Air	34
60				20	Oxygen	20				20	Oxygen	54
60				5	Air	25				5	Air	59
60				20	Oxygen	45				20	Oxygen	79
60	20	Oxgyen	20	5	Air	50	20	Oxygen	39	5	Air	84
60	5	Air	25	20	Oxygen	70	5	Air	44	20	Oxygen	104
60	20	Oxygen	45	5	Air	75	20	Oxygen	64	5	Air	109
60 to 30	30	Oxygen	75	30	Oxygen	105	30	Oxygen	94	30	Oxygen	139
30				15	Air	120				15	Air	154
30	5	Air	80	60	Oxygen	180	5	Air	99	60	Oxygen	214
30	20	Oxygen	100	15	Air	195	20	Oxygen	119	15	Air	229
30	5	Air	105	60	Oxygen	255	5	Air	124	60	Oxygen	289
30 to 0	30	Oxygen	135	30	Oxygen	285	30	Oxygen	154	30	Oxygen	319

[a] The rate of ascent is 1 foot per minute. Do not compensate for slowing of the rate by subsequent acceleration. Do compensate if the rate is exceeded. If necessary, halt ascent and hold depth while ventilating the chamber.

[b] The time at 60 feet begins on arrival at 60 feet. The patient should be on oxgyen from the surface.

[c] The time at 165 feet is total bottom time and includes the time from the surface.

[d] Total time will vary as a function of this stop. The medical attendant should take enough time to accomplish a thorough physical examination, because the ensuing treatment is based on the patient's physical status.

*From *U.S. Navy Diving Manual*

Notes on recompression *

1. General considerations:
   a. Follow the treatment tables accurately.
   b. Permit no shortening or other alterations of the tables except on the advice of a trained diving medical officer or in an extreme emergency.
2. Rate of descent in the chamber:
   a. The normal descent rate is 25 feet per minute.
   b. If serious symptoms are present: rapid descent is desirable.
   c. If pain increases on descent: stop, resume at a rate tolerated by the patient.
3. Treatment depth:
   a. Go to the full depth indicated by the table required.
   b. Do not go beyond 165 feet except on the decision of a medical officer who has been trained in diving.
4. Examination of the patient (see 1.6.2):
   a. If no serious symptoms are evident and pain is not severe, examine the patient throughly before treatment.
   b. If any serious symptom is noted, do not delay recompression for examination or for determining depth of relief.
   c. If Treatment Tables 5, 6, 5A, or 6A are used, a medical officer must be present and a qualified medical attendant must always accompany the patient in the chamber during treatment.
   d. In "pain only" cases, make sure that relief is complete within 10 minutes at 60 feet on oxygen if table 5 is used. If not, table 6 may be used. If table 1 is used, make sure that complete relief has been reported before reaching 66 feet.
   e. On reaching treatment depth, examine the patient as completely as possible to detect—
      1. Incomplete relief.
      2. Any symptoms overlooked.

   NOTE: At the very least, have the patient stand and walk the length of the chamber if this is at all possible.

   f. Recheck the patient before leaving the treatment depth.
   g. Ask the patient how he feels before and after coming to each stop and periodically during long stops.
   h. Do not let the patient sleep through changes of depth or for more than an hour at a time at any stop. (Symptoms can develop or recur during sleep.)
   i. Recheck the patient before leaving the last stop.
   j. During treatment make sure that the patient can obtain all the things that he needs, such as food, liquids, and any other items that he might require.
5. Patient getting worse:
   a. Never continue ascent if the patient's condition is worsening.
   b. Treat the patient as a recurrence during treatment (see 6).
   c. Consider the use of helium-oxygen as a breathing medium for the patient (see 8).
6. Recurrence of symptoms:
   a. During treatment:
      1. Recompress to depth of relief (but never less than 30 feet or deeper than 165 feet except on decision of a medical officer).
      2. If a medical officer is available and the depth of relief is less than 60 feet, recompress to 60 feet and treat on table 6.
      3. If a medical officer is not available or the depth of relief is greater than 60 feet, complete the treatment according to table 4; i.e., remain at depth of relief for 30 minutes and complete remaining stops of table 4.
      4. If recurrence involves serious symptoms not previously present, take the patient to 60 feet and treat on table 6 or take the patient to 165 feet and treat on table 4.
   b. Following treatment:
      1. Recompress to 60 feet and use table 6 if a medical officer is available.
      2. If the depth of relief is less than 30-feet, recompress the patient to 30 feet and decompress from the 30-foot stop according to table 3.
      3. If the depth of relief is deeper than 30 feet, keep the patient at depth of relief for 30 minutes and decompress according to table 3.

* From *U.S. Navy Diving Manual.*

Notes on recompression—Continued

4. If the original treatment was on table 5 or 6, use table 6. If the original treatment was on table 5A or 6A, use table 6, 6A, or table 4. If the original treatment was on table 3, use table 6, 6A, or table 4.

5. Examine the patient carefully to be sure no serious symptom is present. If the original treatment was on table 1 or 2, appearance of a serious symptom requires full treatment on table 6, 3, or 4.

c. Using oxygen treatment tables during or following treatment:

1. Table 6 can be lengthened by an additional 25 minutes at 60 feet (20 minutes on oxygen and 5 minutes on air) or an additional 75 minutes at 30 feet (15 minutes on air and 60 minutes on oxygen), or both. Table 6A can be lengthened in the same manner.

2. If relief is not complete at 60 feet or if the patient's condition is worsening, the additional time above may be used or the patient can be recompressed to 165 feet and treated on table 2, 2A, 3, or 4 as appropriate.

7. Use of oxygen:

a. Use oxygen wherever permitted by the treatment tables unless the patient is known to tolerate oxygen poorly.

b. If a medical officer trained in diving is available, he may recommend the use of oxygen for patients who are known to tolerate oxygen poorly.

c. Take all precautions against fire (see table 1–34).

d. Tend carefully, being alert for such symptoms of oxygen poisoning as—

1. Twitching of the face and lips.
2. Nausea.
3. Dizziness and vertigo.
4. Vomiting.
5. Convulsions.
6. Anxiety.
7. Confusion.
8. Restlessness and irritability.
9. Malaise or excessive tiredness.
10. Changes in vision as blurring or narrowing of the visual field.
11. Incoordination.
12. Tremors of the arms and legs.
13. Numbness or tingling of the fingers or toes.
14. Fainting.
15. Spasmodic breathing.

e. Know what to do in the event of a convulsion:

1. Halt ascent.
2. Remove mask at once.
3. Maintain depth.
4. Protect the convulsing patient from injury but do not restrain or forcefully oppose the convulsive movements.
5. Use a padded mouth bit to protect the tongue of a convulsing patient.
6. If the patient is not convulsing, have him hyperventilate with chamber air for a few breaths.

f. If oxygen breathing must be interrupted:

1. On table 1, proceed on table 1A.
2. On table 2, proceed on table 2A.
3. On table 3, continue on table 3, using air.
4. On table 5, 6, 5A, or 6A, allow 15 minutes after the reaction has entirely subsided and resume the schedule at the point of its interruption.
5. On table 5, if the reaction occurred at 60 feet, upon arrival at the 30-foot stop, switch to the schedule of table 6.

g. At the medical officer's discretion, oxygen breathing may be resumed at the 40-foot stop. If oxygen breathing is resumed, complete treatment as follows:

1. Resuming from table 1A: breathe oxygen at 40 feet for 30 minutes and at 30 feet for 1 hour.

Notes on recompression—Continued

2. Resuming from table 2A: breathe oxygen at 40 feet for 30 minutes and at 30 feet for 2 hours.
3. In both cases, then surface in 5 minutes, still breathing oxygen.
4. Resuming from table 3: breathe oxygen at 40 feet for 30 minutes and at 30 feet for the first hour, and then finish the treatment with air.

8. Use of helium-oxygen:
 a. Helium-oxygen mixtures in a ratio of about 80:20 can be used instead of air (not in place of oxygen) in all types of treatment and at any depth.
 b. The use of helium-oxygen mixtures is especially desirable in any patient who—
  1. Has serious symptoms which fail to clear within a short time at 165 feet.
  2. Has a recurrence of symptoms or otherwise becomes worse at any stage of treatment.
  3. Has any difficulty in breathing.

9. Tenders:
 a. A qualified tender must be in the chamber at all times.
 b. The tender must be alert for any change in the condition of the patient, especially during oxygen breathing.
 c. The tender must breathe oxygen if he has been with a patient throughout treatment using table 1 or 2.
  1. On table 1, breathe oxygen at 40 feet for 30 minutes.
  2. On table 2, breathe oxygen at 30 feet for 1 hour.
 d. A tender in the chamber only during the oxygen-breathing part of table 1 or 2 gains a safety factor by breathing oxygen for 30 minutes of the last stop, but it is not essential. Tenders may breathe oxygen during the use of table 3 or 4 at depths of 40 feet or less.
 e. When tables 5, 6, 5A, and 6A are used, the tender normally breathes air throughout. However, if the treatment is a repetitive dive for the tender or if tables 6 or 6A are lengthened, the tender must breathe oxygen during the last 30 minutes of ascent from 30 feet to the surface.
 f. Anyone entering the chamber and leaving before completion of the treatment must be decompressed according to standard diving tables.
 g. Personnel outside the chamber must specify and control the decompression of anyone leaving the chamber and must review all decisions concerning treatment or decompression made by personnel (including the medical officer) inside the chamber.

10. Ventilation of the chamber:
 a. All ventilation will be continuous and the volumes specified are measured at the chamber pressure.
 b. If ventilation must be interrupted for any reason, the time will not exceed 5 minutes in any 30-minute period. When the ventilation is resumed, twice the volume of ventilation will be used for twice the time of the interruption and then the basic ventilation will be used again.
 c. When air or a helium-oxygen mixture is breathed, provide 2 cubic feet per minute for a man at rest and 4 cubic feet per minute for a man who is not at rest, such as a tender actively taking care of a patient.
 d. When oxygen is breathed, provide 12.5 cubic feet per minute for a man at rest and 25 cubic feet per minute for a man who is not at rest. When these ventilation rates are used, no additional ventilation is required for personnel breathing air. These ventilation rates apply only to the number of people breathing oxygen.
 e. The above rules apply to all chambers that do not have facilities to monitor the oxygen concentration in the chamber. Chambers that can monitor oxygen concentration may use intermittent ventilation so that the oxygen concentration in the chamber does not exceed 22.5. percent. This ventilation also requires no additional ventilation for personnel breathing air.
 f. If an oxygen-elimination system is used for oxygen breathing (see app. B) the ventilation rate required for air breathing may be used and applies to all personnel, whether or not the oxygen-elimination system is used to obtain the correct ventilation rate.

Notes on recompression—Continued

11. First aid:
    a. First aid may be required in addition to recompression. Do not neglect it (see table 1–33 and app. A).
12. Recompression in the water:
    a. Recompression without a chamber is difficult and hazardous. Except in grave emergencies, seek the nearest chamber even if it is at a considerable distance.
    b. If water recompression must be used and the diver is conscious and able to care for himself.
        1. Use the deep-sea diving rig if available.
        2. Follow treatment tables as closely as possible.
        3. Maintain constant communication.
        4. Have a standby diver ready and preferably use a tender with the patient.
    c. If the diver is unconscious or incapacitated, send another diver down with him to control his valves and otherwise assist him.
    d. If lightweight diving outfit or scuba must be used, keep at least one diver with the patient at all times. Plan carefully for shifting rigs or cylinders. Have an ample number of tenders topside and at intermediate depths.
    e. If depth is inadequate for full treatment according to the tables:
        1. Take the patient to maximum available depth.
        2. Keep him there for 30 minutes.
        3. Bring him up according to table 2A. Do not use stops shorter than those of table 2A.
13. The most frequent errors related to treatment:
    a. Failure of the diver to report symptoms early.
    b. Failure to treat doubtful cases.
    c. Failure to treat promptly.
    d. Failure to treat adequately.
    e. Failure to recognize serious symptoms.
    f. Failure to keep the patient near the chamber after treatment.
14. ALWAYS KEEP THE DIVER CLOSE TO THE CHAMBER FOR AT LEAST 6 HOURS AFTER TREATMENT. (Keep him for 24 hours unless very prompt return can be assured.)

Notes on artificial respiration *

1. Start artificial respiration immediately whenever a man is *not breathing* due to drowning or any other cause.
    a. Never wait for mechanical resuscitator.
    b. Delay *only* to stop serious bleeding (if possible have another person tend to such measures while you start artificial respiration).
    c. Send *another person* for a medical officer or other competent aid.
2. Before starting, remove victim from the cause of his trouble; but do not waste time moving him any further than necessary.
3. *Get on with artificial respiration.* Leave details to others or try to get them done quickly between cycles.
    a. Recheck position of victim:
        1. In position for mouth-to-mouth resuscitation.
        2. Head slightly lower than feet if possible, especially in drowning.
        3. Chin pulled toward operator.
    b. Recheck airway:
        1. Remove froth, debris, or other material.
        2. See that tongue stays forward; have someone hold it if it draws back (you can run a safety pin through tongue if necessary).
        3. If *artificial respiration does not move any air, there is an obstruction.* Strangulation must be overcome (see app. A).
    c. Loosen any tight clothing—collar, belt, etc.
    d. Keep victim warm.
    e. Check pulse. Combat shock.

* From *U.S. Navy Diving Manual.*

Notes on artificial respiration—Continued

4. Continue artificial respiration without interruption. (Minimum time is 4 hours unless victim revives or is pronounced dead by medical officer.)
   a. Do not apply *too much* back pressure. (A strong operator can crack ribs of a small victim.)
   b. If you become tired, let another operator take over. Do not break rhythm during shift.
   c. Watch carefully for signs of return of natural breathing movements. If they appear, time your movements to assist them.
   d. Shift to a mechanical resuscitator if one is available, ready, and operating properly.
   e. If victim starts breathing for himself, watch him carefully. Resume artificial respiration if he stops or if movements become too feeble.
5. If victim revives, continue care:
   a. Keep him lying down.
   b. Remove wet clothes; keep him warm.
   c. Give nothing by mouth until fully conscious.
   d. Attend to any injuries.
   e. Be sure he is seen promptly by medical officer.

If victim has been underwater with any kind of breathing apparatus, he *may have air embolism.* This can seldom be ruled out in an unconscious diver, whether he is breathing or not, and recompression should be given if any doubt exists. Do not delay artificial respiration. Give it by some method on way to chamber and during recompression.

Tables 1 through 4 are time-honored, but they are now usually bypassed in favor of Table 5 or Table 6. In most situations, these newer oxygen tables appear to afford better results, and they generally require less time as well. Table 4 remains a refuge for the most refractory problems.

Please read the instructions and note that the basic principles of deciding which table to use are rather simple. Unfortunately, some of the decisions that look simple on paper are less simple in real life. Knowing when relief is complete is one of the greatest problems especially in neurological cases. Anybody can treat a routine case, but there are many times when there is no substitute for the experience and judgment of a diving medical officer—and there are also some times when he will have his fingers crossed along with everybody else.

It should be quite obvious that trying to give adequate treatment of decompression sickness by "recompression in the water" with scuba would be difficult almost to the point of impossibility. Remember, also, that any treatment involving inert gas will probably make matters much worse if it cannot be carried to completion. Knowing the location of the nearest suitable chamber, knowing how to reach it most rapidly, and having lines of communication for advice are almost as important in decompression sickness as in air embolism.

There is considerable debate about the potential value of portable one-man chambers. Undoubtedly, such a vessel would be good to have under some circumstances. One aspect, however, is sometimes overlooked: if a victim of bends or air embolism is so ill that he cannot be transported a fair distance, he may very well require care that cannot be given in a one-man chamber. In any event, a one-man chamber should be designed so that it can be attached to, or carried into, the nearest regular treatment facility.

HELIUM

Helium lacks the narcotic or anesthetic properties of nitrogen, argon, and some of the other inert gases. As has been discussed in connection with narcosis, this is the principal reason for its use as the usual diluent for oxygen in gas mixtures for deep diving. Because of the depths involved, much saturation diving is done with helium-oxygen mixtures. The long duration of exposure makes it important, because of the danger of pulmonary oxygen poisoning, to keep the partial pressure of oxygen from rising very much above that of air at the surface. For example, a mixture for use at more than 20 atm abs might contain 1 per cent oxygen or less.

In addition to its high cost, practical problems with helium include the change in voice that occurs because of the faster speed of sound (and thus the altered resonance of body air cavities) in helium. Unassisted voice-communication becomes almost impossible, but practical electronic "helium speech unscramblers" are now available.

The high thermal conductivity of helium adds to the problem of maintaining normal body temperature at depth. The temperature in a helium-filled chamber or habitat must be kept much closer to body temperature than in an air environment, and increased density at depth further increases the temperature required for comfort. Respiratory heat loss can become such a problem in cold water that a diver's breathing gas has to be warmed under some conditions.

OXYGEN

Can oxygen be harmful? Oxygen is essential to life, and increased amounts of it are beneficial in several types of disease. It may be hard to believe that such a gas could ever be harmful, but it is important for divers to realize that such is the case.

Even at the surface, exposure to an unusually high concentration of oxygen can cause harm if continued long enough. Lung irritation (pulmonary oxygen toxicity) is the usual manifestation. For example, physicians take this possibility very seriously when a hospital patient needs very high inspiratory oxygen levels for more than a short time.

At one time, divers were little concerned about the pulmonary form of oxygen poisoning. They were never "on oxygen" for the longer periods required to bring this about. As has already been mentioned, saturation dives and other long-term exposures make it a matter of concern if the partial pressure of oxygen stays very much above the normal 0.21 atm level for very long.

The form of oxygen poisoning that is of primary concern in short-term exposures is that which affects the brain and causes convulsions. Anyone who has seen a grand mal epileptic seizure or similar episode will not need a definition of this word.

Oxygen convulsions do not occur unless the partial pressure of oxygen is somewhere near two atmospheres. Reaching such an oxygen pressure can come about in a number of different ways.

Open-circuit scuba presents no chance of oxygen poisoning if it is charged with compressed air and used at reasonable depth. Any attempt to use oxygen or high-oxygen mixtures in such equipment, however, makes oxygen toxicity a very real possibility. (Other possibilities, such as explosion of a cylinder on charging must also be considered if there is any thought of using oxygen in ordinary "air" scuba.)

Historically, the possibility of oxygen poisoning has most often been associated with the use of closed-circuit oxygen-rebreathing apparatus. Problems of such equipment have already been discussed in connection with hypoxia and CO_2 intoxication. If a closed-circuit rig is used exactly as intended, the inspiratory concentration of oxygen will not be very much below 100%. Assuming 100%, a depth of 33 feet (or possibly somewhat less) would introduce the possibility of oxygen convulsions. An uncertain number of variables would then determine whether a convulsion would actually occur and, if so, how long an exposure would be required to bring it about. The factors that most dramatically increase the risk of convulsion are increased CO_2 levels and physical exertion.

All U.S. Navy divers who will be exposed to oxygen in their work are given an oxygen tolerance test. This involves breathing oxygen for 30 minutes at rest at 60 feet in a recompression chamber.

The basic Navy rule about breathing oxygen on working dives under normal circumstances is this: Do not breathe oxygen deeper than 25 feet and observe proper time limits. Where it is essential to use oxygen at greater depths or for more than a short time, the limits of this table are applied:

TABLE XIII

TIME LIMITS FOR BREATHING OXYGEN

Depth (ft.)	*Time (min.)*
40	10
35	25
30	45
25	75
20	110
15	150
10	240

These limits apply to normal, moderate work and are generally safe for the average diver, but they do not allow for exceptional exertion, carbon dioxide excess, or unusual susceptibility to oxygen poisoning. And a depth-measurement error of a few feet could make quite a difference.

Limits in terms of oxygen partial pressures in nitrogen-oxygen mixed-gas diving are even more conservative because of additional factors that are not yet fully understood.

What to Breathe

Deciding what breathing medium to use in scuba is seldom a problem. With open-circuit equipment, compressed air is the only logical choice. With simple closed-circuit oxygen-rebreathing scuba, pure oxygen is absolutely the *only* choice. Nevertheless, there seems to be a lot of interest in the possibility of breathing something different, so the subject is worth some discussion.

The risk of hypoxia in a closed-circuit rig charged with something other than oxygen has already been explained.

Why not use oxygen in open-circuit equipment? There are several good reasons:

1. Danger of explosion on charging. Oil and oxygen will cause explosion if they get together under pressure. Oil may have gotten into the gear either during manufacture or repair, or as a residue of oil vapor from a previous air charge.

2. Danger of oxygen poisoning. Use of oxygen imposes severe depth-time limits that are not normally associated with open-circuit gear.

3. There are absolutely no advantages. Oxygen does not decrease the amount of gas you use, and you can't go deep enough to get any decompression advantage from it.

WHAT ABOUT MIXTURES?

Nitrogen-oxygen. Air is a nitrogen-oxygen mixture. Its main drawback is the amount of nitrogen it contains and what this means in terms of decompression. The most obvious way to remedy this is to boost the amount of oxygen present. If you cut the nitrogen percentage in half (40% nitrogen, 60% oxygen), you could theoretically double your absolute depth as far as decompression limits are concerned. But the corresponding increase in oxygen pressure would stop you with oxygen poisoning long before you could take full advantage of this.

In any event, using such a mixture in open-circuit scuba would hardly be advantageous enough to warrant the trouble of mixing and analyzing or the expense of buying the mixture. The short duration of gas supply at depth would keep you from getting much benefit from any extension of depth-time decompression limits.

Helium-oxygen. Granting that the breathing mixture has to contain oxygen and that the oxygen has to be diluted if you are going deep, the question boils down to what you can use for this dilution. Besides nitrogen, helium is about the only practical possibility. As has already been said, the compelling advantage of helium is its lack of narcotic effects. Advantages in decompression are hardly great enough by themselves to warrant the expense of helium and the problems of mixing. The lesser density of helium is a distinct advantage from the standpoint of breathing at greater depths.

Hydrogen. The danger of explosion makes diving with hydrogen a specialized business. Most of the danger can be eliminated by appropriate procedures, but the question remains whether it offers any advantages over the use of helium-oxygen mixtures. The first technique for hydrogen-oxygen diving was developed in Sweden, where helium was not readily available; and, indeed, availability and cost may well be the best reasons for pursuing the matter.

More recently, however, interest has arisen in the possibility that H_2 may have positive physiological benefits by virtue of its mild but definite narcotic properties and its low density and viscosity.

Noble gases other than helium have been tried. *Argon* and *krypton* are more narcotic than nitrogen, and *xenon* is as potent an anesthetic as nitrous oxide. *Neon* appears to lack anesthetic properties, so it would be suitable from that standpoint for deep diving. At the same time, it is relatively dense; and this limits its usefulness at depth. Crude neon is a mixture of neon and helium, a by-product of liquid air production. It appears promising as a gas for moderately great depths.

According to what is now known, any inert gas usable for diluting oxygen in diving will involve much the same decompression problems as nitrogen. The idea of using combinations of inert gases, or of alternating them, may have some merit. It is now recognized, however, that certain switches or alternations of inert gas can provoke bubble formation even without coincident decompression.

Attention is also being given to the possibility that some ill-explained phenomena in diving, such as the "no joint juice" effect on deep descents, may be due to the osmotic effects of dissolved gas.

BREATHING APPARATUS FOR MIXED GAS

As mentioned above, there is not much point in using nitrogen-oxygen or helium-oxygen mixtures in open-circuit scuba, and they absolutely must not be used in simple closed-circuit rigs because of the danger of anoxia.

The drawback with open circuit is the limitation of gas-supply duration. This can be overcome by using a system in which part or all of the gas is rebreathed. But safe rebreathing of mixtures requires apparatus which is far more complicated than the simple oxygen-rebreathing circuit. Such equipment is available and is in use for military and commercial diving, but its high cost and complexity place it outside the realm of practicality for sportsmen. The complexities are formidable, meticulous maintenance is essential, and the potential hazards are very great. This is true even of the best equipment from experienced and reputable firms. A basement genius who has a mixed-gas scheme on his drawing board is flirting with death.

The greatest potential for development of self-contained diving apparatus surely lies in the direction of mixed-gas scuba, but it is difficult to predict whether or how soon this sort of equipment will become practical for sport diving or whether it will be used widely where simpler systems could be employed.

Toward Greater Depths

Hydrostatic pressure effects. It has been known for a long time that pressure could have effects on living tissues that could not be attributed to partial pressures or to local differences in pressure. These hydrostatic pressure effects—effects of *pressure per se*—had been observed only in experimental preparations at pressures much above levels that had been reached by divers. For this reason, they were not taken very seriously in terms of practical diving.

In the 1960's, when divers first made chamber dives to pressures equivalent to 800 feet or more, they experienced neuromuscular phenomena that were at first called "helium tremors." Now, the term "high pressure neurological syndrome" (HPNS) is in more common use. Beyond 1000-ft pressure, tremors were accompanied by alarming brain-wave patterns and unfamiliar mental states. There is good reason, now, to attribute such effects to pressure itself.

These effects are much less prominent in slow descents than in rapid ones, and they disappear, at least in part, with time at a given pressure. At this writing, such effects have not prevented descent to the equivalent of 2,000 feet, but they are now regarded as a major potential obstacle to penetration of much greater depths. Much research may be required to explain the mechanism of these phenomena and to find ways of circumventing them.

ARTIFICIAL GILLS AND LIQUID BREATHING

Aside from problems attributed to "pressure per se," the primary obstacles in the way of diving to extreme depths are presumably those relating to the inert gas required to dilute oxygen in the diver's breathing medium. The total pressure of the gas a diver breathes must be equal to the pressure that surrounds him. Oxygen must be included in that gas, but its partial pressure must be kept within safe limits; and the remainder of the gas pressure must be accounted for by an inert gas such as nitrogen or helium. Helium at high pressure, for exam-

ple, not only causes decompression problems but it may (at the density of high pressure) interfere with diffusion of oxygen and carbon dioxide within the lungs.

Fish are unaffected by oxygen poisoning and inert gas problems even at great depth because they are exposed only to the gas pressures that exist in the water. These, in turn, are essentially the same as in air at the surface. The total pressure of dissolved gas in a liquid, unlike that in a gas mixture, does not have to be equal to the ambient pressure. This fact suggests the possibility that man may be able to go to very great depths if he can only breathe a suitable liquid either with his own lungs or by circulating all or part of his blood through an artificial gill.

FOR ADDITIONAL READING AND REFERENCE

U.S. Navy Diving Manual

NAVSHIPS 0994-001-9010, March 1970. Superintendent of Documents, U.S. Government Printing Office, Washington, D.C. 20402. Price $7.25.

The Physiology and Medicine of Diving and Compressed Air Work

Bennett, P. B., and Elliott, D. H., editors. Baltimore: Williams and Wilkins, 1969. (About $25.)

Underwater Medicine

Miles, S., 2nd edition, Philadelphia: J. B. Lippincott Co., 1966.

Medical Aspects of Sport Diving

Dueker, C. W. South Brunswick and New York: Barnes, 1970.

The Merck Manual, 12th edition

Holvey, D. N., and Talbott, J. H., editors. Rahway, N.J.: Merck Sharp & Dohme, 1972.

Most physicians and emergency rooms have a copy of the *Merck Manual.* It contains a short but useful section "Decompression Sickness and Related Disorders" written specifically for non-diving physicians.

Underwater Physiology

(Proceedings of the Fourth Symposium on Underwater Physiology)

Lambertsen, C. J., editor. New York and London: Academic Press, 1971. The Fifth Symposium on Underwater Physiology was held in 1972, and the Proceedings will be published eventually. The volumes generally cost over $20.

Scuba Safety Report Series published by Department of Ocean Engineering, University of Rhode Island, Kingston, R.I. 02881.

Report No. 2 Skin and Scuba Diving. Fatalities Involving U.S. Citizens

Report No. 3 Non-Fatal Pressure-Related Scuba Accidents, Identification and Emergency Treatment

4

FUNDAMENTALS OF COMPRESSED GASES AS RELATED TO DIVING

Compressed gases are a normal part of our everyday life. Air hoses at service stations, CO_2 fire extinguishers, spray cans, oxygen tanks in hospitals; special gases in school laboratories, and breathing apparatus on emergency vehicles include compressed gas with which everyone is familiar. So commonplace are the various forms of compressed gas that most of us give little thought to the potential energy stored in pressurized containers. A measure of this energy can be sensed by the accidental shattering of a heavy carbonated beverage bottle under a few psig of pressure, the blowout of a passenger car tire with 1 to 3 atmospheres pressure or a heavier vehicle tire at pressures from 5 to 10 atmospheres. Diving tank pressures vary from 122+ atmospheres (1,800 psig) to about 200 atmospheres (3,000 psig). By comparison it should be immediately apparent that gases at high pressures, if not properly managed, constitute a frank hazard. To ensure that compressed gases may be handled safely, there are Federal regulations controlling the specifications for containers and their approval. In addition, the Compressed Gas Association has established procedures for handling compressed gases, gas composition standards, and container testing procedures beyond those established by Federal codes. The U.S. Bureau of Mines further requires that all compressed gas cylinders be registered with it by serial number.

Compressed Air Tanks

Compressed air tanks are made in many sizes and to various specifications as defined in Title 49, Code of Federal Regulations, Department of Transportation Parts 100 to 199. The basic specifications for tanks suitable for diving are given in Part 178.36, with specifications for safety devices and allowable overpressure filling being covered in Parts 173.34(d) and 173.302 respectively.

Each tank must have the tank type, working pressure, date of manufacture, manufacturer, for whom manufactured, and a serial number stamped into the material of which the cylinder is fabricated. In addition the stamped information will indicate any subsequent inspection dates and whether or not the tank is approved for overpressure filling.

These specifications were formerly controlled by the Interstate Commerce Commission. In reading the data stamped into a tank the letters ICC (Interstate Commerce Commission) may be found instead of DOT (Department of Transportation). Tanks properly cared for have a long life potential and some may be found which are still serviceable after more than 50 years of use.

The data stamped into the tank are:

1) Controlling agency (ICC or DOT)
2) Type of tank (intended use) (3A, 3AA)
3) Allowable pressure (working pressure)
4) Date of Manufacture
5) Manufacturer
6) For whom manufactured
7) Pressure test history

Of these data, the important ones for a diver to consider are the type of tank, allowable pressure, and the last test date.

These data may appear on the shoulder, top head or the neck itself. They usually appear as:

DOT-3AA 2015	(Type and pressure)
XX	(Serial number)
YY	(Manufacturer or owner)
7-60	(Inspection date)

Other data required include the words "SPUN" or "PLUG" when an end closure has been made by one of these means, and the identity of the inspector. If the data contains a symbol or character between the month and years, that mark identifies the inspector. The marks may appear in a line instead of a column, as follows:

ICC-3A-1800-XX-YY,

or they may appear in more than one column.

A "plus" (+) sign after the pressure rating indicates that the tank may be filled to a 10% overpressure at 70° F. Dates appearing below the date of manufacture indicate times at which the tank was hydrostatically tested for further service. If a tank is tested and fails to meet the test requirements, it is considered unsafe for further service and no new date is added. DOT requires that a tank be tested at least every five years, and no reputable vendor will fill a tank if more than five years has elapsed since the last test.

Tanks are available in air capacities from 35 cf. to 94 cf. at working pressures respectively from 1,800 psig to 3,015 psig. Manifolds and pack frames are available for mounting two or more tanks as a single dive unit. Tanks outside this capacity range can be used for diving providing they are classified by an ICC or DOT rating as 3A or 3AA and can successfully pass inspection and testing. However, the beginning diver should not invest in any tank without some thought as to the size and type that is best suited to the type of diving that he plans to do. An old tank or one which shows scratches, nicks or corrosion should not be purchased without proper certification that the tank is still serviceable. Foreign-built tanks are not refillable by compressed-air vendors since they have no traceability to DOT materials and processes specifications. In many cases the neck threads are metric and standard valves cannot be directly attached. The neck threading also may be a problem with otherwise acceptable tanks not built specifically to diving tank specifications.

Care and Handling of High-Pressure Tanks

The Compressed Gas Association (CGA) has established certain practices and procedures to be followed by its members. These are in compliance with the controls established by state and Federal regulatory agencies. These guidelines are available to all compressed-gas vendors and to the general public at a marginal cost. If a diver plans to fill and inspect his own tanks, copies of the appropriate CGA pamphlets should be acquired for ready reference. Some of the highlights of these publications are given in the following discussion.

In Pamphlet C-6 "Standards for Visual Inspection of Compressed Gas Cylinders," the CGA identifies a high-pressure cylinder as one having a working pressure of 900 psig or higher. All the usual diving tanks fall within this category. Mentioned earlier, tanks should be examined for evidence of pitting, general corrosion, dents, cuts or nicks, and for heat damage. If a tank shows evidence of fire damage (paint charred) or a burn by an arc or torch, it should be taken to a reliable service shop and the extent of the damage, if any, determined by inspection and hydrostatic testing.

To further inspect the tank it should be cleaned so that all surfaces are visible, i.e., bare metal or tightly adhered coatings. If general corrosion or pitting is present the tank should be examined and pressure tested as for heat damage.

Sharp-bottomed nicks and gouges are stress raisers and should be repaired even if the damaged tank passes a hydrostatic test. A retest is required after the repair.

A general guideline on dents is that they are acceptable up to 1/16″ deep if the diameter of the dent is at least 32 times the depth in diameter. Sharper dents may produce stress damage. If in doubt have a pressure test.

In general, damage which displaces or removes wall material to such an extent that the remaining metal approaches the minimum thickness specified for that tank in the Code of Federal Regulations should be adequate evidence to retire the tank.

CGA Pamphlet P-5 offers "Suggestions for the Care of High-Pressure Air Cylinders for Underwater Breathing." These and other suggestions given below will help ensure a long and safe service period for your diving tanks.

1. Never charge a tank to pressures above its rating. Tank ratings are established for filling at 70° F. The effects of temperature on pressure is given in Table XV on Page 108.

2. Recharge with pure air only. Impure air may be contaminated with toxic or corrosive gases that are harmful to both you and your equipment.

3. Recharge with air only. Even mixtures of pure nitrogen and oxygen that are not at normal concentrations may put you outside the allowable time-pressure limits for no-decompression diving or, on the other side, oxygen poisoning. Be sure your tank is marked "COMPRESSED AIR ONLY."

4. Keep water out. CGA recommends that a tank valve be kept closed after the pressure reaches 25 psi. If the tank shows 30 psig at the surface it is "empty" at about 35 feet in either fresh or salt water. Diving regulators respond to the difference in pressure between ambient and tank pressures. If you work hard at it, you can exhaust a tank underwater. Work done at the University of Rhode Island has demonstrated that water can get back through the regulator and into the tank if this is done. This is why we suggested in Chapter 2 that dive planning be based upon an end-of-dive pressure of 300 psig.

5. Handle the tank carefully, avoid dropping it. Lay the tank on its side if it is unattended, particularly where people are moving about. When transporting tanks, be certain they cannot roll around. Check that other objects which might damage the tank or valve are not "loose gear" that can shift around during transportation.

6. Check for moisture or oil. CGA recommends removing the valve and examining the interior of the tank for liquids at the end of each diving season. If the tank is contaminated, it should be cleaned and dried before storage. The University of Rhode Island recommends more frequent visual inspection. Any time a tank has been emptied during a dive or left empty with the value unseated for a period of time, check for moisture in it.

7. Prevent corrosion. Internal corrosion is prevented, or at least held to a minimum, by the inspection procedures above. If the tank has an internal coating which has become penetrated and is coming off it should be removed. (This is not a "do it yourself" project. Exterior corrosion is best prevented by keeping the tank painted or covered with other suitable coating. Do not allow the tank to lay around unnecessarily long with other wet gear. Rinse salt or salt water off as soon as possible after an ocean dive.

8. Do not lubricate. Lubricants may be a source of toxic materials that could be breathed in. Furthermore, hydrocarbon lubricants (most oils and greases) can combine with air or oxygen under pressure to form an explosive mixture. Oil products also tend to hasten the deterioration of natural rubber that may be a part of your other equipment. Tank threads and other fittings are designed to make leak-tight connections without the aid of lubricants under conditions of normal tightening.

9. Keep cool. Do not store or transport tanks under conditions that may expose them to excessive temperatures. In an overheated condition, the safety valve may actuate due to overtemperature and pressure thus causing the loss of the tank charge and the necessary replacement of the safety device.

One exception to the discussion on tanks should be noted. The Code of Federal Regulations makes no provision for tanks to be fabricated from any material other than steel. Aluminum tanks are manufactured to the accepted safety standards under special permits issued by DOT but no general specification exists for them. Instead of the usual classification, these tanks are stamped DOT-SP-XXX-YYY where the SP-XXX indicates the special permit number and the YYY denotes the working pressure. They will also carry the other data required for steel tanks. These aluminum tanks require the same care, testing, and inspection as the 3A and 3AA tanks.

Compressed Air

Air is the natural atmosphere of the earth. It is an odorless, tasteless, colorless mixture of nitrogen and oxygen containing small amounts of water vapor, carbon dioxide, and several other gases in trace amounts. For practical purposes breathing air can be considered to be 79% nitrogen and 21% oxygen by volume or 76.8% nitrogen and 23.2% oxygen by weight.

Compressed air for breathing may be prepared by the direct compression of atmospheric air or by mixing pure nitrogen and oxygen in the ratio of 79/21 by volume. Where it is made by compressing the air, filters are employed to remove hydrocarbons, CO_2, CO, water vapor, and any other noxious gases. Some of these contaminants may be present in the free air being compressed or they may be produced by the compressor. Filters are therefore necessary between the compressor and the tank being filled. Frequent inspection of the filters is required to ensure that they are in good condition and have not become saturated with the contaminants, thus losing their effectiveness.

Breathing air made by mixing nitrogen and oxygen is sold by some companies which deal in large volumes of pure gases and provide limited quantities of breathing air more as a community service than as a major commodity. This type of air may vary slightly from the 79/21 mixture but will always be within 1 or 2%. This is considered by some dealers to be the purest form of breathing air. However, do-it-yourself mixing should not be attempted. Oxygen under pressure is considerably more dangerous to handle than is compressed air. Getting the correct mixture is also tricky. High or low concentrations of oxygen could lead to unanticipated problems with oxygen toxicity or with nitrogen narcosis or bends respectively.

The regulation of air purity has been slow in developing. A few organizations, such as the University of California, set air purity standards as early as 20 years ago, and enforced their use in diving sponsored by the organization. In 1964, the state of New Jersey passed a regulation controlling the production of breathing air for scuba use (Table XIV) and several similar acts have been passed by a few other jurisdictions.

TABLE XIV

REGULATION GOVERNING COMPRESSED AIR USED IN SCUBA*

Components of compressed air shall not exceed the following limits:

Carbon monoxide	10 parts/million (ppm)—0.001%
Carbon dioxide	1000 ppm—0.1%
Oil	0.02 mg./liter
Water	Saturation
Odor	Free from objectionable odors
Other	Contaminants deleterious to health shall not be present.

* State Department of Health of the State of New Jersey regulation effective April 1, 1964.

In January 1971 the Z86 Committee of the American National Standards Institute (concerned with standards for all aspects of scuba diving) approved a standard for air purity which is similar to the New Jersey regulation except that it reduced the CO_2 concentration from 1,000 ppm to 500 ppm. The committee further recommended that divers use the Compressed Gas Association "Grade E" for all sport diving down to 130 feet of depth. Beyond 130 feet (hardly sport diving) "Grade F" or better should be used.

The Compressed Gas Association lists nine grades ("A" through "J"—the letter "I" is not used) of compressed air. Purity of air (by grade) increases from A to J with D being the minimum grade suitable for ordinary breathing devices such as scuba. Grade E is suitable for use where decompression is required and as noted above is the lowest desirable grade for divers.

Divers should always buy breathing air from a reputable dive shop or compressed-gas dealer. If you maintain your own compressor, keep it in good repair and change the filters before they are overloaded. Most compressed-gas dealers and many dive shops will run an analysis for a nominal charge if you have any reason to question your air supply. (The effects of carbon monoxide, carbon dioxide, and other contaminants in breathing air are discussed in Chapter 3.)

Small portable compressors are available which are designed for charging breathing-air tanks. These compressors may be driven by either electric motors or gasoline engines. Generally speaking, these pumps compress air at rates from

0.3 to 1.5 c.f. per minute. Thus, the filling time required is fairly long. These small compressors are not designed with the pressure capability for filling 3,000 psi tanks. Compressors are available with higher pump rates and higher pressures; however, these are not readily portable units.

When using a compressor driven by a gasoline engine, be sure that the exhaust fumes are downwind from the intake side of the compressor and that there is proper filtering of the compressed air to avoid having exhaust fumes enter the cylinders. In the event an oil-lubricated compressor is used, similar precautions must be taken to prevent oil vapors from entering the breathing air cylinders. See Chapter 3 for reference to carbon monoxide, carbon dioxide, and oil vapors.

Air is considered to be the safest gas and is the one which is used with open-circuit scuba equipment. The term "open-circuit" designates scuba equipment in which the exhaled gases are discharged and not rebreathed. There may be some partial rebreathing equipment available, now or in the future, in which part of the exhaled gases is conserved for the next inhalation and part is discarded. In closed-circuit breathing, the same gas is breathed over and over. Sufficient oxygen is allowed to enter this system to replace that which has been consumed by the body, and the exhaled gases go through a canister containing a carbon dioxide absorbent to remove the carbon dioxide from the gas prior to the next inhalation. The closed-circuit systems are more complicated and require the use of oxygen rather than air. In the open-circuit systems, there is no advantage to the use of oxygen since the lungs cannot absorb more than a small percentage (5%) of the oxygen from the gas which we breathe and normal air (20% oxygen and 80% nitrogen) is more than adequate to supply our oxygen requirements. Also, there is the possibility of oxygen poisoning below the 25-foot level.

Cascade System for Recharging Small Breathing Air Cylinders*

An economical way of filling small cylinders is from a cascade system. This system utilizes several large cylinders (or tanks), e.g., 300 c.f. capacity at 2,400 psi from which air is transferred to the diving tank as described below. These large containers, like the smaller diving tanks, are available in several combinations of volume and pressure. The type to use should be determined by the size and frequency of diving refills as well as the working pressure of the tanks to be refilled.

* The term "cylinder" is used for compressed gas containers as defined in the Code of Federal Regulations by most dealers. In diving jargon the term "tanks" is more commonly used.

In using a cascade system you buy the air only, not the big tanks. Most suppliers allow a reasonable time for using the air purchased. After that period, rent or "demurrage" is charged on the container. Therefore, planning the capacity of a cascade system in terms of the anticipated use is necessary to achieve the greatest economy.

GENERAL INSTRUCTIONS

A system utilizing only one or two large cylinders is neither practical nor economical for the recharging of small cylinders. In order to have efficiency in recharging, it is necessary to set up a bank of at least three large cylinders. (On the other hand, little advantage can be gained with more than three or four.) These cylinders are manifolded together to the charging line for the small cylinder. The high-pressure hose should include a bleed valve for relieving pressure after charging and before disconnecting the charged cylinder.

In setting up the system, a rack should be provided such that the cylinders can be securely restrained by a clamp or chain so that they will not topple over. This system should be permanently located in an area where the cylinders will not be damaged by traffic through the area or by loose gear being thrown around. The small bottle being filled should be immersed in water at room temperature.

This water bath for the small cylinder serves two purposes. First, the water has a high heat capacity and helps prevent overheating of the small cylinder during filling. Second, it acts as an energy absorber in the event of a rupture of the small cylinder. A heavy plastic container such as a garbage can is recommended for the water tank, since the plastic is more resilient and less likely to rupture or fragment than is metal in the event of an accident.

Temperature tends to rise in the cylinder being filled due to the "heat of compression" of the air being transferred. A hot cylinder is more likely to rupture than a cool one. Also, the working pressure of a cylinder is its load pressure at 70° F. If the cylinder heats up during filling, the pressure will drop after it is taken off the line and cools down. The pressure changes with temperature changes given in Table XV below are taken from the *Handbook of Compressed Gases* by courtesy of the Compressed Gas Association.

Copper tubing is frequently used to fabricate the manifold. However, the Compressed Gas Association strongly recommends the use of stainless steel tubing. A typical cascade system is shown schematically in Figure 17 below.

The procedure is to open one of the large cylinders and bring the small cylinder up to full pressure, or until the pressure balances between the 300-cubic-foot cylinder and the small cylinder. After the first and second small cylinders are filled, this pressure may be down to 1,600 psig or less. In this case, the valve on the first large cylinder is turned off, and the valve on the second large cylinder is opened to utilize the higher pressure of the second large

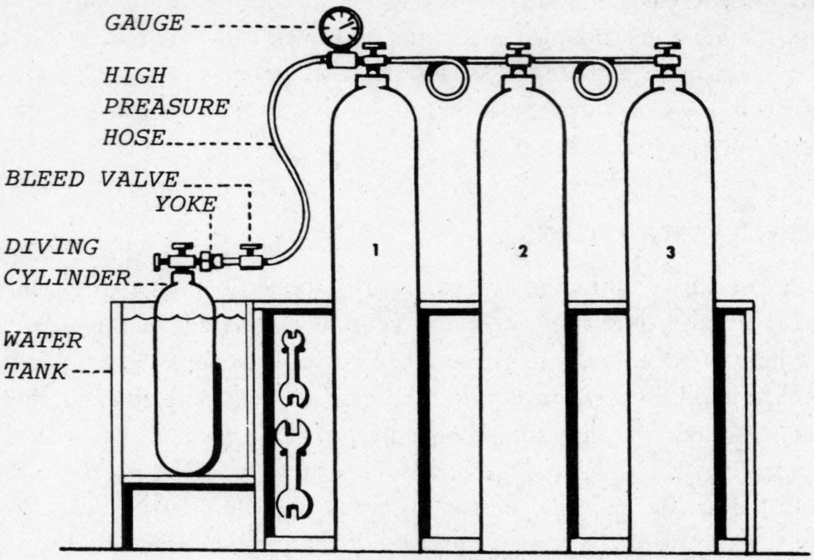

FIGURE 17. CASCADE SYSTEM

cylinder and thus bring the small cylinder up to the desired pressure. After several small cylinders have been filled, it will become necessary to charge from cylinder no. 1 up to whatever the pressure may be, let us say 800 pounds,

TABLE XV

PRESSURE/TEMPERATURE CONVERSION CHART

Settled Temp. °F	*Type I Container Service Pressure (expressed in psig)* 1,800	2,000	2,200	2,265	2,400	2,490	2,640
—20	1,401	1,548	1,694	1,741	1,839	1,903	2,011
—10	1,446	1,599	1,751	1,800	1,901	1,969	2,082
0	1,490	1,649	1,807	1,858	1,964	2,035	2,152
10	1,535	1,699	1,863	1,917	2,027	2,100	2,222
20	1,579	1,750	1,920	1,975	2,089	2,165	2,292
30	1,623	1,800	1,976	2,033	2,152	2,230	2,362
40	1,668	1,850	2,032	2,091	2,214	2,295	2,431
50	1,712	1,900	2,088	2,149	2,276	2,360	2,501
60	1,756	1,950	2,144	2,207	2,338	2,425	2,571
70	1,800	2,000	2,200	2,265	2,400	2,490	2,640
80	1,844	2,050	2,256	2,323	2,462	2,555	2,709
90	1,888	2,100	2,312	2,380	2,524	2,619	2,779
100	1,932	2,149	2,367	2,438	2,585	2,684	2,848
110	1,976	2,199	2,423	2,496	2,647	2,748	2,917
120	2,020	2,249	2,478	2,553	2,709	2,813	2,986

shut off no. 1 and charge from no. 2, which may bring the small cylinder up to, let us say 1,400 pounds, then shut off no. 2 and top off with no. 3 to the desired pressure.

When the pressure in no. 1 cylinder gets down to 300 pounds, it is impractical to use it any further, and the no. 1 cylinder should be replaced. Cylinder no. 2 now becomes no. 1, cylinder no. 3 becomes no. 2, and the fresh cylinder is no. 3. By utilizing this system of three large high-pressure cylinders a recovery of approximately 80% to 85% of the gas in the large cylinders can be made. If there are a large number of small cylinders to be filled, it may be practical to manifold more than four large cylinders together in order to get better efficiency.

Utilizing this three-cylinder manifold system to fill scuba cylinders will effect a saving of approximately 60% over the cost of sending the individual cylinders into a plant for refill.

FOR ADDITIONAL READING AND REFERENCE

Publications of the Compressed Gas Association, 500 Fifth Avenue, New York, N. Y. 10036.

Handbook of Compressed Gases

A valuable and comprehensive compendium concerned with all aspects of preparing, handling and using compressed gases.

C-5 Cylinder Service Life—Seamless, High-Pressure Cylinder Specifications.

C-6 Standards for Visual Inspection of Compressed Gas Cylinders.

G-4. 3 Commodity Specification for Oxygen

G-7 Compressed Air for Human Respiration

G-7. 1 Commodity Specification for Air

G-10. 1 Commodity Specification for Nitrogen

P-4 Safe Handling of Cylinders by Emergency Rescue Squads.

P-5 Suggestions for the Care of High-Pressure Air Cylinders for Underwater Breathing.

American National Standard Minimum Course

Content for Safe Scuba Diving Instructions Z86. 3-1972. American National Standards Institute, Inc. 1430 Broadway, New York, N.Y. 10018.

Scuba Safety Report Series published by Department of Ocean Engineering, University of Rhode Island, Kingston, R.I. 02881.

Report No. 1 Corrosion of Steel Scuba Tanks

5

BASIC SKIN AND SCUBA EQUIPMENT

Since the dawn of history man has had to go into the water and sometimes under the water. From the times of Homer, Alexander the Great, Aristotle, Julius Caesar, and on down through the centuries, men have sought ways to extend their diving time, ways to go deeper into the waters of the world. During these centuries, except for the past decade, the primary objective of the diver has been commercial or military. Because of this the equipment the diver used could be relatively expensive. The techniques of diving practiced then, as well as the equipment itself, required several men in a diving crew, yet diving was still economically feasible because it was being done for gain.

The sport diver, however, receives no gain from the use of his equipment except the pleasure of its use and possibly a limited amount of food for his table. To him one of the primary considerations in the purchase of equipment is cost. Because of this and because of the number of potential divers, the trend in diving equipment has been away from complex and expensive helmet gear toward less expensive and relatively less complex self-contained underwater breathing apparatus—scuba.

Scuba has opened up new fields for the commercial, open-sea, research, and military diver. Contrary to popular belief, the importance of scuba does not lie in the fact that it has replaced, or ever can replace, conventional helmet equipment. For certain types of underwater work helmet equipment will remain the best suited.

Self-contained diving equipment has long been used. The first such equipment was designed by William H. Jones in 1825. Basically this first scuba was a thin copper or leather helmet fitted with a window. To this was attached a short diving dress or suit, having elastic waist and armholes. Air was carried in an iron reservoir in the form of a cylindrical belt. The iron container was charged to about 450 psi, a terrific pressure for those days.

In the years since Jones pioneered scuba many advances have been made; today's equipment does not even remotely resemble that of the early nineteenth century. One can readily see the technological and fabrication advances upon visiting dive shops or consulting manufacturers' catalogues. Diving publications present current and proposed equipment along with evaluations by experts in the field. The vast scope of available equipment and its adaptability to divers and dive conditions would fill a good-sized book. This chapter will deal with basic descriptions and, in some instances, desired features of basic equipment.

Instructors and specific published data must fill the desire for other than rudimentary information. Individual selection of equipment must be guided by fit, function, and adaptability to the diver and proposed activities. Following simple guidelines of fit, function, and adaptability will simplify the selection of basic equipment.

Skin Diving Equipment

An individual becomes skilled in surface and underwater swimming only after he has solved many problems. Even with the help of expert teachers he must ultimately solve these problems for himself by experimentation and practice. Each piece of equipment used by the diver, even though designed to help him in a specific activity, complicates the situation. When he has solved most of the problems, he then becomes proficient in the use of the equipment.

Realizing that some divers hang twelve or more pieces of gear on themselves, it is important that they become familiar with one item before adding another. Eventually the diver may become skilled in the use of all the equipment available to him and then he can knowledgeably select only that which is necessary to his planned activity.

CHOOSING THE MASK

Face masks are designed to fulfill a specific need; to provide a constant layer of air between the eyes and a transparent lens. Since this basic piece of equipment must be adaptable to use with other equipment, mainly snorkel and scuba, the designed shape covers only the nose and eyes. Inclusion of the nose permits pressure equalization of contained air with that of ambient water.

The variations of design are multiple and purposeful. A variety of facial contours must be taken into account and accommodated. Individual needs or desires will dictate size, volume, and lens design. Facilitation of associated functions is provided for by incorporation of purge valves and nose-pinch devices. The majority are built for comfort, efficiency, and durability.

The final choice should be governed by size, shape, comfort, and positive seal. Size and shape are optional; comfort and positive seal are imperative. Essential features are a soft, flexible, face-fitting skirt, shatterproof or tempered glass lens secured by a metal band, an adjustable, head-fitting, well-anchored head strap. Not essential but individually desirable are clearing (purge) valve and construction which permits pinching the nostrils shut.

Before you purchase a mask, place it over your eyes and nose *without donning the head strap.* Observe the skirt contour so as to avoid placing the mask on upside down. The skirt edge should contact your face completely. Inhale slightly with the mask in place. If desirable seal is obtained, the mask will re-

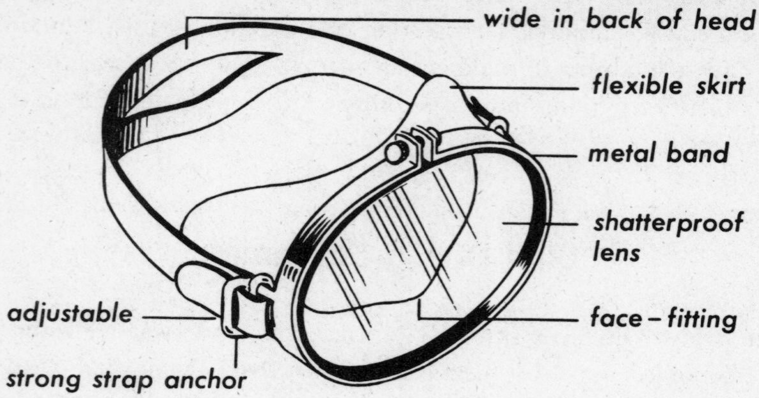

FIGURE 18. MASK

main in place until you exhale. Try several types, keeping in mind adaptability, comfort, and efficiency.

A good mask rates good care. Avoid contact with oil or grease (suntan lotions, hair dressing, and some cosmetics). Rinse or wash as necessary after use. Protect the lens from scratches or cracking. Check all parts, especially purge valves, before and after diving.

CHOOSING THE SNORKEL

Though multiple designs are available, most snorkels are basically designed as J-shaped tubes of rubber, neoprene, plastic, or adaptable combinations. The length of the tube above mouth level is generally 12 to 14 inches. Greater length is superfluous; with it breathing comfort is noticieably decreased, dead air space is increased, and no advantage gained.

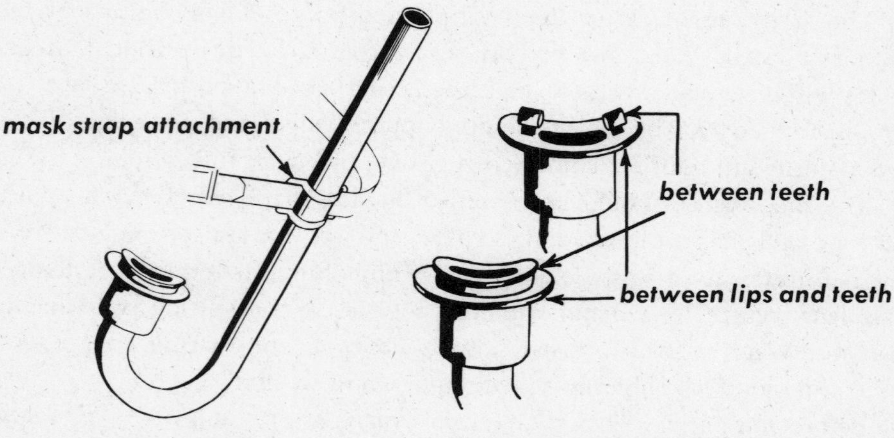

FIGURE 19. THE SNORKEL

Mask and snorkel combinations, mechanical gimmicks to keep water out, and designs alleged to permit several feet of submergence while breathing should be avoided. Most are clumsy and inefficient, and some are just plain dangerous.

Choose a design which is simple, light, adaptable to attachment on the face-mask strap, and which is equipped with a soft, smooth, easily gripped mouthpiece. Most manufacturers of modern diving equipment provide these features, so the choice boils down to comfort and price. Purging valves located below the mouthpiece on a snorkel are a luxury rather than a necessity and add to the "things to be checked" list.

CHOOSING THE FINS

The evolution of this foot-area-increasing attachment from a board on the shoe to the many scientifically designed fins now available is an excellent example of the combined research and development necessary to make man more adaptable to an underwater environment. Variations of total blade area, outline, and curvature, and stiffening of ribs to govern flexibility and increase efficiency of thrust are combined with a slipper or foot pocket and heel strap of such design as to provide positive control and comfort to the wearer. No one design will be satisfactory for all, so the choice must be governed by individual physical

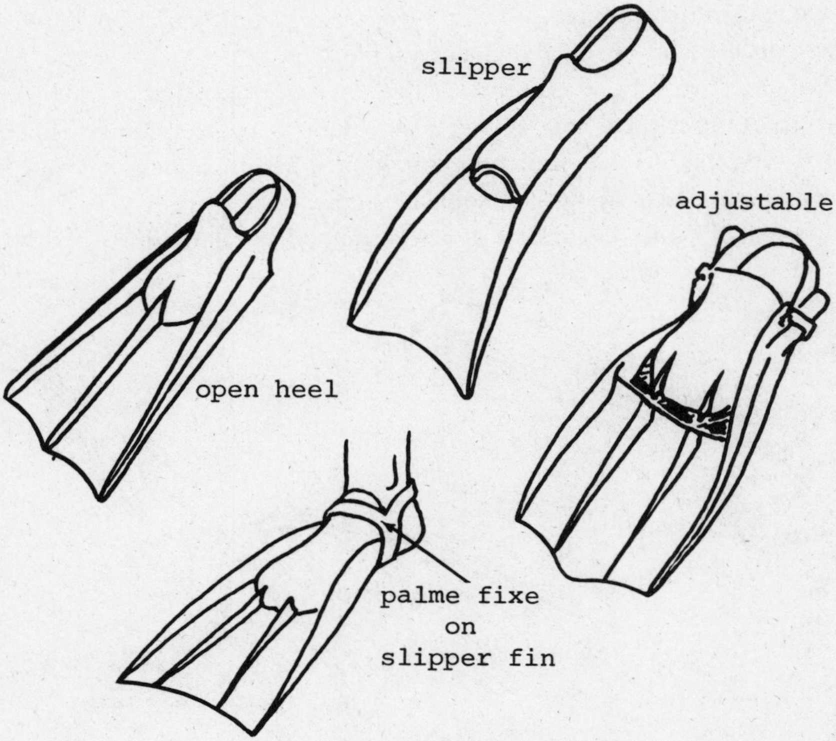

FIGURE 20. FIN TYPES

agility and structure. Some degree of limitation is built in. Since most fins are made in graduated sizes to fit small through large feet (usually two shoe sizes are accommodated by each size) with proportional blade sizes, some regulation is offered.

Choice of fins will be more satisfactory if the individual considers that most of the diving activity will involve wearing neoprene boots or other foot covering. The purchase of fins with fixed heel strap or slipper type should be governed by foot-size plus the boot. If one desires to have fins adaptable to both bare and shod feet, the adjustable heel-strap-type fin is the most logical choice.

CHOOSING THE WEIGHT BELT

An essential item of equipment for those who, because of positive buoyancy, have trouble submerging and remaining submerged, the weight belt should be sturdily constructed, flexible, and wide enough to be comfortable when worn next to the skin or over diving equipment. It must be equipped with a quick-release mechanism or double D rings for the safety hitch. These must permit positive release with one hand. Belt-size (girth) adjustment methods are variable according to buckle design. Such adjustment is necessary, not only to fit the individual but also to provide for additional length when protective clothing is worn and weights added. *Do not tie the belt excess material.* Better to let it dangle than to eliminate the effectiveness of the quick release. Elastic-type belts are available which provide snug fit even though girth variation is caused by pressure during skin or suited scuba dives.

Weights should be so constructed that they can be readily added to or removed from the selected belt. Bilateral distribution in equal amount is desirable for providing stability. Determination of required weight, as described in Chapter 6, prior to purchase may provide some economy.

Important: Fit the weight belt to go on last and come off first.

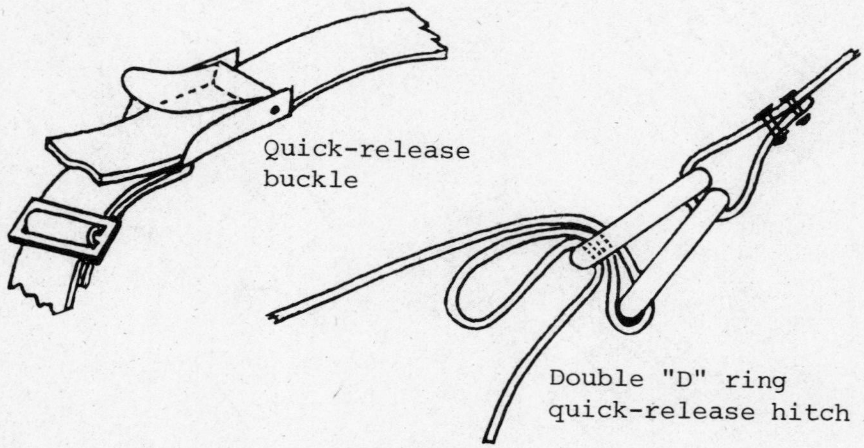

FIGURE 21. QUICK-RELEASE FASTENINGS

Protective Clothing

The prime reason for wearing insulating clothing is the prevention of body-heat loss to the water. Choice of type of clothing and area to be covered will depend on intended use, individual need, and, in many instances, price. Such protective clothing may be divided into three categories: wet suits (foam neoprene), absorbent cloth, and dry suits (sheet rubber).

WET SUITS

These suits are designed to permit a small amount of water between the diver and suit. The fit should be snug enough to prevent a general flow-through of water but not so tight as to restrict movement or cause discomfort.

It is generally conceded that the foam material be covered with "skin" (smooth material, neoprene, or nylon) both inside and out. This smooth surface will facilitate donning and doffing, strengthen the material, and make general maintenance easier. The thickness of material governs the insulating properties. Suit material is offered in thicknesses of 1/8, 3/16, 1/4, and 3/8 inch. The thicker materials afford more insulation, but impose some problems due to bulk. Definite temperature assignment for each thickness would be misleading because of individual tolerance, length of time in the water, tailoring, and total area covered.

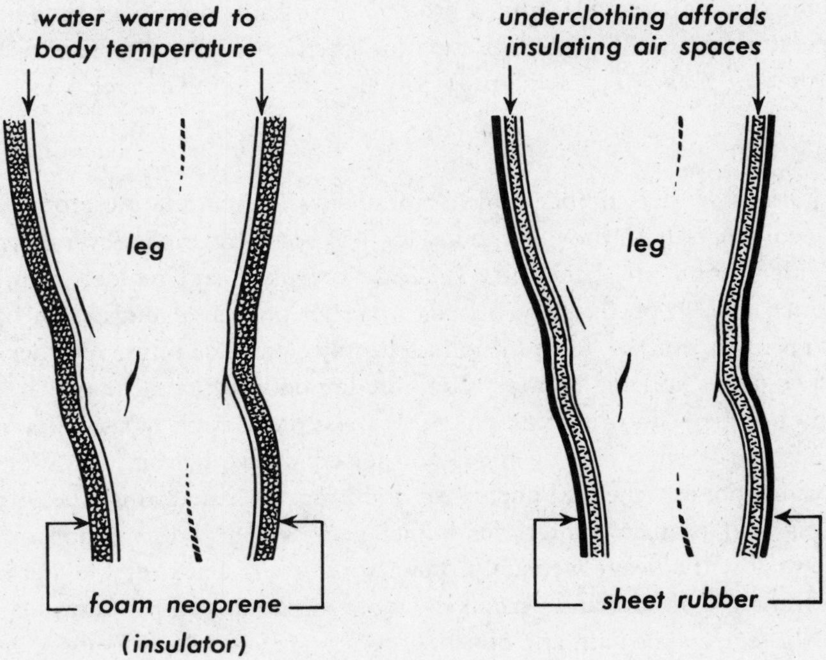

FIGURE 22. WET SUIT (left) AND DRY SUIT (right)

Barring extensive destruction of the suit, no drastic efficiency loss occurs when the material is torn during a dive. Repairs can be easily and quickly made, using liquid adhesives recommended by the manufacturer. (Further discussion of wet suits will be found in Chapter 6.)

BOOTS AND GLOVES

Almost all fins will be much more comfortable if worn over neoprene foam boots (hard or soft sole). There will be less chilling (feet get cold first), chafing, and there is added protection from rough surfaces. However, it must be remembered that boots worn without fins will drastically reduce the efficiency of the leg kick. Do not remove fins until you are supported or free of the water so as not to need their aid.

Gloves, either fingered or mitten type, reduce tactile sense and hand efficiency, but insulate against heat loss which causes the same effects. Therefore, it is wise, if possible, to practice various skills involving hand manipulation with gloves on.

ABSORBENT CLOTHING

Almost any adaptable article of clothing designed primarily to provide insulation against heat loss to air will afford some protection in water. Though some thermal jackets and pants, efficient when dry, give little protection when wet. Generally, close-fitting garments of fibrous or wool-like material, closely woven or tight knit, will provide limited protection for short periods of time in water temperatures above 65° F. Substitution for specifically designed protective clothing is *not implied.* (Types and problems are discussed in Chapter 6.)

DRY SUITS

Fabrications of sheet rubber, which in itself has little insulating properties, are designed generally to provide head-to-toe leakproof covering. Several types are available: Front- and back-entry suits are one-piece and molded seamless or cemented and stripped; entry is made through one large midsection opening which is then gathered, folded, and fastened by clamps or rings. Another design is in two pieces, top and bottom; after donning both sections, the two are rolled together at the waist or sealed by use of a waist ring device. Wrist cuffs or rings and necessarily snug face openings are not conducive to comfort. Worn over adequate wool and thermal underwear and properly sealed, this type of protective suit will provide comfort for longer periods and permit diving in colder water than will a heavy wet suit. Combination of dry suit over wet suit merges the advantages of both and permits diving at minimum temperatures.

Poor seal, trapped air, and possible rupture of material are discussed in Chapters 2 and 6. Regular maintenance should include thorough examination, testing for leaks, and careful storing (dried and powdered with unadulterated talc).

Oil, grease, volatile liquids (gasoline, kerosene, mineral spirits, etc.), and prolonged heat will alter the elastic properties of rubber and must be avoided.

The foregoing description of protective clothing has been of basic nature. Consultation with knowledgeable and experienced divers in your part of the world should provide enough information to guide your selection. Regardless of choice, it must be remembered that none are 100% efficient and that the effects of continued heat loss can be dangerous.

THE FLOAT

The float, whether an inner tube, inflated raft, inflated boat, modified surfboard, or other satisfactory improvisation, should be brightly colored on its above-the-water surface and equipped with a diver flag. The flag standard should be sufficiently high so as to permit adequate visibility.

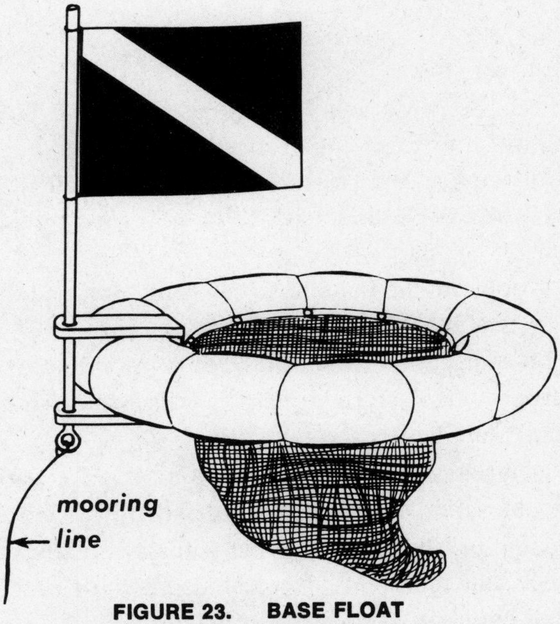

FIGURE 23. BASE FLOAT
Inner tube, diver flag, and carryall net.

This float can be used as a surface base, a resting station, and, in an emergency, as a rescue device. Suitable racks or holding devices can be rigged to attach equipment and to provide out-of-the-water storage for speared fish. If random coverage of a large area is anticipated, and if conditions permit, a tow line from the float to the diver will assure its proximity when desired.

THE VEST

The inflatable vest in one of its many designs is an essential item for safety when skin or scuba diving. Since the diver is constantly confronted with buoyance variations due to depth and equipment, it is essential that some device be worn

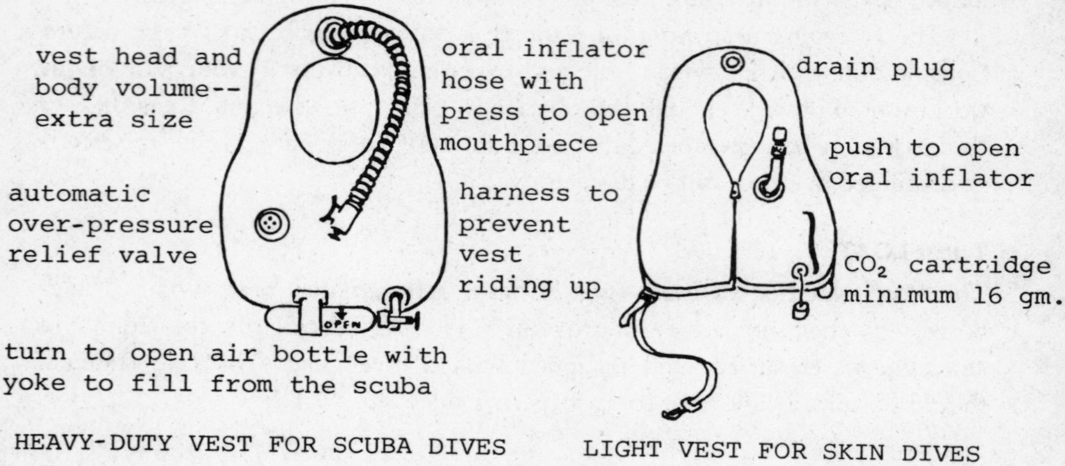

FIGURE 24. THE VEST

which will permit compensation. Positive flotation in a "face up" position on the surface is a must for the resting or incapacitated diver.

Providing for the foregoing has resulted in the manufacture of several basic designs. Selection of any one kind should be governed by the need for some or all of the following factors:

- Sufficient displacement volume, when fully inflated, to provide positive surface buoyancy is a must for all.
- An inflation source, other than oral, for surface employment. This may be provided by carbon dioxide cartridge or by valving air from the scuba bottle, regulator, or small supplementary air bottle.
- A means of inflation under water so as to offset negative buoyancy or to provide positive buoyancy must be provided. This may be accomplished by oral inflation or by high-pressure air from the scuba or smaller air bottle. CO_2 cartridge inflation at average diving (scuba) depths will usually not provide the needed or desired buoyancy change (see Chapter 2).

Oral inflation devices vary in design and placement. The valving mechanism for inflation or deflation is varied. This makes a mutual pre-dive check by all of the dive group mandatory.

An over-pressure relief device (automatic) is desirable so as to preclude vest rupture during ascent. Manual operation of bleed-off valves to produce desired volume requires experience.

The interior of the vest must be rinsed and cleansed so as to prevent bacterial growth caused by expired air. This usually involves a bit of maneuvering if the inflation tube enters in the chest area and no other drain is provided.

In using the vest, care must be exercised to prevent snagging, overinflation, or other material-damaging effects.

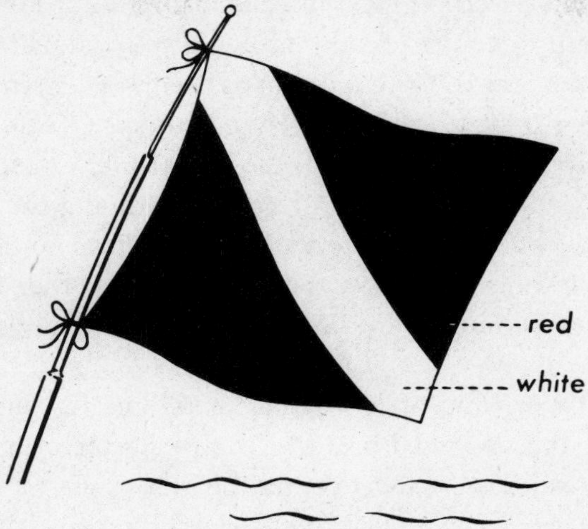

FIGURE 25. DIVER FLAG

DIVER FLAG

This red flag with diagonal white stripe from upper staff to lower outside is widely accepted and used by divers to denote the area in which there is diving in progress. Its use has been widely advertised to boaters through diving clubs and through individual diver effort. Some states have enacted a law which forbids surface craft operators to approach closer than 100 feet to the displayed flag.

The flag is to be displayed on a staff of sufficient (not less than 3 feet) height to be clearly visible and in sufficient numbers so placed as to define the area of diving operations. The placement of the flag(s) must govern the sphere of activity of the diver as well as the boat operator. This is a precautionary device to protect both diver and boat operator. Neither will benefit from its display if its meaning and restrictions are not known and obeyed.

Diving Tools and Instruments

The definition of diving tools and instruments would have to include almost every item available to the diver, and the detailed coverage of all such would involve a book in itself. Since this is intended to be a basic text and to leave detailed coverage to the instructor or to the individual's research, the following items are representative of basic needs:

Watch: Constructed so as to be waterproof and pressure resistant to at least five atmospheres (132 ft.) by actual test. The dial should be easy to read, have a clearly visible sweep second hand and adjustable bezel to measure elapsed time. The case should be noncorrosive and be equipped with a large-enough band to permit attachment over the wrist of a wet suit. Time passage is of utmost importance to the diver in every phase of his activity. Your need and the price of the watch will of course greatly influence your selection.

Depth gage: Depth, equally as important as time, is an essential factor to be known and controlled in practically all diving activity. Granted this could be done less expensively by a surface-based line of calculated length, as may be done during initial open-water dives, but since scuba diving is classed as "free," the average diver will want to dispense with the umbilical cord of surface supply or restraint. Following his desire, the diver adds another tool, the depth gage. The depth gage is available in three basic types:

1. Capillary: This consists of a small-diameter plastic tube, open to the water on one end, mounted on or in the perimeter of a calibrated dial. Pressure-increase causes water to enter the tube as air volume in the tube is reduced (Boyle's Law). It is sensitive, cheap, easy to maintain, and accurate enough for skin and basic scuba diving.

2. Bourdon type: Ambient pressure is transmitted into a curved metal tube which tends to straighten as pressure increases. The change of tube curvature through linkage moves a gear system to move the gage indicator needle. This gage must be protected against loss of seal and thoroughly

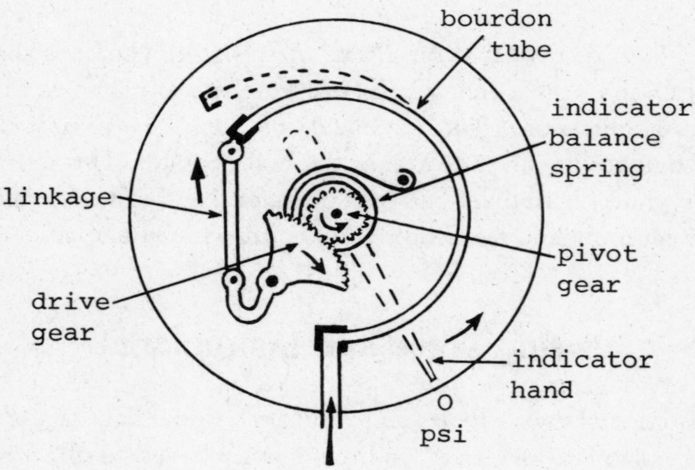

FIGURE 26. BOURDON TUBE-TYPE PRESSURE-GAGE ACTION

rinsed to prevent obstruction of water-entrance ports. Some recent gages of this type have an oil-filled tube capped with a diaphragm at the pressure port. These are said to be more sensitive and less subject to corrosive effects.

3. Oil-filled: These depth gages rely on pressure variance upon an outer surface of the body of the gage which is designed to be flexible. Such movement of the flexible area is then transmitted to the internal mechanism which, in turn, activates the indicator on the calibrated dial face. Though sealed against water, the gage should be rinsed thoroughly in fresh water, kept free of dirt and crystallized materials, and treated as a reasonably delicate instrument.

Each of the foregoing depth gages has merit. Price and your need will be the governing factors in purchase. More detailed descriptions of these gages may be offered by instructors or can be found in technical manuals.

The compass: A waterproof and pressure-resistant cased magnetic needle or disk which should be free to rotate in a reasonable plane other than true hori-

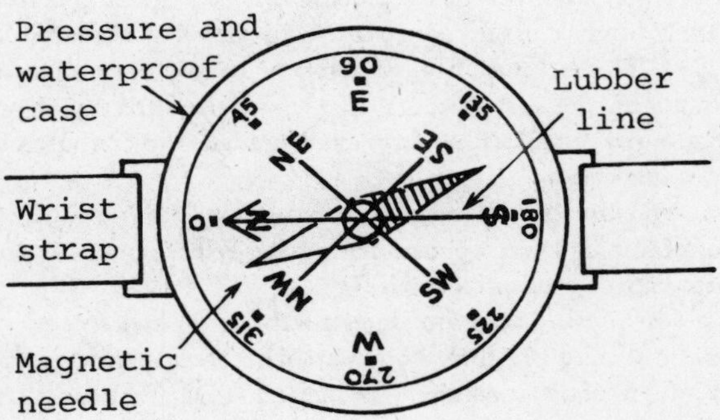

FIGURE 27. DIVER'S COMPASS

zontal. All markings should be easily read. Also, there should be a clearly visible "lubber line" for orientation of sight line. Dives made in open water where known landmarks either do not exist or may be obscured by poor visibility, and dives made in areas requiring constant awareness of specific direction, make this an essential instrument. Without means of directional orientation the diver can be faced with an exhausting swim or, still worse, possible entrapment.

Decompression meter: Considered by many divers to be an essential instrument when performing repetitive or deep dives which may require decompression stops. This instrument, when properly maintained and periodically checked, provides visual decompression information to the diver. Although eliminating much of the sometimes impractical consultation of dive tables during dive operations, it should not be used to take the place of a dive plan. Properly used, it will serve to double-check on preconceived dive plans.

The knife: Considered by most experienced divers to be an essential tool of the trade, it probably should have been given priority over the foregoing instruments. Whereas instruments may not be considered necessary because of some diving conditions, the knife often takes an essential role in what may have been

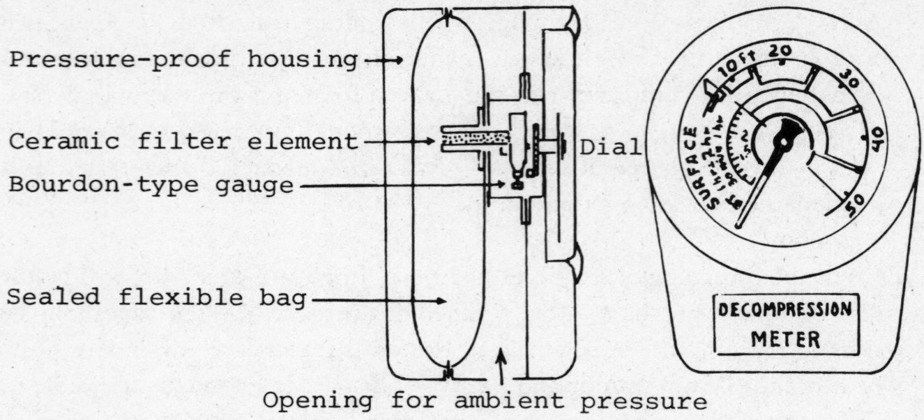

FIGURE 28. DECOMPRESSION METER

As ambient pressure increases, the flexible bladder is compressed, causing air to flow through the ceramic filter at a rate approximating nitrogen absorption by the body tissues (an average). This pressure change activates the bourdon-type pressure gauge causing the indicator on the dial to move in a clockwise direction from the starting point (atmospheric pressure). The flow and gauge indication continues while ambient pressure is increased.

When ambient pressure is reduced, the reverse flow from gauge to flexible bag through the filter occurs at a rate approximating the release of nitrogen from the tissues. The indicator moves counterclockwise.

The pressure-proof housing accommodates compression and subsequent reinflation of the flexible bag to surface pressure. Both start with atmospheric pressure contained. (The diagram is only to show function (mechanical). Detailed function, reading and use of the decom meter is left to the reader and the instructor.)

planned as a simple, basic skin or scuba dive. Encounters with kelp, grass, derelict lines, and the nightmare of monofilament fish line—all of which require the services of a good blade to prevent or undo entanglement—will prove the worth of a good knife.

The knife is a useful tool and should not be considered a weapon by the diver. The well-designed knife should have a reasonably sharp edge, a serrated or saw-like edge, strong blade, hilt, and easy-to-hold handle. Most knife blades are made of stainless steel. When not in use the knife should be carried in a dependable sheath which may be firmly attached in an accessible location on the diver's person. Though considered by many to be "just something else to snag," a lanyard from handle to sheath will guarantee retention and still not seriously hamper use.

An alternative to the knife is a similar tool but has a stronger blade. Instead of the usual knife point the end is chisel shaped for prying or digging. It also has a sharp and a serrated edge.

By this time the novice diver may be overwhelmed by the presentation of so many accessories classed as either essential or desirable. It must also be remem-

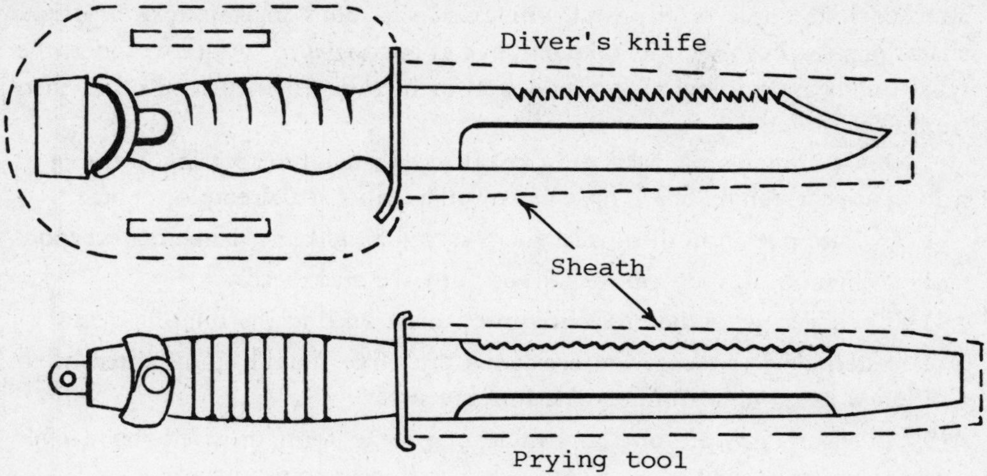

FIGURE 29. KNIFE AND PRYING TOOL

bered, however, that each one alone, or in combination, has its use. It must also be remembered that no advantage is to be gained by simply having or wearing these accessories. Need and the knowledge of each gained through experience will dictate selection and placement for best employment. Basic use of the foregoing items will be further discussed in Chapter 9.

Spearfishing, underwater photography, gold-mining, live-specimen collecting, finding and recovery of relics, exploring underwater caves, and archeological expeditions are all diving activities. Each employs specifically designed and manufactured equipment, tools or instruments. In order to take game such as fish, shellfish, or crustaceans, it is often necessary to have specialized tools. They can be divided into spearing, prying, and cutting devices. Since this is a basic text, detailed description or recommendation of choice will not be attempted. The brief discussion which follows will leave details to the instructor and for later research by the diver entering a specific field.

SPEARS AND SPEAR GUNS

Before purchase or employment of any of the available pole spears or spear guns, the prospective spear fisherman would be wise to determine legality of their use and seek the experienced advice of area divers.

Pole spears, whether of the hand or rubber-sling thrust type, are designed for impalement of the fish at little more than arm-thrust range.

Spear guns, whether powered by elastic sling(s), CO_2 cartridge, or explosive cartridge, are designed to propel a shaft with penetrating force. Distance of effectiveness is variable with design. The effective underwater range is rarely more than several times the length of the shaft.

Accuracy is attained by practice. Shaft length, projecting force, spearhead, attached line, angle of fire—all will cause variations in trajectory or flight characteristics. Even with its minute range as compared to surface weapons, the spear hunter must know his weapon well or be satisfied with food other than fresh fish.

A few common-sense rules must be observed when transporting, carrying or storing a spear gun on beach or boat as well as in its actual employment:

1. All are made to kill so treat them as you would any dangerous weapon.
2. When not in use, remove (if possible) the spearheads.
3. Do not activate the projecting mechanism until at the hunting site.
4. Safety devices to prevent accidental discharge should be inspected often and relied upon "only at the hunting site."
5. If spearpoints are not removable, put some form of safety hood over them to prevent an accident during storing or transporting.
6. Practice in a safe area in the water. Beach practice is taboo and would yield no experience except that the projectile travels a great deal farther in air than in water.
7. Remember to take only that which you can consume and *not* all you can kill.
8. Lines should be attached to the gun or device designed for retrieval. Never attach the line to yourself, you may become the catchee instead of the catcher.
9. Be sure your target is a fish and that other divers are not endangered.
10. Handle the thrust-type spear with care at all times, but particularly when going through breaking surf. When ascending from a dive without a fish, avoid pointing tines upward. Surface swimmers have been speared by careless divers. Always look up when surfacing. Avoid thrusting spearpoints against rocks. When you are swimming through kelp, the spear can be trailed to avoid tangling.

CAMERAS

Photography under water requires a camera either encased in a waterproof pressure-resistant case or one specifically designed to operate efficiently under water. The scope of available housings for adaptable cameras is far beyond this basic text treatment. Underwater cameras (self-encased) are available in a myriad of sizes for practically any use.

Unlike land photography, underwater stills and movies require that the prospective photographer be well versed in varied light, color, clarity, width, and depth of field conditions which exist in the water environment. More than mediocre results are obtained only by study, practice, patience, and consulting with experts.

* * *

The other special pursuits mentioned involve specialized equipment and a great deal more skill than the basic diver has mastered. All have been written about by experts. Before embarking on any new diving venture, read, consult the experts, heed their advice, and practice as directed until you are equipped mentally, physically and technically to safely dive with the experts.

Discussion of diving equipment to this point has dealt with basic diving gear and accessories which are common to skin or scuba diving. Man has, for centuries, sought to prolong his underwater activities. Thanks to modern technology we are now able to realize this dream. The creation of modern scuba has released us from the restrictions imposed by surface-supplied breathing apparatus as existed for the helmet or bell diver previously. Granted, there were many advantages in that type of underwater activity. Time, depth and, to a large degree, safety were (and are) indisputable advantages. Cost, limited field, and surface base limited it, however, to commercial and military use. Although depth, time, and comfort are limited by the volume and components of the breathing apparatus which can be carried and by the type of insulating clothing, the freedom of movement obtained by the use of scuba is ample compensation.

Selection of scuba to fit individual needs must be governed by a knowledge of function and limitations, and by trial use of the types available. Having determined the type, one is then faced with numerous manufacturers who offer standard and deluxe models. Consultation with experienced and impartial divers and with your pocketbook will usually result in a satisfactory choice. Following are basic descriptions of type and function of available gear.

Open-Circuit Scuba

Since the open-circuit demand-type scuba is the most prevalent in use today, it will receive initial and extensive coverage. Components and basic function tend to define the term. Its components are a container of compressed air, a valve, and regulator. These are fastened to a back pack which has an attached harness to fit the diver. The basic function is to supply the diver with the needed volume of ambient pressure air during inhalation. Exhaled gases are exhausted into the water.

The most recent trend is toward the plastic, back pack. Tank attachment devices are simple and adjustable as desired. Harness is uncomplicated, adjustable, and equipped with quick-release fastenings. These features provide for convenient adjustment or disassembly when desired, usually without special tools. Cost will be one of the factors affecting selection, but whatever the choice may be, it must feature necessary quick-release fastenings of all harness. Complete knowledge of design and function peculiarities prior to any diving is a necessity.

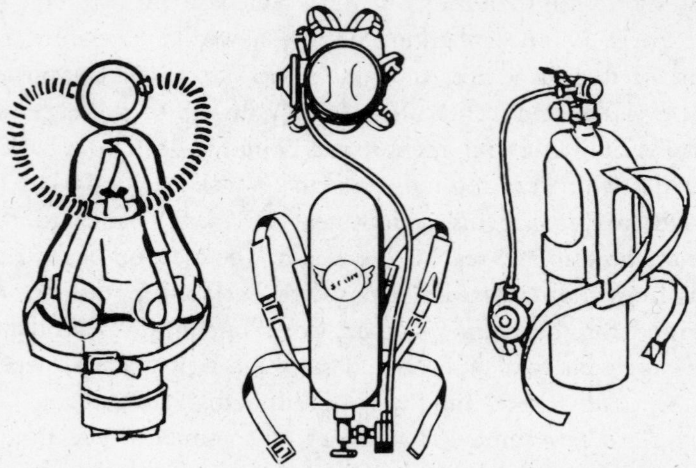

FIGURE 30. OPEN-CIRCUIT SCUBA TYPES

A variety of bottle volumes, pressure, metallurgy, internal and external surface coating, offers a wide choice for selection.

Bottle valves of simple ON and OFF type ("K") differ in design but not in function. Bottle valves which contain mechanism to "hold back" or "reserve" the flow at pre-set low pressure (300 to 600 psi) and provide a means for releasing this (pressure—volume) manually are termed "J" valves. This type of valve may be bottle-attached (as the "K") or be a part of the first stage of the regulator (single-hose type).

Demand flow regulators are basically of two types: double hose and single hose. The one-housing design of the two-hose-type regulator made it possible to engineer both a single-stage and a two-stage mechanism. The single-stage type was simpler and less expensive, but generally lacked the uniformity of required breathing effort afforded by the two-stage design. The two-stage type, because of the first-stage reduction of bottle pressure to a set working pressure (100 to 125 psi), plus ambient pressure, serves to permit uniform function of the second-stage reduction to ambient pressure regardless of bottle pressure.

The single-hose, two-stage regulator provides for bottle-pressure reduction to a set working pressure (100 to 125 psi) plus ambient pressure in the first stage (attached to bottle valve) with delivery of air (at first-stage reduction pressure) via the single hose to the second-stage reduction mechanism at the mouthpiece. This second stage reduces the hose pressure to ambient pressure upon inhalation demand.

The foregoing is little more than definition. The following is intended to explain *basic* mechanical function of each type. Detailed or specific design de-

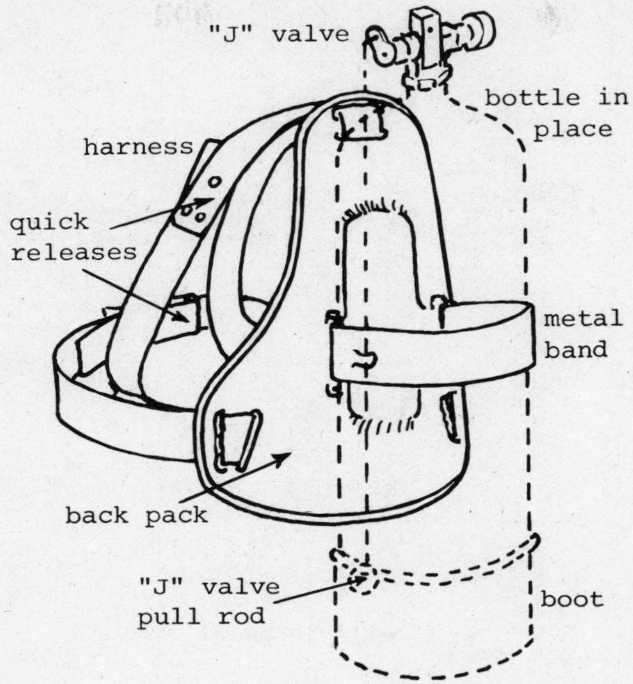

FIGURE 31. BACK PACK AND HARNESS

scription or drawings have been left to the instructor or to research of manufacturer's technical manuals by the reader.

Bottle, tank, cylinder (synonymous) have been previously discussed in Chapter 4. Size, volume, pressure, metal, lining, and color are items of individual determination. Single, double or, more rarely, triple joining for greater volume must be limited by actual need, common sense and ultimately by safety considerations. Regardless of choice, it must be remembered that a hydrostatic test is mandated by law each five years and the visual inspection of the interior should be performed at least once a year, or more often if use and conditions indicate need.

Valves, whether "K" or "J" (constant reserve), are equipped with a safety plug and disk designed to rupture before the burst pressure of the bottle is reached. Most of these safety devices were set for approximately 3,200 psi for bottles rated 2,250 psi. Filling to 10% over rated pressure (with a plus hydro test indicated) still keeps pressures within acceptable levels. Pressure rise because of heat or careless overfill will result in an ear-assaulting report and the escape of contained air. This is the least that can happen. Your dive activity is abruptly altered, but your anatomy and surroundings hopefully are intact. If the safety has been altered or damaged and pressure goes to danger levels the story

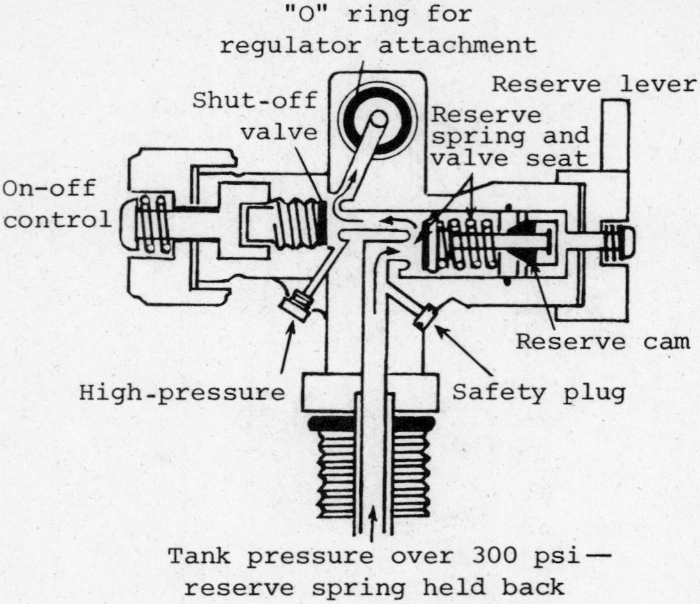

FIGURE 32. CONSTANT RESERVE "J" VALVE

may have a disastrous and messy conclusion. Careful handling (the valve is *not* a handle) of valve and tank will pay off in continued safety.

Recent valves made to be used on now available 3,000-psi bottles should not be fitted to bottles having lower rated pressures.

"J" valves are constructed so as to permit flow of air from the bottle to the regulator until bottle pressure is reduced to the *constant reserve* level if the reserve lever is in the ON position (up). A valve held in the forward position by a calibrated spring is kept open by air pressure in excess of reserve level (300 to 600 psi determined by spring strength). When this level is reached, the spring action forces the valve forward, thus closing the flow. Pulling the reserve rod (or lever) rotates a cam which compresses the spring and removes the restricting valve from its seat. The flow is thereby resumed and will continue until pressure is insufficient to supply ambient pressure to the diver (zero psi gage at surface or more at greater depth). Once this restriction of flow or "reserve" has been opened the dive must be terminated. Calculation will show that 300 psi in a 71.2 cu. ft. (at 2,475 psi) bottle will yield 8.7 cu. ft. of one-atmosphere air. Depth decreases this volume yield as you already know. Smaller bottles yield less reserve volume. A few minutes of arithmetic to determine "reserve" volume will be well spent. It must also be remembered that the "reserve" is no more constant than the condition of the spring which imposes the shut-down of flow.

Submersible pressure gauge. Since the "J" valve constant reserve is not in-

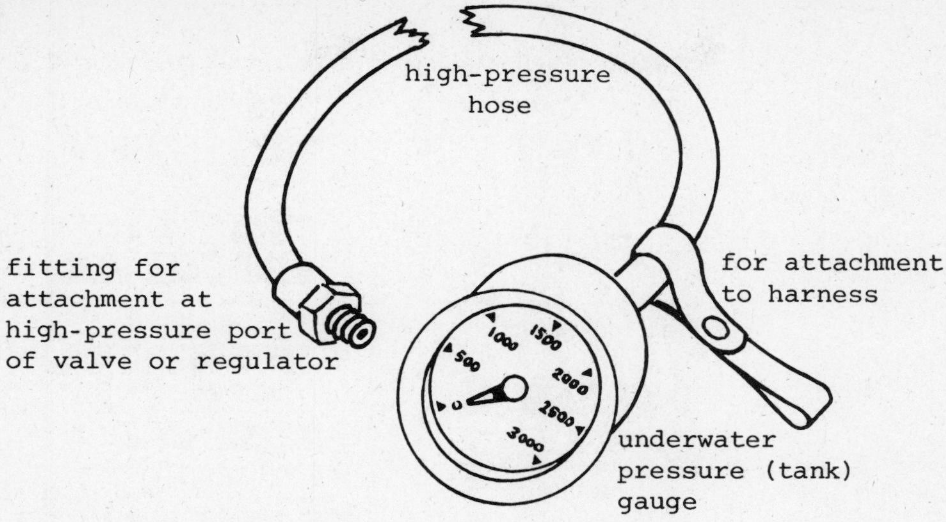

FIGURE 33. VISUAL PRESSURE GAUGE

fallible, the experienced diver resorts to the use of a visual pressure gauge. This adds one more hose from the bottle valve or high-pressure port of the regulator to the gauge. However, being able to read the exact bottle pressure at all times should preclude the necessity for emergency ascent due to air-supply shortage.

Reducing the high-pressure air carried in the scuba bottle to the ambient-pressure air necessary to diver safety and comfort requires one of the previously defined regulators. In order to have better understanding of the function of these regulators it is desirable to become acquainted with some of the requirements for satisfactory functioning. The following will serve as basic information. More specific instruction and updating of available equipment must be the aim of the instructor or the desire of the reader. Technical manuals and papers are myriad and are available from many sources. These sources include manufacturers' repair manuals, and impartial or specific reports appearing in diving magazines.

REGULATOR AIR-FLOW REQUIREMENTS

There is a great deal of misunderstanding and misinformation regarding the meaning of easy breathing in a regulator. Few people actually understand what is necessary to give a diver the large volumes of air flow needed when he is working underwater. As a result, many divers are selecting their regulators on the basis of a "pretty case" or a "nice-looking mouthpiece." Others attempt to judge regulator performance and "easy breathing" by the slight effort necessary to depress the regulator diaphragm and start an air flow. Such effort has very little to do with actual performance.

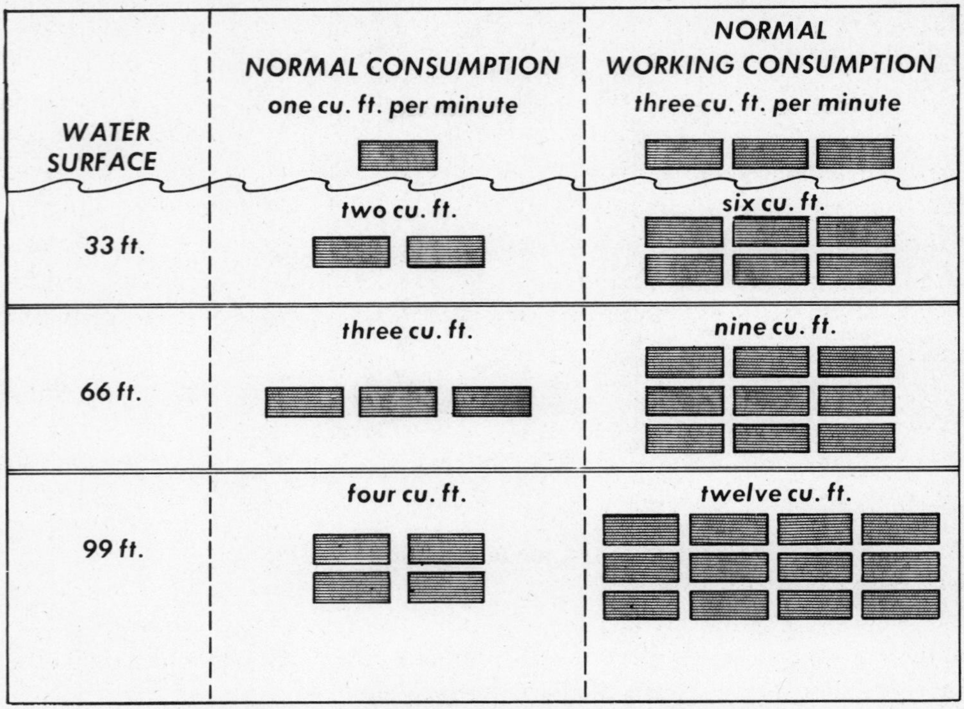

FIGURE 34. REGULATOR AIR-FLOW REQUIREMENTS

As an illustration of this, put a straw in a person's mouth while he is sitting quietly and he will have no difficulty in breathing through the straw. This is "easy breathing." But let that person try running while breathing through the same straw and you will have an example of the requirement in regulator performance.

In a regulator, we are concerned with great volumes of air flow with *no increase in suction effort.* The extremely large volumes of air flow demanded from a regulator are illustrated in Figure 34.

Increase in air flow. The figure of 1-cubic-foot-per-minute normal consumption is not accurate, as air consumption varies between individuals. But 1 cubic foot per minute is close enough to illustrate the tremendous increase in volume of flow required during exertion. The estimate of three times normal consumption during exertion is conservative. At 100 feet a diver under working conditions may consume as much as the illustrated 12 cubic feet per minute. This is a tremendous air flow. Any restriction to breathing in a regulator will give the same effect as trying to run around the block while breathing through a straw. The large air flow must be obtained with *no increase in suction effort.*

Actually our lungs do not occupy a greater volume under pressure. The molecules are pressed closer together, air becomes thick, and forcing it through an opening is somewhat the same as the flow of syrup through a straw as compared to the flow of water through a straw. Another comparison is the flow of light traffic through a subway door as compared to the congestion of traffic during the rush hour. The size of the opening determines the number of people who can travel easily through a doorway and it also determines the amount of dense air which can flow easily through an orifice.

The result of such restriction to breathing with insufficient volume of air flow is air "starvation." The diver's inhalation effort increases tremendously in an attempt to increase the flow. This increased effort accelerates the process of exhaustion and causes demand for an even greater volume of air flow. At this point even stopping to rest while still under pressure will not appreciably reduce the demand for a large volume of flow. The diver is left gasping for sufficient air until shallow water or, better yet, surface is reached.

This example is extreme, but degrees of exhaustion from restricted breathing are experienced every day by divers working in moderately deep water with inadequate regulators. This exertion in breathing also uses air at a faster rate and cylinders are more quickly exhausted.

Upstream and Downstream Valves

An engineer designing a two-stage regulator, whether of the two-hose or single-hose type, must consider, basically, the type of valve which will best perform the desired function as the air flows from tank to diver.

Two-stage regulators of either type must primarily deal with tank pressure variance from high to low in such manner as to provide a nearly constant intermediate (first-stage) pressure. This is usually adjusted to approximately 8 atmospheres absolute. The second stage must be designed to regulate the flow of the constant pressure first-stage air in such manner as to match the ambient pressure on the diver when he inhales.

A look at the diagrammatic valves in Figure 35 will help to clarify the "upstream" and "downstream" connotation. The *upstream* valve opens against the flow and requires two springs or counterforces: one to force the valve open against high pressure and another to guarantee closing force as high (tank) pressure reduces. The *downstream* valve opens with the flow and requires a counterforce (calibrated spring) to close it against the flow pressure. Understanding the principle of each type should make clear why the upstream valve is used in most first stages (tank pressure reduction) and the downstream valve is used in the second stage (intermediate to ambient).

The mechanical parts of the regulator coupled with the employment of air-flow openings of calculated area (calibrated orifice) regulate the air-flow force and volume under varying pressures. Explained simply, these calibrated orifices are similar to openings which permit small numbers (low pressure) to pass but slow the passage of vast numbers (high pressure). The following descriptions of various types of regulators will further illustrate *how, why* and *where* valves, springs and calibrated orifices are employed.

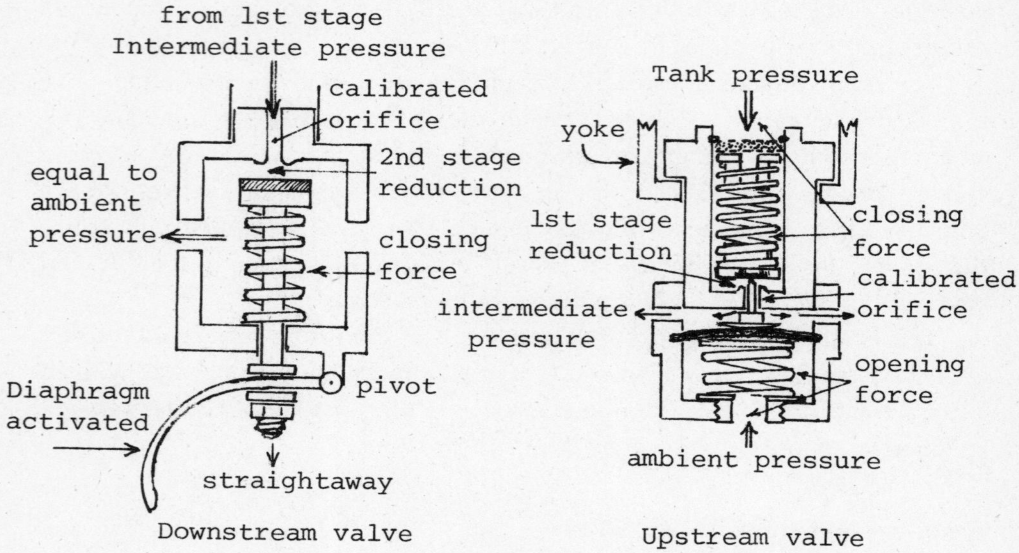

FIGURE 35. UPSTREAM AND DOWNSTREAM VALVE

The diameter of the orifice is extremely important in regulator design. Too great a variation in breathing between high and low pressures cannot be tolerated. In the two-hose type of regulator, large orifices and a degree of variation can be tolerated because of the extremely large diaphragm and the space available inside the case for a mechanical leverage advantage. Since the great area of the diaphragm makes it extremely sensitive to slight differences in pressure, a variation in effort required in opening the valve is not noticed. Because of the size of the diaphragm, large orifices can be used and no restriction to breathing is encountered.

One-Stage, Two-Hose Type

A single-stage demand regulator is one in which there is only one valve mechanism between the cylinders and the mouthpiece. It can be made with fewer parts and therefore be less expensive than a two-stage unit. This is one of the primary advantages, provided the design features of the regulator take into consideration the inherent characteristics of a single-stage regulator.

All demand regulators must provide a more or less constant volume of air from the cylinder regardless of the pressure within the cylinder. Orifices within the regulator have a fixed diameter and can, therefore, deliver only a fixed amount of air at any given pressure. The amount of air that can pass through an orifice of a given diameter varies with the cylinder pressure and with depth. If

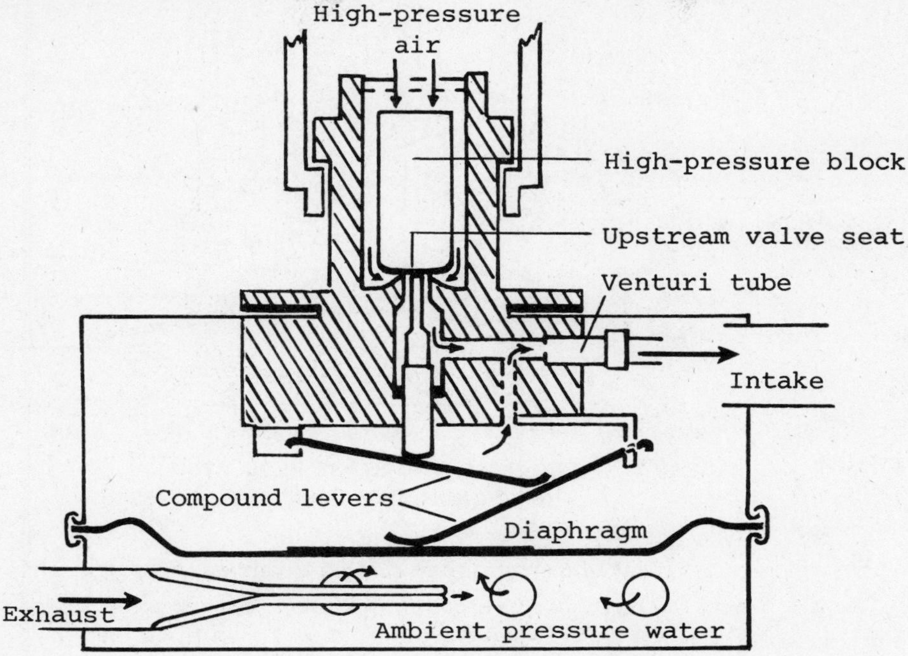

FIGURE 36. ONE-STAGE, TWO-HOSE REGULATOR WITH "OVER-BREATHING" VENTURI ACTION

the orifice in a single-stage regulator is not large enough to pass adequate amounts of air at all cylinder pressures and depths, breathing may be considerably restricted. This tendency has been overcome in most single-stage regulators by systems of compound levers, larger orifices and other means such as:

The Over-Pressure Breathing Device. Demand regulators release air as a result of a reduction of pressure in the air chamber created by the diver's inhalation. The effort required to activate the demand valve depends not only upon the "stiffness" of the demand system but also upon the difference in water pressure existing between the lungs and the diaphragm of the regulator. Normally, this amounts to only 6 or 7 inches, or about one-quarter pound of pressure per square inch. However, this muscular exertion must be maintained as long as air is required and may create a considerable strain on the chest muscles.

A development known as "over-pressure breathing" eliminates part of this required effort except at the very beginning of inhalation. The "over-pressure breathing" device is a *venturi tube system* designed so that air from the regulator, rushing through the venturi tube, creates a slight reduction in pressure in the air chamber, much as occurs on inhalation. This allows the water pressure to continue to hold the diaphragm in an open position, giving an increased flow of air with less effort.

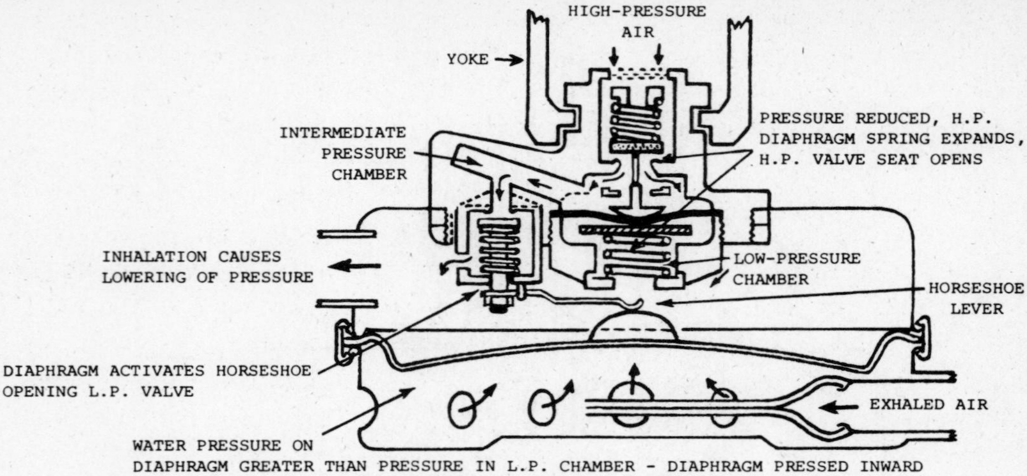

FIGURE 37. TWO-HOSE, TWO-STAGE REGULATOR (DIVER INHALING)

An over-pressure breathing system may be used to advantage, particularly at great depths, where the resistance to breathing increases because of increased air density. However, such a system may reduce the duration of the air supply considerably. The possibility of such reduction should be taken into account when planning dives involving depths beyond average.

But diving engineers, not satisfied with the single-stage solution, developed a regulator which gave less variation and permitted larger flows. The result is the two-stage, two-hose regulator.

Two-Stage, Two-Hose Regulator

The two-stage regulator sketch is intended to show basic function and *not* specific proportions or construction.

In this type, high-pressure cylinder air is reduced to breathing pressure in two stages. The first-stage valve reduces cylinder pressures to a lower predetermined pressure in the intermediate chamber leading to the second-stage valve. The large diaphragm activating the second-stage valve is then balanced against a much lower and more consistent intermediate pressure.

In the first stage, high-pressure cylinder air acts as a closing force tending to push the valve through the orifice. Counteracting the closing force of the cylinder air is a large spring pressing against a small diaphragm with a stem attached to the valve. Movement of the diaphragm up or down moves the stem up and down and opens or closes the valve.

The heavy spring is manually adjusted to hold the valve open against the closing force of a full cylinder of air until the intermediate pressure increases sufficiently to compress the spring and close the valve. When intermediate pressure reaches a predetermined point, usually around 110–125 psi *over ambient pressure,* the diaphragm is depressed and the valve closes.

In the second stage, a slight inhalation causes the large diaphragm to be depressed by ambient water pressure. This opens second-stage valve and allows air to flow to the mouthpiece. In this case, the large diaphragm controls only the low, intermediate pressure leading to the second-stage valve.

But once again we have a variation in pressure in the intermediate chamber due to variation in cylinder pressure.

The heavy spring against the first-stage diaphragm is adjusted against a full cylinder to give a calculated intermediate pressure. When cylinder pressure falls, the force of high-pressure air seating the valve also falls. Then the spring holds the valve open longer and the intermediate pressure increases to a point above the predetermined pressure. The intermediate pressure must increase sufficiently to depress the diaphragm and the spring until the first-stage valve again closes.

Once again the diameter of the orifice in the first stage determines the degree of pressure variation in the intermediate chamber. The large-diameter diaphragm in a two-hose regulator permits a degree of variation from large orifices. Thus adequate volumes of air flow are obtained with no increase in effort.

The first stage is depth-compensated, as air pressure in the housing is always equal to the surrounding water pressure. As this pressure increases with depth, it adds to the pressure of the spring against the small diaphragm and opens the first-stage valve. The valve stays open until intermediate pressure equals the surrounding water pressure plus the predetermined pressure at the surface.

The "downstream" type of valve in the second stage opens more easily with an increase in intermediate pressure. Since intermediate pressure increases as tank pressure falls, a two-stage, two-hose regulator of this design will breathe easiest when cylinder pressure is low—at the end of a dive when fatigue is a factor.

Non-return, or check-valve. A check-valve mouthpiece has been designed to prevent water from entering the inhalation tube of the breathing hose. Also, the check valves keep any water that may enter the exhalation tube from returning to the mouthpiece and thus make clearing a flooded circuit much easier.

Unbalanced Single-Hose First Stage

The unbalanced first-stage valve used with single-hose regulators works very much the same as the first stage in two-hose regulators. The hose leading to the second stage at the mouthpiece carries the intermediate pressure.

The sketch is diagrammatic only. This type of valve has been phased out and may be rarely encountered.

Here again, high-pressure cylinder air acts as a closing force seating the first-stage valve.

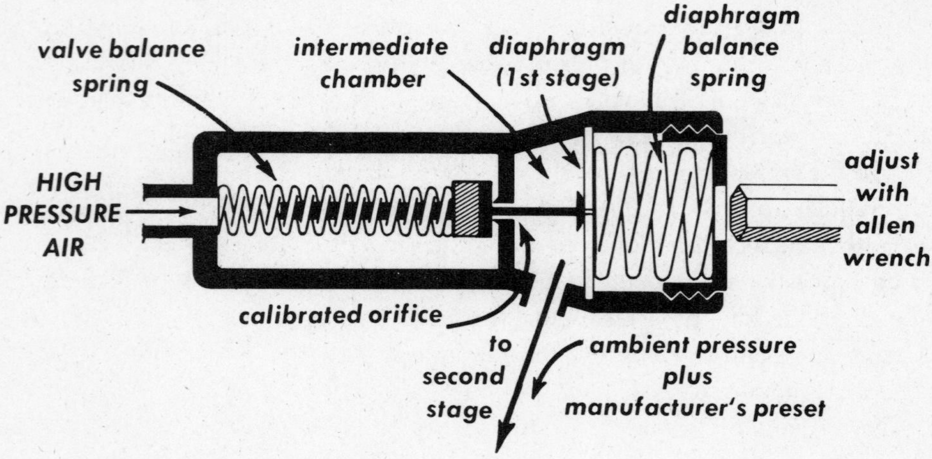

FIGURE 38. UNBALANCED SINGLE-HOSE FIRST STAGE

The spring pushing against the diaphragm counteracts this force and must be adjusted to open the valve against the maximum pressure from a full cylinder. When intermediate pressure increases to a predetermined pressure, the valve closes.

When the cylinder is opened, air flows through the orifice into the intermediate chamber and into the hose leading to the second stage. When this intermediate pressure reaches the preset level (110–125 psi), it pushes against the diaphragm, compresses the spring, and the valve closes.

The single-hose first stage is depth-compensated by water pressure which enters the spring area, presses the diaphragm upward, and opens the valve. The valve will remain open until air in the intermediate chamber is equal to surrounding water pressure plus the calculated predetermined pressure.

But, again, we have variation due to changing cylinder pressures. A low cylinder pressure exerts less closing force on the valve. The spring will hold the valve open until intermediate pressure in the hose increases sufficiently to depress the diaphragm and close the valve. In some regulators the increase in hose pressure is as great as 50%.

In single-hose regulators the diaphragms are much smaller than in two-hose regulators and are extremely sensitive to variations in pressure. The number of square inches of surface area in single-hose diaphragms is so small that slight variations in hose pressure make a great difference in breathing effort.

In order to reduce the amount of variation it is necessary to reduce the size of the orifice in the first stage. Remember the closing force seating the first-stage valve is the area of the orifice times the cylinder pressure plus the spring pressure. Using a smaller orifice reduces the effect of cylinder pressure in closing the valve. However, a small orifice adds resistance to breathing

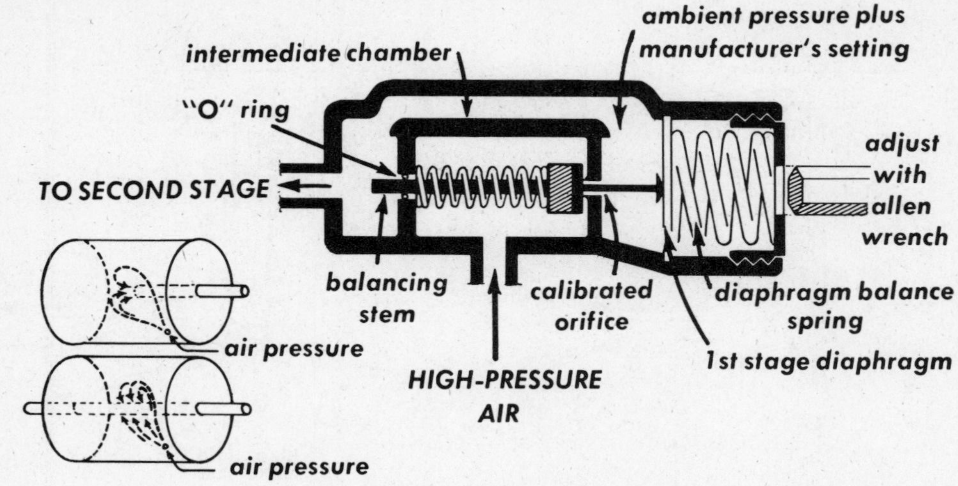

FIGURE 39. BALANCED FIRST STAGE

when large volumes of air flow are required. It is similar to breathing through a straw.

Balanced First Stage

In the balanced first-stage valve, cylinder air pressure has no effect in seating the valve. Remember that in an unbalanced first-stage valve the closing force *normally* exerted by cylinder air is calculated by multiplying the area of the orifice times the cylinder pressure.

Closing the orifice in a first-stage valve would neutralize the effect of this air pressure in seating the valve. The same effect as closing the orifice is achieved in the balanced valve.

The small drawing in Figure 39 showing a stick inside a can illustrates what has been accomplished. The can with the end of the stick inside illustrates an unbalanced valve. Pressure applied into the can tends to drive the stick outside. The diameter of the stick determines the force with which it will be expelled.

The can that has the stick completely through it illustrates a balanced valve. Pressure inside the can has no effect on the stick as it is neutralized in all directions. The diameter of the stick makes no difference.

In a balanced valve, a valve stem of exactly the same diameter as the orifice is extended *outside* the chamber. High pressure is not exerted on the end of the valve stem, and we have the same result as the stick extended completely through the can.

With cylinder air pressure neutralized, only the mechanical force of springs affects operation of the valve. These springs can be set to give exactly the desired intermediate pressure. And this pressure will remain the same over all stages of cylinder pressure.

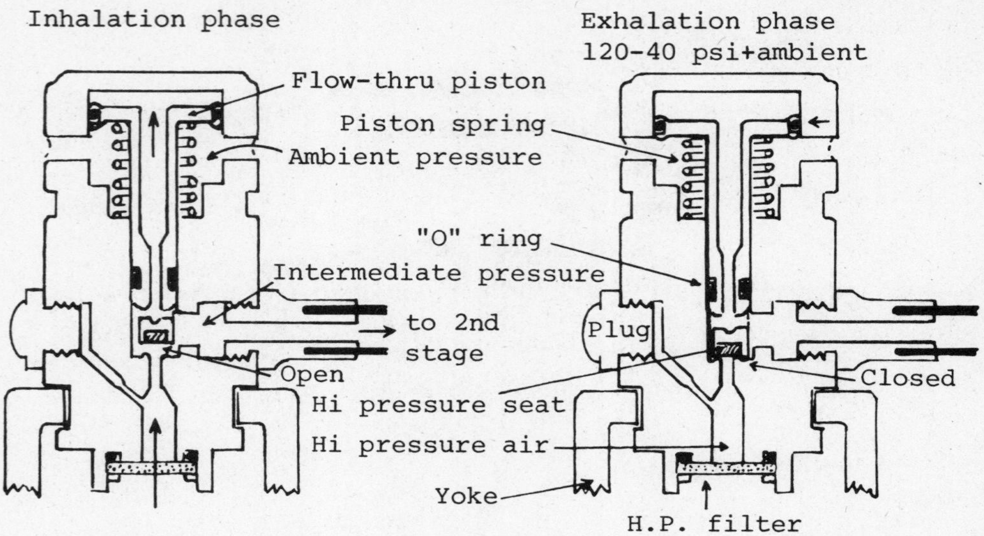

FIGURE 40. SINGLE-HOSE REGULATOR FIRST STAGE—PISTON TYPE

Inhalation phase: Intermediate pressure is reduced in the dome by the inhalation. Ambient pressure and the piston spring push the piston upward toward the dome. The high-pressure seat opens to admit high-pressure air into the intermediate-pressure area. The flow continues to the second stage until the exhalation phase.

Exhalation phase: As inhalation ceases, high-pressure air continues to flow into the intermediate area and through the stem of the piston until the pressure increases to the predetermined 120–140 psi, plus ambient. The piston is pushed away from the dome and closes the high-pressure seat.

(*Note:* The high-pressure accessory port is shown closed by a threaded plug.)

What is more important to a scuba diver, with the valve unaffected by variations in cylinder pressure, large orifice diameters can be used to give *large volumes of air flow with no increase in suction effort.* The resistance to breathing caused by straining air through a tiny opening has been eliminated.

The balanced valve is also depth-compensated. The pressure in the intermediate chamber and air hose is always equal to the pressure of the surrounding water *plus* the factory setting. To protect the valve stem and "O" ring from contamination due to contact with salt water, sand, and dirt, a special housing has been developed to contain the valve stem *inside* the housing and still maintain depth compensation.

Piston-type (Flow-Through) First-Stage Valve

This type of first-stage valve is currently in use on many single-hose regulators. The single moving part (piston) and "O" ring seals provide relatively troublefree function and reportedly make for easy maintenance. Thorough rinsing with fresh water after each use is essential for continuous troublefree performance as is the case with all regulators. Rinsing should be done with the tank-valve attachment high-pressure port sealed with the attached dust cap.

Now let's look at the second stages commonly used in conjunction with an unbalanced first stage and with the balanced valve.

Single-Hose Second Stages

Development of the single-hose first and second stages brought changes in diver breathing comfort and increased efficiency.

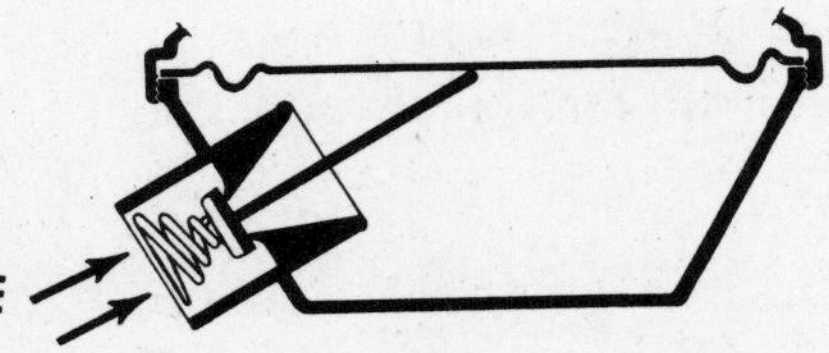

FIGURE 41. SINGLE-HOSE REGULATOR SECOND-STAGE "TILT VALVE"

Second-stage development saw the introduction of the upstream valve activated by a simple lever which caused the valve to "tilt" from its seat to open. Reviewing the principle demonstrates the shortcomings of this type of valve. Combined with an unbalanced first stage, and its less-than-ideal function, any increase in hose pressure tends to increase the inhalation effort necessary to open the tilt-operated upstream valve. The downstream valve type (straightaway) needs only to move one-fourth of the diameter of the orifice to obtain full flow. The "tilt" valve needs to tilt to an angle of 30° to the orifice before a full flow equal to the area of the orifice can be obtained.

Use of the upstream valve, which closes more firmly as flow-pressure increases occur, made it necessary to provide a safety valve to prevent bursting pressure in the hose. Function of such relief valves could become impaired or nonexistent because of corrosion and/or fouling. Lack of testing or poor overpressure in the hose would generally occur when bottle pressure was lower than bursting pressure of the properly maintained hose.

Later development of more efficient second-stage operation utilized the downstream type of valve which permitted easier breathing and, at the same

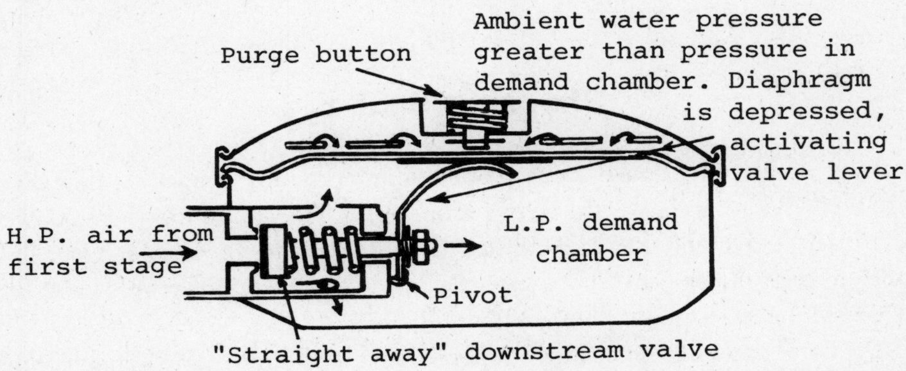

FIGURE 42. SECOND STAGE OF TWO-STAGE, SINGLE-HOSE REGULATOR, WITH DOWNSTREAM VALVE

time, served to prevent pressure buildup in the hose in the event of first-stage malfunction.

Increased popularity of the single-hose, two-stage regulator has prompted designers to develop first- and second-stage mechanisms with sensitivity and flow characteristics more than adequate for most diving activities. Since exhalation requires considerable physical effort, much attention has been directed to perfection of exhalation exhaust ports and to "away-from-the-face" direction of exhaled air for unimpaired vision.

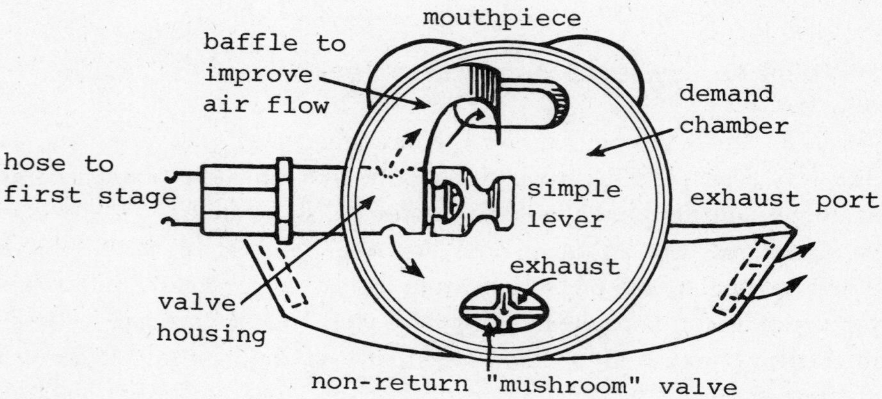

FIGURE 43. SECOND-STAGE, SINGLE-HOSE REGULATOR (TOP VIEW—OPEN)

Research and development by reliable manufacturers has produced nearly troublefree (when properly maintained) single- and double-hose regulators. Choice of a name brand will be influenced by trial use, knowledge of function, and troublefree operation records. Impartial evaluations by instructors and such reports as may be obtained from diving publications will greatly assist in satisfactory selection of either type or manufacturer.

Choosing Scuba

As previously mentioned, a check of equipment catalogs leaves the new diver confused and at a loss as to which regulator is best. The choice may be narrowed by considering average use, adaptability to need, and ease of maintenance. Cost is not a major factor, since there is little difference between double-hose and single-hose types of comparable quality.

If general use will be confined to sport diving in shallow or moderate depths, with no extended activity planned or foreseen, the less expensive single-stage, double-hose type of approved design and manufacture or the less expensive single-hose, two-stage unit should be adequate. Modern equipment, even the least expensive, is generally tested for continual satisfactory function at depths far below the recommended sport-diving limits.

Reserve valves, either tank-valve or regulator-attached type, are desirable if not mandatory for sport divers in the above instance.

If deeper, extended working dives are contemplated, it naturally follows that the best and most adaptable scuba outfit should be selected.

One does not expect the same over-all performance from both jalopy and high-priced auto, though both may yield adequate performance under average conditions. Similar (though not the same) comparison may be made when choosing scuba. Modern technology, manufacture, and competition have removed the scuba "jalopy" from the scene, but we still have the equivalents of the standard and deluxe models.

SCUBA CHECK PRIOR TO USE

A thorough check and test of all equipment should be standard procedure when the equipment is purchased and prior to any dive. The use of a checklist may be warranted under certain conditions of sport diving involving a number of participants. The list should cover essential points of each piece of equipment. Particularly important, however, is a thorough check of the scuba itself.

Perhaps most important is testing or checking the scuba cylinder pressure. A slow, almost undetectable leak may be present from a faulty fitting or from the valve's having been opened slightly during transportation. After the pressure has been determined, even though there may have been some loss of air, a safe dive can be planned.

Next, check the hoses, mouthpiece, mask, and other parts of the assembly for cracks, punctures, or other indications of weakness. Check to see that the harness is adjusted properly and free from signs of excessive wear, and that it is equipped with quick-release-type buckles.

After attaching the regulator to the cylinder, open the cylinder valve and check to see that there are no leaks from around the high-pressure block of the regulator. This may be determined by listening for the sound of escaping air. If there is any doubt about there being a leak, submerge the regulator and top of the cylinder in water and visually check for leaking air, indicated by the presence of bubbles.

Also, check for air leaking through the regulator. Sometimes the regulator may be dirty, or a part may become worn, allowing a constant flow of air. This not only wastes the air supply but may indicate serious mechanical trouble in the regulator that could become hazardous.

Inhale and exhale through the regulator before you enter the water to determine whether or not the unit is functioning properly.

When attaching the regulator to the cylinder valve, use caution to prevent damage to the high-pressure valve seat or "O" ring. If these parts become damaged, air will probably leak, causing a waste of air and allowing only a dive of considerably shorter duration.

Again check the proper operation of the scuba when just below the surface of the water by inhaling and exhaling through the regulator and hoses.

POST-DIVE CHECK AND CARE

All parts of the scuba should be thoroughly washed in clean, fresh water after use. This applies after use in either salt water or fresh water because saliva that may find its way into the breathing apparatus is as corrosive as salt water. Also, there is the possibility that the fresh water in which the dive was made contained silt or other foreign matter that should be rinsed from the unit before storing.

Most modern regulators are equipped with an attached "dust cap." The cap (plastic cone), attached to the yoke by a metal ring, should be inserted over the high-pressure seat and maintained by the thumbscrew whenever the regulator is not attached to the tank valve. The cap serves to prevent entrance of dirt or water into the regulator through the high-pressure chamber.

Particular care should be taken to cleanse exhaust, and check valves of all particles of dirt or grit. Even a small particle in one of these valves will hold it open, allowing water to enter the breathing system.

The rubber parts of the unit, such as breathing tubes and mouthpiece, should be washed, dried, and sprinkled with soapstone (crude talc) to help preserve the rubber. Any indication of cracking of the rubber parts, or stiffness, would be reason for replacement of rubber parts.

When tightening fittings, use a wrench of the correct size and design to prevent damage to the threads or sides of the nuts that may cause serious weakness.

A pipe wrench should never be used on the neck of a scuba cylinder, for it can cause nicks in the metal wall that will weaken the cylinder's strength by as much as 50 per cent or more. There have been several instances where cylinders have failed to pass recertification tests because of damage to the neck of the cylinder.

No work should ever be done on a cylinder, valve, or high-pressure fitting of any kind when the cylinder or fitting contains a gas under pressure.

Repair Procedures

Unless you are qualified to work on high-pressure regulators and fittings, maintenance and repair of scuba should be limited to that required to prevent corrosion or other damage. The exception may be any necessary replacement of breathing hoses, mouthpieces, or exhaust valves. Avoid leaving the regulator in direct sunlight, as the ultraviolet rays may cause the hoses to deteriorate quite rapidly.

Current Department of Transportation (D.O.T.) regulations require that the scuba bottle be hydrostatically tested every five years. More frequent hydrostatic tests will produce metal fatigue that will drastically reduce the average life of the bottle. If damage or excessive internal or external corrosion indicates the likelihood of structural weakness, the bottle should be retested. As has been previously mentioned, visual inspection (VIP) by a qualified person should be done at least once each year, or more often if use and conditions warrant.

Attempted repair or adjustment of regulators by persons not qualified by virtue of extensive training and experience is definitely not recommended.

Lubrication of working parts or fittings must be governed by the following: *Never use oil or grease on any high-pressure fitting or mechanism. Use only Dow Corning silicon lubrication or similar recommended product. Even this must be used sparingly.*

Compressed Air Cylinders

The potential energy (and hazard) of a fully charged cylinder is very great, and cylinders require special precautions in handling and storing.

In one accident involving a high-pressure cylinder, the valve was accidentally broken from the cylinder. The force of the escaping air (2,000 psi) jetted the cylinder through the roof of the shop and through the air for a distance of about two city blocks. The cylinder then struck a lawn, dug a trench six feet long, and richocheted into the side of a house with sufficient force to penetrate several inches. The blast of escaping air tore the clothes off the man who was working on the cylinder and might have caused serious injury.

When transporting cylinders, whether by automobile, boat, or other means, be sure all cylinders are securely tied, blocked, or held in place to prevent damage. Equal care should be taken to see that no heavy object can fall on the unit and cause damage to the cylinders or fittings.

When transporting in a car, place the cylinder so that the valve is toward the back of the car. The bottom of the cylinders should be blocked or resting against the front wall of the trunk. Cylinders should be prone and properly blocked to prevent side motion.

Considerable care should be taken to avoid accidentally striking the cylinders against a sharp object that could cause nicks or scratches, which might produce a weak spot that would be a potential site of cleavage or explosion.

High-pressure air cylinders must be filled slowly, preferably while submerged in cold water to prevent a radical buildup of heat and pressure. They should never be filled more than 10% beyond their rated working pressure. The 10% overfill is only permitted when the last hydrostatic test date is accompanied by a "plus" symbol.

All filling tubes, hoses, and fittings must be of high-pressure construction. Work should not be done on any cylinder, valve, or fitting while it is under pressure.

Cylinder harness should be in good condition. Inspect it frequently to see that all rivets and sewed fastenings are secure. Fasten all straps so that they can be released quickly.

Closed-Circuit Scuba

This is definitely not recommended for use by sports divers. This type of scuba utilizes pure oxygen as the breathing medium and is equipped with an absorbent canister which removes carbon dioxide from the medium as it is exhaled. Oxygen repletion is generally regulated by preset flow valves with a manual over-ride provided for emergency need.

Depth limitation, oxygen-tolerance variation, failure to purge the respiratory system of nitrogen, CO_2 absorbent failure—to mention only a few—are reasons enough to avoid use of this device.

Maintenance and repair require high technical skills and access to restricted materials.

Semiclosed-Circuit Scuba

As the name implies, a semiclosed system permits partial rebreathing of the gas. This provides duration of a gas supply longer than can be achieved with open-circuit gear. A semiclosed system uses a mixed gas supply and has all the components of a closed-circuit system. In addition, two other features must be present. These are the reliable automatic-injector system and a special exhaust-valve system. Generally, a semiclosed system uses continuous injection of breathing gas and continuous exhaust.

USE OF CLOSED- AND SEMICLOSED-CIRCUIT SYSTEMS

Closed- and semiclosed-circuit scuba are considered unsafe for use by the average sport diver. The safe use of such equipment requires extensive knowledge and training acquired under close supervision. Disadvantages are imposed by depth limitation, gas-supply control, and continuous maintenance problems. Semiclosed units involve purchase or manufacture of mixed gases in specific proportion and present too complex a problem to be considered for sport diving.

The dangers of anoxia due to insufficient oxygen content or lowered partial pressures, or oxygen poisoning due to high-percentage content plus partial-pressure increase during descent, are ever present. Errors in depth calculation or incorrect valving might bring about either condition. Carbon dioxide accumulation due to failure of absorbent material or incorrect valving is another likely situation.

Whether due to design or human failure, the dangers inherent in the use of these types of scuba are not offset by low purchase price or do-it-yourself economies.

Helmet Diving Apparatus

Helmet diving apparatus involves equipment and techniques that require training by, and supervision of, a qualified instructor. The equipment is not generally considered suitable for sport diving, but will be discussed briefly for comparative purposes.

Helmet equipment (hard hat) may include open or closed helmets. The closed helmet, traditional gear of the so-called deep-sea diver, is attached directly to the suit. Additional parts of the dress are heavy weight belt, weighted shoes, necessary valves, fittings, air hose, intercommunication system wires, and a lifeline firmly attached so as to insure recovery of the diver in the event of accident.

All these hoses, wires, and lines act as a heavy, cumbersome umbilical cord from diver to base vessel. The diver is dependent on his base crew for air supply, timing, ascent, and hose payout—in short, this type of diving is work, and not sport.

Open (shallow-water) helmet equipment utilizes a weighted helmet, air hose, frequently communication lines, and clothing suitable to water temperatures. Unlike the closed-helmet type, in which both helmet and suit are pressurized, only the helmet receives pressurized air. The helmet is open at the bottom (as a bucket inverted) and dependent on internal air pressure to keep the water level below the diver's face. Sudden loss of internal pressure or loss of nearly upright position would result in flooding of the helmet.

All mask- or helmet-type diving rigs dependent on base-supplied air, particularly continuous-flow, have inherent features that would be disadvantageous to sport diving. The main advantages of scuba are its relatively low cost, generally safe use, ease of mobility, and ease of maintenance.

Manufacturer's Instruction Manual

Each manufacturer of the various models of scuba furnishes an instruction manual setting forth recommended procedures for the maintenance, repair, and use of his equipment. The instructions contained in the manual should be carefully studied and fully complied with.

6

SKILLS OF SKIN AND SCUBA DIVING

Diving with modern breathing equipment may be deceptive because of the ease with which untrained persons can perform under ideal conditions. Their attempts might be compared to flying small modern aircraft which are designed in such a way that they almost fly themselves. The operator is safe until an emergency arises. It is then that knowledge, skill, and experience in flying may mean the difference between survival and a serious accident.

A major difference between flying and diving, however, is that in the water the individual may abandon or lose his equipment and still survive, providing he is skilled in handling himself in the water. This represents the one and only advantage a skilled diver has over a skilled pilot. An unskilled pilot and an unskilled diver are about equal risks.

Basic water skills (or "watermanship") are essential to safe diving, with or without breathing apparatus. It is the purpose of this chapter to provide the reader with two safeguards: (1) suggest skills and knowledge for safe diving without breathing apparatus and (2) combine these with scuba skills and associated equipment as taught in many basic scuba diver courses.

The potential skin diver should be able to swim and handle himself well in the water. He should have reached a degree of physical and mental development and co-ordination which makes it possible for him to be safe under most swimming conditions, and he should have a thorough physical examination before entering into a diving class or diving activity.

Basic Skin Diving

Diving without the benefits of an air supply is a basic skill. Though not complicated by the indirect effects of pressure, it still requires the acquisition of theory and development of skills in order to assure safe, intelligent pursuit of the sport. Proficiency attained will materially aid in later scuba diving. The need to develop good techniques is apparent if we visualize the predicament of the scuba diver with air supply exhausted and his base some distance away. Prior planning should preclude such a circumstance, but even the best plans sometimes go awry.

Satisfactory demonstration of ability to perform the dive-related swimming skills without aids, as described in Chapter 1, is usually considered prerequisite to diver-course participation.

Even the skilled swimmer may experience initial difficulty in adapting to basic diving equipment, both on the surface and below. Many will attempt to adapt equipment to skill rather than the reverse. Realization of the philosophy of obtaining best results with the least expenditure of energy will immeasurably assist in the adapting.

Since this is not a swimming manual, only minor attention will be devoted to arm strokes and rarely used kicks. However, those which are the most used and adaptable to diving will be treated more fully.

ARM STROKES

It must be remembered that, due to water resistance, some conventional arm strokes are difficult and inefficient if employed under water. Experienced divers rarely find need to supplement fin action with arm strokes. However, both the experienced and the new diver should become proficient in the use of underwater arm strokes to supplement or replace fin action if needed. The following strokes are suggested, not as the only way, but as a way.

Breast stroke. This is one of the most adaptable of arm strokes and will permit smooth, forward motion with minimum exertion. Arms are extended forward, then with fingers together, palms slightly cupped, the arms are swept backward and slightly downward. Recovery is made when the hands reach about shoulder level. Hands move toward chest center. Forward extension is made and the stroke repeated. This stroke may be combined with the flutter or dolphin kick.

Underwater dog paddle. This arm stroke is so called because of its resemblence to the alternating extension and downward pulling of the forepaws of a swimming dog. Varying degrees of efficiency can be developed, most strokes beginning with the fully extended arm forward. The pull may then be in a downward sweep (elbow straight) or (with elbow bent) a pull toward the chest. In either case, recovery is made when the hand reaches shoulder or chest level. During recovery the other arm is extended and pulls as described.

When swimming on the side, the lower arm may be used alone as described above. This results in what is generally called the *"side arm pull."* It may be used quite effectively when towing equipment or another diver. The side flutter (or scissor kick if without fins) is used in conjunction with this arm pull.

Elementary back stroke. This stroke is not restricted to, but is usually most helpful on, the surface. The surfaced diver, with vest inflated, may, for many reasons, find this desirable in order to maintain motion while resting the legs. The stroke is performed while face up. The arms are extended to the sides just above shoulder level, then swept toward the hips where they are momentarily held for a glide. Recovery is made close to the body. The simultaneous stroke is then repeated. As in the breast stroke, the arms may be swept to shoulder level and recovery made there. More strokes are required but progress is faster.

FINS

Transition of the surface swimmer to the underwater swimmer or diver, as has been noted, will involve quite a change in leg strokes. The addition of many square inches of surface to the foot when fins are worn makes some conventional kicks undesirable from an efficiency standpoint. Although the loss of efficiency is not agreed upon by everyone, experimentation with the frog, whip, trudgeon, and scissor kick may be convincing.

Before experimenting with the following kicks, learn to don your fins properly. Wet your feet (with or without boots or socks), wet the fins. Hold the ribs of the blade and push your foot firmly all the way into the pocket.

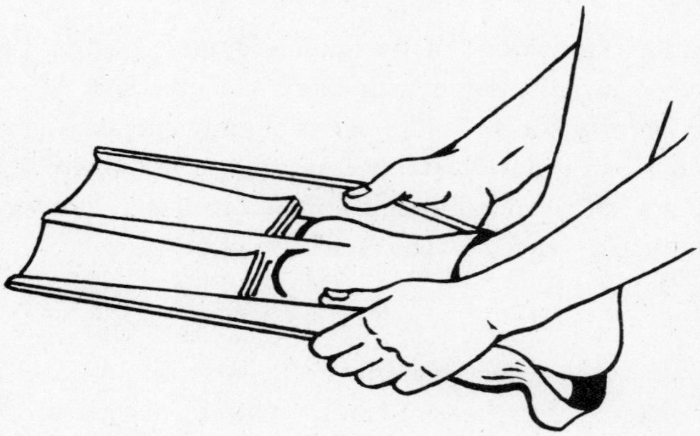

FIGURE 44. DONNING THE FINS

Next, pull the heel strap or back of the slipper into position. If slipper-type fins are being used, turning the heel portion inside out will help. When the foot is in the pocket, gently pull the heel part up to position.

Kicks

The flutter and the dolphin are the most adaptable and versatile kicks to use with fins. Since the flutter kick is readily adaptable to face up, face down, and either left- or right-side swimming position without any change, it will be considered first.

The flutter kick. Adaptation of this kick, commonly used in the crawl stroke, is relatively easy after observation of the fin action during up- and down-beat phases. While standing in waist-deep water, raise one leg from the

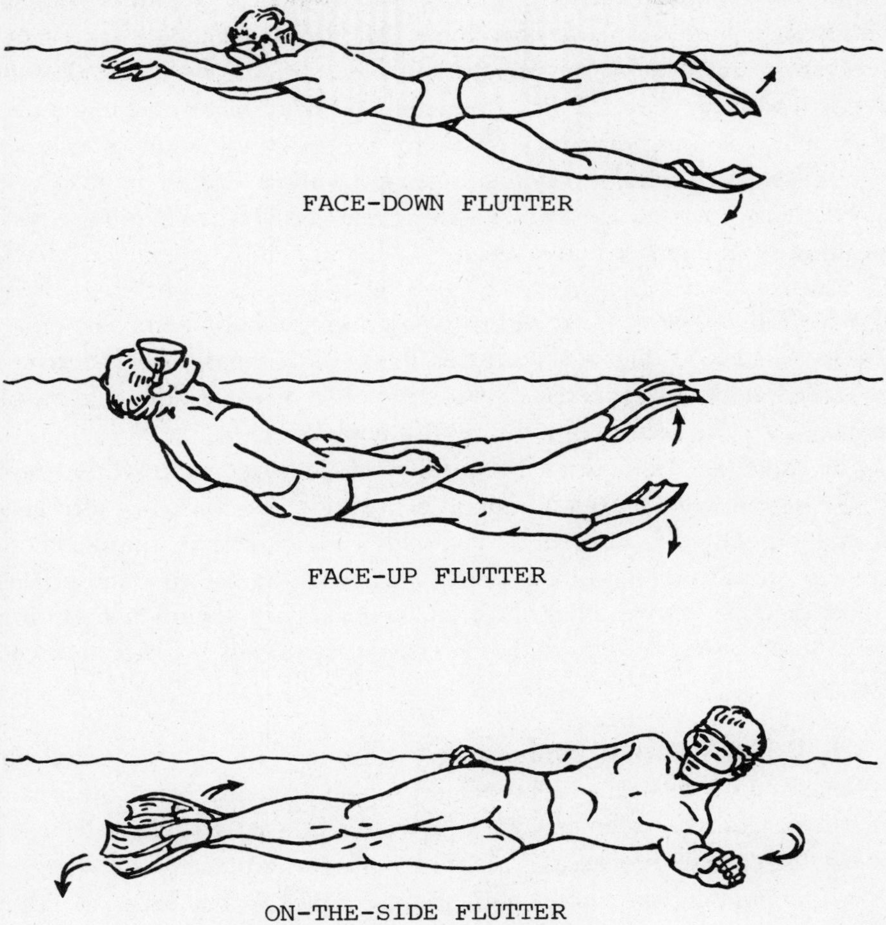

FIGURE 45. FLUTTER-KICK POSITIONS

bottom and comfortably point the toe. Move the leg, knee straight, toward the surface. Note the resistance and flexing downward of the fin blade. This result is the driving force during the down beat. Now, start the leg near the surface, knee straight, toe pointed, and move the leg toward the bottom. Note the resistance and the upward flexing of the fin blade. This is representative of the driving force of the up beat. The blade flex and return serves to smooth the motion and provides some added drive.

Repeat the foregoing with a bent knee and toes not pointed. The results will demonstrate the effectiveness of the straight knee and pointed toe.

Now, while holding on to the poolside or being held in position by your buddy, execute the flutter slowly. The greatest opening (heel to heel) of the kick should be between 18 and 24 inches. The frequency of the beat should be about 20 per minute. The foregoing having been observed and tried, now may be applied to the front, back, and side positions.

Face-down flutter. The body position should present a comfortable curve with hips and buttocks at the low point (see Figure 45). The arms may be trailed at the sides or placed straight forward from the shoulders. The body arc will tend to prevent the fins from coming out of water, thereby reducing splash and promoting efficiency. Now try the kick. Variation of width and frequency, so as to achieve maximum comfort without loss of propulsion, will require some practice. Remember, maximum force with minimum energy expenditure is the goal, and *not* speed.

Back flutter. The body arc in this position should be smooth. The hips and buttocks will be down but *not* bent as in the sitting position. The arms are best trailed at the sides. During pool practice, it may be advisable to place one hand over the head to prevent head to pool contact.

The flutter in this position is basically the same as in the prone position. Avoid the tendency toward assumption of a sitting position. Kick efficiency is lost and propulsion hampered by increased body profile to the direction of travel. As in the prone position, practice will develop comfort and efficiency of the kick. This is an excellent kick for on-the-surface towing or returning to base. The one disadvantage is the necessity for pausing to determine course adherence.

Side flutter. The body position, while on either left or right side, should be a compromise between the prone and supine positions. Since the legs and feet will generally be submerged, the body can be nearly straight. The lower arm may be extended overhead, the hand serving as a plane.

In this position, the flutter will be more efficient and easier to perform than is the conventional scissors kick. The forward drive is continual and smooth.

When combined with the previously described "side-arm pull" a most satisfactory towing stroke results. The lower arm performs the side pull.

Dolphin. Simulation of the undulating movements of the caudal fin and lower portion of the dolphin's body, after some practice, will provide the diver with a strong leg kick. Since forward motion is delivered almost equally on the up as well as on the down phase of the stroke, maximum efficiency can be developed. The following description of movement is basic and will require individual practice in order to develop continuous, smooth, non-tiring, propulsion. Initial practice will be best accomplished underwater.

As illustrated, start with the knees slightly bent, toes pointed. Thrust downward by straightening the knees and bending slightly at the waist. The return (upward) stroke is made with toes pointed, legs straight. About halfway up, the knees begin to bend, and at the peak of the stroke the knees are again in the starting position. Avoid extremes in bending the waist or knees. Practice

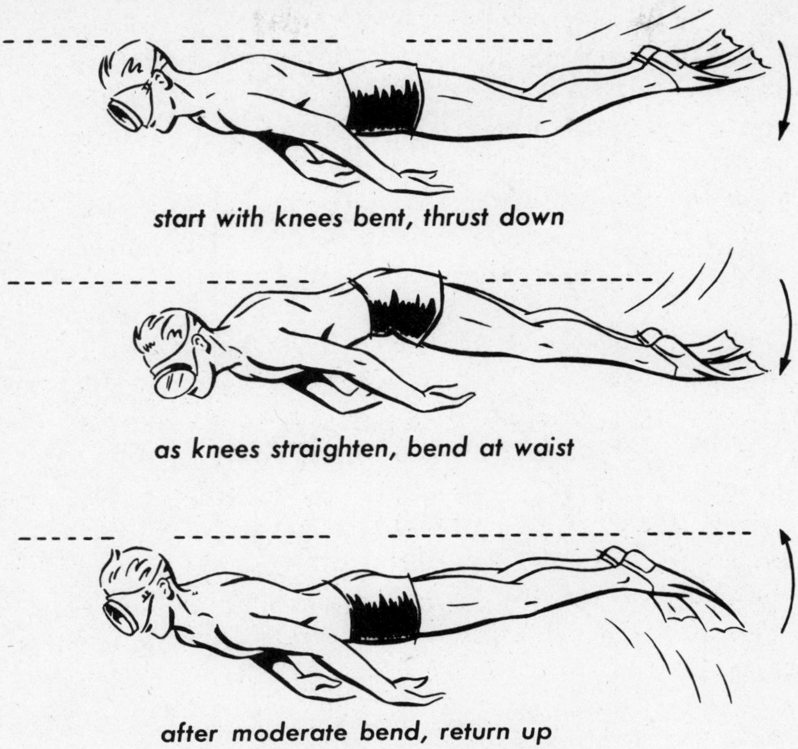

start with knees bent, thrust down
as knees straighten, bend at waist
after moderate bend, return up

FIGURE 46. DOLPHIN KICK
This is a continuous, slow, waving movement affording fast, smooth, porpoiselike motion.

will bring about a slight flip of the fins at the peak of upward and downward motions, affording additional thrust. This is accomplished by ankle movement and will come with the development of timing.

Holding Position

Maintaining position on the surface, unless you are positively buoyant, will require some kicking, arm strokes, or both. The following are suitable for this purpose:

Treading. The flutter kick is easily adapted to a vertical position. The beat frequency can usually be reduced since the diver needs only enough upward force to overcome negative buoyancy. Unless grossly overweighted, this should be easily accomplished with fin action only. If an arm stroke is necessary (or desired) the following is efficient and energy conserving.

Sculling. This is a useful supplementary skill for use while treading water and holding position on the surface or submerged. One or both hands may be used. The hand or hands move to form a figure eight. The palms are slightly

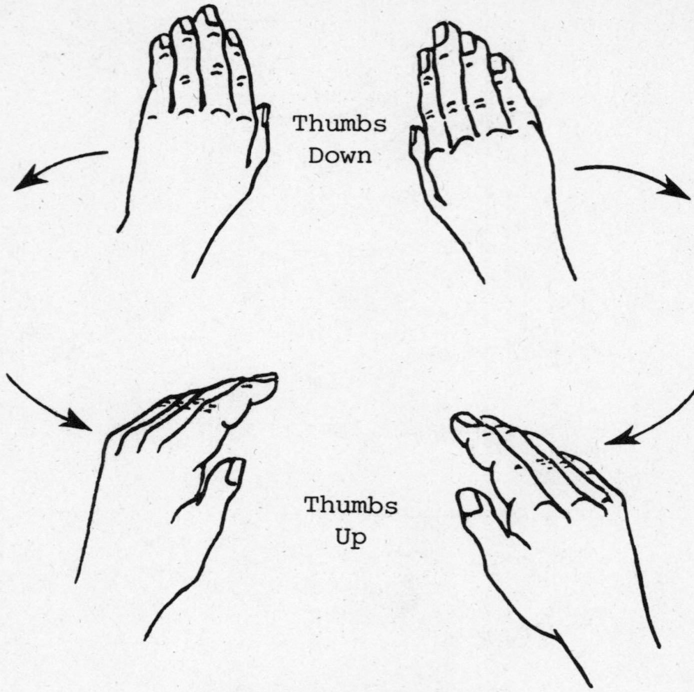

FIGURE 47. SCULLING

cupped, fingers together. When moving through the figure eight, the palm should be inclined with *thumb up* during inward motion and *thumb down* on outward motion. The resultant alternate angle of the palm provides continuous lift. Experimentation will prove this to be an efficient, versatile, energy-conserving stroke.

THE MASK

The mask is an essential item in both skin and scuba diving. Without this window, and the air space behind it, the diver's vision would be practically nil. Keeping the window clear and the air space free of water and in pressure balance will involve some care and practice. Practice means repetition until the following actions are automatically performed as needed.

Preparation

Since the seal of the mask to the face was checked at the time of purchase, it should only be necessary, at this time, to adjust the head strap. This adjustment should be made to hold the mask gently but firmly in place. Do not attempt to seal an improperly fitted mask by drastically tightening the head strap. Before wearing the mask in the water, it will be necessary to apply a fog preventative to the inside of the lens. Some of these antifogging substances are saliva, seaweed, tobacco, raw potato, or one of the commercial preparations designed for this purpose. Application of other than the commercial preparations should be followed by rinsing with clear water until the lens is clear. In using the commercial preparations follow the directions of the manufacturer. Some of the commercial preparations which do not advocate rinsing may be irritating to the eyes, *so check the label carefully.* Most of the foregoing will provide a fog-free lens for a limited time. If and when fogging occurs during the dive a small portion of water may be introduced into the mask and swished across the lens by moving the head back and forth. Leave this water in the mask and repeat if necessary.

Pressure Equalization

With the mask on, dive to the bottom at several different depths and, as the mask is pressed to the face by water pressure, exhale lightly through the nose until ambient and mask pressures balance. Overcorrection will result in the escape of air. Undercorrection will be apparent with a continued feeling of tightness. During descent this equalization may have to be done several times. During ascent the contained air volume will expand and escape without effort on the part of the diver.

Clearing

Clearing a flooded mask involves replacing the water with exhaled air. The air, being lighter than the water, will force the water out at the lower portion of the mask if the upper portion is held firmly to the face by hand pressure to prevent escape of air at the top of the mask. The amount of hand pressure and the position of the hand will vary depending upon the mask type and size. Head position during clearing will vary for the same reasons. Prior to performing the following clearing methods, don the flooded mask above water and perform the clearing action without submerging. *Note:* With varied head positions the uppermost portion of the mask must be held to the face so as to prevent the escape of air.

Vertical clearing for masks not equipped with a purge valve. With the mask flooded, hold the top rim firmly to the forehead (slight separation of the lower skirt from the upper lip may occur due to this pressure). Now, while looking down, start the initial exhalation through the nose. The chin-down position will prevent the water in the mask from entering the nasal passages, since it is blocked by the air in those passages. Continue exhaling while inclining the face toward the surface. The displacement of water by air will be seen. Continue until air escapes at the bottom portion of the mask. The mask should then be free of water. The degree of head inclination toward the surface during exhalation will vary depending upon shape and size of the mask. This variation will be greatly altered if the mask is equipped with a purge valve.

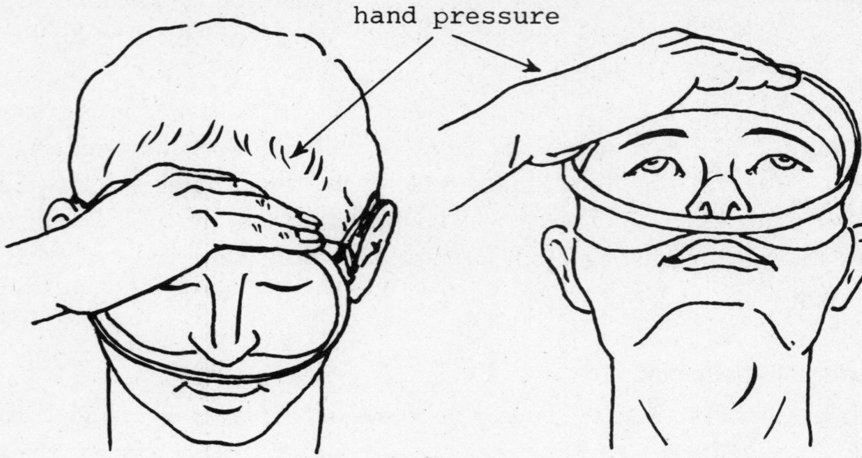

FIGURE 48. MASK CLEARING—VERTICAL

Vertical clearing for masks equipped with a purge valve. Since purge valves are generally located in or below the lower portion of the mask, it is generally only necessary to apply sufficient pressure to the top portion of the mask to prevent the escape of air at that point. Most types require little or no inclination of the face toward the surface while exhaling to clear the mask. Due to the size and placement of the purge valve, experimentation to determine the best head position and hand pressure will be necessary to achieve the best results.

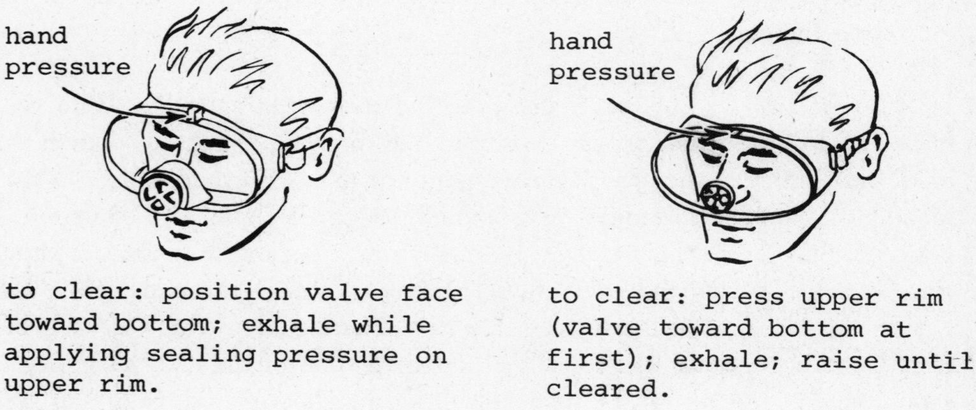

NOSE PURGE VALVE
hand pressure
to clear: position valve face toward bottom; exhale while applying sealing pressure on upper rim.
PURGE VALVE IN LENS
hand pressure
to clear: press upper rim (valve toward bottom at first); exhale; raise until cleared.

FIGURE 49. MASK PURGE VALVES

Horizontal roll clearing. This method is least preferred, but is effective. Exert firm pressure on one side of the mask rim (right or left) with hand. Roll the body downward and around so that the shoulder *opposite* the side being held is moved toward the bottom. Exhale gently and continuously. This causes the water to be displaced by air. Continue the roll until all water is purged. This will generally be accomplished in the first 90° but may require a complete 360° until experience and practice indicate adequate hand pressure on the rim and satisfactory exhalation rate. (*Note:* Failure to achieve complete clearing is usually due to change of body and head position to other than horizontal.)

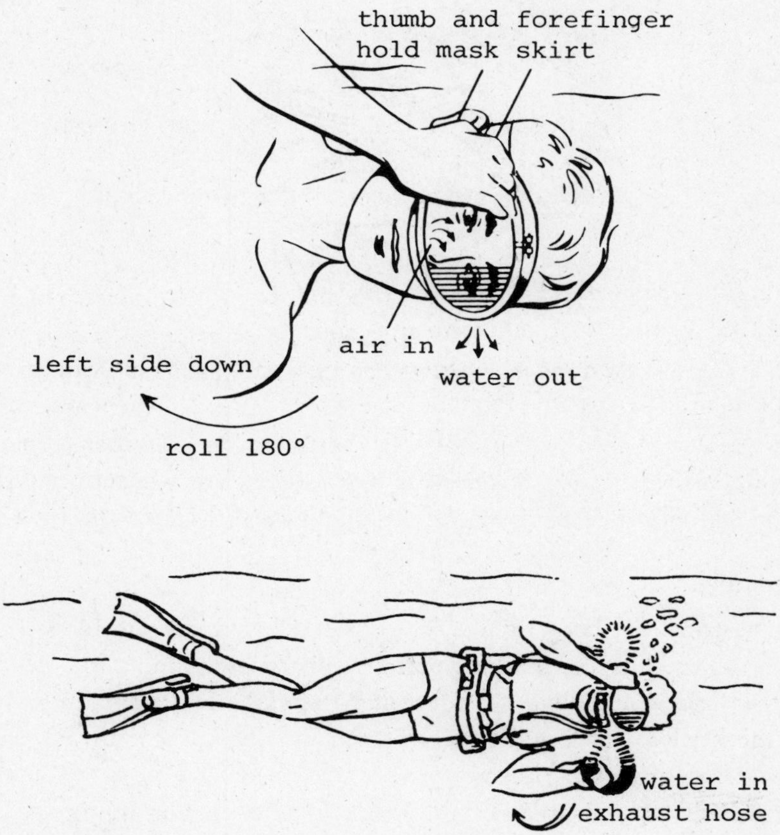

FIGURE 50. HORIZONTAL HOSE AND MASK CLEARING

The above-described method of clearing was found to be more successful than other methods when wearing a full mask (entire face enclosed). Even though equipped with a purging device, few wearers were successful in complete clearing attempts. Vertical clearing attempts usually resulted in clearing down to the exhaust port or nose level. The remaining water (about nose level) made the first breath more than annoying. The horizontal roll (exhaust port down) permitted visible clearing. This method of clearing is adaptable to modern full masks which are best adapted to voice communications systems.

It should be noted that many masks are designed to permit sealing of the nostrils by pinching or finger pressure. This convenience will assist measurably when middle-ear squeeze prevention via sealed-nose exhalation is attempted.

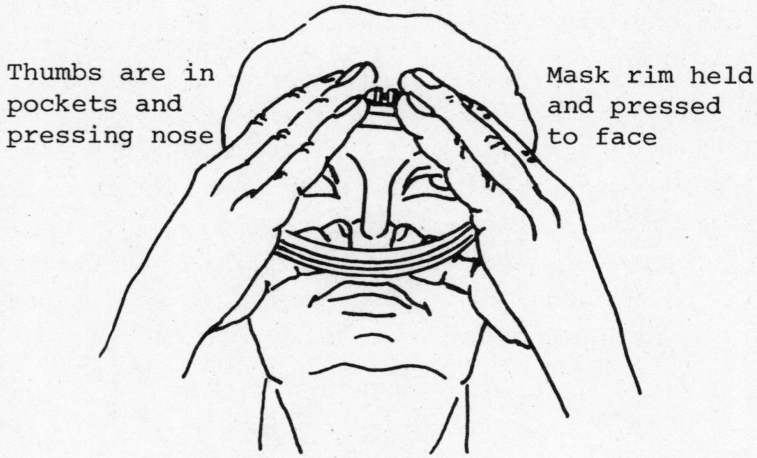
Thumbs are in
pockets and
pressing nose
Mask rim held
and pressed
to face

FIGURE 51. NOSE "PINCH" POCKETS

A skills note at this time is desirable: Early introduction of higher pressure into the eustachian tubes *before* the need is felt, rather than when the need is indicated by discomfort or pain, may make the descent easier.

THE SNORKEL

This extension of the body's airway is considered by most divers to be nearly as essential as the fins and mask. It permits normal breathing without interruption of the snorkeling diver's underwater viewing. It eliminates raising or turning the head to get a quick breath when moving on the surface. In short, it makes surface travel a pleasure.

The smaller bore in most of the snorkels as compared to the human air passages, plus the added distance which air must travel both in and out, often makes initial use difficult. Practice will result in development of a deeper inhalation and heavier exhalation than in normal breathing. This will serve to provide desired volume on inhalation and prevent possible buildup of carbon dioxide. Snorkel fatigue may be further reduced by selecting a type which has a more comfortable mouthpiece and/or larger bore. This last statement may be contested by some when the subject of clearing water from the tube is discussed. The validity of such contest will literally "not hold water" if final clearing procedures are prefaced by at least partial displacement of the water (usually about ½ cup) at or near the surface. The following methods will be applicable to most of the circumstances encountered:

Snorkel clearing. The easiest clearing method, both to learn and perform, is the water displacement ("downhill") action. The action is simple and its advantages many. Clearing becomes a part of the ascent procedure of looking up to see that the way to the surface is clear.

The ascending diver, snorkel in mouth, looks upward. This puts the open end of the snorkel below the mouthpiece. Just before surfacing (a foot or two below) the diver starts to gently exhale into the tube. Water is displaced by air and gravity. The head-back position is kept until the chin is clear of the surface. Generally, this will result in the open end being out of water also. Since you have exhaled, you may now inhale and assume normal surface position. During initial practice the diver should make that first inhalation with caution in case water displacement was incomplete or the open end was not kept down until above the surface. When properly performed, the above method is natural and effortless regardless of bore size.

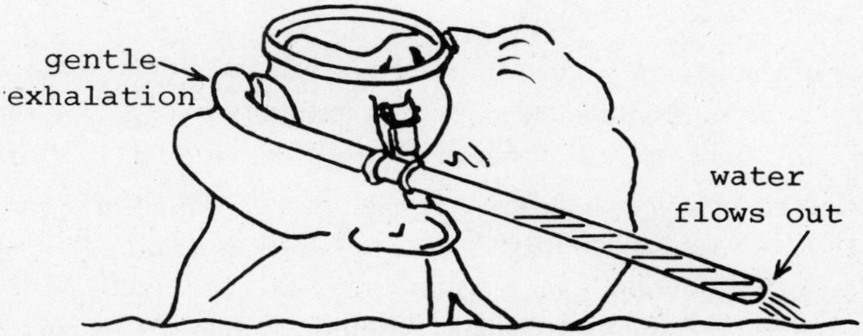

LOOK UP ("DOWNHILL") METHOD

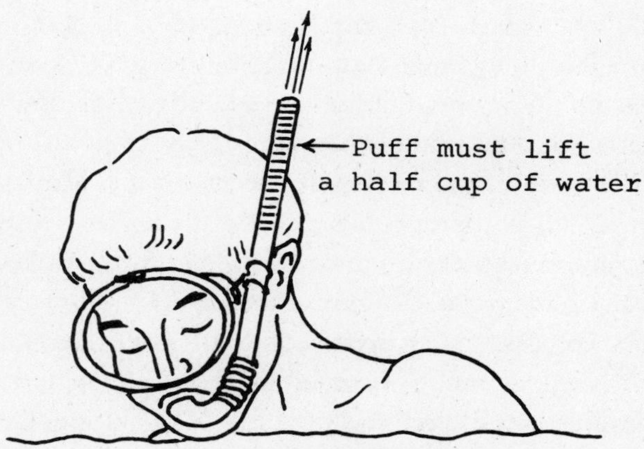

"PUFF" METHOD

FIGURE 52. SNORKEL CLEARING

The "puff" method of clearing, though not so effortless as the above, still is preferred by many divers. Perhaps this is because the natural instinct is to hold the breath until the next breath is readily available. Following this instinct, the skin diver arrives at the surface with a lungful of air and a snorkel filled with water. Two alternatives exist: 1) to remove the snorkel, exhale, inhale and maneuver so as to drain the snorkel (hopefully) before replacing it; 2) forcefully exhale (puff) through the snorkel so as to move the column of water up and out. Quite often this method results in a small quantity of water remaining in the bend of the "J." This necessitates another puff which may or may not be successful in total clearing. The larger the bore, the less chance of success. If the bend of the "J" is flexible, pinching the upper surface so as to reduce the bore size will facilitate total clearing in many instances. Obviously, practice in the use of this method will be necessary to achieve the desired results.

The advice by some to drink the remaining small portion of water remaining in the snorkel is hardly advisable since the water may not be of drinking quality. It must also be remembered that the snorkel should be thoroughly cleansed after each use.

The foregoing instructions for the individual use of the basic items—fins, mask, and snorkel—is not intended to restrict progressive combination of the three. These items have been discussed separately only for the sake of clarity. This does not mean that they should be covered in the order shown. Depending upon the instructor's or reader's preference they may be taught or learned in any sequence or combination. Practice combining all three items will initiate the basic skin-diving techniques. Practice should include the wearing of all three and the employment of all the described techniques while swimming on and under the surface. Having mastered the combined use of the fins, mask and snorkel, the student diver should now start to develop a sense of underwater thinking. This may be accomplished by learning to recover and don the equipment on the bottom of the pool. And, finally, to don all and clear the mask and snorkel in one breath. The order of donning will be governed either by individual choice or by direction of the instructor. Most students will find it easier to satisfactorily perform this exercise if the mask-clearing is performed during the ascent. Mask-clearing must be accomplished in such a manner that sufficient breath remains to clear the snorkel upon surfacing. The preceding exercise may be complicated by positive buoyancy which could make remaining on the bottom while donning the equipment a difficult procedure. There are two methods which can be used to overcome this situation. One, the least desirable for the beginner, is to limit the air intake so as to reduce buoyancy. This will usually result in the feeling that there is insufficient air supply to perform the clearing actions. The second is to employ a weight belt of sufficient weight to provide neutral or even slightly negative buoyancy. Prior to the use of the weight belt as suggested, it will be necessary to become acquainted with this piece of equipment.

THE WEIGHT BELT

Since neutral buoyancy is often desirable in both skin and scuba diving, many divers must resort to making themselves heavier. This necessitates the use of a weight belt equipped with a *quick-release-type* buckle or double "D" rings with a *safety hitch.*

Determine the amount of weight needed by stringing 1-lb. weights on a line. Take a deep breath and submerge with the weights. While on the bottom, remove one of the weights at a time until you become slightly buoyant. The amount of weight retained on the line should be sufficient to give you the desired buoyancy when diving on a normal breath.

Practice quick removal of the belt. This involves learning to make and undo the safety hitch if the double "D" ring-type belt is used or to unfasten the quick-release buckle if that type is used. Both are described in Chapter 5. It must be noted and thoroughly impressed on the diver that *weight belts must be worn outside protective clothing and any other equipment requiring harness. The quick-release device must be readily available for "Last On—First Off" use.*

SURFACE DIVES

Learning the use of basic diving gear has left little time to really enjoy the freedom and ease of skin diving. Diving from the surface to the bottom to emulate the fish, while being able to see and to move about with little effort, will be a profound pleasure. Following the concept of obtaining maximum results with minimum energy, the prospective diver should learn to perfect the initial descent techniques of "surface dives."

Head-First Surface Dive

If properly performed, this dive will permit the diver to drop a couple of body lengths before beginning to swim. The dive may be started with some forward motion on the surface. When the dive point is nearly reached, the head should be bent downward, the hands brought to the area of the hip with palms facing downward. The body is bent at the waist and the hands swept toward the head to move the body to vertical position. The legs may be extended above the water at this point by straightening the body and legs when the body is vertical. An alternate method is to pull the legs into a tuck position and, when the body is vertical, straighten the legs above water. The latter, unless practiced, is more splashy but generally delivers greater downward push. Hands and arms move to extended position to protect the head. When downward motion slows, start kicking until the desired depth is reached.

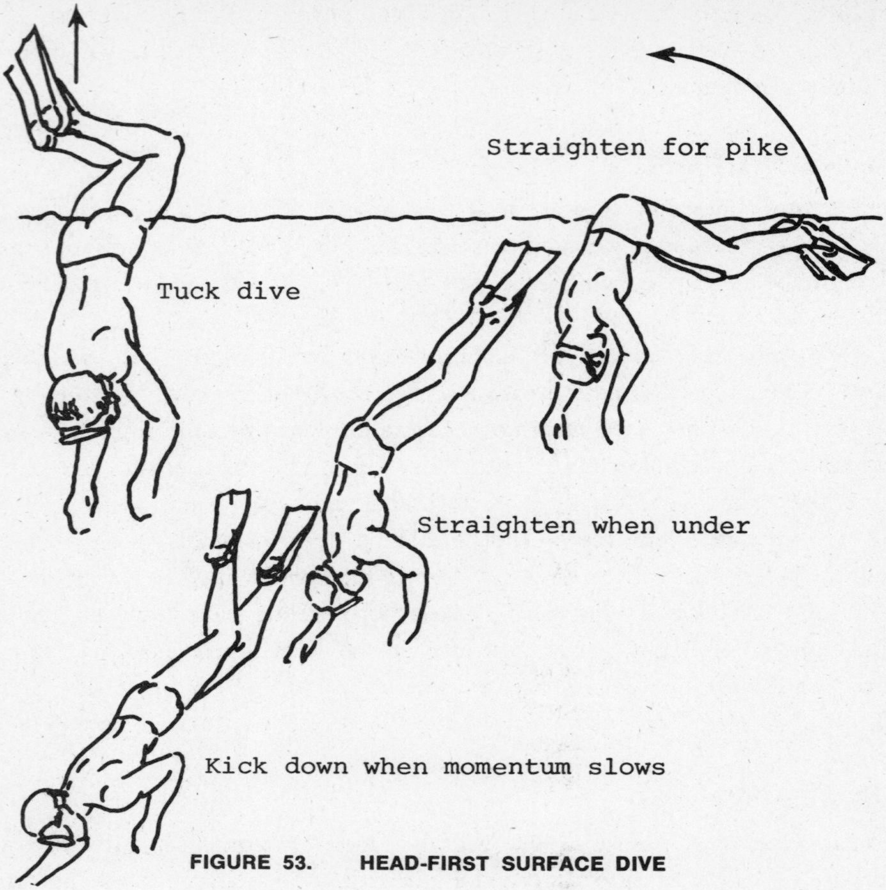

FIGURE 53. HEAD-FIRST SURFACE DIVE

With practice, the head-first dive may be performed without forward motion. While face down and motionless, bend the head down, bend sharply at the waist, and extend the arms downward. A strong downward push with both fins (as in the dolphin kick) as the body is bent, will start the vertical descent. Straightening the body as the kick is completed, plus a stroke with the arms results in good initial descent.

Practice, timing, and adaptation will result in splash-free, nearly effortless descent to a considerable depth (depending on buoyancy factor) before kicking is necessary.

Vertical Drop Dive (Feet-First)

When practiced and perfected, this maneuver permits dropping nearly straight down from the surface. The feet-first attitude gives added protection when water depth is not known or obstructions or a heavy concentration of water plants exists in the dive area. Neutral or slightly negative buoyancy acquired during descent may eliminate the need for reversal of position and permit a continued feet-first drop.

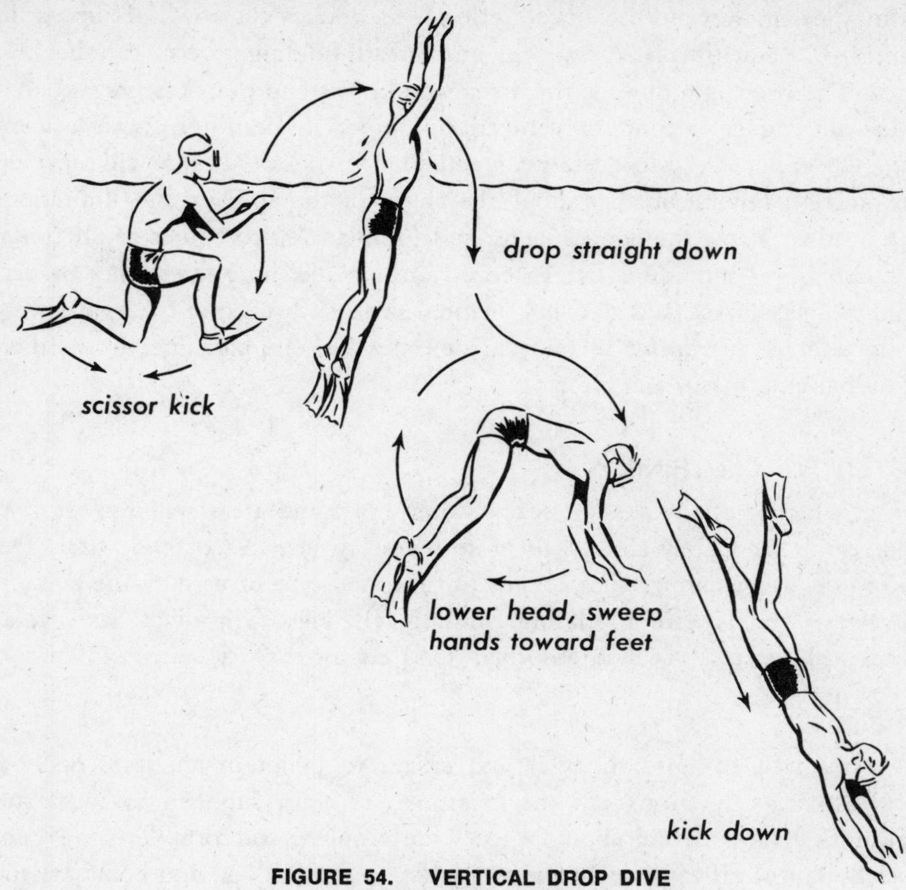

FIGURE 54. VERTICAL DROP DIVE

Starting from an upright position (as in treading water), give a strong kick with the fins and, if possible, a downward stroke with the hands to lift the body upward above the surface. Immediately following the lift, straighten the legs, body, and hands, as illustrated in Fig. 54. This attitude is maintained as long as downward motion continues. Leveling off or reversal of position, as indicated, will facilitate further sloping or vertical descent.

When the surface dive techniques have been mastered and the other basic skills have been developed to the point of minimum expenditure of effort, the new diver will be ready to put it all together and prolong his underwater activities.

HYPERVENTILATION

The purging of as much carbon dioxide from the system as possible, so as to suppress the "desire to breathe," will add to underwater time. It must be realized, however, and remembered, that this technique alters normal physiological function and that if breath-holding is pushed to extremes or repeatedly performed without recognition or heed as to symptoms, partial or total incapacitation may occur. Review the "direct effects" section of the medical aspects in Chapter 3. Remember that squeeze and breath-holding effects can be prevented. The good skin diver is the diver who knows and practices prevention.

Do not engage in contests of breath-holding or underwater distance-swimming. Underwater comfort, skill and endurance to safe limits will develop with practice. Diving buddies should be aware of the abilities and limitations of each other, know the danger signs, and follow safe procedures at all times.

Limited breath-holding dive practice can be made more interesting by performing object search and recovery, manual skills such as knot-tying, assembly of nuts and bolts, transfer of buoyant objects from one container to another, and exchanging masks and clearing.

PROTECTIVE CLOTHING

Diving, whether of the skin or scuba variety, in some areas will require that the diver be adequately clothed to protect him against loss of body heat. Depending on water temperature, length of time, and type of activity the amount of coverage and type of insulating clothing will vary. The diver has several choices such as: the wet suit, absorbent clothing, or the dry suit.

Wet Suit

The wet suit is the most popular and easiest to maintain and presents few problems. Properly filling out the measurement chart supplied by most suit fabricators upon ordering should ensure the required comfortable, snug (not too tight) fit of all components. Hood, jacket, pants, gloves, and boots are the complete outfit. Depending on the need, any or all parts may be worn. Regardless of material thickness and parts worn, positive buoyancy will be noticeably increased. Some of this buoyancy will be due to trapped air which must be eliminated by manipulation of the suit parts and alteration of body position so as to force air to flow upward and out of the openings. Wearing such a suit will, in most instances, involve the use of a weight belt to reduce buoyancy to slightly positive. No firm rule can be made governing the amount of weight to be used. Various thicknesses and varied combinations make the correct choice of weights one of experimentation. A rough estimate for selection of desirable weights when wearing a full ¼-in. wet suit would be about 10% of the body weight when diving in salt water. Final selection of weight to be worn should be made with all gear on in a shallow and safe area. The chosen amount of weight should provide slightly positive buoyancy, since it must be remembered that *buoyancy will be lost as depth is increased.*

Absorbent Clothing

Though not so efficient as the wet or dry suit, such items as long underwear, tight sweaters, or other tight-fitting cloth garments may be suitable to provide short-time insulation in not-too-cold water. Loosely woven, baggy garments provide little or no insulation. Most items of clothing will increase buoyancy when on the surface, but have little effect when the pockets of air have been eliminated by submersion. Little dependence can be put on this type of insulation and, as in all diving activities, one should be alert to signs and symptoms of chilling. As soon as any are noticed get out of the water.

Dry Suit

This type of suit requires complete exclusion of water along with adequate undergarments if maximum efficiency and safety are to be obtained. Practice donning and sealing the suit before going into the water. This will require ample powdered talc to facilitate entry and short fingernails to prevent tearing. After learning the best way to don and seal the suit, you should make the following pool and shallow-water experiments, for the knowledge you will gain from them may be invaluable later.

1. Enter the water gradually and in a vertical head-up position. Permit air to escape (without letting water in) by stretching the uppermost opening at the neck, or face if hood is attached. Release air from the arms in a similar manner by stretching open the wrist cuff.

2. Note the buoyant effect attained even with the air excluded. Select the necessary weights to provide a slightly buoyant state.

3. Prior to any open-water diving do the following: In warm, chest-deep water without weights, deliberately flood the suit. Note the change in buoyancy. Swim in shallow water noting the difficulties. Now don the selected weight belt and note the extreme loss of buoyancy.

The foregoing will illustrate the need for proper sealing and regular examination of the thin rubber in order to detect holes. Unlike the wet suit, where a hole only involves slight loss of heat and negligible loss of buoyancy, a hole in the dry suit produces considerable loss of insulation, buoyancy, and swimming efficiency. *Note:* Air not excluded from the dry suit, which also envelops the feet, may concentrate at the feet during a head-first descent. This may necessitate a swimming somersault maneuver to shift the air before a head-first ascent can be made. Air which is not excluded may also result in areas of "suit squeeze" as described in the chapter on the medical aspects.

THE VEST

Every diver, whether skin or scuba, should consider this as basic equipment. The skin diver's use of the vest is limited to oral or cartridge inflation while on the surface for purposes of positive flotation. If the depth is relatively shallow (less than 30 feet), inflation by gas cartridge under water will, in some instances, provide positive buoyancy sufficient to surface the incapacitated skin diver. Attempts to orally inflate below the surface will give negative results

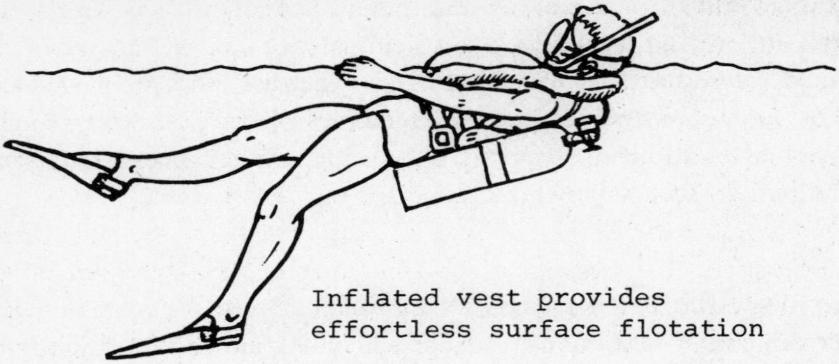

Inflated vest provides effortless surface flotation

Buoyancy adjustment with the vest

FIGURE 55. USES OF THE VEST

since this is merely moving the displacing air from the lungs to the vest with no change in buoyancy.

The scuba diver's employment of the vest is much more versatile. First, he may inflate it orally to the desired volume at any depth since he has an adequate air supply. Second, depending upon the construction, he may inflate it directly from his breathing air supply. Third, he may also inflate it below the surface by valving air from a supplementary bottle incorporated as part of the vest for that purpose. Adequate inflation by gas cartridge is generally not effective at other than relatively shallow depths.

If the diver is wearing protective clothing, the vest is donned after the clothing and before any other equipment. If he is not wearing protective clothing, the vest is donned next to the diver's skin. *Harnesses must be adjusted so as not to restrict inflation of the vest.*

The number of possible uses and the variety of vests available make practice mandatory. In using scuba, oral inflation while submerged, to provide greater buoyancy and the necessary release of this expanding air upon ascent, must be practiced. This use will probably be the most common. Slightly positive buoyancy throughout the descent is maintained by periodic oral inflation. This requires complete familiarization with the oral-inflation mechanism. Preventing overinflation of the vest due to expansion of air introduced into the vest involves manual operation of the bleed-off mechanism. If the vest is equipped with an over-pressure release, which functions properly, no manual control should be necessary. Familiarity with diving physics should indicate the need to relieve the expanding volume during ascent.

Inflation from the air supply or supplementary bottle is less difficult than oral inflation, but involves the same principles.

Due to the variety of vests, diving buddies and teams should familiarize themselves with the types worn by others so that they can be operated successfully in the event of emergency need.

Use of Open-Circuit Scuba Types

Having mastered skin-diving techniques and equipment, which are essential and basic to survival in all free-diving pursuits, you are now in a position to advance to the use of scuba. There is, as described in Chapter 5, more than one type of scuba. Each has its own peculiarities and techniques due to variations in construction. Closed-circuit and semiclosed-circuit techniques will not be discussed, since they are not considered, at this time, as adaptable to sport diving. Their employment is usually restricted to specialized occupations or purposes. Techniques and training for their use requires specific, intense supervision by qualified specialists in the field. Open-circuit scuba types include double-hose units of one- or two-stage demand regulator design. The two-stage, single-hose regulator type is the most popular. The two-stage, single-hose type which incorporates the second stage in a full-face mask is uncommon, but is used for some specialized purposes, the main one being voice transmission.

All of the aforementioned scuba types have some things in common and will be discussed generally. Special techniques, developed as a result of design variation, will be given specific attention. Techniques for use of the available equipment should be repeated and practiced until they become as natural as everyday living. The following is a summation of the essential knowledge which should prepare you for the specific and general coverage of discussion, instruction, and illustration of scuba use.

1. Know how your equipment operates.
2. Know the limitations of your equipment mechanically, physiologically and environmentally.
3. Know the importance of breathing normally throughout the dive.
4. Know how to clear flooded scuba while submerged.
5. Know the importance of cautiously inhaling after a clearing operation.
6. Become thoroughly familiar with doff and don procedures.
7. Know how to clear mouthpieces, hoses, and full masks of all scuba that you use or may use on special occasions.
8. Know and habitually perform pre-dive and post-dive checks of equipment, diver, and dive plan (all chapters).

Previous editions of this text gave prominence to the two-hose regulator. Original techniques of use were developed for this type. Since most were readily adaptable to the use of the single-hose type, the prominence continued. Now, although many still prefer the two-hose type, the single-hose, two-stage regulator is the one most used by the sport diver.

Comparison of the advantages and disadvantages of each type would bring as much debate as a major political confrontation. Let it suffice to say that each has qualities which make it more desirable than the other in certain specific circumstances. Whenever possible, the new diver should practice training techniques with both types. This dual familiarization will broaden his ability and materially assist in progress toward advanced diving and its specific needs.

Some of the basic techniques for the use of the full-face mask-type scuba have been kept in the text. Full-face masks are still being made and used. Though not so numerous or popular as other types, this type adapts well to voice communication systems and to situations which make the use of a mouthpiece undesirable. Not many will ever use such a unit, but having a basic knowledge of its peculiarities may someday be advantageous.

PRE-DIVE PROCEDURES

Proper assembly and check of scuba is the initial technique to be learned and perfected. This routine will be performed totally or partially before every dive. Diver and dive-plan check are fully discussed in Chapter 9, so they will not be covered here except to state that they are absolutely essential to safety.

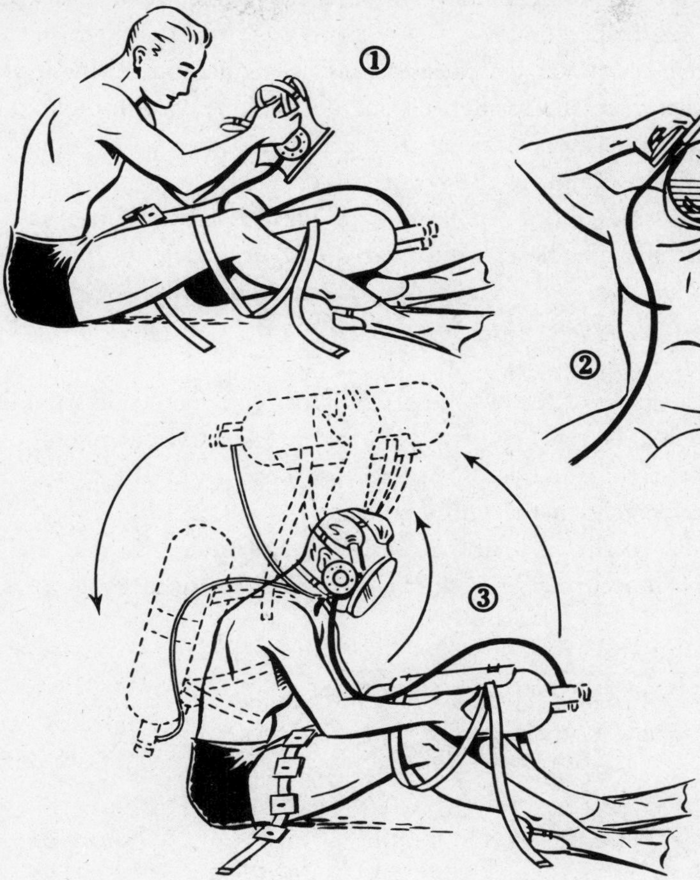

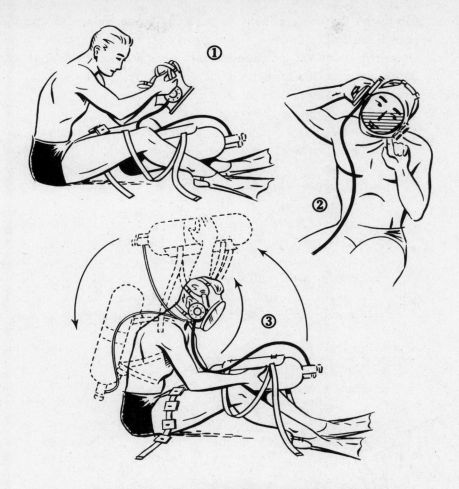

FIGURE 56. DONNING FULL-FACE MASK SCUBA

(1) Surface dive or drop feet first to unit when you have a mental picture of the donning procedure. Assume a sitting position with valve toward feet, and grip tank with legs. Slip on the mask—be sure it is straight—and tighten the lower straps.

(2) Bend forward and turn your head so that your chin is toward your right shoulder. The exhaust valve on the left side of the mask is now the lowest part. With thumb and forefinger of the right hand pressing the right edge of mask to your face, press the purging button with palm. Lifting edge of mask adjacent to the exhaust valve slightly with finger of left hand will allow water to be forced out. Look toward exhaust valve—*you can see last of water go out.* Remove left finger as soon as water level is below left eye, allowing remainder to go out valve. Exhale and inhale shallowly to test. Adjust mask and repeat clearing if water seeps in. Transfer weights to thighs.

(3) Reach through shoulder harness and grasp tank with both hands. Swing tank over head to back, smooth end close to head. Shoulder harness drops in place. Check air line (turning mask over in doffing or donning will cause it to kink) before fastening waist belt. When everything is checked put on weight belt.

Clearing the mask is easily done while in a prone swimming position by merely repeating the head roll described above in Step 2. (Doff and Don developed by Subcommittee, YMCA, Washington, D.C.)

1. Check the physical condition of the scuba bottle, valve, "O" ring, and reserve lever operation.
2. Gage the contained air pressure and have definite knowledge of its purity. Estimate the available (one atmosphere) air volume.
3. Check the physical condition of the regulator.
4. Attach the regulator to the bottle valve.
   a. The single-hose regulator is assembled to the bottle valve so as to have the hose come over the *right* shoulder. *If assembled to come over the left shoulder, the exhaust port of the second stage will be uppermost. Attempts to use it in this position will not be satisfactory.*
   b. Assembly of the two-hose regulator with the bottle valve must be such that the hose from the body (demand chamber) comes to the right shoulder. The exhaust hose from the water chamber cover goes to the left shoulder.
5. Open the bottle valve to pressurize the regulator. Inhale and exhale from the mouthpiece. Check for leaks may be made by immersing the

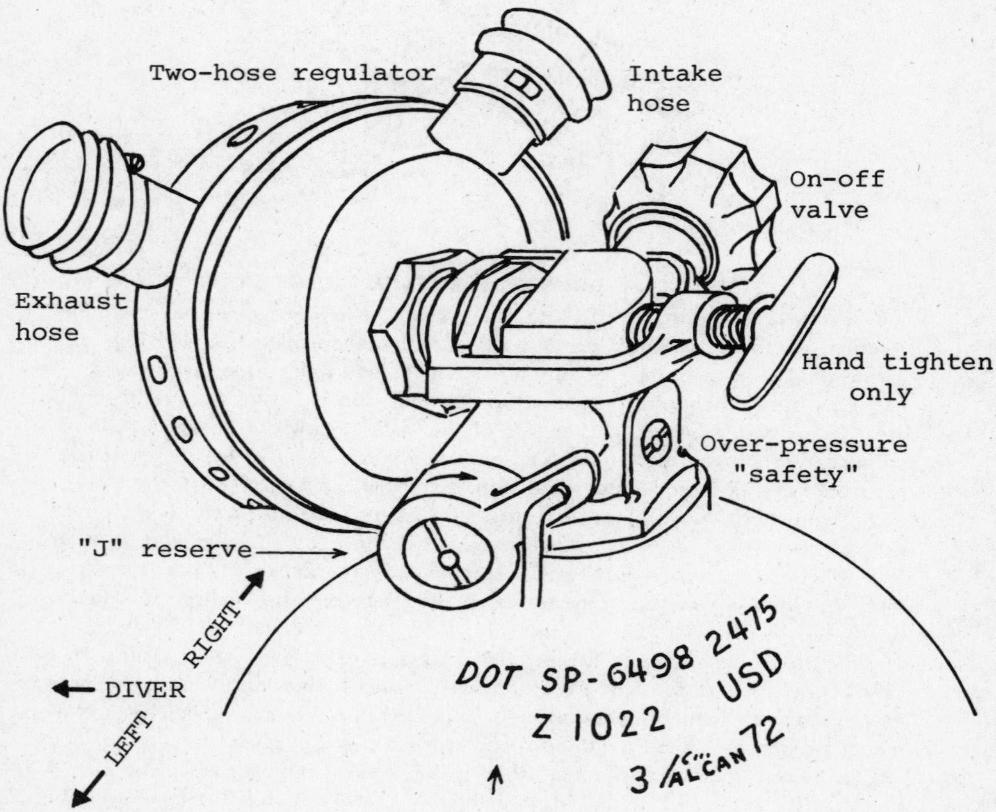

FIGURE 57. REGULATOR TO BOTTLE ASSEMBLY

entire unit. If the two-hose type is being tested, "free flow" of air from the mouthpiece should occur when the regulator is immersed fully with the mouthpiece above the surface. If the single-hose type is being tested, press the purge button, release and observe the interval of continued flow, if any, after release.

6. Check back-pack attachment to bottle. Check all harness and quick-release devices. Try to get a mental picture of the origin and function of all harness.

Of equal importance in the pre-dive check are the fins, mask, snorkel, weight belt (weight and fastening), and a complete check of the vest (fabric, seams, oral inflator and other types, CO_2 cartridge and puncturing mechanism).

Note. Repetition of the check procedure before each training session by buddy team will help establish it as a habitual practice to promote safety.

POST-DIVE PROCEDURES

Following the use of scuba and all dive equipment, proper disassembly, examination and storage are of equal importance to the pre-dive check. Establishing the habit of post-dive check and care will add measurably to the life of the equipment and to the planned activities of the user.

1. Upon completion of the dive activity removal of equipment on base or shore should be carefully performed so as to prevent loss or damage. Care exercised here will prevent marring an otherwise enjoyable dive.

2. Shut off the scuba-tank valve. Inhale from the mouthpiece to reduce regulator pressures (all stages) to atmospheric. Now the yoke may be loosened and the regulator removed from the scuba tank. Failure to "breathe down" the regulator will make loosening the yoke difficult and will usually result in a noisy dislodgment of the "O" ring.

3. Examine the physical condition of the regulator. A short blast of air from the bottle across the high-pressure port will usually remove any moisture or particles. Put the dust cap in position and fasten with yoke screw. Rinse the regulator in fresh water.

4. Check the physical condition of the bottle, back pack and harness. Check bottle pressure (total consumption can be recorded). Rinse with fresh water.

5. Check and wash fins, masks, snorkel and weight belt. Powdering with talc later will help to preserve the rubber.

6. Check the vest thoroughly for damage. Check the operation of the cartridge-puncturing mechanism and cord. Rinse the inside with fresh water and drain. Slight inflation will facilitate drying and prevent sharp creasing. Rinse the outside and hang to dry.

7. Thoroughly rinse and dry any protective clothing that was worn on the dive. Hang carefully to dry.

Note. Many of the foregoing will have to be done at home following a diving trip. Don't procrastinate, do it *when you arrive,* not later. The post-dive care you take will govern the success or disappointment of your next pre-dive check.

Scuba Orientation

The following orientation is offered as a suggested procedure. Instructors develop techniques and progressions which adapt best to their program. This suggested procedure is, however, the product of many of these adaptations.

After completing pre-dive checks and assembly of equipment, buddy teams should, while in shallow water, each don all equipment with the assistance of the other. This initial donning should emphasize the vest position, proper fastening of quick-release devices and the positioning of the weight belt so as to permit instant doffing if necessary.

Special care must be taken during the following exercises to prevent unvented ascent after breathing compressed air while submerged. Even in the shallow end of the pool there is potential hazard and such an ascent could cause some form of lung injury.

Recheck the regulator function before submerging. With the mouthpiece in place, breathe normally. Lay on the bottom face down. Alter the breathing volume and note the change in buoyancy which results. Roll to the side and to the face-up position. If using the two-hose regulator, free flow will be noticed, but volume intake can be controlled by shortening the breath and permitting the excess flow to escape around the mouthpiece. If using the single-hose regulator, free flow does not occur regardless of position, so it is not a problem.

After completing the initial breathing exercise, the trainee should surface while breathing normally. Return to the bottom, remove the mouthpiece and surface while exhaling continuously.

Clearing the flooded mouthpiece and resumption of breathing is the next phase. The flooded single-hose regulator may be cleared after inserting the mouthpiece by pushing the purge button or by puffing into the mouthpiece. Inhalation following either method should be of the cautious, trial type rather than a full breath.

Double-hose regulator clearing may be accomplished by raising the mouthpiece above the level of the regulator (with mouthpiece opening down) until free flow occurs. Immediately insert the mouthpiece, exhale and take a cautious inhalation. The mouthpiece may also be cleared by the "puff" method: with mouthpiece in and exhaust hose lower than the mouth, exhale vigorously to displace the water in the exhaust hose. Inhale cautiously.

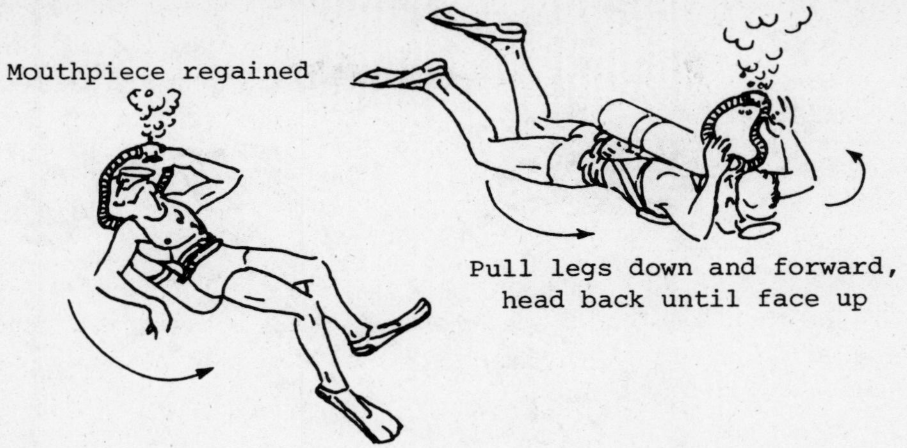
Mouthpiece regained
Pull legs down and forward,
head back until face up

FIGURE 58. REGAINING THE MOUTHPIECE

Clearing methods are simple and usually accomplished on the first attempt. Ridiculous as it may seem, however, the trainee must be impressed with the fact that inhalation cannot be made if the lungs are already full. Complaints of regulators not functioning, no air, or inability to breathe after mechanically purging the mouthpiece are, in many instances, traceable to this human failure. The trainee again submerges. Practice the appropriate clearing procedures until complete ease is achieved with each. Now flood the mask and clear. Flood the mask and remove the mouthpiece. Clear the mouthpiece and then the mask. Repeat for familiarization. Surface while breathing normally or exhaling continuously.

After initial orientation, the trainee will appreciate and benefit from swimming several lengths of the pool while on bottom, breathing normally. If the trainee desires and is comfortable enough, he should flood and clear the mouthpiece and mask several times during this excursion. Experimentation with and regulation of breathing volume during the excursion will demonstrate the desired buoyancy control.

STATION BREATHING

All trainees should come back to the shallow area and remove the scuba. Scuba should be placed on the bottom so as to form a square in the shallow water. The divers will, in rotation, start at one unit, get several breaths, swim to the next unit while exhaling slightly but continuously, reserving enough breath to perform necessary clearing at the next unit. The circuit should continue until all trainees have made the tour of all units while continuously submerged.

This station breathing exercise can then be repeated in the following manner. Starting at the shallow end, anchor the units progressively to the

FIGURE 59. STATION BREATHING AND MASK DONNING

deepest portion of the pool. Operating as a "buddy team" with one member snorkeling over the submerged member, begin the exercise at No. 1 in the shallow end. Since the progress is downward, the event of breath-holding between the stations presents no problem. When the last unit is cleared and breathing is satisfactory, have the trainee flood his face mask and cease breathing. Insert snorkel mouthpiece. While ascending along a predetermined 25 to 30 degree sloping line, clear the face mask (this guarantees exhalation during ascent), clear the snorkel, and return to the starting point while snorkeling. Repeat the circuit with a flooded face mask. Clear at the last station and breathe out (maintain an open airway) continually during the sloping ascent. Snorkel to starting point.

Station breathing, though most easily accomplished while wearing a weight belt, may also be done without the weight belt. When done without the weight belt, the valve should be held close to the body in the chest area, letting the scuba serve as a weight belt while the mouthpiece is cleared and a breath taken.

The preceding exercises should impress upon the trainee: *a*) the necessity for keeping an open airway when not breathing from scuba, *b*) the mouthpiece-clearing procedure, and *c*) the need for breathing volume control to achieve the desired degree of buoyancy.

Utilization of the foregoing skills (and their necessity) will be featured in the next exercises, involving donning and doffing scuba while under water.

Before attempting the doff-and-don procedures under water, a full review of both should be demonstrated on the deck and the illustrations (Figures 60 and 61) should be studied carefully. Again review the origin and function of all harness because underwater doff and don will involve feeling, rather than seeing, much of the harness. Initial performance of the exercises will be easier if the mask is left on and if it is done in shallow water.

DONNING

Place the scuba on the bottom with the weight belt placed over the bottle near the base. If the two-hose regulator is being used, the mouthpiece must be placed under the valve or the air turned off.

Overhead Method:

Dive to scuba. Grasp the valve, hold it close to the chest so as to maintain bottom position. Clear the regulator and breathe. While still face down, grasp the scuba and move it, parallel to the bottom, to the area of your thighs. Roll to your back and sit up. Place the scuba on or between your thighs with the back pack up. Transfer the weight belt to your lap. If using the two-hose scuba, it will be desirable to reduce the distance between the mouthpiece and regulator to a minimum. This permits control of the free flow. This may be accomplished by raising the regulator or bending the body forward as far as possible. Make up the shoulder harness. When the shoulder harness has been assembled to fit the individual, the hands and forearms are inserted into the straps and they, in turn, grasp the scuba bottle. *If the single-hose type is being donned, the right arm must be OUTSIDE the hose before placing into the harness.*

The bottle is now lifted through an arc into position on the back. Position the shoulder straps. Grasp and pull the waist strap into position and fasten it. If a crotch strap is part of the harness, it may be used to pull the base of the bottle into position. The crotch strap may be held until needed by anchoring it beneath the buttocks or between the legs. With harness in place, adjusted, and fastened, the weight belt may now be donned. This can be done while still in the sitting position but is better accomplished in the face-down "knee-chest" position. Using this latter position permits putting the belt into the desired position and facilitates snug fastening without a lot of juggling.

Incorrect donning of the single-hose scuba may result in the hose being caught under the shoulder harness or coming from beneath the armpit rather than over the shoulder. This may be corrected by removing the mouthpiece and repositioning the hose to its proper path. Insert and clear the mouthpiece.

In the two-hose scuba, unnecessary turning of the mouthpiece or cross-

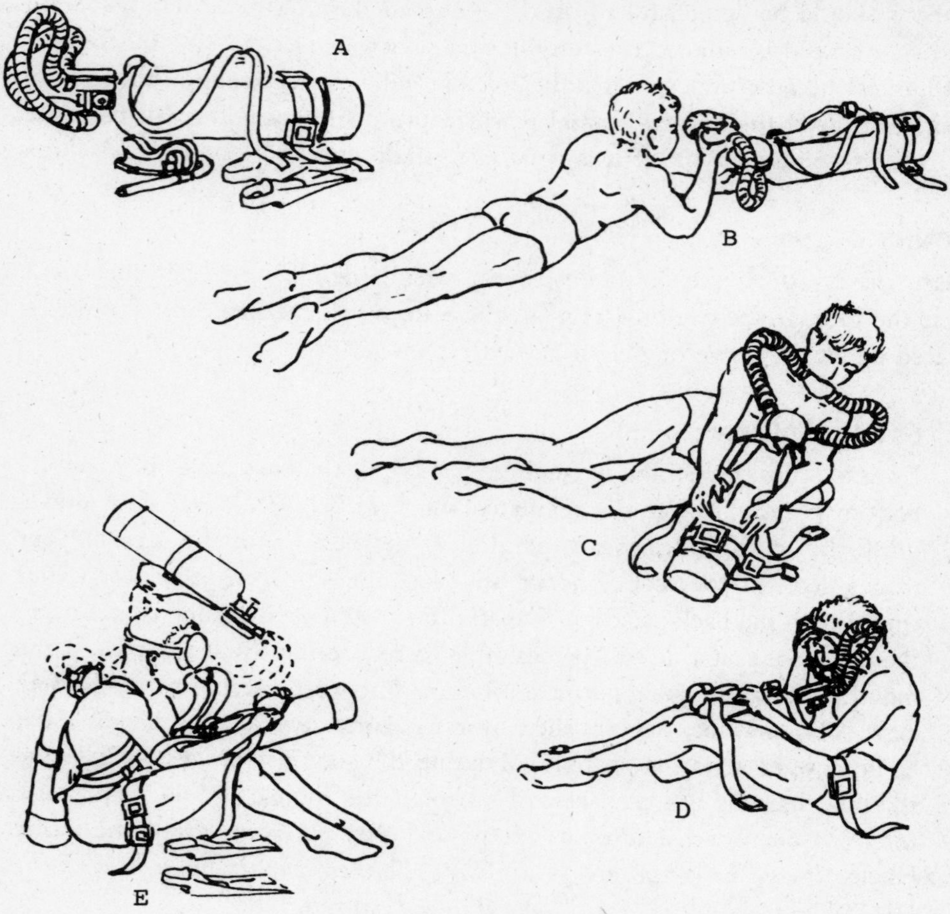

FIGURE 60. THE OVERHEAD METHOD OF SCUBA DONNING

A. Scuba and other equipment is placed neatly on bottom so as to facilitate donning (basic gear should be on side away from swing—see C). The mouthpiece of a two-hose scuba must be placed under the regulator to prevent free flow if air is on.

B. Diver places hand under regulator to assist in remaining on bottom. Mouthpiece is cleared and breathing started. Scuba is pulled toward diver. Either bottle or pack is grasped and diver rolls to his side.

C. Bottle is swung to the side and to legs and lap. Diver sits up. Weight belt transfer from tank to diver's lap can be made before or after full swing, depending on control and preference.

D. Mask is donned and cleared. Harness is prepared for donning. Forearms are inserted into shoulder harness as far as possible. *If donning a single-hose scuba, the right arm must be OUTSIDE the hose before insertion into shoulder harness.* Pack is held and scuba lifted from lap.

E. Scuba is lifted in an arc from lap to back. All harness is adjusted and fastened. The weight belt and fins are donned.

Note: The knee-chest position makes weight-belt donning easier.

ing the hoses when initial clearing is done will result in partial or total closure of the hoses. If this occurs, the mouthpiece should be removed and the excess turn or crossing corrected. Clear the mouthpiece and resume breathing. Continue the donning.

Making these kinds of corrections during the initial exercise often impresses the trainee with the *need to pre-plan and think* when attempting a new technique.

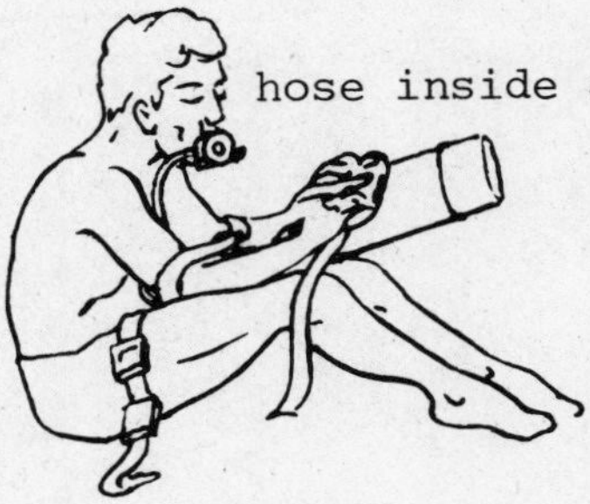

FIGURE 61. SINGLE HOSE—OVERHEAD DONNING

NOTE: Described doff-and-don procedures are a way, but not the only way. Many variations have been devised. Kneeling, kneeling on one knee, prone and supine donning-and-doffing methods are taught and all have merit. Physique, buoyancy, dress, and equipment design may indicate change to another satisfactory procedure. The goal is flawless performance. The route of achievement may vary.

Side Donning of the Single-Hose Scuba:
In this method the initial contact and clearing is the same as in the previous donning exercise. While in the prone position, draw both knees forward to the area of the scuba valve. Keep the body inclined forward. Draw the tank and weight belt up between the thighs. The right hand holds the weight belt. Raise the right knee and move it to the right so that you are in the kneeling-on-one-knee position. Place the weight belt across and high on the right thigh. The mask may be donned and harness made up at this point. Insert the right arm into the right shoulder harness. *"Be sure that the scuba hose is above the arm."* Left hand assisting, the scuba is moved up and around the right shoulder to the back. Right hand assisting, the left arm finds and enters the left shoulder harness. When both shoulder straps are in place, fasten the remaining scuba harness. The right hand removes the weight belt from the thigh and to the back. The kneeling-on-both-knees position is reassumed with the body leaning forward. The weight belt is fastened. The fins are now donned. Raising each knee, thus bringing the foot forward, helps in donning the fins.

FIGURE 62. SINGLE HOSE—SIDE DONNING

A. Approach the valve end of the scuba. Hold close to the chest to aid in achieving bottom stability. Clear the mouthpiece either by "puff" or by purge button. Restrict air-volume intake to achieve negative buoyancy.

B. Draw the knees forward to the sitting-on-the-heels position. Draw the scuba and weight belt between the thighs. Raise the right knee and transfer the weight belt to high on the right thigh. Extending the raised knee to the side and leaning forward improves stability. The mask may be donned and the harness made up if necessary.

C. Place the right arm through the right shoulder strap. Left hand assisting, the scuba is moved up and around the right shoulder to the back. *Be sure that the scuba hose is above the right arm throughout the maneuver.*

D. Right hand assisting, locate and slip the left arm through the left shoulder harness. Locate and fasten the remaining harness.

E. Holding the end of the weight belt on the inside of the right thigh with the right hand, reassume the sitting-on-the-heels position. Lean the body forward, position the weight belt across the back and fasten. Don the fins. Raising the knee and bringing the foot forward will aid in fin donning.

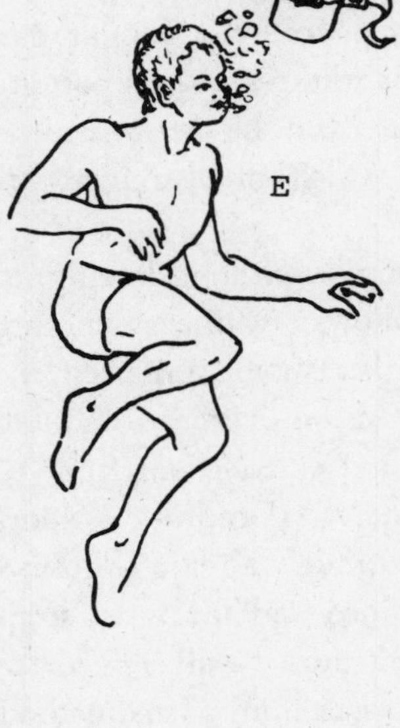

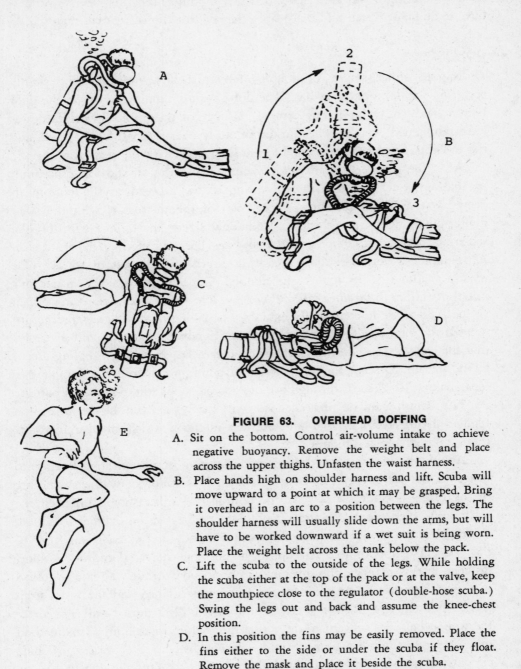

FIGURE 63. OVERHEAD DOFFING

A. Sit on the bottom. Control air-volume intake to achieve negative buoyancy. Remove the weight belt and place across the upper thighs. Unfasten the waist harness.

B. Place hands high on shoulder harness and lift. Scuba will move upward to a point at which it may be grasped. Bring it overhead in an arc to a position between the legs. The shoulder harness will usually slide down the arms, but will have to be worked downward if a wet suit is being worn. Place the weight belt across the tank below the pack.

C. Lift the scuba to the outside of the legs. While holding the scuba either at the top of the pack or at the valve, keep the mouthpiece close to the regulator (double-hose scuba.) Swing the legs out and back and assume the knee-chest position.

D. In this position the fins may be easily removed. Place the fins either to the side or under the scuba if they float. Remove the mask and place it beside the scuba.

E. *Start exhaling continuously* while you swim to the surface on a long sloping course.

Both methods work well with a little practice if the trainee is bare-skinned. If he is wearing a wet suit jacket or other clothing, the shoulder straps will have to be maneuvered into place since they do not slip easily over material.

DOFFING

Doffing of either single- or double-hose scuba is accomplished by simply reversing the donning procedure. The doffed scuba should end up on the pool bottom with the valve in the area of the face of the prone diver. Harnesses are straightened, weight belt adjusted carefully over the base of the tank, and the mouthpiece placed so it will be readily available for the next donning.

After the trainee has satisfactorily performed the doff-and-don procedures in shallow water, he will then, wearing scuba, proceed to the bottom in deeper water. Under the direct supervision of the instructor, with the skin-diving buddy directly overhead for additional safety, the trainee will doff the scuba and any other equipment as may have been directed by the instructor. All equipment doffed shall be neatly arranged on the bottom so as to be readily available when it is to be donned. Depending upon the instructor's initial direction, the trainee will either leave the scuba at this time and return to the surface while continually exhaling, or he may immediately proceed to don all the equipment which has just been removed. Many instructors prefer that the trainee, after doffing scuba and other gear, do a long exhaling ascent to the surface. Descent for the purpose of donning can follow a similar pattern, making the descent through a long, gradual slope to the scuba on bottom.

The donning-and-doffing exercises will rarely, if ever, be performed in regular diving activities, but are teaching methods which involve many of the regular diving techniques.

An alternative way of doffing and donning scuba without having to interrupt the air supply can be accomplished as follows: While swimming in the prone position, at or near the bottom, the diver should unfasten the waist strap (and the crotch strap if present) and, as in the overhead method, bring the scuba to a position in line with the body and extended in front of the body. The mouthpiece is retained in position. After proceeding a short distance in this manner, the diver moves the scuba through an arc overhead to the back position. The shoulder straps are repositioned and the waist strap is then refastened. If there is a crotch strap involved, it must be slipped *under* the weight belt and upward to the waist strap before refastening. This method may be used in initial training to preclude possible unvented ascent. In some circumstances this could be a practical application of doff-and-don procedure.

VEST DRILL

Inflate the vest orally before entering the water. This serves as part of the pre-dive check. After entry is made, deflate the vest (the method depends

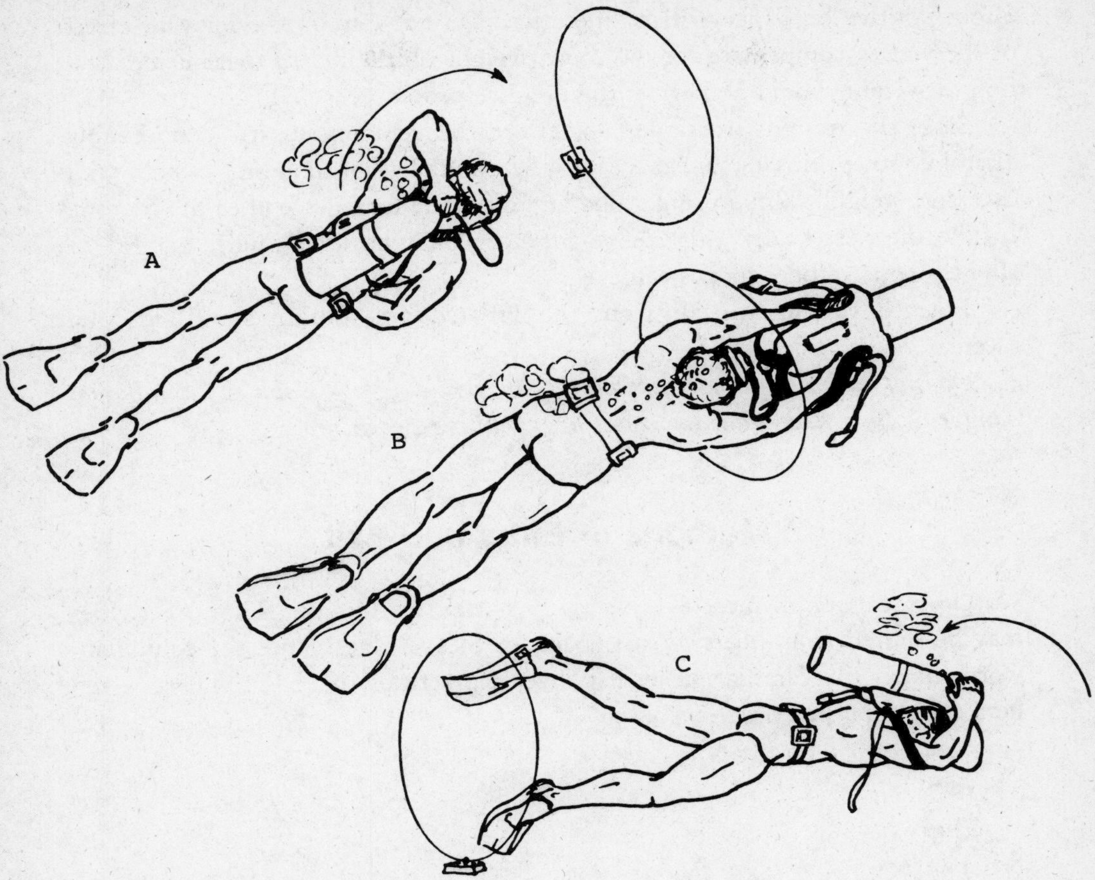

FIGURE 64.
CONTINUOUS BREATHING DOFF-AND-DON ALTERNATIVE PROCEDURE

This alternative method of doff and don is performed without removal of mouthpiece or weight belt. The chance of unventilated ascent or floating upward is thus considerably lessened. Modern back packs without crotch straps are easily adapted to this method. It can be performed with either single- or double-hose scuba. The illustrations indicate doffing before passing through an anchored hoop and donning after passage is completed. The shoulder harness is shown in black.

A. As the hoop is approached, the waist harness is unfastened and freed. The scuba is lifted toward the head. It is then moved to a position in front of the diver and held by the pack.
B. The diver moves through the hoop with scuba extended forward. This position is kept until passage is complete.
C. The scuba is lifted in an arc toward the back. The hands can be moved from the pack to the valve to facilitate positioning the pack and shoulder harness as the arc is completed. The waist straps are retrieved and fastened to complete the cycle.

on the make and design) until descent may be comfortably accomplished. Slight positive buoyancy will be the safest. Do not rely on the buoyant effect of the vest to compensate for too much weight on the belt. Proper determination of weight should be part of the pre-dive procedure.

Since the training area does not afford the depth necessary to noticeably alter buoyance, this circumstance can be simulated by donning a belt with excessive weight. While using scuba and overweighted, descend to the bottom. Inflate the vest orally (air source inflator could be used) until neutral or slightly positive buoyance is achieved.

Practice valving off air from the inflated vest during simulated long ascents.

Do not attempt rapid buoyant ascent while using scuba. The inherent danger of lung damage rules it out as a training procedure.

Methods of Entry and Exit

Up to this point most every activity started in the pool. Future activities may be started from boats, floats, docks, or rocky ledges. Since the equipment worn makes the familiar head-first dive impractical, the basic entries given here should be practiced.

FIGURE 65. FRONT ENTRY—GIANT STRIDE

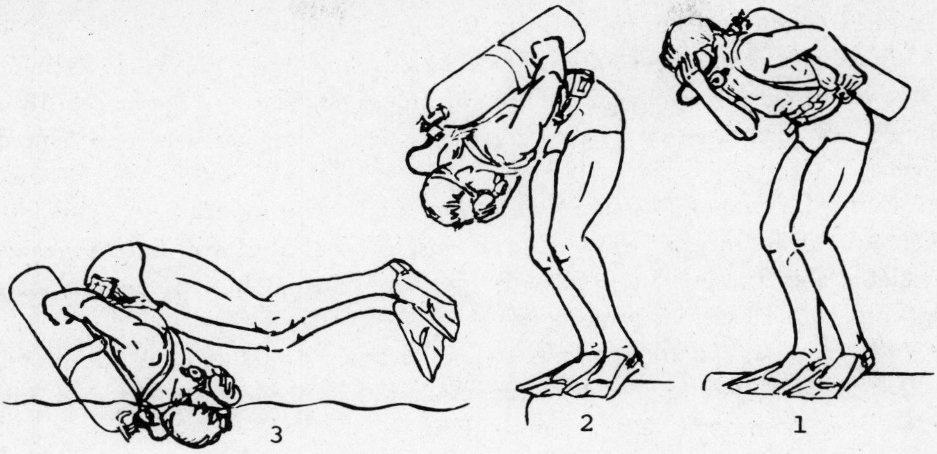

FIGURE 66. FORWARD (QUARTER-TWIST) ROLL ENTRY

With all gear in place, hold the mask firmly with one hand covering the lens, elbow close to the chest. When using scuba, it may be desirable under some conditions to also hold the lower part of the tank harness so as to prevent upward collision with the neck or head. Most entries are made from a few feet above the surface, so the following should suffice:

Front Jump. Feet first and together. Designed for immediate descent in water of sufficient depth and clarity.

Front Step. 1) Hold the mask firmly with one hand covering the lens, elbow close to chest. 2) Feet first with legs spread wide, as in a long stride. 3) When the fins touch the surface, the legs are brought quickly together, toes of fins pointed, as in a kicking stroke. Downward motion is stopped, after a little practice, before head and shoulders are submerged.

Forward (or Quarter-Twist) Roll. This is best performed from areas close to the surface. Face forward while standing at the edge of the entry area: 1) Place one hand firmly on the mask, elbow close to the body. 2) Bend at the waist, head down. 3) Either roll forward or drop the shoulder of the hand holding the mask as the forward roll is made. Turning the head and face away from the water helps to make the quarter twist. This latter method will result in the dropped shoulder entering first and that side of the body making initial contact with the water. Do not jump or throw the body into a somersault. This is simply a roll entry.

Standing Back Entry. With back to water and making sure that no one is under you, the jump or step-off methods used in front entry may be made in reverse.

Back Roll. From a crouched or sitting position close to the surface, merely roll backward. Care and practice should be exercised when making this type of entry, as straightening or opening up too quickly could result in bumping the head on the wall, boat, or float.

Entry or exit in a rocky area or at a beach through surf presents too many variables to permit description of simple procedures. The inexperienced diver should only attempt this type of entry or exit in company with experienced divers.

Exit to any area higher than the surface while wearing all the scuba equipment would be, in most instances, a clumsy maneuver. If you have someone available above, remove and pass the heavier items to him. Keep your fins on until you are sure of positive exit.

Exit to a stage at surface level should present no problems. While prone, pull with the hand and push with fin action. When aboard to waist level, roll to a sitting position to rest or remove gear.

Buddy Breathing

This is an emergency procedure. Sharing a buddy's air supply would only be done because of a regulator failure, exhausted air supply, or other situation which precludes the use of the scuba. Since any of these conditions would usually necessitate an ascent, precautions must be observed to prevent occurrence of any lung damage.

Obviously, the sharing of air from one regulator will alter the normal breathing rate. *Pressure decrease between each makes it mandatory that continual exhalation be made between inhalations.*

Though not always the case, it may be assumed that the "airless" diver is least able to control the situation. The air donor must retain control of his regulator (or mouthpiece and hoses if the two-hose scuba is being used). He must indicate that exhalation between inhalations is necessary. He must govern, as well as possible, equal and rhythmic sharing of air. When possible, he should govern the rate of ascent. He must always be in position to assume physical control of the assisted diver if conditions warrant.

Although there are many variations of buddy breathing techniques, each, to be effective, must provide control of the mouthpiece by the donor, a position which facilitates sharing and at the same time permits observation and physical control by the donor. Physical difference of the single hose and two-hose scuba requires separate techniques for each.

SINGLE-HOSE SHARING

The "airless" diver should be positioned on the left side of the donor and at about a quarter turn to the donor. This position can be maintained and regulated by the donor's holding onto the back pack or harness of the "airless"

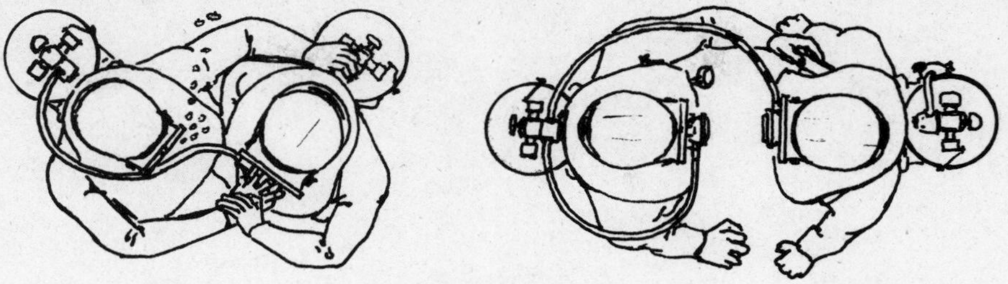

FIGURE 67

SINGLE-HOSE SHARING   OCTOPUS-RIG SHARING

diver with his left hand. The regulator is positioned at the "airless" diver's mouth by the donor, who retains control of the regulator. The "airless" diver may position the mouthpiece so as to get his breath but not so as to have complete control of the regulator. When the mouthpiece is in the desired position, either the donor or the "airless" diver may activate the purge button for clearing. The "puff" method of clearing should be used by both the donor and "airless" diver, when possible, to conserve air supply. The described exchange from donor to "airless" diver should be continued at a rhythmic rate with both exhaling continually between inhalations. This procedure should be practiced while stationary and while swimming.

OCTOPUS SHARING

Many single-hose regulators now have two intermediate (low) pressure ports and a high (tank) pressure port on the first stage. This permits attaching two second-stage hoses and a submersible (tank) pressure gauge. Adaptors are available for increasing the number of low pressure ports so that a vest inflation hose may also be added. Obviously, so many hoses stemming from a central point give credence to the name. When such a rig is made up, the spare mouthpiece or hose should be identified with bright tape. Many users provide a longer than standard hose on the spare. Individual needs and experience will produce many variations of identification, attachment, modification and employment.

The following is one way of using an octopus rig made up of standard stages. First, the spare is positioned over the left shoulder. The mouthpiece should be kept from dangling by securing it to a readily available area by means of a simple and reliable "quick release" device. Having this spare second stage instantly available makes sharing a much less complicated and safer procedure. The donor should maintain control contact by grasping the right shoulder harness as shown in Figure 67. This contact serves to bring the airless diver and donor face to face or to position and maintain constant distance while moving to the surface. Sharing (buddy breathing) is an emergency situation and should be a signal to terminate the dive.

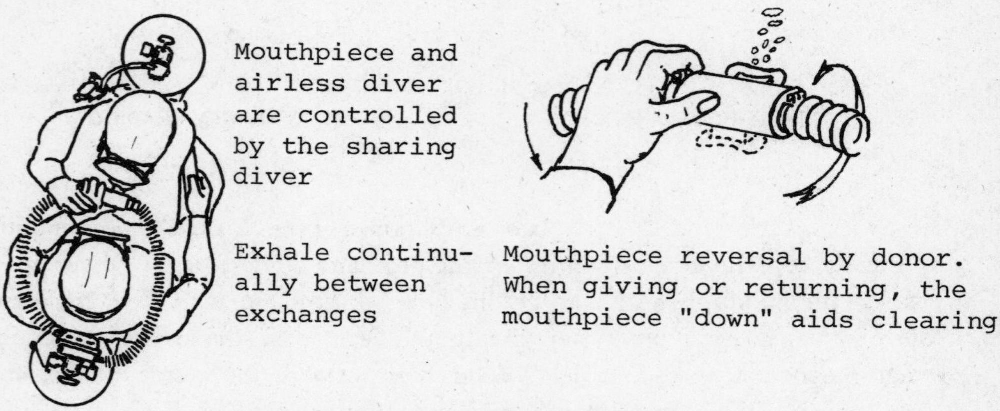

Mouthpiece and airless diver are controlled by the sharing diver
Exhale continually between exchanges
Mouthpiece reversal by donor. When giving or returning, the mouthpiece "down" aids clearing

FIGURE 68. TWO-HOSE REGULATOR SHARING

TWO-HOSE SHARING

Using this type of scuba involves face-to-face position of divers. Although difficult to achieve during vertical ascent, the breathing is facilitated with the exhaust hose (left side) lower than the mouthpiece. The donor must control the turning of the mouthpiece to the "airless" diver's mouth area. Physical contact is maintained by the donor holding the harness or arm of the "airless" diver. The construction of the two-hose mouthpiece makes it necessary to revolve the mouthpiece away from the donor about 180° to the "airless" diver. The "airless" diver will insert the mouthpiece to the desired degree without assuming complete control of the hoses or mouthpiece. When accomplished in the swimming position, breathing is facilitated if the donor swims with his left side down. The free-flow method of clearing (mouthpiece higher than the regulator) may be used, but the "puff" method of clearing is more desirable since it conserves air supply.

Dark-Water Diving

Although diving in areas of poor or no visibility is not recommended as safe, such conditions may occur. Rather than have the trainee cope with this situation for the first time in open water, it is best to simulate such a condition while in the safety of the training area. This may be accomplished by placing aluminum foil inside the mask so as to effectively black out any vision. If the trainee is disoriented by being rolled and turned prior to swimming to a designated area with his mask blacked out, he will experience nearly the same conditions as if in open water without visibility. Prior to performing this exercise, the scuba diver *must be impressed with the need for regular breathing.* The reason for this is that the diver may be unaware of the fact that he is ascending and that breath-holding in this situation is a dangerous procedure.

The trainee will be more aware of his "lost" condition if continued contact with the pool sides is avoided. Prevention of head injury and facilitation of passage around obstructions is accomplished by extending the arms forward, hands together. This is contrary to the instinct to crawl or feel the way. Yielding to this instinct usually results in cessation of forward motion and mask contact with obstructions. This exercise can be further complicated by creating minor emergencies such as removal of the mouthpiece, unfastening of harness, and flooding of the mask by the instructor. *Note:* The foregoing is *not* intended to become a hazing or harassment initiation, the intent is to test reaction and co-ordination of response to emergencies. Observation by the instructor should be critical of panic indication or misjudgment. Primary consideration should be given to the possibility of an unventilated ascent and every precaution must be taken to prevent this.

All of the foregoing techniques of skin and scuba diving, although individually described, should be combined in repeated practice sessions. These practice sessions should be designed so as to simulate, as nearly as possible, diving in open water.

Rescue Skills

Prevention of accidents by careful planning, preparation, and by always diving with a competent buddy is of equal importance with knowledge of what to do in case of an emergency. Whether diving with a group or as a single pair, the practice of knowing where your buddy is and staying in close proximity to him may serve to avert a regrettable incident.

It should be realized that rescue problems involving divers may be quite different from those involving swimmers. Much diver activity takes place in areas not normally used for recreational swimming. These areas may be characterized by rocks, reefs, marine animals or plants, and unusual currents or surges, generally or around wrecks. Many of these areas are far from any organized lifeguard or beach protection service. Many are remote, with no normal access routes. It is, therefore, quite necessary that divers learn and practice rescue skills and first-aid measures. Every diver should acquire a working knowledge of lifesaving techniques. The following descriptions, though not nearly complete, should prepare the basic diver to initiate the necessary procedures, both in practice and in the event of actual emergency.

MISSING DIVER

An emergency situation may exist if a diver has not been seen or his exhaust bubbles have not been noted for a period of time longer than normal. A lookout (dive master) should be stationed so that he may maintain constant check of every diver's location. If the mandatory "buddy system" has been maintained, the absence of the diver should be quickly noted. Suggested action is as follows:

A. Immediately determine where the diver was last seen.
B. Move to that area and look for bubbles.
C. A bottom search team should immediately cover the area. Use the appropriate search pattern. Take into consideration existing currents which may alter the assumed location of the missing diver. Work in the downstream direction from the area in which the diver was last seen.
D. Determine the possibility that the diver has left the area (gone ashore) without notifying the group.
E. If available, send for additional help to aid in the search.

SURFACE EMERGENCY

A victim struggling on the surface. A person while diving may encounter difficulty that would cause him to panic even after returning to the surface. Suggested action is as follows:

A. Move toward the victim shouting encouragement.
B. Extend a floatable object to the victim if available.
C. If necessary to make a swimming rescue, approach from the rear.
D. Grasp the victim's tank at the valve, press up on the opposite end, and level the victim to the surface.
E. Inflate the victim's vest and remove his weight belt if necessary. Inflate your own vest if necessary.
F. Tow the victim to safety in such a manner that control can be maintained at all times and the victim constantly observed.

Non-struggling victim on the surface. A non-struggling victim is likely to be unconscious and may be in need of immediate resuscitation. The following action is suggested:

A. Reach the victim in as short a time as possible.
B. Position the victim so that his face is up.

FIGURE 69. APPROACH AND TOWING

1. Approach the struggling victim who is on the surface from the rear and underwater. Contact and hold.
2. Level the victim by holding scuba valve and pushing up on lower part of the bottle.
3. Side-flutter tow while holding scuba valve or shoulder harness.
4. Back-flutter tow while holding scuba valve, hair or harness with one or both hands.
5. Side-flutter and side-arm pull while holding hand of extended arm of victim. The victim's palm is rotated upward.

C. Inflate his vest and remove the weight belt if necessary. Inflate your own vest if necessary. Remove his mouthpiece and mask and test for breathing.

D. If not breathing, immediately clear the mouth and proceed with oral resuscitation.

E. Move the victim toward shore while continuing resuscitation. If more than one rescuer is present he may perform the towing.

F. Arrange for transfer of the victim to medical facilities. Continue resuscitation if necessary. This includes cardiac resuscitation if the need has been determined and the rescuers know the procedure.

SUBMERGED DIVER EMERGENCY

While submerged, divers may be involved in emergency situations as a result of being entangled in weeds, wire, fish lines, nets, etc., or they may become trapped in wrecks or caves, or may have been injured by marine life, coral or boats. Action suggested is as follows:

A. *Entangled diver.* Cut the diver loose with your knife, being sure that you do not become entangled yourself. Buddy-breathe if necessary.

B. *Trapped diver.* Enter with a guide rope, locate and lead the diver to safety.

C. *Injured diver.* Assist the diver to the surface, remaining in such position as to be in control in the event that the victim panics.

D. *Conscious diver.* Constantly observe to ensure that regular breathing is maintained during the ascent.

E. *Unconscious diver.* If not breathing, efforts must be made during the ascent to induce exhalation. This may be accomplished, with the mouthpiece in, by positioning the head and neck so as to open and straighten the airway and by exerting pressure on the lower ribs and diaphragm by hand.

Upon surfacing, tend and reassure the conscious diver and, if necessary, begin resuscitation of the unconscious diver. Proceed toward base. Give first aid and arrange for proper transportation to medical facilities.

OTHER EMERGENCIES

Diving when or where conditions are contrary to safety should be avoided. If diving under dangerous conditions is necessary, every precaution possible should be included in the planning. Unforeseen emergency situations may arise even during the best-planned dive. Good judgment and calm action by all concerned can prevent many a possible tragedy.

A. *Loss of equipment.* Though unlikely, this can occur. Depending on the equipment lost, it may be necessary to provide air, provide mobility, and provide guidance and/or buoyancy.

B. *Loss of lifeline under ice.* The diver should remain at the area of loss and ascend to the ice cover. The search party, *with lifelines attached,* should enter and search toward the area of last contact with the diver. Surface search should also begin if the ice is clear enough to detect the lost diver through its surface. An emergency escape hole should be cut if the diver is located by surface observation.

Search Patterns

CIRCULAR

Search of a limited area can be efficiently made visually or by feel while progressively covering concentric bands radiating outward from a fixed center. The search pattern, beginning at the fixed center with short radius, is expanded by systematically lengthening the radius after each complete circle is made. The number of searching divers employed will determine the number of circle completions necessary to thoroughly cover the area.

GRID

The grid, as illustrated, should be constructed of line sufficiently strong and visible as to permit handling and/or visual contact. Whether constructed in or out of the water, the grid should be moved to the search area and anchored so as to preserve the size and shape, either on or off the bottom as the need indicates. Sufficient surface markers should be provided to ensure complete coverage and to provide a direct route of descent to the grid. The size of the blocks will be determined by visibility and bottom conditions. Searchers cover the area assigned. When all have completely covered their area the grid is moved.

IRREGULAR SHORE-LINE PATTERN

An assistant walks along the shore holding a line extending to a diver who is searching the visibility range from the shore; by keeping the line taut and at right angles to the shore the area may be thoroughly searched. Successive tries, each spaced to the limit of visibility, will complete the search. Two or more divers may search, providing the line remains taut and at right angles from shore. Attendant sould be given hand-pull signals for information related to the search.

SEARCH PATTERN FOR CURRENTS

Search should cross current on an angle so as to eliminate energy necessary to fight water movement. Two or more divers could cover width of visibility. After crossing current, return also on a diagonal. Second and successive searches may be started downstream from first starting point and parallel to it. It is important to search quickly as object of search may drift with the current. Depending on the speed and force of flow, it may be advantageous to institute the initial pattern downstream and work back to the area of last sighting.

FIGURE 70. RECOMMENDED SEARCH PATTERNS

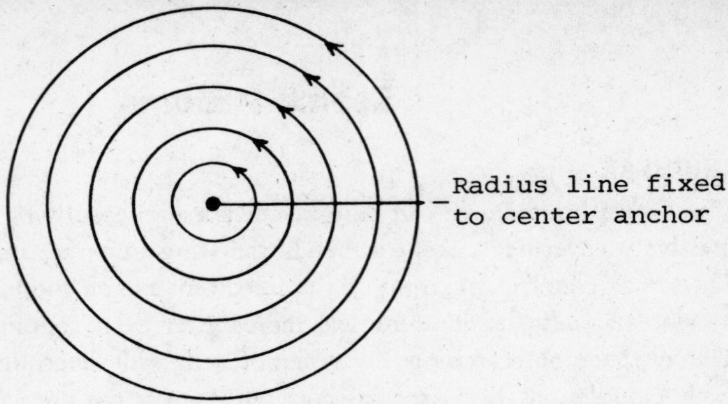

CIRCULAR SEARCH PATTERN

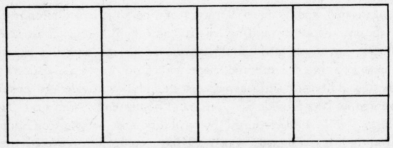

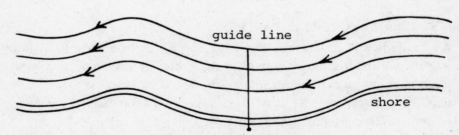

GRID SEARCH PATTERN

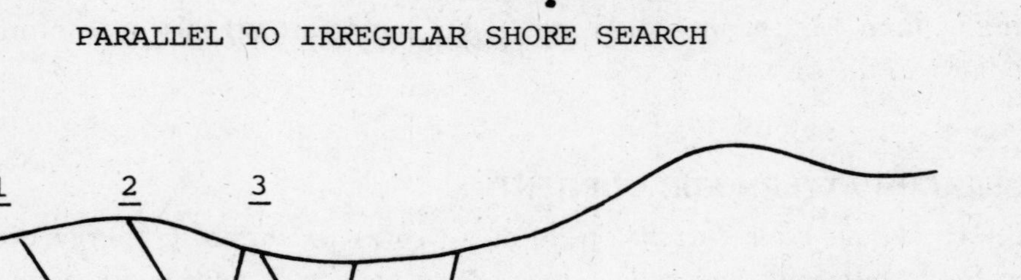

PARALLEL TO IRREGULAR SHORE SEARCH

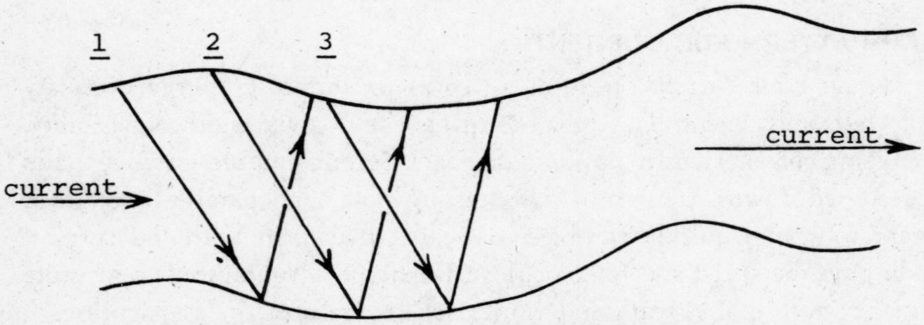

CURRENT SEARCH - PROGRESSIVE OVERLAP

Summation

This is a general summary and review of all previously learned skills. Discussion of several planned dive activities and the possible danger involved will set the stage for planned safety.

A. Pre-dive check: equipment, diver, planned activity. Include the emergency situations and course of corrective action, role of the "safety man."

B. After appropriate entry to fit indicated condition, the designed conditions are encountered and corrected according to plan. Following are suggested situations that can be set up using imagination, experience, and simple props.

   1. Entrapment—net, bag, large plastic trash can, snarled line, etc.
   2. Dark-water loss of safety guide line or buddy line.
   3. Air supply cut off or exhausted. Long ascent with no air.
   4. Continual flooding of mask.
   5. Loss of one or both fins.
   6. Remove scuba, pass through area just big enough to wiggle through; don and continue.
   7. Send and receive communications—visual hand signals, written, sound. React accordingly.
   8. Buddy-breathe with a disabled diver (conscious) to a distant location.
   9. Locate and rescue an unconscious diver. With history of the dive reviewed, determine the most likely cause of the diver's condition; act accordingly.
   10. Set up and carry out a grid search for a hard-to-find object.
   11. Devise methods for lifting a heavy object from the bottom with simple, readily available equipment and materials.
   12. Use hand tools underwater to make a box; assemble pipes; tie objects together or disassemble objects previously tied.

The relative safety and close observation possible in a pool should be used to every advantage before the open-water checkout is made. Acquirement of skills and know-how, when emergencies occur, will make the future activities of the diver safer and full of pleasure.

7

FIRST AID FOR DIVING ACCIDENTS

Most diving accidents can be prevented, but even the best-trained diver on the best-run dive may get into real trouble when he least expects it. So it is not enough to know how to "do it right" in the first place. You also have to know what to do if things go wrong. Whether a mishap on a dive turns into a full-blown tragedy or not can depend entirely on you or your buddy. There won't be a doctor down there to handle a medical emergency and there may not be a hospital within miles; so you're on your own. If you've had good first-aid training and have some emergency plans ready in the back of your head, doing the right thing will be almost automatic. Otherwise, you may be the one who panics and needlessly loses his own life or his buddy's.

Just how important it is to *know what to do* was shown on a dive made by Jim Stewart and Ron Church, both long-time ace divers from Scripps Institute of Oceanography. They were making scientific observations off Wake Island in the Pacific. Suddenly Jim was attacked by a black-tip shark and bitten badly on his right arm and elbow. The bite took off muscle down to the bone and even opened the joint. Blood gushed from the severed blood vessels, but Jim applied hand pressure to the brachial artery and stopped the flow. Ron helped him to shore and gave further first-aid care. Later, much surgery and weeks of healing were required. The scars are something to see, but Jim is back to his valuable work almost as if the attack had not happened. Without his knowledge and presence of mind, he could have bled to death before reaching shore.

Diving alone places the whole burden of decision, action, and conclusion on the individual. None of us is so self-sufficient that we can exclude a helping hand or the added safety afforded by diving with a competent buddy.

Prevention

This chapter deals with first aid—what to do *after* an accident. Knowing a good deal about this is vital, but remember that the best way to handle an accident is to keep it from happening. Most of the contents of this book are concentrated on just that: *prevention.* Accident prevention starts with being sure you're fit for diving and does not stop until you're back on shore after a dive *made safe* by your training in handling yourself underwater and knowing how to plan dives and stay out of trouble. If trouble comes in spite of all the preparations, you must know how to keep mishaps from becoming accidents. One definition of first aid is, "How to keep an accident from becoming a tragedy."

No chapter—not even a whole book—could possibly take the place of the hours of training and practice necessary to make a good first-aid or life-saving and water safety man. Although these take time, it's hard to think of a cheaper form of diver's life insurance. This chapter will be a guide to things divers should know about first aid, review the essentials, and serve as a place to look up certain facts (such as care of injuries from marine animals) that can be very important but hard to remember.

General First Aid

Very few serious accidents can be handled entirely without professional medical assistance. However, the fact that such assistance is not immediately at hand hardly ever needs to result in loss of life. A few fairly simple first-aid procedures can almost always handle the situation in the meantime. Calmly applying proper first aid on the spot is far better than madly rushing the victim to the nearest doctor or hospital. This does *not* mean that there should be any *needless* delay in getting professional help.

DO THE RIGHT THING FIRST

In taking care of the victim of any accident, the first step is to *size up the situation* rapidly but accurately. This will tell you what to do first, and doing the right thing first can be a matter of life or death. Splinting a broken bone is useless if the victim dies within minutes because his breathing has stopped, and artificial respiration won't help a victim who is rapidly bleeding to death. If you have someone to help you, all the really important things can be done almost simultaneously provided you know what *needs* to be done. Ask yourself these questions:

1. *Is he breathing?* If not, artificial respiration takes precedence over absolutely everything *except* the need to control massive bleeding—which you are not likely to miss.
2. *Is he bleeding?* Rapid loss of blood can cause death in a few minutes, so it clearly must be controlled at once. Even less obvious bleeding can cause shock or death in a relatively short time, so it must be discovered and stopped.
3. *Is he in shock?* Shock can and does follow almost any type of injury and can cause death even though the initial injury was unlikely to do so.

If none of these problems which demand immediate attention is found, then proceed to examine the victim as thoroughly as possible so as to find *all* the injuries that he may have sustained. Be extremely gentle and do not move him any more than absolutely necessary in the process of examination or when loosening clothing. Be particularly careful to avoid unnecessary moving of the head and neck. If the neck happens to be broken, such movement can cause death or permanent paralysis. If a broken bone is found or suspected, immobilize the part before moving the victim.

In general, the victim should be kept lying flat with head level with the body—at least until you are sure of the full extent of his injuries. Unless circumstance demands prompt removal to a safer place, do not move him unless you are *sure* it is safe to do so or until he can be moved properly by means of a stretcher or suitable substitute.

In everything that you do, remember that *your first duty is not to do harm.* It is better to do nothing than to do something that makes matters worse. Send for medical help immediately if you can. Never delay getting help while you do things like nonessential bandaging. It is always possible that some condition you may have overlooked, such as internal bleeding or a head injury, demands medical attention urgently.

All these things may seem too obvious and basic to be worth mentioning. Perhaps that is why they are so often forgotten and need emphasis as much as specific first-aid procedures.

BLEEDING

Nothing is more urgent than stopping rapid loss of blood, and only artificial respiration is more important than control of even moderate bleeding. Four different methods of control can be employed, either singly or in combination, using materials at hand:

1. *Direct pressure on the wound* either by hand or dressing (sterile or clean cloth in several folds) bandaged in place. It is desirable to use sterile dressings on any wound to reduce the danger of infection. However, serious loss of blood caused by waiting for or transporting to such a dressing may prove far more dangerous than an infection. Bandages should be applied firmly but not tightly enough to hamper circulation.

2. *Hand or finger pressure on the artery* supplying the area of the wound will slow or stop most bleeding from the extremities until a dressing and bandage are applied. The pressure points located on the inner side of the arm, which cause the brachial artery to be compressed against the arm bone, and pressure points on either side of the groin, which cause the femoral artery to be compressed against the front of the pelvis, are most easily found and most widely used. Others are

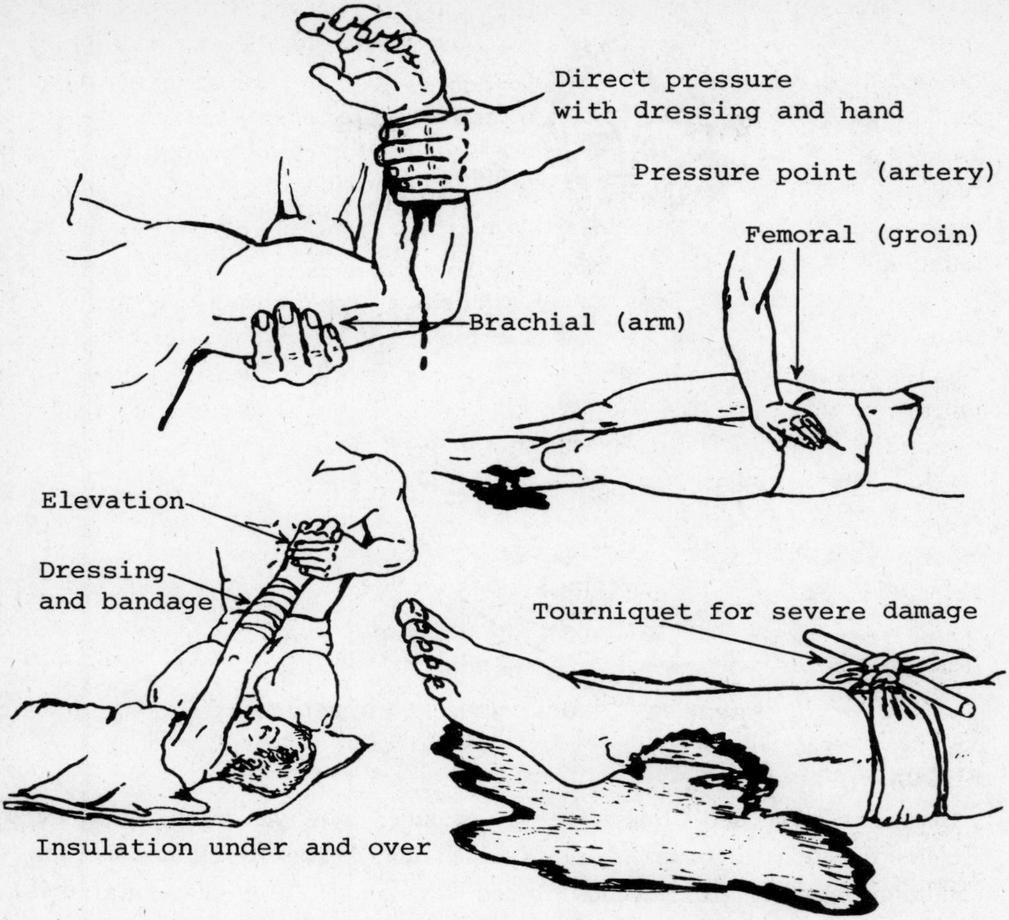

FIGURE 71. SEVERE BLEEDING CONTROL

described in older manuals but have little value, or are difficult to find and hold for any length of time.

3. *Elevation of the affected part* will serve to slow serious bleeding at its onset and during subsequent transport.
4. *The tourniquet is the last resort.* It must be remembered that when a tourniquet is incorrectly placed venous bleeding is increased and arterial bleeding is unaffected. *When a tourniquet is placed correctly,* several inches above the wound, the blood supply to the area *below* the constricting band is completely shut off, and the tissues will die from loss of oxygen and food unless surgical attention is obtained within a short time. Contrary to past technique, the *tourniquet should not be loosened* except by the doctor. If, as a last resort, a tourniquet is applied, it should be of flat material about 2 inches wide, tightened till bleeding stops and fixed to continue pressure. The attending physician must be notified that the tourniquet is in place.

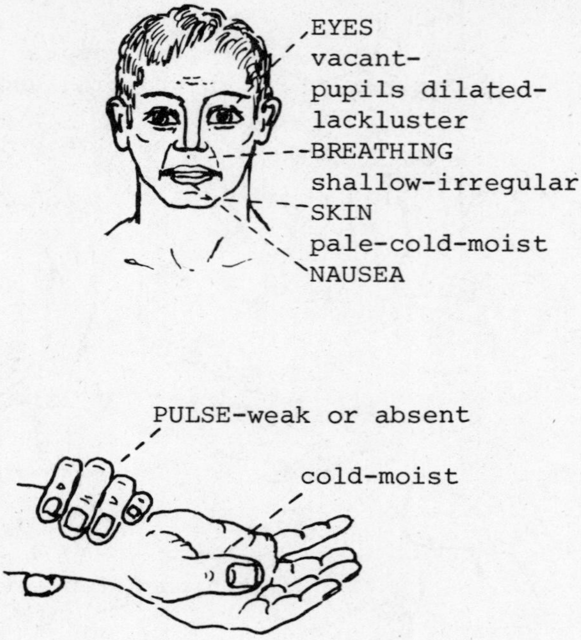

FIGURE 72. SHOCK: SIGNS AND SYMPTOMS

SHOCK

All injuries or sudden illnesses are accompanied by some degree of shock. Reference here is to *traumatic shock* which may be briefly defined as "the condition resulting from reduced blood circulation." The anatomical and physiological causes of this reduction in circulation are complex. The resultant diminishing of circulation causes the slowing down of all the body functions. This slowing down of the vital functions must be reversed or the condition may become more serious than was the original injury or illness. The first-aid steps necessary to reverse shock are relatively simple and become a part of first-aid procedures. Briefly, the following steps will serve to start the reversal:

1. Place and maintain the victim in a lying down, quiet, comfortable, position. If nausea or vomiting is present, the head should be turned to the side to permit drainage from the mouth. Whenever possible, the lower extremities should be elevated to promote return of blood to the heart.
2. Body heat should be preserved by placing insulating material under and over the victim as needed. Insulating material should be such as to prevent heat loss to the ground and to the air. If the victim or the surface is wet and cold, insulation under the victim is of greater importance than insulation over the victim.

3. Perform necessary first aid with as little disturbance of the victim as possible.

4. When and if conscious, the victim may complain of thirst. Fluid intake should be restricted to small sips of water. Abdominal injury or conditions which may involve immediate surgery, and the presence of extreme nausea would preclude giving any fluids to the victim. Alcohol should not be given.

STOPPAGE OF BREATHING (ASPHYXIA)

There are many causes for the stopping of breathing associated with diving accidents. Whatever the cause, when breathing has stopped, the victim must be supplied with air by some method. Many methods of artificial respiration (causing an alternate increase and decrease in chest expansion) have been devised and practiced since man recognized the need for such action. Most have succeeded in moving little or no air, although they have on occasion been used successfully.

Very careful and exhaustive research has shown that the oldest method of all—inflating the victim by mouth—can be by far the most effective, with no gadgets whatever, provided that the head and neck are placed in the proper position. This method (now called Rescue Breathing) of "mouth-to-mouth or mouth-to-nose" artificial respiration utilizes the rescuer's exhaled air. The exhaled air has more than enough oxygen to supply the needs of the victim. The rescuer knows positively at every instant whether air is going in and out adequately, so that if obstruction occurs he will know it at once and take action. A child can successfully ventilate even a large adult, and the method can be used anywhere (even in the water) and under conditions where other methods would be difficult, damaging, or impossible.

The sole objection to Rescue Breathing stems from squeamishness, bashfulness, prejudice, and fear of acquiring an infection. Only fear of an infection is an obstacle that intelligent people should be willing to admit, and the actual danger of contracting a serious disease is extremely slight. It should not deter you for one instant from using the method on a fellow diver or on any apparently healthy person. When properly done, the method does not involve inhaling the victim's breath. The chances that the victim has a communicable disease or, if so, that the rescuer could contract it are remote. Fire, police, and hospital personnel deserve the added protection of mask-and-tube devices that are available. Such devices, in almost every other circumstance, must be condemned because they add nothing to the effectiveness of the procedure and only increase the likelihood of fatal delay in starting or of ineffective application. The possibility of infection may be a legitimate objection to frequent or extensive practice of the method, but fortunately most individuals can do it prop-

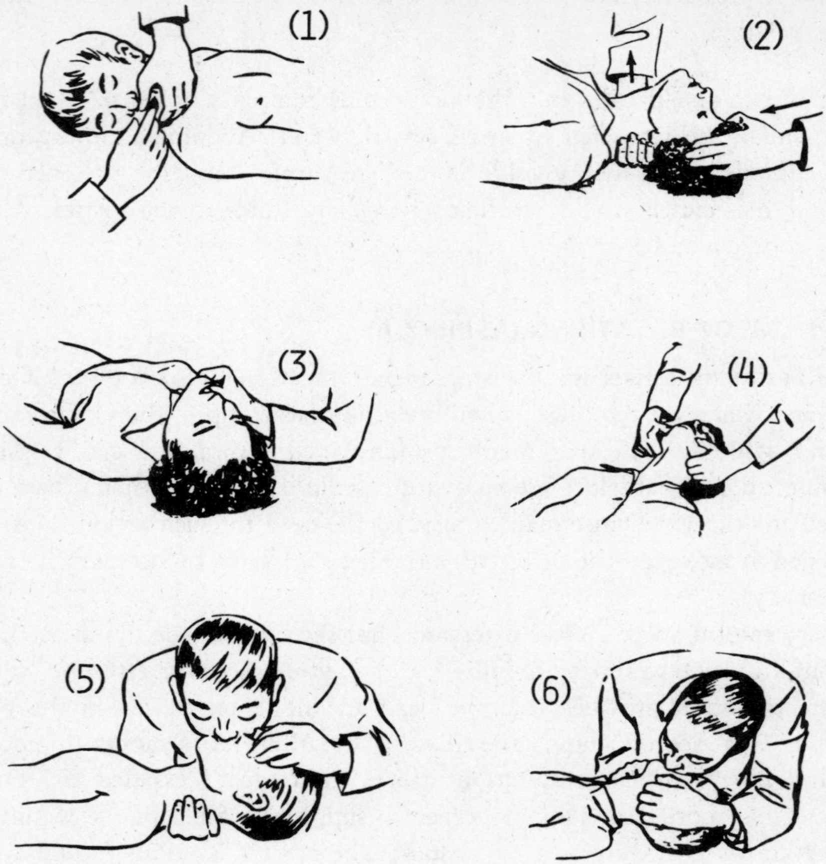

FIGURE 73. MOUTH-TO-MOUTH RESUSCITATION
(Figures 73 & 74 used by courtesy of the American Red Cross)

erly after instruction and very limited trial. Manikins for safe and realistic practice are available, which solves the problem of practice.

The following concise description of the method was combined from the American Red Cross *First-Aid Text* and the American Heart Association *Discussion Guide,* both 1970.

1. If possible, place the victim on a firm, flat surface (do not put anything under the shoulders or let the head hang over an edge), preferably with the lower extremities higher than the head. Remember that the head and neck position in relation to the body is essential and can be achieved properly under any conditions, even when both victim and operator are in the water. Turn the head to one side and clear the mouth of any regurgitated food or foreign material. This may be accomplished by opening the mouth with one hand and inserting one or two fingers to sweep the material from the mouth as shown in Fig. 73, No. 1.

(7) (8)

FIGURE 74. EXAMINATION OF MOUTH AND REMOVAL OF OBSTRUCTION
Jaw is held forward by finger in mouth to permit examination (7), followed by attempt to remove obstruction (8).

2. Tilt the victim's head backward as far as possible to provide an open airway. This may be accomplished by lifting the neck close to the head with one hand and pushing the forehead with the palm of the other, the neck is extended and the airway straightened. This action serves to "jut" the jaw as shown in Fig. 73, No. 2. The palm so placed on the forehead puts the thumb and forefinger in position to pinch-seal the nose. Alternate straightening and opening of the airway can be achieved by pulling or pushing the lower jaw into a jutting position as in Fig. 73, Nos. 3 and 4.

   Opening the airway way promote voluntary breathing. Watch for rise and fall of the chest, listen for sounds of exhalation, or feel the exhaled air against your cheek or ear. If no respiration is detected, start breathing for the victim as follows:

3. With the head tilted back, jaw jutted forward as described and illustrated in Fig. 73, No. 5, pinch the nostrils closed, or close the nostrils with your cheek. Take a deep breath, open your mouth wide and place it tightly over the victim's mouth and blow. Observe to see that the chest rises. Following the rise of the chest, remove your mouth, maintain the "jutted" jaw and extended neck condition, observe the fall of the chest. This is the exhalation phase caused by natural relaxation of extended chest muscles. If the expansion and contraction of the chest occurred, repeat the process at a rate of once every five seconds (12 times per minute) for adults. Infants and small children will require that the inflation or expansion phase be restricted in volume but increased in rate up to 20 times per minute. If resuscitating a baby or small child, the neck and jaw position straightening the airway must be maintained. The nose and mouth can be covered by your mouth or the nose sealed by your cheek. Inflation is controlled relative to the size of the victim. A slight puff may be all that is necessary to obtain inflation.

If inflation does not occur, or is inadequate and difficult to attain, the jaw and neck position should be rechecked and the mouth examined for any obstruction without delay. Having corrected position and cleared the mouth, renew the effort to inflate the lungs.

If regurgitation of water or stomach contents occurs, the head should be turned to the side to permit drainage so as to prevent forced aspiration of foreign material into the airway. If, after checking the jaw and neck position and clearing the mouth, obstruction is still present the victim should be rolled to the side and a sharp blow or blows delivered between the shoulder blades as shown in Fig. 74, Nos. 7 and 8. During the foregoing operations, care should be exercised to maintain the open airway. Even with the victim turned on the side, the resuscitator can effectively function from behind by leaning over the victim.

4. If conditions exist which do not permit the preceding mouth-to-mouth procedure, mouth-to-nose resuscitation may be accomplished. The jaw may be jutted forward by placing fingers under the chin and lifting the jaw upward and forward. The thumb and forefinger may be used to seal the mouth. This jutting of the jaw may be assisted by the other hand lifting at the angle of the jaw as shown in Fig. 73, No. 6. The mouth covers the nose and nostrils and the inflation is performed at the same rate as in the mouth-to-mouth. Remember to keep the jutted jaw, open airway position throughout the process of inhalation and exhalation.

Every diver should be familiar with Rescue Breathing and should, when possible, practise applying it under a number of circumstances. The rescue of an unconscious non-breathing diver or swimmer may be made at quite a distance from shore. Resuscitation efforts should be started as soon as the victim has been brought to the surface. The vest of the victim and/or the resuscitator should be inflated, weight belt or belts should be dropped, if necessary, to promote positive buoyancy. The resuscitator, supported by the inflated vests, should experience little difficulty in attaining the required head and neck position and performance of mouth-to-mouth or mouth-to-nose resuscitation. Experimentation will disclose that the procedure may be performed and progress made toward shore or base. See Fig. 75, Nos. 1, 2, 3. Similar efforts may be performed using an inner tube, surf board, or the side or stern of a small craft as a supporting medium. See Fig. 75, Nos. 4, 5, 6. Regardless of the flotation used, it must be remembered that the mouth must be cleared and the aforementioned open-airway position maintained. This is critical for an unconscious victim, while almost any position of a similar nature will work on a conscious "volunteer" victim.

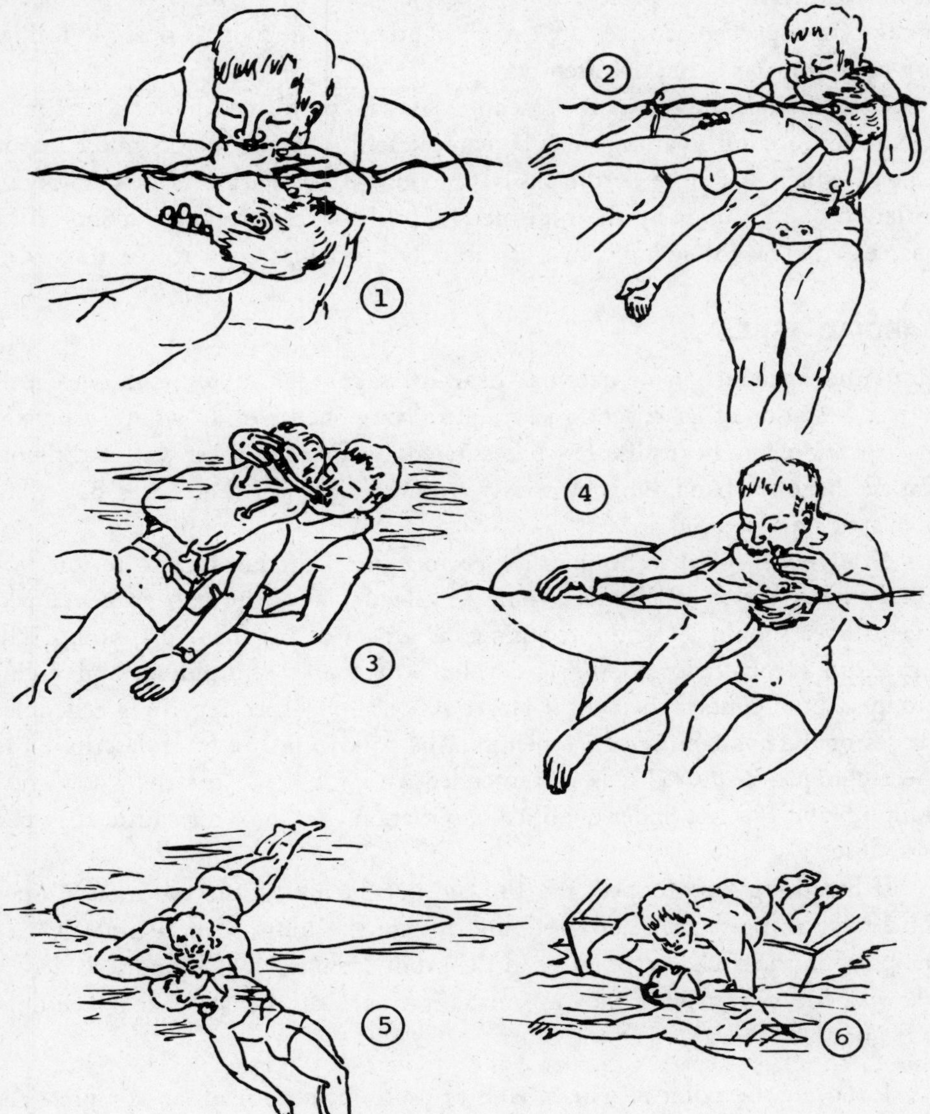

FIGURE 75. RESCUE BREATHING IN WATER

Nose pinch and neck lift with vest inflated (1). Head back and cheek seal; forearm levels (2). Snorkel airway; fingers position snorkel, seal lips and jut the lower jaw (3). Tire-tube float—tube serves as neck support (4). Surfboard support (5). Boat support (6).

The victim should be observed closely after revival and kept quiet, lying down, with body heat preserved (insulation under and over). By all means, obtain (transport to, if necessary) medical attention as soon as possible following or during resuscitation attempts.

Even though resuscitation procedures may be performed in an expert manner, restoration of breathing may be complicated by other factors, most important of which is failure of the heart function. Resuscitation efforts involving inflation of the lungs by the oral method will not restore heart action which has ceased. The following course is the only procedure open to the rescuer.

CARDIAC ARREST

Until the introduction of external heart-massage (cardio resuscitation) techniques, cessation of heart action (a frequent consequence of drowning, asphyxia, electrocution, and heart disease) necessitated opening the chest wall and pumping the heart by hand. This obviously required a physician and was not a layman's first-aid technique.

Now, nonsurgical techniques for performing heart massage to restore voluntary heart action or produce some blood circulation have been developed. Every diver should learn the technique as a part of his first-aid training. The American Heart Association has developed a course of training, and diving groups should contact their local Heart Association office regarding scheduled classes or the availability of instructors. The following is a brief description of the technique. *Note:* This is not intended as a substitute for the knowledge, training, and practice-under-qualified-observation necessary for satisfactory performance.

If breathing has stopped, the first-aid person must clear the mouth, open the airway as previously described, and inflate the lungs several times. Check the pulse in the neck (carotid) or in the groin (femoral). If no pulse is detected, with the victim lying face up on a firm surface, the following technique is begun:

1. Locate the point at which hand pressure must be made to compress the chest and heart. Feel the lower half of the breast plate to the point at which it ends. The pressure point is centered on the lower half of the breast plate just above its soft lower end where it meets the abdomen (about three fingers width). Pressure must be applied here and nowhere else to be effective and prevent damage. This is extremely important.

2. The resuscitator positions himself at either side of the victim. The long axis of the heel of one hand is placed on the long axis of the breast plate at located pressure point. The other hand is placed atop the first, fingers not touching the chest. The resuscitator positions his body so that as

the shoulders are moved forward his body weight will be exerted downward on the pressure point.

3. Firm, heavy pressure is applied through the heel of the contacting hand as the resuscitator brings his shoulders directly over the hands (required pressure for an adult is between 80 and 120 pounds). Pressure required to achieve desired compression (about 1½ to 2 inches) will vary with the anatomy of the victim. Compression is held for about a half second and then rapidly released. Each compression phase must result in maximum depression to achieve heart pumping action. Anything less will not be adequate.

   Artificial circulation must be repeated at least once each second and may be applied at an even faster rate (60 to 80 times per minute). Slower rates will be ineffective. Rhythmic compression and release can only be interrupted for a few seconds.

4. If there is only one resuscitator available to administer both cardiac and pulmonary resuscitation, the cardiac compressions must be started immediately following several inflations of the lungs by the oral method. Fifteen compressions are made at 1 per second, then two quick inflations of the lungs are completed. This cycle (15 to 2) must be continued until help is available.

   When two persons are performing heart and pulmonary resuscitation five chest compressions are made at the one-per-second rate. Then one lung inflation is made by the second operator. This cycle must be continuous, even during transport to medical facilities.

The foregoing brief description should impress divers with the necessity for being taught and trained to perform the combined resuscitation procedures necessary in the event of cessation of breathing and of heart action. Recognition of the need for knowledge of what-to-do-and-how-to-do-it until professional care is obtained may save a life which would otherwise be lost.

The victim must be transported as soon as possible to adequate medical facilities. A suitable vehicle must provide a firm surface for the victim and sufficient room for the first-aid person or persons to continue resuscitation efforts throughout the transport.

The combined techniques of resuscitation of breathing and heart action are referred to as Cardio-Pulmonary Resuscitation (C.P.R.). Complete working knowledge and training should be regarded as essential by every diver. Attempts by untrained persons may be useless and may result in further injury.

WOUND CARE

Aside from bleeding control, which has been discussed, here are a few general directions for the care of wounds. Following these will greatly reduce the chance of infection and add to the comfort of the victim, as well as making the later medical attention less complicated.

1. Whenever giving first-aid care to any opening in the skin the first-aid person should have clean hands.
2. Soap and clean water (preferably boiled) may be used to cleanse the area of the wound. Care must be exercised to prevent dirt or foreign material from entering.
3. If the wound will receive further care by a physician, it is best that no antiseptic be applied. Consult your doctor concerning antiseptics to be placed in first-aid kits.
4. Cover the wound with a sterile dressing, and bandage in place snugly but not so tightly that circulation is impaired.
5. Even in minor wounds, if any sign of infection appears (redness, swelling, pus) bring it to the attention of a physician.

PREVENTION OF TETANUS

Tetanus (lockjaw) is a commonly fatal disease caused by germs found in soil, dirt, mud, and elsewhere. These germs enter the body through a break in the skin. Minor wounds, particularly punctures, can be dangerous if sustained where contamination is at all likely; this makes it mandatory that the victim be protected against the disease. This is certainly true of divers injured in mud or dirty water. There are two methods of protection: use of *tetanus antitoxin*, which requires several injections at the time of injury and can cause troublesome reactions; and the use of *tetanus toxoid*, which seldom causes any difficulty. Tetanus toxoid is given as a routine immunization, and most people have had it either as children or as members of the armed forces. If the individual has received a "booster" *within three years,* all that he needs to be given at the time of injury is a small additional dose. Unfortunately, very few adults keep their boosters up to date and, if injured, must receive the antitoxin instead. Very few divers are aware of the danger of tetanus in underwater injuries. A sensible diver will get the protection of tetanus toxoid immunization and will apply for the additional dose if he is injured on land or in the water.

Since much diving water is contaminated to some degree, divers are also exposed to all waterborne diseases, including polio. It therefore makes good "safe diving sense" to see your doctor and make sure that all your immunizations (which everyone should have, anyhow) are up to date.

FRACTURES

First aid for fractured bones consists mainly of careful handling (or no handling, unless necessary) so as not to increase the injury. If the victim must be moved or transported other than in an ambulance under expert supervision, the fracture should be immobilized. Using whatever *suitable* materials are at hand (appropriate length, weight, and strength) for splints; apply these in such a manner as to keep the broken bone ends from moving and at the same time prevent movement of the adjacent joints. Careful transportation and treatment of shock are essential.

BURNS

First aid for burns is dependent on the degree and the amount of area involved. Burns are classified as:

First Degree—reddening of the skin.
Second Degree—blisters.
Third Degree—charring or deep destruction of tissues.

Pain of burns involving less than 20% of the body surface may be greatly reduced by immersion in clean, cold water (preferably ice). If immersion of the area is not practical, ice-cold wet applications may be used. Immersion or packs should continue until pain is eliminated.

Regular burn care should follow ice-water immersion. The area should be covered with a sterile pad bandaged firmly in place and of sufficient thickness to exclude air.

A small first- or second-degree burn may be cared for by the application of a medically approved preparation and a sterile dressing.

The commonest type of burn suffered by divers is sunburn. Long exposure, both in and out of water, has taken all the pleasure out of many a well-planned and well-executed diving trip. Gradual tanning may be accomplished by an initial short exposure, which is increased daily until the desired protective pigment layer has been built up. Shielding the skin with light clothing or applying tanning lotions or creams will prevent painful or even serious burns.

Shock care is imperative when large areas of any degree are involved and shock is generally a threat even where relatively small areas have suffered third-degree burns. Since infection and other complications may be involved, the attention of a physician should be sought.

FIRST AID FOR DIVER AFFECTED BY CHILLING

Symptoms are mentioned in Chapter 3, along with a warning to avoid being so affected. Loss of tactile sense, loss of muscle control, and uncontrollable shivering may progress to complete inability to function, with a loss of consciousness. Indicated first-aid care is prompt removal from water to an adequate outside heat source such as a bonfire or a heated enclosure. Merely wrapping in blankets or drinking hot liquids will not suffice.

Prevention is important. Wear adequate insulating clothing and don't ignore the primary warnings. Get out while you are able.

FIRST AID KIT

A simple metal, or well-constructed box of some moistureproof material, to contain first aid materials should be standard equipment on every dive. The following items are suggested:

1 box adhesive compresses (assorted sizes)
1 pkg. 3-in. x 3-in. sterile gauze pads (individually packaged)
2 2-in. roller bandages
2 large gauze dressings 12-in. x 12-in. (sterile)
2 or 3 triangular bandages
1 pair scissors
1 pair tweezers
1 dowel ½-in. x 6-in. for tourniquet use
1 box or plastic container of baking soda
1 bottle of aspirin (5 gr. tablets)

Antihistamine tablets and ointment (obtainable without prescription) Meat tenderizers containing papaya extract, dissolved in water and applied locally, have been successfully used to allay the discomfort of some coelenterate stings (jellyfish and man-of-war).

Injuries From Contact With Marine Life

It would be virtually impossible to cover all the injuries possible and their care in a manual such as this. Many books, research papers, and technical reports available are the product of patient, trying, and costly experiments and research compiled by scientists, professional divers, and amateurs.

The following information is a general coverage for first aid which may be administered by the diver with subsequent attention by a physician:

TABLE XVI

MARINE-LIFE INJURIES—CAUSE AND TREATMENT

Cause	*Prevention*	*Symptoms*	*First Aid*
Marine Plants	Avoid fast, entangling movements.		Move straight up to surface. Look for clear spot. Drop straight down and swim to clear area. Repeat till clear of plant bed.
Coral	Wear shoes, gloves protective clothing around coral. Avoid contact, be especially careful of surge effects toward coral heads.	Cuts, abrasions, welts, pain, and itching. Severe reactions are not usual.	Rinse area with baking soda solution, weak ammonia, or plain water. Apply cortisone or antihistamine ointment. Antihistamine may be given by mouth to reduce initial pain and reaction. When initial pain subsides, cleanse the area with soap and water, apply an antiseptic, and cover with sterile dressings. Severe cases or those not responding readily should be referred to a physician.
Sea Urchin	Avoid contact. Spines will penetrate most forms of protective covering.	Often immediate and intense burning sensation followed by redness, swelling, and aching. Weakness, loss of body sensations, facial swelling, and irregular pulse may be noted. Severe cases involving paralysis, respiratory distress, and even death have been noted.	Remove as many spines as possible with forceps (tweezers, pliers). Cleanse the area and cushion with large, loose dressings. If signs of infection appear, seek medical attention promptly.
Cone Shells	Avoid contact with soft parts of the animal.	Puncture wound. Reduction of blood supply (cyanosis). Stinging, burning sensation at first. Numbness, abnormal sensation begins at wound and spreads rapidly. In severe cases: paralysis, respiratory distress, coma, heart failure.	No specific care. Remove from water immediately. Keep lying down. Get medical attention as soon as possible. See section on first aid for venomous fish sting (general).
Jelly Fish (Coelenterates), Sea Nettles, Portuguese Man-of-War, Sea Wasp	Be alert—avoid contact. Wear protective clothing when present, also on night dives. Avoid whole or partial "dead" parts either in or out of water.	Variable, according to species. Vary from mild stinging to intense burning, throbbing, or shooting pain; may be accompanied by unconsciousness, reddened skin, welts, blisters, swelling, skin hemorrhage. In some	Obtain buddy assistance and leave water. Remove tentacles and as much of stinging material as possible, with cloth, seaweed, or sand. Avoid spreading. Apply weak ammonia solution saturated solution of baking soda in water or fresh clean water.

TABLE XVI—*Continued*

Marine-Life Injuries—Cause and Treatment

Cause	*Prevention*	*Symptoms*	*First Aid*
		cases, shock, cramps, loss of tactile senses, vomiting, paralysis, respiratory difficulty and convulsions, and death. The SEA WASP has caused death within several minutes.	Apply cortisone or antihistamine ointment. Anesthetic ointment to relieve pain. Obtain medical attention as soon as possible in severe cases. If the Portuguese Man-of-War or Sea Wasp is the cause, medical help is essential.
Octopus	Avoid being trapped by tentacles. Porous clothing will hinder action of cups. To prevent bite, avoid mouth area at tentacle origin.	Beak bites (two) produce stinging, swelling, redness, and heat. Bleeding out of proportion to size of wound.	Apply cold compresses. Keep lying down, feet elevated. Get medical attention as soon as possible if bitten. No specific care other than bleeding control if profuse.
Sting Rays	Avoid stepping on in shallow water. Shuffle fins to scare away. Avoid contact with barb at base of tail.	Pain within 4 to 10 minutes. Fainting and weakness. Pain increases and may affect entire limb within 30 minutes. Pain maximum in 90 minutes. Wound may be of puncture or laceration type.	Remove from water immediately. Wash with sterile saline solution or cold, clean water. Remove remaining portions of barb sheath. Soak in plain hot water for 30 minutes. Hot compresses may be used if soak is not practical. Get medical attention promptly if wound is in chest or abdomen or if symptoms do not subside with heat application.
Venomous Fish: Horned Sharks, Catfish, Weeverfish, Scorpion Fish, Rabbit Fish, Ratfish, Toadfish, Zebra Fish, Surgeonfish, Stonefish	When diving in unfamiliar areas, consult local divers or appropriate information source regarding existing harmful marine life native to the area.	Variable with type and contact. Usually of puncture type but may be lacerations. Poison introduced by spines causes redness, swelling, pain, general malaise, muscle spasm, respiratory distress with convulsions, and death in severe cases.	Three objectives of care are to: (1) alleviate pain, (2) combat effects of venom, (3) prevent secondary infection. Remove from water immediately. Irrigate with clean, cold water. Make small incision across the wound, apply suction. Soak in water as hot as can be tolerated (without scalding) for 30 to 60 minutes. Epsom salts added to water may be beneficial. Further cleansing should be done after soaking. Obtain medical aid as soon as possible. Ice-water treatment has not been included because of impracticality at average divesite.

TABLE XVI—*Continued*

Marine-Life Injuries—Cause and Treatment

Cause	*Prevention*	*Symptoms*	*First Aid*
Bite Wounds: Shark, Barracuda, Moray Eel, Orca, others	Avoid attracting the predators. Swim quietly while surveying the underwater area. Avoid wearing shiny equipment or sun reflecting on face plate when predators are near. The best prevention is to get out of the water when possibly harmful fish are present.	Serious lacerations from curved bite of shark, straight bite of barracuda, and jagged combination of puncture and laceration by moray eel usually cause severe bleeding, loss of tissue, and extreme shock.	Control serious bleeding by whatever method or methods are possible, immediately. Remove from water immediately. Treat shock and get medical (surgical) aid as soon as possible. Remember loss of blood can be deadly in a short time, and only immediate control can prevent death.
Sea Snakes	Avoid handling or contact with netted specimens. Their reported docile nature may be overrated.	Little local sign at bite area. Toxic signs appear within 20 minutes after bite. Malaise, anxiety, euphoria, muscle spasm, respiratory distress, convulsions, unconsciousness, all signs of shock. Mortality rate, 25 per cent.	Leave water immediately. Place restricting band above the bite so as to slow the venous flow to the heart. *This is not a tourniquet.* Loosen every 30 minutes. Keep victim at complete rest. Get medical aid quickly. If possible, identify the snake (IT MAY NOT BE A POISONOUS TYPE).
Inedible poisonous marine animals (too numerous and variable to list)	Consult local divers, fishermen, state or federal bulletins if planning to dive, spear fish, in unfamiliar area. Seafood edible in one area may be poisonous in another.	Variable. Usually start with tingling about lips and tongue, spreading to extremities. Nausea, vomiting, diarrhea, and thirst are common. Muscular incoordination, numbness, paralysis, and convulsions are not uncommon. Symptoms may occur any time within 30 hours after eating the fish.	Empty the stomach as soon as possible. Large amounts of water (5 or 6 glasses), warm and with salt added, should be swallowed. A touch of the finger on the palate will then usually bring up the stomach contents. More water will aid in cleansing the intestinal tract. If rash or welts appear, and the victim is able, cool showers may give some relief. If poisoning is due to eating clams or mussels, baking soda added to the water is beneficial. Obtain the services of a doctor. Save a small quantity of the fish for analysis and possible aid to medication in severe cases.

Pressure-Related Illness or Injury

The effects of oxygen, carbon dioxide and carbon monoxide, when breathed at higher than normal pressures, were discussed thoroughly in Chapter 3. First aid for conditions brought about by lack or excess of breathing components, unless complicated by stoppage of respiration and circulation, usually consists of rest, fresh air and, if indicated, oxygen. Oxygen poisoning, though unlikely to occur when using open-circuit scuba, may definitely occur if the closed-circuit scuba is employed without compliance with oxygen dive tables. A convulsing diver below, on, or above the surface is hardly a subject for routine first aid and may require expert knowledge and execution by the rescuer and first-aid person. Prevention is the key word. These are less common than some of the other illnesses or injuries due to pressure variance, but merit your acquiring knowledge of cause and effect. Unlike some physical injuries which are readily apparent and require first-aid measures which are a part of the average first-aid course, management of injuries resulting from pressure variance during diving operations is more complex.

The least serious are the variety of squeeze injuries. Little can be done for ear or sinus squeeze since treatment by a physician is necessary. First-aid measures are limited to making the victim comfortable and advising that further diving activities be suspended. Mask and suit squeeze areas respond to cold wet-packs initially and later to warm wet-packs.

Lung squeeze, though certainly serious, should rarely occur in either skin or scuba diving. Unless uncontrolled sudden descent has occurred with insufficient inhalation during a scuba dive, the condition would be difficult to imagine. Deep skin dives (breath-holding) which would approach depths at which lung-air-volume reduction was critical would rarely occur unless of an involuntary nature. Either case would be likely to cause such lung-tissue damage as to preclude any action (first aid) other than rescue from the area of injury and immediate transport to adequate medical attention.

Most serious and, unfortunately, not so rare as the foregoing are the injuries associated with ascent from the dive.

Air forced from the lungs into the surrounding area of the chest cavity may:

—cause collapse of portions of the lungs resulting in much reduced respiratory processes,

—occupy the center of the chest area thereby restricting heart function with resultant circulatory impairment,

—occupy the space at the apex of the cavity in such volume as to constrict the airways enough to preclude adequate respiration.

Determination of these conditions is facilitated if the victim is conscious and able to describe the symptoms and events which preceded the condition.

Here, again, little can be done except to keep the victim quiet, reassured and in whatever position is most comfortable and conducive to improvement of the condition. Body heat should be preserved by adequate insulation over and under the body. Comfortable and immediate transportation to adequate medical facilities must be arranged. Oxygen, if available, may be beneficial.

All of the above—pneumo-thorax, mediastinal emphysema, and subcutaneous emphysema—are caused by continuous or intermittent unvented ascent. Though far from being "not serious" they are the least serious of the ascent-oriented respiratory, circulatory, or central-nervous-system injuries (impairment).

Air embolism and decompression sickness (bends) are the most damaging and require immediate (as soon as possible) recompression if permanent damage or even death is to be averted. Since the symptoms and signs of both are similar, accurate determination of the condition must be influenced primarily by events preceding the collapse, suddenness of collapse, and visual signs indicative of lung damage and/or central-nervous-system involvement. Initial confusion relating to rescue operations or sudden collapse of a diver may delay the amassing of information which will influence the ultimate treatment. If the victim is unconscious or unable to communicate, the first-aid person must make every attempt to learn the history of the dive and the events leading to the collapse so that they may be passed on as accurately as possible to the recompression facility. The signs, symptoms, time elapsed from onset, and first-aid measures instituted must be forwarded with the victim.

The depth and bottom time of dive or dives, the conditions under which the ascent was made (breathing normally or not breathing), scheduled decompression not taken—all are facts to be determined and forwarded with the victim to the recompression facilities. Lay diagnosis is an educated guess of condition guided by events and evaluation of observed signs. Making such a diagnosis or evaluation of condition is a desirable procedure for facilitating treatment and report making, but must not delay transportation to a recompression chamber or to first-aid care. If air embolism or decompression sickness is a possibility, time is an all-important factor. The victim must be transported as soon as possible to recompression and adequate medical attention. Knowledge of the agency to contact for such transportation and the location of the nearest hyperbaric facility capable of handling the probable condition is necessary to every planned dive.

First-aid procedure is to place the victim in a lying-down position, rolled partially toward his left side with lower extremities raised. The mouth should be cleared and the airway opened as in the first step of preparation for artificial respiration. Respiration and heart action are determined immediately and at such intervals as necessary. Equipment should be removed. The wet-suit hood should be removed and the zippers opened to facilitate breathing and circulation. Body heat should be preserved by insulating under and over the body as the ambient temperature demands. If convulsions occur, efforts must include prevention of further injury during the spasmodic motion of the body and extremities. Envelopment in a blanket or similar covering will facilitate control. Attempts to restrict arm and leg movements by hand may be futile or even result in injury to the victim or the first-aid person. If the victim is conscious and rational, reassurance should be given. Cessation of breathing or heart function must be anticipated and must receive immediate care.

BIBLIOGRAPHY

American Heart Association, *Cardio-Pulmonary Discusssion Guide, 1970 —Training of Life Guards.*

American National Red Cross *First-Aid Manual.*

Dangerous Marine Animals, Bruce W. Halstead, M.D. Cambridge, Md.: Cornell Maritime Press, 1959.

Reader's Digest, November, 1960 (article from "Today's Health" in the American Medical Association *Journal*).

Skin Diver Magazine, P.O. Box 111, 11200 Long Beach Blvd., Lynwood, Cal., June, 1961.

Spectrum (New York: Pfizer Laboratories), July, 1960 (Vol. 8, No. 7).

U.S. Navy Diving Manual, NAVSHIPS, 1970. (Out of print.)

8

ENVIRONMENT AND MARINE LIFE

Since approximately three-quarters of the earth's surface is covered by water, both fresh and salt, there is, in most instances, a body of water close to every potential diver. The variety of environmental conditions existing in the earth's waters is noted, studied, and recorded in detail by word and photography in countless volumes. World-traveling divers become veritable storehouses of environmental lore. The new or untraveled diver cannot help envying the broad experience and activity of scientists, explorers, sportsmen and military divers. Yet, it must be remembered that all the experts began, even as you and I, by learning the fundamentals.

No one book, let alone one chapter, can do more than introduce the myriad changes between the land and water environments. Instructors, books, experienced divers, watermen, and guided personal experience will, in time, broaden the basic knowledge set forth here.

The influence of weather, seasonal changes in temperature, water movements, salinity, and marine life will be covered generally in basic form. Knowledge of a specific environment and its influence on diving activity in a given locale must be acquired by consulting available data and by accompanying knowledgeable divers. Observance of safety, local laws, regulations, regard for the rights of others, preservation of nature's balanced community, and upholding a high standard of conduct and performance are all incumbent on a good diver. Respect for and care of our relatively new environment will help to make each entry into it a pleasant and memorable occasion.

Weather

Continuous changes in barometric pressure and air-mass movements bring about a variety of conditions broadly referred to as *weather.* Man has not yet learned to control the elements, but he has done much to analyze and predict the path of, and conditions resulting from, changing atmospheric highs and lows. Divers are not expected to be meteorologists, but should consider predicted conditions (weather forecasts and maps) when planning dives.

Seasonal changes of temperature, probable weather conditions, plant growth, and marine creatures' habits are more or less predictable. Dependent on the earth's climatic zones, weather conditions and temperature (water and air) follow a general pattern for a given area. The pattern, though often interrupted, generally influences seasonal behavior of all living things. The seasonal changes often influence planned diving activities. Temperature variation (air and water) and atmospheric changes create situations of physical importance to the diver.

TEMPERATURE

Variation of water temperature in the oceans and connecting inland seas is far less dramatic than that of air. Divers readily adapt to water temperature variations by wearing appropriate protective suits. Contrary to air temperature variations, water temperature is relatively uniform. The range is from 28.5° F. in the polar regions to 85° F. in some tropical areas. Three-quarters of the sea's surface has a seasonal change of less than 9° F. Since not all diving is done in ocean waters, the diver must consider the temperature conditions which may be encountered in inland bodies of water.

THERMOCLINES

Surface temperature variation in many of the lakes, quarries and rivers often occurs with seasonal weather. Depending on depth and source of water, there may be dramatic temperature variations which, when known, will influence dive planning and choice of protective clothing. These temperature gradients are known as *thermoclines.* Webster's dictionary defines the word as "a temperature gradient, especially one making a sharp change. A layer of water in a thermally stratified lake or other body of water separating an upper warmer, lighter, oxygen-rich zone from a lower, colder, heavier, oxygen-poor zone." This may result in temperature reduction from 75° F. at the surface to as little as 36° F. at the bottom even in quarries or lakes less than 100 feet in depth. If the dive plan involves such a body of water it must obviously include adequate protective clothing along with the diver's awareness of the gradients. Temperature variations in both water and air, either known or anticipated, may be compensated for by wearing suitable garments and exiting to a source of heat if chilling occurs. However, other facets of weather variation may also influence the dive plan. Wind generated by changes in atmospheric conditions has a decided effect on the surface of bodies of water.

Waves

Waves generated by wind, currents, high- and low-pressure atmospheric conditions may drastically alter the surface and bottom contour of dive sites located in the relatively shallow waters adjacent to ocean beaches. Planning dives to wrecks located in such areas should include a study of prior weather and predicted dive-time weather, both local and general. Nothing is quite so disappointing as to find that wave action has all but covered it with sand. Dives

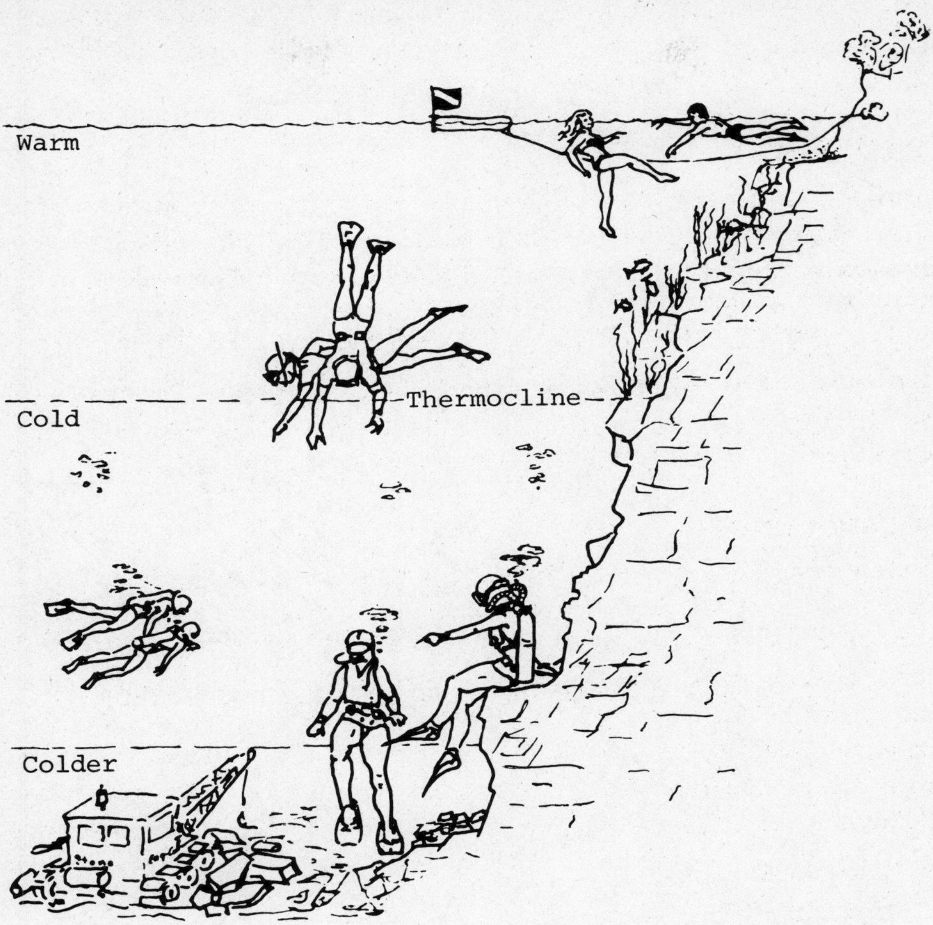

FIGURE 76. THERMOCLINES

planned for visits to offshore deeper sites, where surface-wave action has little or no effect on bottom topography, should still include assessment of weather conditions. Surface travel to and from the site, mooring at the site, entry and exit can be made pretty miserable, if not actually dangerous, by wind and waves. Much more could be written about the effects of weather conditions relative to diving environment. This basic manual can do little more, however, than encourage the new diver to acquire more knowledge from studies made and reported by experts. Since there is so much water and so many possible and probable conditions existing, this manual can only generalize and advise that divers obtain specific knowledge relative to their areas before diving. The following is basic and generalized information:

The formation, structure and action of waves is a study in itself. The surface waves we see and the deeper waves resulting from tides, earthquakes and large displacements of bottom contours influence the diver's environment. Waves

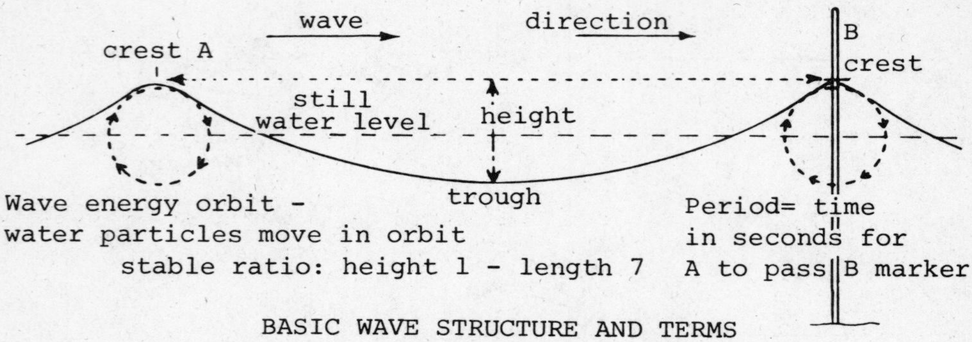

BASIC WAVE STRUCTURE AND TERMS

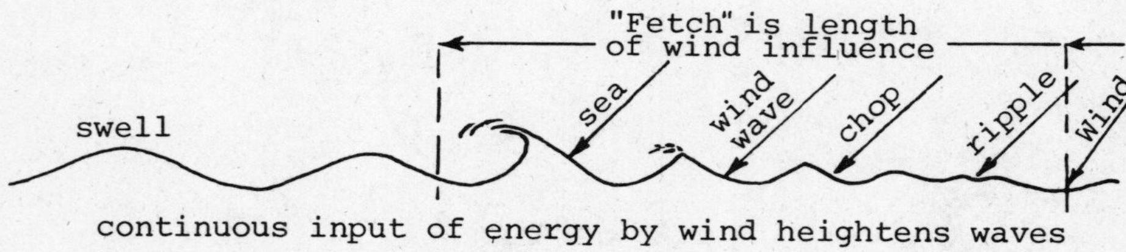

WAVE GENERATION BY WIND (FETCH ABBREVIATED)

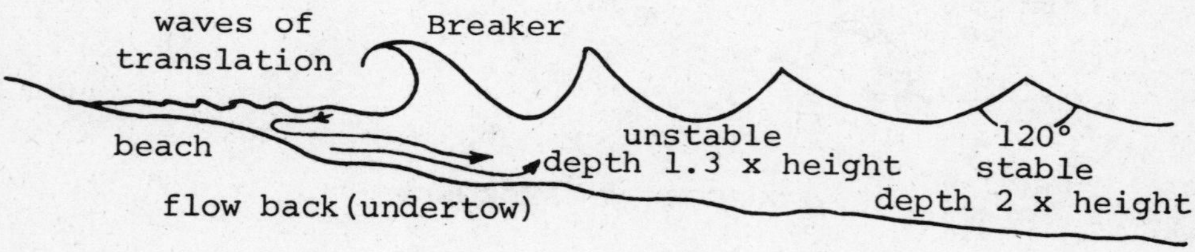

WAVE ACTION ON EVEN SLOPE BEACH

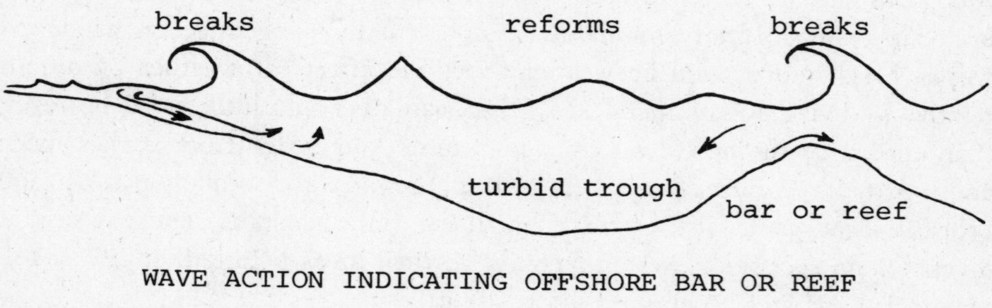

WAVE ACTION INDICATING OFFSHORE BAR OR REEF

FIGURE 77. WAVE STRUCTURE AND ACTION

created by wind are of most importance to sports divers. The accompanying diagrams in Figure 77 should convey a general idea of the anatomy and evolution of the wind-formed wave.

Currents

Entry and exit for shore-based dives should be planned so as to prevent exhausting battles with tidal flows. Remember, a diver's speed generally averages less than one knot. Trying to gain distance against a one-knot current will be an exhausting and losing battle. Work with the current, angling in or out as desired. Keep in mind that a long walk on land is safer than an exhausting swim.

Local peculiarities in current caused by jetties, coves, prominences, reefs, and bars should influence planning for entrance, exit, and activity. The accompanying sketches in Figure 79 will probably make the conditions clearer than could words. This knowledge, coupled with the advice or company of divers having experience in the area, should influence planning and execution.

Regular water flows, such as those caused by rise and fall of tides, should be a part of every diver's environmental knowledge. Tide tables are available for practically every body of water having such a rise and fall of level. Tides are attributed to the influence of the gravitational pull of the moon and sun which cause bulges in the sea's surface. Though not so pronounced in the deeper portions, tidal influence is definitely observable in the more shallow areas adjacent to land masses. Resultant movements of water are anticipated and may influence operational dive plans. Ebb (falling) and flow (rising) of tides is accompanied by slack (no motion). Slack tide is usually within one hour of high or low water. This slack period varies with the tide tables and, even if the timing is accurately determined for a particular tide and activity, the plan should include anchored safety lines, adequate mooring, and secured downstream floats.

Ocean currents along shore (parallel to, or nearly so) can be observed prior to making an entry. Such currents are often wave generated. Waves arriving obliquely to the shore generate a current which runs before them and parallel to the shore (see Figure 79). Determination of such flow should influence entry and exit points so as to prevent exhausting swims against the flow. Observation of water surface prior to entry should be a must for any safety-minded diver. Bottom contour characteristics, currents, wave height and patterns can be determined by visual observation for five or ten minutes before making entry. See Figure 77.

Surface-water movements in rivers and streams can generally be determined by watching floating objects. However, subsurface water movement is often dramatically influenced by bottom contours. Knowledge of such possibilities

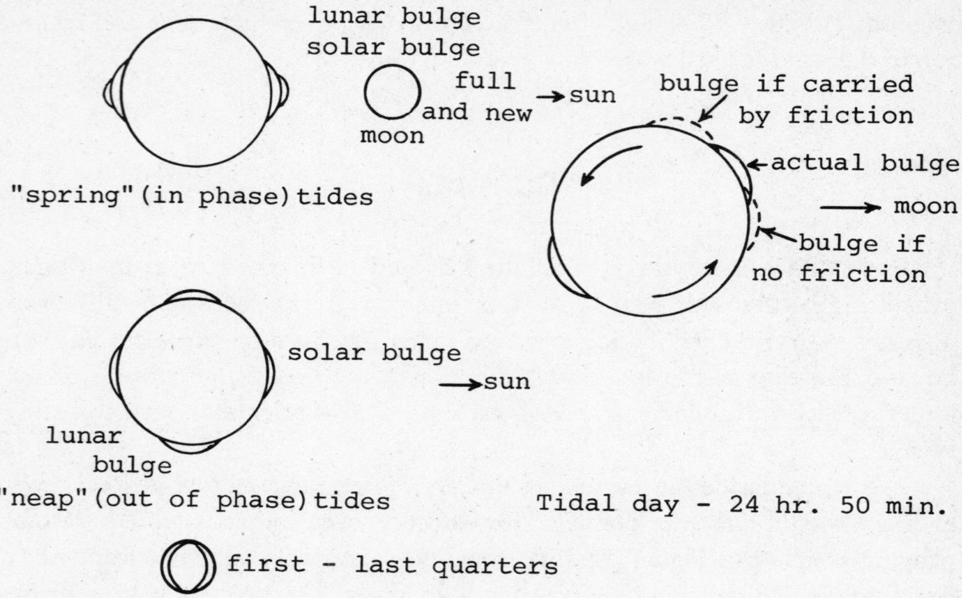

FIGURE 78. SUN AND MOON GRAVITY TIDES

should be obtained from experienced sources prior to diving. If such information is not available, adequate safety lines should be rigged to permit remaining at the proposed site during the dive and to provide direct exit to base.

Water movement near dam spillways, level control valves, or gates (at or below surface) can be quite swift and should be avoided. Attempts to escape from such a flow or eventual pinning against an opening could be exhausting or humanly impossible.

UNDERTOW

Undertow might be more appropriately called back wash or back flow. Water deposited on the beach by breaker action and the resultant waves of translation flows back as indicated in Figure 77. The back flow is shortlived and only extends to the line of breaking waves, usually in no more than waist-deep water. A more definite and sometimes troublesome flow seaward may occur and be detected in areas having an offshore bar or reef.

RIP CURRENT

Perhaps one of the greatest contributing causes to drownings and swimmers in trouble off ocean beaches is the rip current. This particular type of current is caused by water flowing seaward through a gap in a bar or reef, setting up a swirling action inshore leading into a strong current outward which carries the unwary or uninitiated rapidly away from the safety of shallow water. Experi-

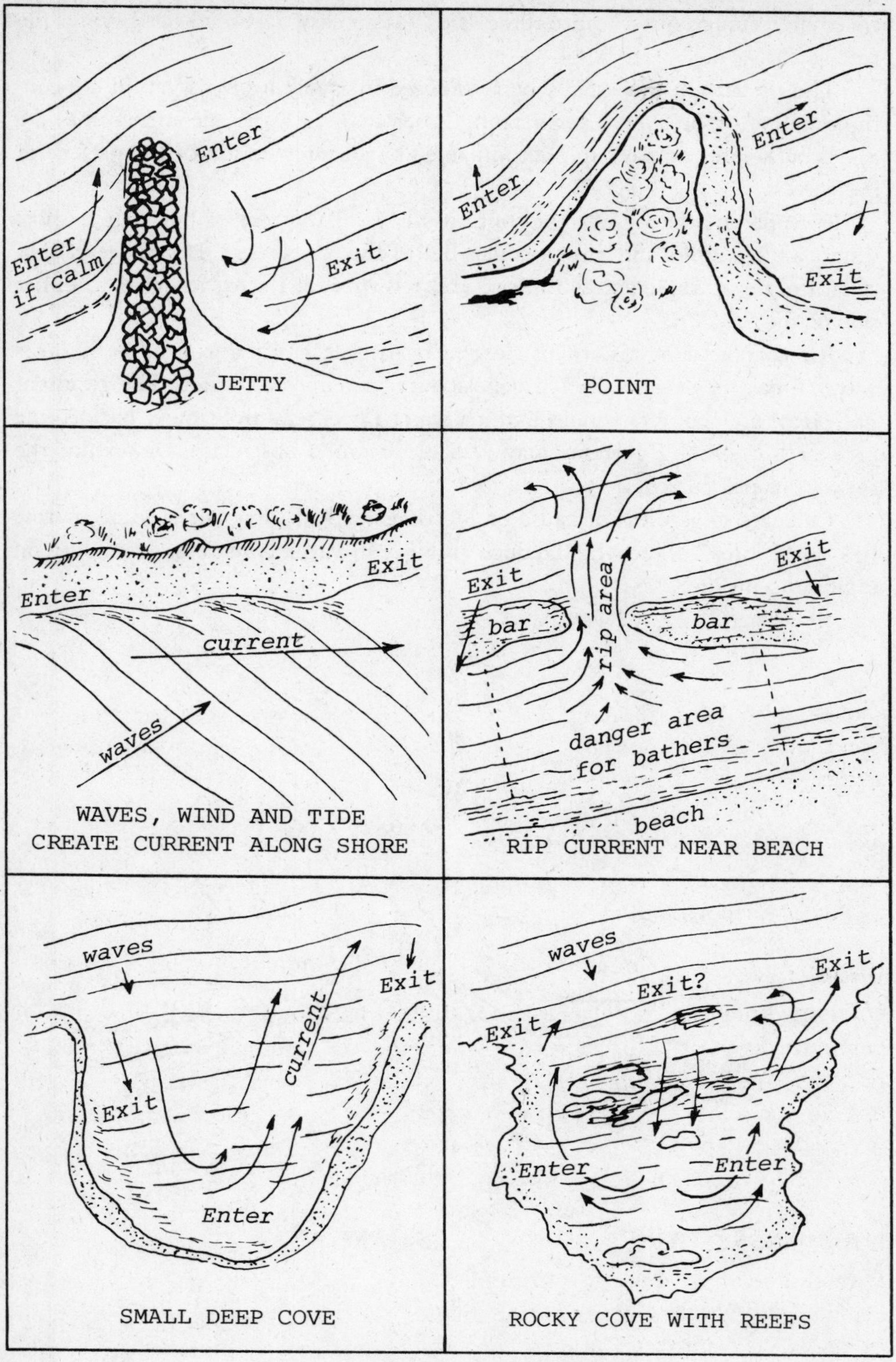

FIGURE 79. ENTRIES AND EXITS

enced divers quite often utilize these "rips" as an easy, fast road out beyond the reef or bar.

The rip current can usually be recognized by watching for a gap in the continuous line of breakers over a reef. Closer inshore some turbulence may be noted in the area of the "rip," accompanied by an interruption of the pattern of the waves.

Fortunately, the rip current continues beyond the reef or bar only a short distance, then splits and disperses parallel to the reef or bar. If you are caught unaware, relax, angle across the rip, and return with the waves well to either side of the "rip."

Rip currents may also occur close in to the beach when exceptionally large waves breaking near the beach deposit large volumes of water. The resultant back flow may cut a channel in which water flows seaward rapidly back to the breaker line. Strong currents may also result when obstructions interrupt the flow of lateral currents.

Currents, regardless of cause or location, tend to carry silt, minute marine life, and debris—all of which reduce visibility in varying degrees, depending on their concentration.

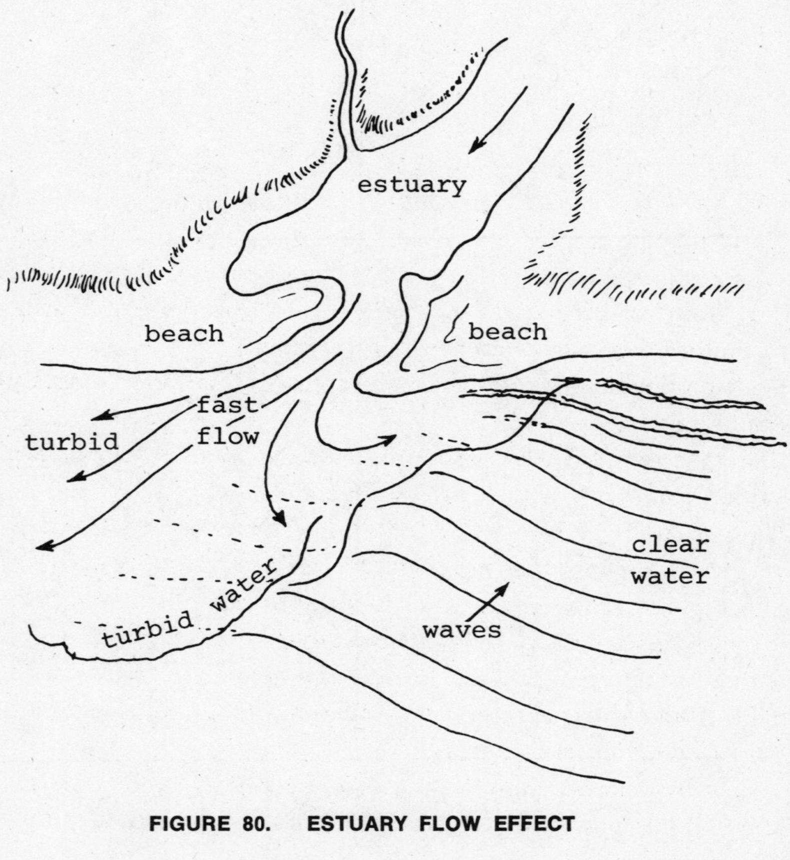

FIGURE 80. ESTUARY FLOW EFFECT

Visibility

Open water and silt-free lakes and streams many times are as clear as glass, but, again, they can become almost as dark as a clothes closet when currents or streams stir up or carry in small particles which bar penetration of light. Harbors, rivers, estuaries, and open water in their vicinity are often near zero in visibility ranges and not conducive to safe diving. Often these murky waters carry products of pollution which could be injurious to the diver. Sharp and jagged metal or glass, old pilings, rocks, and long-abandoned sunken hulks endanger skin and equipment. If circumstances demand diving in water of poor visibility, extreme caution before, during, and after diving should be the order of the day. Guide lines should be used in area searches. Buddies should maintain contact by a short length of line. Waterproof lights should be used. A lookout topside with boat or float and diver's flags to keep surface craft clear is a safety must. It is better to travel a little farther to clear water than to risk injury or infection in dirty, dark waters. Even open water can be dangerous when visibility is poor. Remember there are others in the sea who may mistake you for a choice dinner or an undesirable companion, or may inflict injury merely because you unwittingly touched their protective mechanism.

Entering the Water

Entry made from docks or boats—whether from a ladder, platform, or by one of the step, jump or roll methods—usually presents little difficulty. However, the safety-oriented diver considers water depth, possible obstructions, presence of other divers, and his own preparedness prior to actual entry. Hasty, inadequate preparation may make even the simplest entry complicated or dangerous.

Entries made from shore should be preceded by observation and knowledge of existing conditions, as well as the probable changes which may occur while diving. Having made the decision as to the best entry and exit points, entry is made in such a manner as to prevent loss of equipment and to work with the water action rather than against it. Because of the wide variety of shore, wave, and bottom characteristics existing throughout the world, no one simple plan or method would cover all such entries. The new diver, or even an experienced diver in a strange locale, should rely on the advice and assistance of qualified instructors or divers in that area.

A few basic considerations relative to surf entry from a sandy beach will make initial attempts somewhat more comfortable. Entering through breaking

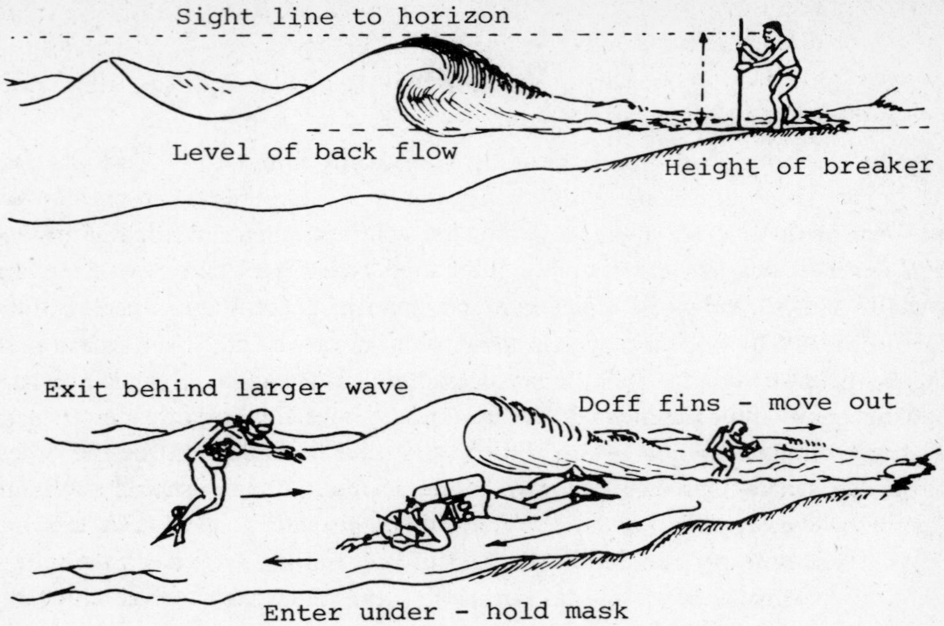

FIGURE 81. ENTERING AND EXITING PROCEDURES

waves while wearing fins, with or without boots or socks (unless boot tops are tight fitting) will usually result in some pretty uncomfortable filling with sand. This will necessitate removal of the collecting equipment once the breaker line is passed. Unless the breaker line is difficult to maneuver through or other equipment is being carried, the entry will be more comfortable if the fins are donned beyond the surf line. The mask should be held firmly to the face when negotiating breaking waves. Timing the entry so as to take advantage of the back flow from the larger waves will assist the passage under a smaller breaker.

So far, the major discussion has been relative to shore-based diving. This seems a logical place to introduce the new diver to open water. However, unless the bottom is rock, coral-covered or such as to provide food and shelter for marine life, the physical acts of diving will not be enhanced by an uninteresting environment. Flat sandy bottoms, barren of plants or fish, leave much to be desired. Inland waters offer a variety of bottom contour and life. Quarries, lakes, rivers, and streams lend themselves to a myriad of diving activities.

QUARRIES

Quarries, with their sharp temperature gradients, often precipitous borders, and depths many times in excess of 100 feet are, in some areas, the only available local spots suitable for scuba diving. Water clarity is variable, ranging from good to poor. Aquatic life may be limited to algae which covers nearly everything. Contact with sides or bottom usually results in clouding of the area to near zero visibility. Since most quarries are private property, permission must be obtained from the owner before use. Indiscriminate trespassing and misuse of such areas has, regrettably, reduced the many available diving areas to a painfully few, or even none, in many cases.

LAKES

Lakes, man-made or natural, often provide an interesting and suitable diving area for both skin and scuba divers. Some are stocked with fish, have a variety of plant growth, varied bottom topography, and in general lend themselves to marine nature study. Here again is the problem of ownership and restrictions. Lakes are often sources of drinking water or stocked for sports fisherman and as such are off limits to divers. Some of our great inland lakes provide nearly as much variety of diving activity as the continental shelf. Newcomers to the lake areas, no matter how experienced, should seek the company and advice of the knowledgeable divers in the area. Storm effect, currents, local laws, restricted or dangerous areas, and advisable technique changes are but a few of the things to be considered in lake diving.

RIVERS

Rivers and streams in populated areas usually offer somewhat less than ideal diving conditions. The water is often turbid and the carrier of many forms of pollutants. Surface traffic adds to the diver's problems, even when the diving area is properly posted with "diver down" flags. Debris often litters the bottom. This makes "dark water" diving somewhat of an obstacle course and, in many instances, a pretty hazardous activity. River diving and mining in streams often involves special knowledge, equipment, and techniques which the basic, and even advanced, diver must acquire from those who are experienced.

Safety Summary

Every body of water, regardless of size or location, presents its own peculiarities and environment. Volumes have been written and will be written by knowledgeable divers in all parts of the world about specific water environments. The basic diver has literally just begun to window shop in this often complicated new world. He starts with safety as the prime objective, moves with caution, and builds skill and confidence as his ability and knowledge increase. The best divers are those who never cease learning.

BUOYANCY CONTROL

Remember that fresh water is less buoyant than salt water. Determine the amount of weight needed in both and remember to change accordingly when diving. Having too little weight with you on a diving trip may present some problems, but being over-weighted in water may call for quick action and some anxious moments before the desired buoyancy is attained with the inflatable vest. A few minutes spent in surface preparation of the weight belt, rather than partial inflation of the vest, will be well spent.

UNDERWATER OBSTACLES

Submerged trees, wreckage, cable, rope, nets, and fish line (particularly monofilament) present entanglement hazards even in relatively clear water. The surge of waves, or careless passage while maneuvering through or around such areas in which this occurs, may result in entanglement and a workout for your knife. Careful and methodical disentanglement or removal with minimum motion gives best results. Areas of poor visibility and possible bottom trash should be avoided as diving sites. Diving is fun; leave the dangerous jobs to the experts.

SURFACE CRAFT

"Stop, look up and listen when ascending" is good practice during dives anywhere. Surface craft users will be unaware of the location of divers unless the area is adequately indicated with diver's flags. Even then the diver must exercise caution because not all surface craft operators know the meaning of the flag. Avoid diving in areas of surface craft travel. Maintain a plainly visible surface safety and lookout man. Post the area adequately, stay within the posted area, and obey prearranged sound signals for caution, surfacing, or recall to base.

FIGURE 82. ALERT ASCENT—BUDDY SYSTEM—DIVE BASE

Skin divers must be even more cautious. Delays in ascent are limited in time. Plan for safety, dive the plan, and be able to safely plan again.

SUDDEN STORMS

Some shallow lakes and bays may be rapidly transformed from placid to rough by wind squalls. This makes surface travel difficult. Area divers, residents, and weather maps should be consulted before diving in such areas.

SOFT MUD

Soft mud covers the bottom of many diving areas. Stirring it up will greatly reduce visibility. Sinking into it while working on bottom makes freeing oneself a real job sometimes. A safety line securely attached to a surface craft or float would be a wise precaution for divers working in such an area.

Marine Life

The continental shelf, although partly beyond the reach of the free diver using present-day equipment, supports the abundance of the ocean's available supply of food, the smallest to the largest forms of life.

One-celled plants called *diatoms*, microscopic in size, utilize the silica washed down by the rivers. Other microscopic organisms called *dinoflagellates*, animal larvae, and a myriad of small floating animals which feed on the diatoms are collectively called *plankton*. The plankton is the food of larger sea life, even for some whales and members of the shark family. Most of the inhabitants of the sea feed upon one another, which thereby prevents overpopulation. Thus is established a balanced community in the sea. Man observes this balance and wisely (in most instances), either by law or by agreement, does not upset it. As on land, the variety and abundance of life is determined by environment, temperature, and the availability of food. Even slight temperature changes have a marked effect on sea life; therefore most forms are restricted to certain temperature areas. There are so many varied pursuits open to divers in the underwater world that each is worthy of further study. Geology, photography, zoology, marine biology, archaeology, spear fishing, treasure hunting, or just plain sightseeing are full-time paying jobs for many. Whether professional or amateur, all would be wise to become acquainted, through research, with the creatures of the underwater world.

This chapter can only begin to present some of the vast storehouse of knowledge available to the interested diver. As before, the following descriptions, though perhaps not in the order of importance to many, will serve as basic background for study.

Rather than attempt to introduce all the undersea creatures, only those considered to be harmful to the diver will be covered. Some are nonaggressive and only cause injury when their defensive mechanism is contacted by accident or through ignorance. Others, by nature of their habits, may be aggressive and a threat to the safety of the relatively defenseless stranger in their underwater world.

RAYS

The ray family, though not all venomous or equipped with specialized defense mechanism, comprises a large portion of the harmful sea creatures. They are possessed of a cartilaginous skeleton and, for the most part, feed on plankton and crustaceans. The larger forms, such as the manta ray, are rarely seen by the average diver. The smaller forms are so numerous in species that discussing all would not be feasible in this text. Since it is responsible for numerous injuries to divers reported annually, the *sting ray* will receive some attention. Most of these can be found in relatively shallow water. Since they are bottom feeders, they may be observed lying on or partially submerged in the sand or mud with only their eyes, spiracles, and a portion of the tail exposed.

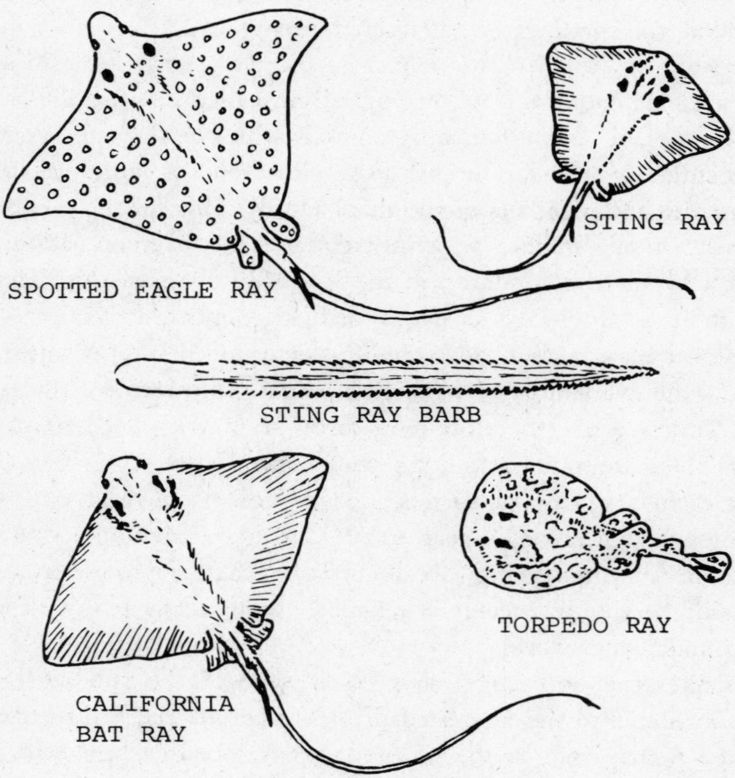

FIGURE 83. TYPES OF RAYS

Their defense mechanism consists of a barb or barbs located on the tail adjacent to its junction with the body. When disturbed or molested, the barb is raised by erectile tissue from its normally flat position. The barb is bony, grooved in the center, sharp, and with serrated edges. It is covered by a thin sheath which retains the venom within longitudinal grooves on the underside of the barb. Even if the sheath is worn away, venomous material may remain in the longitudinal grooves.

Since the sting ray is not aggressive and, by nature, is easily frightened, the diver seeking to avoid puncture by the barb can cause its flight by shuffling his fins on the sand or mud. The sting rays thus disturbed will generally swim a short distance away and again bury themselves in the sand or mud. Since they are difficult to detect in murky water, divers should proceed with caution over the bottom when they are known or suspected of being in the area. Their barb is sufficiently strong and sharp to cause a severe laceration or puncture in the foot, hand or body. The unfortunate diver so injured should exit from the water immediately and receive first aid.

Another species known as the *torpedo ray,* often found on sandy bottom off Northern California, is equipped with an organ capable of giving an electric shock severe enough to stun a large fish.

Despite these defenses, however, the entire ray family is nonaggressive and will avoid contact with the diver when possible.

COELENTERATES

The coelenterates are invertebrates which are dangerous because of their numerous stinging cells. They are grouped into four major categories: hydroids, jellyfish, corals, and sea anemones. The major portion of this group of dangerous or harmful animals is probably coral. Coral exists in practically all the warm waters of the seas.

The coral, with its many brilliant hues and its varied and beautiful formations, is made up of many millions of living and dead polyps of the coelenterate family. Utilizing the calcium deposits in the water, a small shell-like cup is built at the base. This is the living polyp's home. As the polyps reproduce and die, successive layers of these shells are deposited in a variety of formations. Concentration of these coral growths results in the formation of reefs and atolls.

Beautiful as coral may be, it becomes a menace to the diver when contacted with bare skin. Stings and lacerations resulting from contact with coral may vary from annoying to serious. The lacerations and stings must receive first aid and, when necessary, medical treatment. Prevention of such injury should be practiced by avoiding contact or wearing protective clothing and gloves.

Fire coral, often called *stinging coral*, is not a true coral. It is a colony of hydroids called *millepora* which grows among true corals and may be recognized by its bright yellow color and branching colonies.

Portuguese Man-of-War

This is a colonial hydroid. The specialized organisms make up what appears to be a single individual. The stinging cells in the tentacles are particularly dangerous to man since they create extreme pain, partial paralysis, and systemic reactions which may make hospitalization necessary. Having been once stung, a victim may be more seriously affected if stung again.

The Portuguese man-of-war is easily identified by the brilliant, iridescent float which appears above the surface and supports the tentacles that may attain a length of many feet. The float, though usually much smaller, has been known to attain a length of 12 inches and the tentacles may reach lengths in excess of 30 feet. The stinging tentacles, even when broken away from the main colony, should be avoided, since they are still capable of inflicting severe stings.

Jellyfish

These free-swimming coelenterates are quite numerous in rivers, bays and, to a lesser extent, open water during late spring and summer in temperate zones. In the warmer seas these creatures may be found at any time. These jellyfish vary in size from one inch to many feet in diameter, with tentacles streaming down several inches or even feet below their umbrella-shaped body. Since they are capable of moving up and down in the water, they may be found near the surface or quite deep.

Contact with the tentacles of a jellyfish can cause a wide variety of discomforts to the diver. These vary from mild, local stinging to violent systemic disturbance. The latter is rare. Since they are difficult to avoid, especially in limited visibility areas, adequate protective clothing should be worn if their presence is suspected.

The *sea wasp* is an extremely dangerous jellyfish which inhabits the warmer waters of Australia, the Philippines, and the Indian Ocean. An apparently less deadly but closely related form may be found in northern Australia, the Indian Ocean, and the Atlantic Ocean from Brazil to North Carolina (cf. Halstead's *Dangerous Marine Animals*). It may be identified by its dome-shaped bell, which may grow to heights of 10 inches or more, but is usually much smaller. The sting of this species is capable of causing death in less than 10 minutes. Most recently reported in *Skin Diver* Magazine by James Mead is another deadly jellyfish closely resembling the sea wasp but apparently not the same. Mead refers to it as a *box jelly.* This species can be as large as a man's head and transparent, except for a bluish tinge. It originated in the Timor Sea and spread through the islands of southeast Asia and into the tropical waters of Australia.

Sea Anemones

Some sea anemones are capable of inflicting venomous stings which can be harmful to man.

Some other marine creatures which may be harmful to divers when contacted are as follows:

MOLLUSKS

These broadly include clams, mussels, oysters, snails, abalones and cone shells. Though not venomous, with the exception of the cone shell, many have sharp or serrated edges which are capable of inflicting painful and easily infected wounds. Gloves should be worn when collecting any specimens. Some of the mollusks are inedible, particularly in specific areas. This may be determined by consulting local sources of information or Government bulletins. Some of the cone shells possess a venomous stinging apparatus which can produce a variety of systemic effects that in some cases may even result in death.

BARNACLES AND TUBE WORMS

These have hard shells which, in many instances, are sharp and capable of inflicting easily infected wounds when contacted.

SEA URCHINS

These belong to the family of the starfish, sand dollar, and the sea cucumber, but are considerably more dangerous. This spiny burr may be found on the bottom, on and under reefs and wrecks in all warm waters. They are equipped with spines which, in some instances, are long and needle-like. Because of their sharpness, the spines of the sea urchin may penetrate skin or light clothing and often break off. Every effort should be made to extract each spine as soon as possible and the puncture wound should be immediately cared for to prevent infection.

CRABS AND LOBSTERS

Many of these have specialized equipment in the form of large claws for capturing their food. The unwary diver may find himself painfully attached to even one of the smaller species. The larger species are capable of breaking or even severing a finger with their large claws. When attempting to collect these by hand wear heavy gloves and know how to capture your prey lest you be caught instead. Local divers usually develop safe procedures and will generally share their knowledge with you.

OCTOPUS

The octopus has been the villain in many an ancient sailor's tale, with its size greatly magnified and its aggressiveness said to be so great that whole ships were pulled under by its tentacles. Skin divers have found no evidence to support such tales. The octopus is nonaggressive and—except for the largest of the species, which may measure 20 feet from arm tip to arm tip—are usually small, timid, and, because of its nocturnal habits, seldom seen. Handling an octopus should be done carefully so as to avoid the center-placed beak, which in some species secretes a venom that paralyzes its prey.

SQUID

The squid has ten arms, two longer than the others, and, unlike the octopus, swims about. It is capable of inflicting severe bites with its beak when annoyed or caught. Because of its size, the giant squid, which grows in excess of 50 feet, may well be responsible for the atrocities placed at the door of the peaceful octopus.

SCORPION FISHES

The venomous scorpion fishes have been divided into three main groups. Halstead in his *Dangerous Marine Animals* groups these fishes on the basis of the structure of their venomous organs as follows: zebra fish, scorpion fish proper, and stone fish. Zebra fish are beautiful and inhabit coral reefs. The scorpion fish proper are not nearly so beautiful and may be found in a variety of species in practically all the oceans and seas. The stone fish, the most venomous of all, is found along coastal areas in shallow, warm water in the Eastern Hemisphere.

All these fishes are equipped with venomous spines in various numbers in the dorsal, pelvic, and anal fin areas. Due to the extreme effect of the venom, the utmost caution should be exercised when moving about in areas known to be inhabited by these fishes.

SEA SNAKES

The sea snake is usually brilliantly colored with a flattened tail. They may be seen in tropical waters, particularly the Pacific and Indian Oceans. They secrete a venom similar to but stronger than cobra venom. Regardless of their reputed docility, handling and contact with these snakes should be avoided. If bitten, avoid exercise and seek immediate medical help.

SHARKS

Although considered by many experienced divers as not being worthy of the considerable space given it in discussions and descriptions, the shark still remains one of the most popular subjects of conversation during talk of diving by non-divers and new divers. The existence of the technical and nontechnical volumes written about sharks attests to the importance of this creature of the sea. Following is a quote from *Sharks and Survival* which would certainly lend more than just casual coverage to the shark story:

"Probably only a few species have made unprovoked attacks on humans in clear water that does not contain blood or refuse. But in turbulent or murky water, or under conditions in which a man is bleeding or is transporting a

FIGURE 84. TROUBLE AHEAD

wounded fish or is attempting to net, spear, or otherwise capture a shark while in the water, many species are capable of inflicting injury to humans. Even the common nurse shark (*Ginglymostoma cirratum*), which many consider completely harmless, will occasionally bite man."*

The Smithsonian Institute has documented accounts of shark attacks around the world numbering over 1,000 in the last 50 years. The majority of the attacks were on persons in waist-deep (2 to 4 feet) water or who were involved in sea disasters. Relatively few authenticated attacks have occurred involving divers, unless provoked. From available data it appears that most attacks occur during daylight hours between 10 A.M. to 6 P.M. in water of 70° F. or higher. It cannot necessarily be assumed, however, that the night would be less dangerous. Night can even be more dangerous because of greater feeding activity and because the human in water is perceived by the shark by lateral line sense and smell. These shark senses are more acute at night, probably because their night vision is reduced.

* Perry W. Gilbert, ed. *Sharks and Survival* (Lexington, Mass.: D. C. Heath Company, 1963).

Before describing some of the members of the shark family assumed to be most dangerous, it may be advisable to present some preventive measures. The following are expressed as personal opinions in Cousteau's *The Shark*:

"Every species of shark, even the most inoffensive, is anatomically a formidable source of potential danger.... The youngest sharks—and therefore the smallest—are the most brazen. Even a small shark, two feet in length, can inflict dangerous wounds.

"Sharks race in from great distances to devour any fish in trouble. They can perceive the fish's convulsive movements by the rhythm of the pressure waves carried to them through the water. At a short distance, sharks are also extremely sensitive to odor, and particularly to the odor of blood. For both these reasons, underwater fishermen should not attach their catch to their belt."*

A buddy team, when confronted by sharks, can best keep sharks in view and achieve protection by working back-to-back. Although many measures have been put forth to prevent attack, such as striking the water forcefully, shouting under water, directing a stream of bubbles, or banging on air tanks, their collective worth is questioned by many authorities. A solid object two or three feet long, such as a shark billy, may provide effective protection against the shark. The end of the shark billy should be studded with short points or nails so as to prevent slipping off the shark's skin. It serves the purpose of repelling the shark and, at the same time, increases the distance between the diver and the shark. In order to avoid any defensive reaction, the shark billy should not be used with the intent to strike or wound the shark.

The best protection lies in ease of movement when diving, swimming slowly and softly, and avoiding any abrupt change of position. Observe the area behind and to the extreme sides. Do not try to outswim a shark. Face the menace, extend the shark billy and, when possible, keep the shark in view while you quietly retreat to your boat. If there is blood in the water from speared fish or from human injury, leave the water immediately. Also, do not carry speared fish close to your body. Tow your catch on a minimum of 20 feet of line or, better yet, remove it from the water immediately.

There are 250 or more identified species of shark. Because of their variety, size, distribution, and unpredictable behavior, no hard and fast rules can be given for handling an encounter with a shark which apply in every case. Remember that all sharks, even the smallest, possess the ability to inflict harm, with or without provocation.

Here are some brief descriptions of the better known sharks:

White Shark. Length: 30 feet. Black or slate gray dorsally and white on the belly, but may occur as leaden white entirely. Feeds on large fish and turtles. Generally found in temperate seas in deep water, but often comes into shallow

* Jacques-Yves Cousteau & Philippe Cousteau, *The Shark: Splendid Savage of the Sea* (New York & Garden City: Doubleday & Co., 1970).

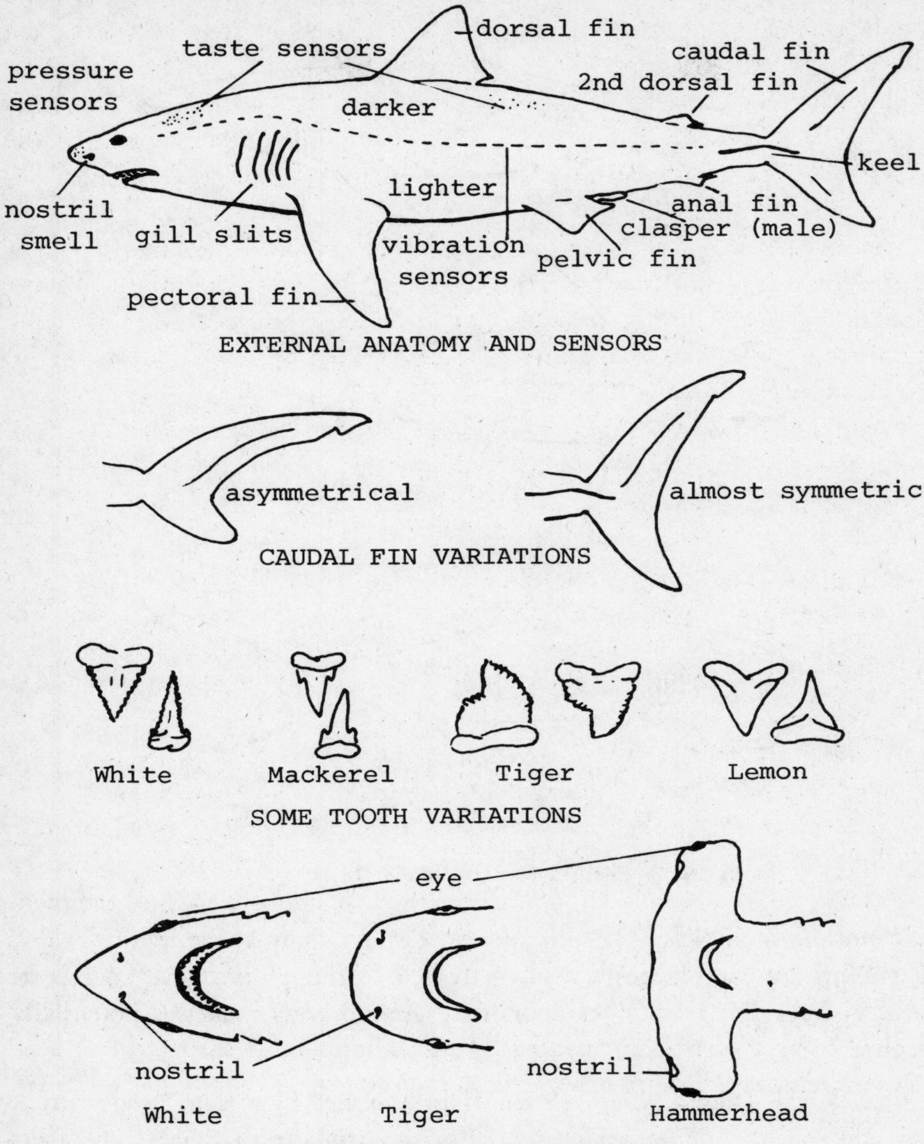

FIGURE 85. THE SHARK—GENERAL INFORMATION

water. Aggressive and considered most dangerous. More attacks on men and boats have been laid to this species than to any other. The majority of these were unprovoked attacks.

White-Tip Oceanic Shark. Length: 11 feet. Bluish gray or brown above, yellowish to white below. Fins are white-tipped and mottled with grey. Has very large pectoral fins. Authenticated reports of unprovoked attack are on record.

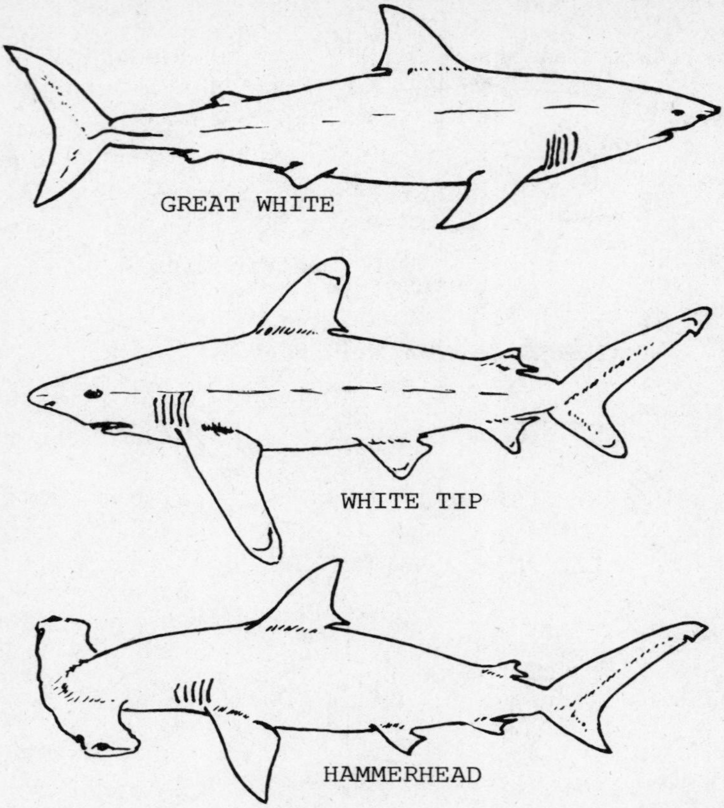

FIGURE 86. SHARKS (1)

White-Tip Reef Shark. Length: 8 feet. Color is gray above, white below, and the fins are conspicuously white-margined. Although we have no reports of attacks from this species, its abundance around reefs makes it potentially dangerous.

Tiger Shark. Length: 12 to 15 feet. Distinguished by a large head, convex snout, and wide overhanging jaws full of sickle-shaped teeth. Smaller members may have conspicuous color patterns on back and fins of dark brown blotches or bars on a gray or gray-brown background. These markings fade with growth so that larger specimens may be patterned on the caudal fin or not at all. This shark ranges throughout tropical and subtropical areas of all oceans, both in-shore and off-shore. It may be found in temperate belts during the summer. There are authenticated unprovoked attacks on record.

Mako Shark. Length: 12 feet. It has a pointed snout and is streamlined and fast. Its color is dark blue or blue-gray above and white below. It has a bilateral keel forward of the caudal fin. There are authenticated reports of attacks on men and on boats.

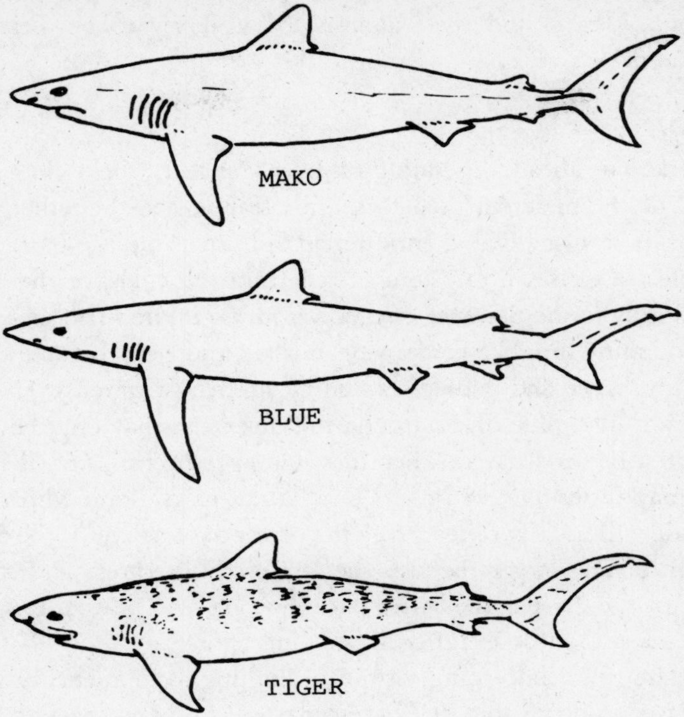

FIGURE 87. SHARKS (2)

Hammerhead Shark. There are several types of hammerhead shark. The largest is known as the *Great Hammerhead* and may exceed 17 feet in length. Hammerhead sharks are found in most warm waters throughout the world. They are easily distinguished by their unusual head shaped like a tack hammer with eyes and nostrils at the outer portion. Because of their nostrils in front of the hammer, they are, if nearby, the first on the scene where blood is spilled. There are authenticated records of unprovoked attacks on men.

Blue Shark. Length: 12 feet. This shark is indigo blue above, lighter on the sides and snow-white below. Found in tropical, subtropical, and warm temperate seas of all oceans. There are numerous authenticated reports of unprovoked attacks on men and on boats.

Black-Tip Shark. Length: 6 to 8 feet. This shark is gray or bronze gray above, white to yellowish below. Fin tips are dusky to black, particularly in the smaller specimens. Occurs in all warm waters of the world. Authenticated reports of attack are meager.

Lemon Shark. Length: 11 feet. Color is varying shades of brown above, paler brown below—sometimes yellowish. Characterized by second dorsal fin almost as large as the first. This species' identified range is strictly inshore in enclosed sounds, bays, and river mouths, New Jersey to northern Brazil in western Atlantic.

BARRACUDA

Next to sharks (or ahead, depending on how you feel) these are probably the most feared of the undersea predators. This fear is not altogether unwarranted. There have been many authentic reports of attack by the barracuda. However, in almost all cases it can be assumed from the evidence that the attacks were due entirely to the presence of blood from an injured fish or a human being, bright or shiny lure-like equipment, mistaken identity because of poor visibility, or disturbance and bubbles caused by surface swimming. The barracuda will swim over, alongside of, or around the diver and may only be tempted to rush in when a fish is speared. Then it is not so respectful, and if the catch is disputed it may easily remove fingers or adjacent parts along with the fish.

Barracuda will usually retreat from the presence of a diver if the diver makes a bold advance. The larger the fish the less easily it scares; and sometimes a slow retreat of the diver is the better part of valor—no headlong, splashy, surface retreat but a slow deceitful back-pedaling type.

Stick to the rules concerning visibility, clothing, equipment, blood, and injured fish. If you don't panic, the barracuda will probably be just another inquisitive member of the underwater population.

There are twenty or more species of barracuda, but only one, the *great barracuda*, is of concern to the skin and scuba diver. Ranging from 3 to 10 feet long, the fish is long and cylindrically built for speed. Its wedge-shaped head (about one fourth of the body length) is half occupied by the knife-edged front and rear grinders. These are displayed almost constantly since the barracuda has

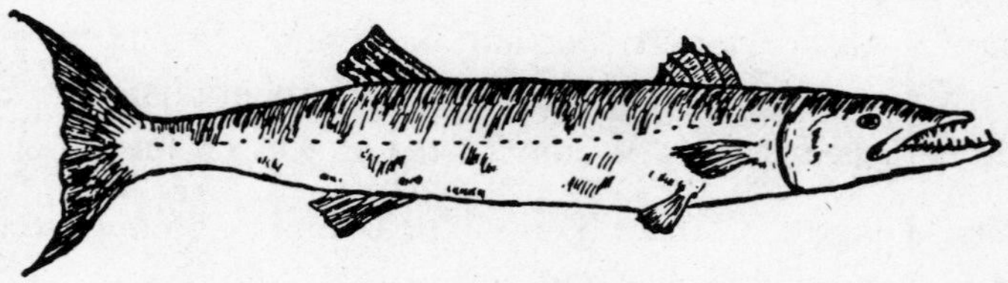

FIGURE 88. GREAT BARRACUDA

two mouth vents which permit it to swim with mouth open. The coloring, though changeable with environment, is usually dark green or blue on top, the sides are silver or yellow, and the belly is white. Dark bars and blotches mark the back and sides. It may be found around wharves, buoys, coral beds, and wrecks, usually near the surface. The range of the great barracuda is the West Indies and the coast of Florida.

MORAY EEL

The six-foot *green moray* is covered with thick, leathery skin. The basic color is bluish slate but this is covered with a yellow mucus thereby blending to green. Some brownish or slate-colored specimens may be observed, because of an absence of yellow in the mucus. They are usually found in holes or crevices of the reefs of the West Indies and Florida Keys.

Three species of spotted morays are found as far north as Charleston, South Carolina. Still another which inhabits deep water may be found as far north as New England. The Pacific moray eel ranges off the southern coast of California.

The moray eel poses no problem to the skin diver unless he carelessly puts his hand into a hole or crevice without first cautiously assuring himself of its contents. If the eel does bite, he is tenacious and capable of producing severe lacerated wounds.

Some of the tropical species are known to be poisonous if eaten. Consult local fishermen and divers as to the edibility of local eels.

AQUATIC MAMMALS

Whales, Dolphin and Porpoises. These aquatic mammals are generally not considered to be a menace to the skin or scuba diver. One of the dolphin fam-

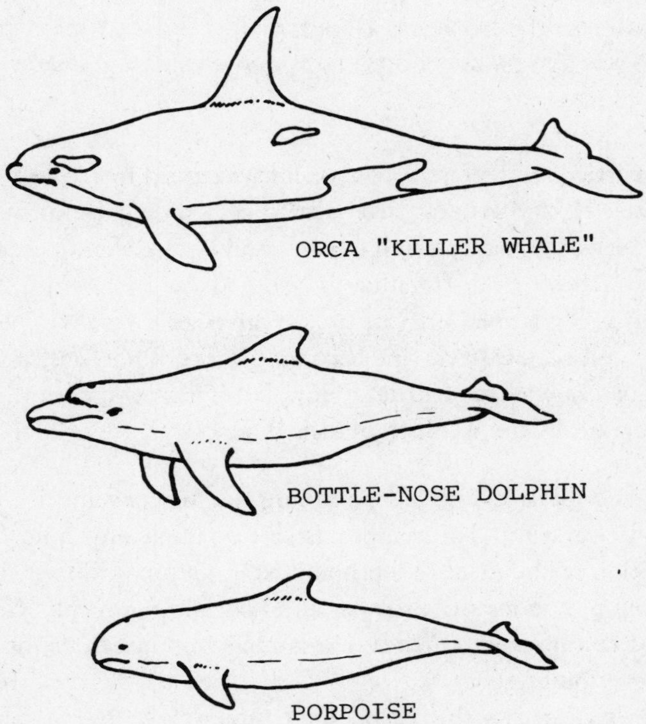

FIGURE 89. MARINE MAMMALS

ily *(grampus orca)*, known as the "killer whale" because of its size and hunting habits, usually in schools, can be a danger, however. They are characterized by a bluntly rounded snout, high black dorsal fins, a white patch just behind and above the eye, and the striking contrast of jet-black color of the head and back with snowy white underparts. Records of their attacks on herds of seal and other large creatures indicate their danger potential. It would be wise for divers to leave the water if killer whales are sighted.

Seals and Sea Lions. Although these animals are not normally a menace to divers, they may be aggressive to the danger point if they are guarding a harem or if the herd is near by. Avoid areas in which there are large groups and stay out of trouble.

PLANT GROWTH

Plant growth in the form of seaweed or kelp, particularly in heavy concentration, can be annoying or even dangerous to the inexperienced or panic-stricken diver. Rising from the bottom, kelp may spread out and cover large areas of the surface. A diver coming up from kelp should keep his hands overhead, part the kelp, look for a clearer area, then drop feet first, and move to the clearer area underwater. Eel grass may be long enough to entangle equipment in heavy surge.

If entangled in either kelp or grass remain calm and methodically disentangle or cut away the plants, drop below, and swim to a clearer area.

FOOD FISH

Food fish of particular interest to the spearfishing skin or scuba diver are so numerous in species and habitat that local divers should be consulted or Fish and Wildlife Service booklets obtained and read before diving so as to comply with custom and law. Also, fish that is good to eat in one area may not be edible in another. A planned activity usually gives best results.

Since skin and scuba divers are becoming more numerous, and many, because of lack of knowledge, will take any fish which becomes a target, there may be an increase in the number of sick diners.

Ichthyotoxism. This is internal poisoning due to consumption of fish, and resembles food poisoning. The symptoms can occur at any time from shortly after consumption of the meal to ten hours later, and may vary in intensity, depending on how poisonous the fish was and how big the meal. Nausea, vomiting, abodminal cramps and diarrhea, even numbness, paralysis, or impairment of the senses may be present.

Since little is known of this particular poisoning, the best treatment is prevention. Consult local sources to ascertain the presence of poisonous species. If symptoms appear, large quantities of water by mouth will help flush the alimentary tract and speed recovery. All cases should be brought to the attention of a physician as soon as possible.

PARASITES

A parasite known as the flat-fish tapeworm has one of its intermediate life cycles in the muscle tissue of the freshwater fish. It can be dangerous to human beings only if the fish is eaten raw. Cooking destroys the parasite.

BIBLIOGRAPHY

Bascom, W. *Waves and Beaches.* New York & Garden City: Anchor Books, Doubleday & Co., 1964.

Cousteau, J.–Y., Philippe Diole. *Life and Death in a Coral Sea.* New York & Garden City: Doubleday & Co., Inc., 1971.

Cousteau, J.–Y., and Philippe. *The Shark.* New York & Garden City: Doubleday & Co., Inc., 1970.

Gilbert, P. W., ed. *Sharks & Survival.* Lexington, Mass.: D.C. Heath & Co., 1963.

Halstead, B.W. *Dangerous Marine Animals.* Cambridge, Md.: Cornell Maritime Press, 1959.

Meade, James, "Killers From Beyond Time," *Skin Diver* Magazine, Vol. 23, No. 1 (January, 1973).

Secrets of the Sea. Reader's Digest Association, Pleasantville, N.Y. 10570.

9

PLANNING A SCUBA DIVE

The simplicity with which scuba can be utilized with only a minimum of essential training by no means reduces the hazards intrinsic in diving. Simplicity of operation is no measure of safety. On the contrary, it tends to develop within the individual a false sense of proficiency which can lead to disaster. The early cultivation of safe scuba diving habits predicated upon sound knowledge of the basic laws pertaining to the physics and physiology of diving is essential to counteract this incipient danger.

Safe scuba diving habits are assured when sound knowledge and good judgment are exercised in planning a scuba dive. Plans need not be elaborate or restrictive but should provide for a systematic means to consider essential elements of diving safety. The essential elements are those which determine whether or not a scuba dive can be conducted without endangering human life. The purpose of this chapter is to present and discuss these essential elements as they affect the individual, the environment, and the scuba. Planning a scuba dive ensures maximum safety within the means available.

The Individual

The individual is the foundation upon which safe scuba diving procedures are formulated, but they are of value only insofar as the individual demonstrates a willingness to implement them. Safe-diving procedures are not new; they are established techniques based upon long experience and scientific study by scientists, doctors, professional divers, and in particular the United States Navy. The safety record established and maintained by our Navy in deep- and shallow-water diving is above reproach and one every scuba diver should endeavor to match.

In planning a scuba dive, consideration should be given to the individual's physical capacity or fitness to perform the dive. Physical fitness should include periodic physical examinations to ascertain the individual's state of health and assurance by a qualified medical doctor that scuba diving will not be harmful or injurious. Prior to the actual performance of a dive, the scuba diver should have obtained adequate sleep and abstained from alcoholic beverages. Under no circumstances should he dive while under the influence of alcohol, sedatives, or any drug which impairs alertness. Diving with a common cold, ear fungus infection, external skin abrasions, or similar handicaps should be avoided. The damage which may result to the upper respiratory system, the middle ear, or other portions of the anatomy could cause permanent disability. Scuba divers should exercise regularly, utilizing exercises which demand physical exertion and endurance, and which provide an opportunity to increase their proficiency in the water. A partial list of recommended exercises includes distance swims with fins and mask, skin diving, water polo, cross-country running, and other active athletic endeavors. Good health habits and exercises plus a periodic physical examination will ensure the individual's physical fitness for scuba diving.

No less important than physical fitness is mental fitness. Each individual should have a sincere desire to perform a scuba dive and should have demonstrated the quality of emotional stability. The unfamiliar natural phenomena to be encountered in the fluid, comparatively silent world underwater coupled with the scuba diver's own awareness of his solitude may create panic reactions even in voluntary divers. Individuals who coerce, shame, or ridicule another person into involuntarily performing a scuba dive are inducing him to risk self-destruction needlessly. Unfortunately, specific rules cannot be applied which will positively determine an individual's mental fitness or emotional stability in reference to scuba diving. Certain factors can, however, give indications as to mental fitness for diving and should be subjected to critical evaluation by the individuals concerned. These factors include a sincere desire to dive, no personal history of or tendency toward claustrophobia, no fear of darkness or isolation, an alert mind capable of formulating and implementing decisions, respect for danger, and a capability for normal fear reactions without a tendency to panic.

Very few emergencies arise in scuba diving that cannot be successfully concluded with the proper timely application of corrective actions. Physical and mental fitness offers the best assurance that an individual can competently and expeditiously extricate himself from a hazardous or untenable situation.

The next essential element to be considered and evaluated in planning a scuba dive consists of the individual's academic knowledge of the theory of diving, aquatic proficiency, and experience in scuba diving. These factors, aside from the physical and physiological limitations, necessitate the establishment of safe boundaries commensurate with the degree of knowledge, training, and skill possessed by the individual. When planning a scuba dive, the individual must carefully evaluate these factors and establish safe boundaries. Clubs and other organizations will find it useful to establish a classification of divers on the basis of their knowledge, aquatic proficiency, and experience. The following is offered as a suggested rating scale:

A. The student is an individual who is attempting this endeavor for the first time or who has limited knowledge of the physics and physiology of diving, possesses only meager aquatic proficiency, or is unfamiliar with scuba equipment. Novice scuba divers should confine their activity to indoor swimming pools under the supervision of a competent scuba diving instructor.

B. The second degree, or classification of skills, which may be applied to scuba divers in general is that of BASIC diver. This individual has achieved adequate knowledge of the theory of diving, demonstrated sufficient aquatic proficiency, and become familiar with the operation of scuba equipment. Experience in scuba diving is inadequate. Basic scuba divers should restrict their diving to optimum environmental conditions and do their open-water training under the supervision of capable, experienced scuba divers and instructors.

C. Continuing the classification of skills essential to the scuba diver, necessitates the listing of criteria for qualification as a SENIOR or ADVANCED scuba diver. This designation represents outstanding proficiency, knowledge of the theory of diving, aquatic ability, and acquisition of extensive open-water scuba diving experience. In addition, the Senior or Advanced diver must exercise good leadership and accept personal responsibility for the safety of individuals with lesser knowledge, ability, or experience. The Senior or Advanced scuba diver sets the example by insisting on the establishment of safe scuba diving procedures based on sound knowledge of the essential elements and the application of good judgment predicated upon a continuous systematic evaluation of the diving conditions as they exist. When a Senior or Advanced scuba diver is accompanied on a scuba dive by a Basic scuba diver, the restrictions applicable to the lesser qualifications must apply to ensure maximum safety to all concerned.

The next consideration in planning a scuba dive after determining that the individual scuba diver is physically, mentally, and technically qualified to dive within prescribed boundaries is to evaluate those essential elements of diving safety which must be accomplished in conjunction with another scuba diver. No live scuba diver has ever been, nor should he ever consider himself to be, a completely self-sufficient, self-sustaining individual. Those essential elements of diving safety which must be considered, evaluated, and established with another individual in planning a scuba dive are: the "Buddy" System, an Underwater Communications System, and the Emergency Assistance Plan.

The Buddy System

The buddy system is a mandatory safety diving procedure which must be recognized, understood, and established prior to each and every skin or scuba dive. Quite simply defined, it means that no individual skin or scuba diver, regardless of proficiency or experience, should ever undertake a skin or scuba dive alone but must in the interest of self-preservation be accompanied by at least one other similarly qualified diver who has acknowledged and accepted the responsibility for the safety of his partner under any circumstances requiring mutual assistance.

1. To facilitate the most effective safety measures when utilizing the buddy system demands the utmost confidence in each other's knowledge, ability, and judgment, and the strict observance of a well-defined diver-distance range. Diver-distance range is that distance which separates one buddy from another during performance of a scuba dive. This range may vary, depending upon visibility, depth, and dive-site conditions, but should normally not exceed 10 to 12 feet, even with good visibility. Greater distance and more freedom of travel are often desirable, but the widened interval between buddies reduces the chances of rendering immediate assistance if an emergency situation occurs. Remember the buddy system is for mutual safety and benefit. Why lessen its potential benefits? Scuba dives at night, or in conditions of limited visibility, should be avoided. If the circumstances warrant a night scuba dive, buddies should maintain contact with each other by utilizing a "buddy line." This technique requires two divers to employ a held line 3 to 10 feet long, depending upon conditions, over which they can transmit simple signals relative to their condition and the direction of the dive.

FIGURE 90. MAINTAINING BUDDY CONTACT

2. The mutual protection and responsibility accepted by dive buddies also requires the observance of rules of underwater conduct. These rules should include:

(a) Signal intended actions, such as ascent, descent, and change of direction. Such signals must be previously arranged so that the intended actions may be executed simultaneously.

(b) Signal when visual contact is lost by tapping on scuba cylinders with metal or rock, listening for a reply in similar fashion. Surfacing, if rapid re-establishment of visual contact is not made, should be done according to prior arrangement.

(c) Signal at the earliest possible moment any circumstance or situation which might tend to create a hazardous or untenable condition.

(d) Provide confidence and reassurance to a buddy in a hazardous or undesirable situation while maintaining self-control and implementing proper corrective action.

(e) Coordinate and achieve mutual agreement and understanding of the communication signals to be employed, the depth-time limitation to be observed, and the underwater activities contemplated.

(f) Have working knowledge of your buddy's regular and safety equipment, including his vest.

Underwater Communications System

The communications system to be employed by scuba divers should offer a simple means of conveying ideas and direct actions between individuals underwater. Signals must not be complicated or easily misunderstood, but may vary to meet specific objectives. The significant factor, regardless of the communications system employed, is that complete understanding can be maintained by dive buddies, surfaced or submerged, during all free diving operations. The most readily available method of underwater communications for scuba divers is a system composed of hand or line signals. Hand and line signals have been employed by military and commercial organizations in diving operations with considerable success for decades, and may still be considered the free diver's most effective means of communication. The following may serve as a guide for diver communication:

BUDDY LINE SIGNALS

1 pull	"Are you OK?" or, when going down, "Stop."
2 pulls	"Going down."
3 pulls	"Come up."

From scuba diver B to scuba diver A *in reply.*

1 pull	"I'm all right."
2 pulls	"Going down."
3 pulls	"Coming up."
Signal repeated by receiver	"I understand you."

LINE EMERGENCY SIGNALS

1-1-1 pulls	"Must surface—Emergency."
2-2 pulls	"Air out" or "Air low."

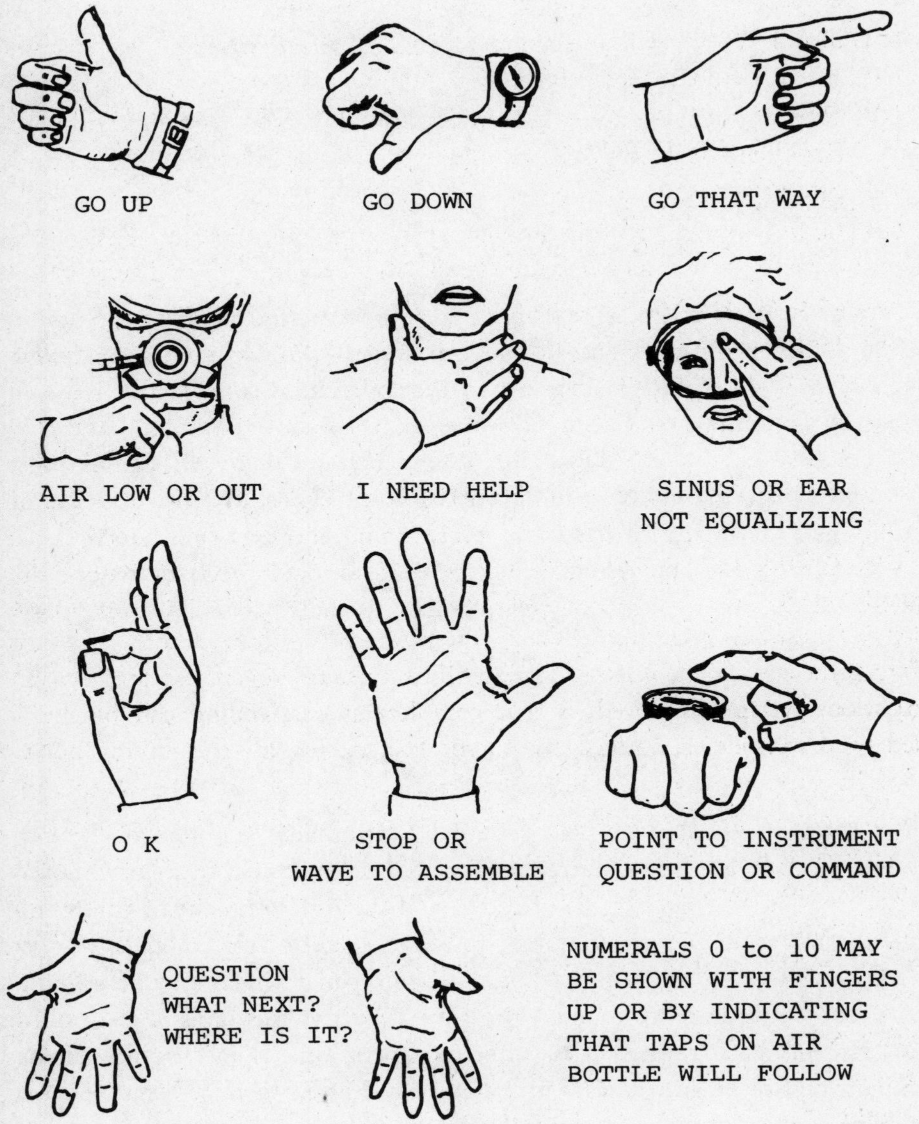

FIGURE 91. MANUAL COMMUNICATION

HAND SIGNALS

1. Thumbs up	"Go up."
2. Thumbs down	"Go down."
3. Hand points horizontal direction	"Go that way."
4. Hand drawn knifelike across the throat	"I need air." or "I'm hurt."
5. Point to compass	"Which way from here?"
6. Point to watch	"Time to ascend."
7. One or both hands palm up	"What's next?" or "Question."
8. One or both hands pointing to ear or face.	"Having difficulty clearing."
9. Numbers formed by fingers	As needed.

SOUND EMERGENCY SIGNAL

Tapping on cylinder with metal or rock	"I'm going to surface. Join me."

The use of hand or line signals does not allow the transmission of complicated messages or instructions. It does, however, provide a simple system which can be codified and memorized by the individuals concerned for use in a variety of circumstances. The signals must be absolutely understood and diligently practised by dive buddies before commencing a dive. All signals must be promptly answered or returned exactly as given. Thus, a positive means of determining that the signal has been received and correctly understood is assured. A communications system, properly utilized, does much to reduce the hazards of scuba diving and is of great comfort to the wary scuba diver apprehensive of isolation or solitude.

Emergency Assistance Plan

The emergency assistance plan should be formulated simultaneously with the selection of dive buddies and/or tenders and the adoption of a communications system. The selection of dive buddies and the establishment of communications are in fact two basics essential to rendering effective emergency assistance. It is not feasible to define each specific emergency which may be encountered in scuba diving and recommend positive corrective measures to be applied in each circumstance. Rather, it is better to depend on the intelligence of the individuals and offer guidelines which have application to many emergencies.

Effective emergency assistance plans will make provision for one man, ideally the most proficient scuba diver accompanying the diving party, to exercise complete supervision over the dive and the divers. This individual should maintain supervision from a surface craft or position, and be completely equipped to render emergency asistance at a moment's notice. The instructions of the dive master must be clear, concise, and instantaneously obeyed before, during, and after a scuba dive, but emphatically so during actual emergencies. It must be clearly understood that the dive master occupies the position of authority. *In addition to his other responsibilities the master should know the location and nature of all natural and man-made hazards in the vicinity of the diving site and caution all divers accordingly. He should also know the name, location, and telephone number of those organizations which can render emergency assistance, such as police department, fire department, lifesaving stations, first-aid stations, hospitals, and the nearest recompression chamber.*

Personnel within the scuba diving group must be accomplished in the techniques of artificial respiration and first aid. Equipment essential to lifesaving must be at hand. Scuba diving accidents seldom just happen; they are caused by inadequate knowledge, ability, experience, planning, or preparation. Most underwater situations which are likely to cause accidents can be anticipated.

Planning can prevent an unfavorable circumstance from developing into an accident or fatality. The greatest danger of all is to be emotionally, physically, or materially unprepared to render emergency assistance when a life may be in the balance.

The Scuba Dive

In planning a scuba dive, the essential elements of diving safety applicable to scuba units must be systematically considered and evaluated to ensure the safety of the individual. These essential elements include the reliability of the scuba, calculation of the air supply, its certified purity, determination of the unit's proper functioning, operation of the mechanical safety features, and care and storage of equipment.

One of the essential elements with respect to the scuba itself is its inherent reliability. Reliability means that it will function as intended with only a minute possibility of mechanical failure when properly maintained. Adequate standards of reliability seldom, if ever, can be obtained in any homemade rig or with components designed for other purposes.

Selection of diving equipment is mostly a matter of personal choice and fitting the price to the pocketbook. A wide field of competition has led to production of good quality, trouble-free, safe equipment. Well-known manufacturers offer a variety of such equipment to suit the needs and desires of divers at practically any level of experience. Evaluation and selection should be made after consulting more experienced divers, check of warranties, and, whenever possible, actual check of more than one brand or type. This latter can often be accomplished by renting or borrowing the chosen brand. The U.S. Navy evaluates apparatus only for its own purposes and in no case publicly approves or disapproves commercial items. No manufacturer is authorized to use "Navy Approval" as an advertising claim.

If new or unfamiliar equipment is acquired, adequate and extensive testing should be performed in a safe area. Before testing, manufacturer's instruction booklets on proper care, maintenance and function should be consulted to ensure that proper attention is given to any peculiarities of the specific unit.

The following pre-dive check items are applicable to any of the current type of open-circuit air-breathing apparatus:

A. Ascertain that the cylinders contain only certified-pure breathing air. Air which contains contaminants such as carbon monoxide can cause serious trouble, even death.

FIGURE 92. PRE-DIVE CHECK AND PREPARATION

B. Know the pressure in the cylinders before each dive. Calculate the depth-time limitation for the deepest depth contemplated. Include the decompression time, if any, and a positive margin of safety. Whenever possible, plan each dive to avoid the necessity of decompression. Exceeding the depth-time limitations without adequate provision for decompression is especially foolhardy when adequate facilities for recompression treatment of bends are not immediately available.

C. Immediately preceding the dive, before entry, the individual using the particular scuba should ascertain by personal inspection that the main high-pressure valve is open and that the demand regulator is functioning properly. Any malfunctions or imperfections in operations, such as hard breathing, erratic valve fluctuations, or loose fittings, justify suspending the diving plans until proper corrective measures have been applied.

D. Mechanical safety features on most contemporary-type scuba units include a reserve air feature and a quick-release harness assembly. The individual utilizing the scuba should be double-checked by his swim buddy on the operation of the reserve air feature and the proper assembly of the harness quick-release feature. The actual operation of both these safety features should then be demonstrated to the dive master who should personally check that the reserve air supply control valve is in the OFF position. The pre-dive check of equipment must include the condition of the inflatable vest. All valves should be checked. This includes oral inflation and, if present, the over-pressure release. The gas cartridge or air-bottle mechanism and available supply should be checked. Buddies and the dive safety man should be thoroughly familiar with all features of the vests worn. The pre-dive test can then be concluded by a shallow dive in the immediate vicinity of the diving site to ascertain that the units are properly functioning before descending to the desired depth and task.

Planning a scuba dive does not end with the descent of the diver into the depths. The plan must also include provision for the proper care and storage of the equipment upon completion of the dive. Generally, the accomplishment of a few simple tasks will ensure the readiness of equipment for the next day of diving. Upon surfacing, the individual should first close all high-pressure valves. If this is the concluding dive of the operation, then in sequence the following steps should be accomplished:

1. Wash the scuba in fresh water, being careful to stop the high-pressure inlet on the demand regulator.
2. Clean all rubber components of grease, oil, or other organic solvents.
3. Drain and dry the apparatus.
4. Store the equipment in a clean, safe place where the cylinders can be protected from dropping, sharp blows, and excessive heat.
5. Vest, wet suit, mask, hood, boots, gloves, and metering devices should be washed, dried, and stored to prevent deterioration or damage.

Diving Safely

Safety and survival underwater are achieved by careful planning. This must be based on a good understanding of the environment, the equipment, and the limitations of the individual. The newcomer to the underwater environment is, at first, thrilled by his ability to breathe and move about comfortably in a nearly weightless fashion. The mere physical wonder gives way to the desire to explore, to do something. This desire, in turn, gives rise to the need for more extensive planning. Where to go, what to do, what to see, and how to put all of his or her training together for pleasure completes the planning.

The dive plan evolves from the simple and not too arduous to the more extensive and complex operations. Whether it be simple or complex, the basics will always be present. Appropriate equipment, entry point, depth, bottom time, objective, exit and *over-all safety* are outline items for proper planning. Most of these have been discussed, and recommendations made, in the preceding text.

One fact for consideration here is another basic: *direction.* Up and down are not usually a problem. Direct passage is quite a different matter. There are no roads, signposts or (for lack of a better word) landmarks. The lack of these things may make unguided travel rather haphazard. Swimming in a straight line in an unmarked void is, for most, nearly impossible. If the dive plan calls for travel in a given direction it must include knowledgeable employment of a compass. The following is basic information and must be enlarged upon by practice and further study.

The Compass

Initial employment of the compass should be preceded by a check of the instrument itself. As has been noted, it should have a plainly visible "lubber" line, an easily read card, and be reasonably sensitive to directional change. Some are arranged to display the heading toward the diver, others away from the diver. Check its sensitivity to objects containing iron. Hold the compass in front of you, lubber line in line with sighting and long axis of the body. Walk (or swim) in a straight line by maintaining the original heading on the lubber line.

Now, pick out a definite object to your right, sight along the lubber line, record the heading. Turn to your left about 90 degrees, similarly sight another definite object and record the headings. Walk straight to the first object, counting the steps. Reverse your position, south to north for example. Follow the

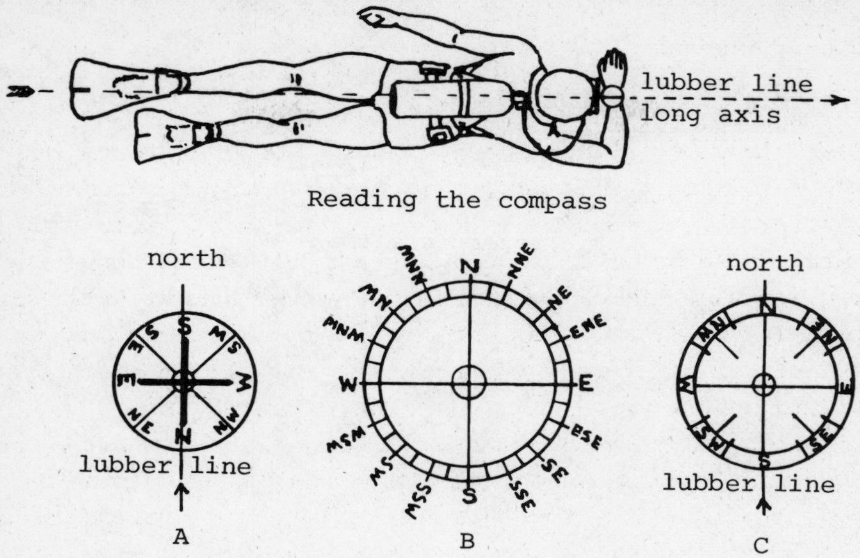

A-Basic division makes precise navigation difficult. Reversed.
B-Finer division increases accuracy. "Boxing" the compass.
C-30 degree division not ideal but better than A. Direct.

FIGURE 93. DIRECTION BY COMPASS

new heading for the same number of steps. Without looking at your original position marker, take a heading on the other object. If you've been reasonably consistent, the heading should very nearly coincide with the original reading and you should be very nearly on the original position.

Another method, not quite as accurate, may be used. Following the leg out from the first object until you reach a point which approximates (by sight) the original angle between the objects, then taking a bearing on the second object, is more involved. You may have to backtrack or continue on course and repeat several times before the desired intersection is found.

Swimming distance may be determined by traveling a known distance (in a straight line) and counting the bottom of each kick of the right or left fin. Divide the number of counted kicks into the distance and you have the distance traveled per kick cycle. This will vary depending on the equipment worn—the more resistance the less distance. Establish an average for both skin and scuba diving with and without a wet suit (suited cycle is shorter). Use the compass regularly, check your accuracy, you can then depend on arrival by the shortest route at a desired location. Chart locations of specific spots or areas on maps, or make your own for specific areas. The foregoing is basic. Much more might be learned before you can consider yourself an underwater mariner, but you at least can give "direction" to the dive plan.

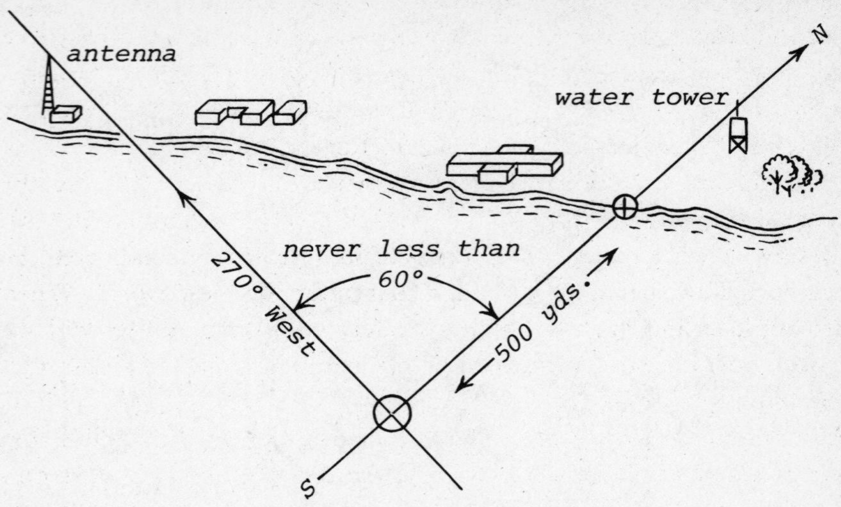

FIGURE 94. COMPASS BEARINGS AND DISTANCE TO SITE

The dive plan can be designed for so many possible underwater ventures that complete coverage in one chapter would fall far short. This is a text for *basic* diving. Further training, experience gained from diving with experts, and continued research *must* follow basic training before planning and conducting advanced activities.

The Variety of Diving

The following are broadly descriptive of some of the more publicized activities of scuba divers:

CAVE DIVING

This is a specialized activity which requires specific training by qualified instructors. The very nature of such activity makes it different in many respects from open-water diving. Since the operation is performed in an area of confinement with no natural light and is often completely dependent on guide lines to prevent becoming lost, one must be psychologically conditioned to these circumstances. Open-water divers usually have the option of up or down as desired, not so the cave diver. The path is defined and his only options are in or out by *that* path. An error in foresight, planning or execution could be disastrous. This is a specialty. Even highly competent open-water divers require special instruction and training to dive in caves with safety.

WRECK DIVING

One of the largest fields for dive planning is visiting a wreck. The wreck may be old, new, large, small, deep or shallow, in fresh water or salt water. If the body of water is large enough to accommodate a floating vessel, then there is probably an ill-fated craft on the bottom. Regardless of monetary worth, any part or content of a wreck which can be removed and displayed is "treasure."

Since wrecks provide protection, food, and a home for marine life, the diver can observe a wide variety of aquatic life in a relatively small area. He can photograph, draw, paint, or just plain marvel at this new world. Where and when permitted and in accord with all safety rules, many divers will spear or otherwise catch their dinner. All this is fascinating and beckons—*but not without planning.*

Wrecks are quite often but a dot on a map or vaguely seen below the intersection of two lines (compass or sight). An error of a couple of degrees (or even feet) in course or calculation may result in viewing a nearly barren bottom or the near exhaustion of air supply before "hitting the jackpot." Currents, usual or temporary, may turn leisurely enjoyment into work or create hazardous conditions which call for aborting the original plan. Even if the wreck is "virgin" to divers, it probably isn't to local fishermen. This means remnants of fish lines, hooks, larger line, nets, and any other gear that might be snagged by wreckage. Planning must include diver briefing, selection of necessary equipment and, as always, emergency handling. Old wrecks get their share of debris

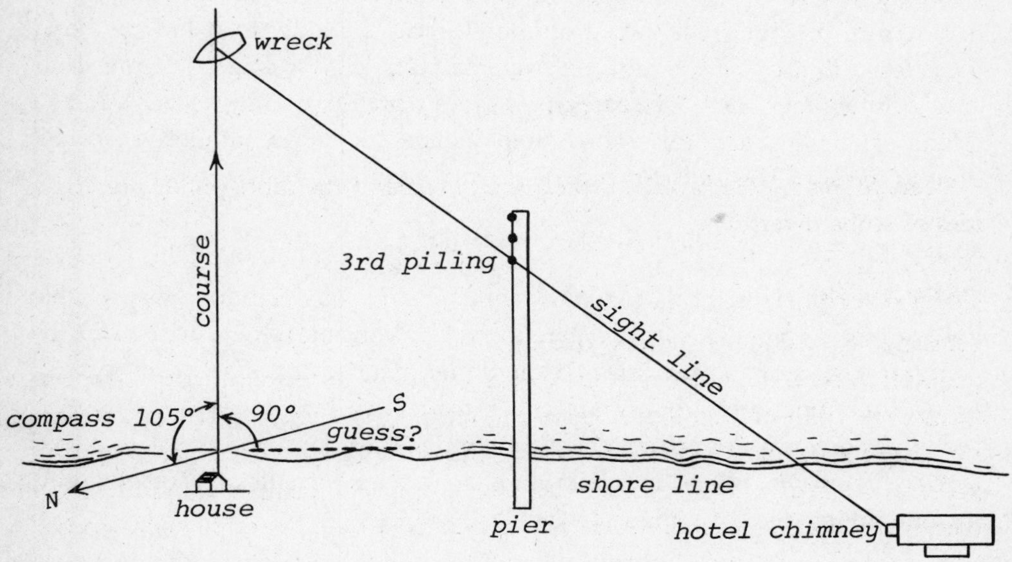

FIGURE 95. COURSE BY COMPASS AND SIGHT

and dismemberment by prior visitors. Plan ahead to provide utmost safety. Hatchways, doors, deck manhole covers and parts moved by surge should be secured so as to prevent entrapment. Adequate guide and safety lines should be used and placed. Bottom time should be within safe limits and adhered to. Deep wrecks may involve decompression dives. This circumstance calls for minute planning which will provide every foreseeable safety factor.

Wreck diving can be fun or work and safe or hazardous. Proper planning and adherence to the plan will make the next dive less precarious.

ICE DIVING

Aside from the prospect of being frozen stiff before and after the dive, many divers enjoy this facet of the sport. The water isn't, generally, any colder than the lower temperature gradient found in many lakes and quarries. Planning includes adequate insulation during the dive and, hopefully, before and after.

Since there is no way to breach that overhead cover, planning and operation must foresee any hazards. Strong safety lines must be firmly attached to immovable anchorage atop the ice or ashore. The water end of the line should be secured to the diver, not his equipment. Line signals must be rehearsed and thoroughly understood by divers and line tenders. A fully equipped and ready safety man must be stationed at the hole in the ice and, if needed, must respond immediately on a safety line. Snagging on bottom debris, uncontrolled movement by unforeseen currents, and serious chilling are only a few of the hazards.

The diver unfortunate enough to lose his safety line when out of sight of the entry hole should remain at the spot of loss rather than start moving about in search of the hole. The advice of knowledgeable ice divers is for the "lost" diver to go to the ice level directly over the point of lost contact. If the ice is clear of snow and fairly transparent, a surface search party may locate him and cut an exit hole. Plans relative to safety should correspond to existing conditions at the site. This calls for experience and good judgment.

NIGHT DIVES

These dives obviously call for sufficient and detailed planning. Dependable lights, careful compass course adherence, depth control (where necessary) by meter or surface-supported lines all should be planned for. The buddy system, using buddy lines and group contact, is a *must.*

Night dives in the oceans or seas are more hazardous because of increased marine-life activity. Areas in which there are strong currents are not favorable for safe diving either by night or day.

DEEP DIVES

These are work all the way from planning through execution. Basic divers should refrain from deep dives. Light is generally poor in many areas. Activity and bottom time are limited by increased air consumption. Inherent risks are greater. Decompression stops, when involved, require experienced planning.

FREE ASCENTS

Since there is considerable controversy about the need for practice of the "free ascent" something must be said about it. Most knowledgeable doctors advise against the procedure, except as an emergency measure to be employed when there is no alternative. Practice, even when a recompression chamber is in the immediate vicinity, can be a risky planned event. Definition of the term might make this clearer.

The "free ascent" is one in which no inhalation is made. The ascent is made from the point of last breath to the surface while depending on slight positive buoyancy and minimum effort. Positive buoyancy is maintained by controlled volume *continuous* exhalation all the way to the surface. The ascent rate should be hopefully kept within the 60 ft. per minute range.

If practice is considered essential, simulated ascents of the continuous exhalation type can be made in shallow water for a variety of distances with a non-critical depth differential involved. Even this simulation should be well supervised. Some experienced (and most basic) divers find it pretty difficult to keep their cool when they reach the "empty" point with some distance still to go. Having the regulator mouthpiece readily available and operable in case of an abort may seem to be a crutch but it's still better than panic.

BUOYED ASCENTS

These ascents are last resorts and, hopefully, not a part of the planned events. Purposeful or accidental inflation of a flotation device to the extent of producing immediate positive buoyancy at any depth could be dangerous. Attempts to breathe normally during an ascent marked by increased velocity can produce dangerous pressure differentials. Spreading the arms and legs and bending at the waist will present more profile with some attendant velocity decrease. Controlled venting of expanding flotation gas, either manually or by an automatic over-pressure valve helps to slow velocity. Unless the precipitate upward flight is drastically slowed, "continual exhalation must be made from the very beginning to the surface." The greater the depth, the more open the airway must be.

Many other planned events for both skin and scuba divers could be discussed. All could be summed up by simply saying: PLAN THE DIVE FOR SAFETY AND DIVE THE PLAN SAFELY.

APPENDIXES

A. UNITED STATES NAVY AIR DECOMPRESSION TABLES *

SECTION 1.5 DIVING TABLES

1.5.1 GENERAL

The tables and procedures outlined herein have been developed to provide safety from the hazards of decompression sickness and oxygen toxicity described in section 1.3. At the same time, the tables have been made as efficient as possible in order that they will be the least possible hindrance to diving operations.

1.5.2 AIR DECOMPRESSION TABLES

General

(1) The air decompression tables are comprised of—

(*a*) Decompression Procedures (table 1–9).

(*b*) U.S. Navy Standard Air Decompression Table (table 1–10).

(*c*) No-Decompression Limits and Repetitive Groups (table 1–11).

(*d*) Surface Interval Credit Table (table 1–12).

(*e*) Repetitive Dive Timetable (table 1–13).

(*f*) Standard Air Decompression Table for Exceptional Exposures (table 1–14).

(2) For all dives where air is the breathing medium, regardless of the type of diving apparatus, use these tables as prescribed.

(3) Use these tables in conjunction with the Equivalent Air Tables (table 1–15) for dives where a nitrogen-oxygen mixture is the breathing medium.

(FORMERLY TABLE 1–4, 1963 DIVING MANUAL)

TABLE 1–9.—*Decompression procedures*

GENERAL INSTRUCTIONS FOR AIR DIVING

Need for Decompression

A quantity of nitrogen is taken up by the body during every dive. The amount absorbed depends upon the depth of the dive and the exposure (bottom) time. If the quantity of nitrogen dissolved in the body tissues exceeds a certain critical amount, the ascent must be delayed to allow the body tissue to remove the excess nitrogen. Decompression sickness results from failure to delay the ascent and to allow this process of gradual desaturation. A specified time at a specific depth for purposes of desaturation is called a decompression stop.

No-Decompression Schedules

Dives that are not long or deep enough to require decompression stops are no-decompression dives. Dives to 33 feet or less do not require decompression stops. As the depth increases, the allowable bottom time for no-decompression dives decreases. Five minutes at 190 feet is the deepest no-decompression schedule. These dives are all listed in the *No-Decompression Limits and Repetitive Group Designation Table for No-Decompression Dives* (No-Decompression Table (table 1–11)), and only require compliance with the 60-feet-per-minute rate of ascent.

Schedules That Require Decompression Stops

All dives beyond the limits of the *No-Decompression Table* require decompression stops. These dives are listed in the *Navy Standard Air Decompression Table* (table 1–10). Comply exactly with instructions except as modified by surface decompression procedures.

Variations in Rate of Ascent

Ascend from all dives at the rate of 60 feet per minute.

In the event you are unable to maintain the 60-feet-per-minute rate of ascent:

(*a*) If the delay was at a depth greater than 50 feet: increase the bottom time by the difference between the time used in ascent and the time that should have been used at a rate of 60 feet per minute. Decompress according to the requirements of the new total bottom time.

(*b*) If the delay was at a depth less than 50 feet: increase the first stop by the difference between the time used in ascent and the time that should have been used at the rate of 60 feet per minute.

*From *U.S. Navy Diving Manual*

TABLE 1–10.—U.S. NAVY STANDARD AIR DECOMPRESSION TABLE

Depth (feet)	Bottom time (min)	Time to first stop (min:sec)	Decompression stops (feet) 50	40	30	20	10	Total ascent (min:sec)	Repetitive group
40	200						0	0:40	(*)
	210	0:30					2	2:40	N
	230	0:30					7	7:40	N
	250	0:30					11	11:40	O
	270	0:30					15	15:40	O
	300	0:30					19	19:40	Z
50	100						0	0:50	(*)
	110	0:40					3	3:50	L
	120	0:40					5	5:50	M
	140	0:40					10	10:50	M
	160	0:40					21	21:50	N
	180	0:40					29	29:50	O
	200	0:40					35	35:50	O
	220	0:40					40	40:50	Z
	240	0:40					47	47:50	Z
60	60						0	1:00	(*)
	70	0:50					2	3:00	K
	80	0:50					7	8:00	L
	100	0:50					14	15:00	M
	120	0:50					26	27:00	N
	140	0:50					39	40:00	O
	160	0:50					48	49:00	Z
	180	0:50					56	57:00	Z
	200	0:40				1	69	71:00	Z
70	50						0	1:10	(*)
	60	1:00					8	9:10	K
	70	1:00					14	15:10	L
	80	1:00					18	19:10	M
	90	1:00					23	24:10	N
	100	1:00					33	34:10	N
	110	0:50				2	41	44:10	O
	120	0:50				4	47	52:10	O
	130	0:50				6	52	59:10	O
	140	0:50				8	56	65:10	Z
	150	0:50				9	61	71:10	Z
	160	0:50				13	72	86:10	Z
	170	0:50				19	79	99:10	Z
80	40						0	1:20	(*)
	50	1:10					10	11:20	K
	60	1:10					17	18:20	L
	70	1:10					23	24:20	M
	80	1:00				2	31	34:20	N
	90	1:00				7	39	47:20	N
	100	1:00				11	46	58:20	O
	110	1:00				13	53	67:20	O
	120	1:00				17	56	74:20	Z
	130	1:00				19	63	83:20	Z
	140	1:00				26	69	96:20	Z
	150	1:00				32	77	110:20	Z
90	30						0	1:30	(*)
	40	1:20					7	8:30	J
	50	1:20					18	19:30	L
	60	1:20					25	26:30	M
	70	1:10				7	30	38:30	N
	80	1:10				13	40	54:30	N
	90	1:10				18	48	67:30	O
	100	1:10				21	54	76:30	Z
	110	1:10				24	61	86:30	Z
	120	1:10				32	68	101:30	Z
	130	1:00			5	36	74	116:30	Z
100	25						0	1:40	(*)
	30	1:30					3	4:40	I
	40	1:30					15	16:40	K
	50	1:20				2	24	27:40	L
	60	1:20				9	28	38:40	N
	70	1:20				17	39	57:40	O
	80	1:20				23	48	72:40	O
	90	1:10			3	23	57	84:40	Z
	100	1:10			7	23	66	97:40	Z
	110	1:10			10	34	72	117:40	Z
	120	1:10			12	41	78	132:40	Z
110	20						0	1:50	(*)
	25	1:40					3	4:50	H
	30	1:40					7	8:50	J
	40	1:30				2	21	24:50	L
	50	1:30				8	26	35:50	M
	60	1:30				18	36	55:50	N
	70	1:20			1	23	48	73:50	O
	80	1:20			7	23	57	88:50	Z
	90	1:20			12	30	64	107:50	Z
	100	1:20			15	37	72	125:50	Z

*See Table 1–11 on page 259 for repetitive groups in no-decompression dives.

TABLE 1-10.—U.S. NAVY STANDARD AIR DECOMPRESSION TABLE (*Cont.*)

Depth (feet)	Bottom time (min)	Time to first stop (min:sec)	Decompression stops (feet) 50	40	30	20	10	Total ascent (min:sec)	Repetitive group
120	15						0	2:00	(*)
	20	1:50					2	4:00	H
	25	1:50					6	8:00	I
	30	1:50					14	16:00	J
	40	1:40				5	25	32:00	L
	50	1:40				15	31	48:00	N
	60	1:30			2	22	45	71:00	O
	70	1:30			9	23	55	89:00	O
	80	1:30			15	27	63	107:00	Z
	90	1:30			19	37	74	132:00	Z
	100	1:30			23	45	80	150:00	Z
130	10						0	2:10	(*)
	15	2:00					1	3:10	F
	20	2:00					4	6:10	H
	25	2:00					10	12:10	J
	30	1:50				3	18	23:10	M
	40	1:50				10	25	37:10	N
	50	1:40			3	21	37	63:10	O
	60	1:40			9	23	52	86:10	Z
	70	1:40			16	24	61	103:10	Z
	80	1:30		3	19	35	72	131:10	Z
	90	1:30		8	19	45	80	154:10	Z
140	10						0	2:20	(*)
	15	2:10					2	4:20	G
	20	2:10					6	8:20	I
	25	2:00				2	14	18:20	J
	30	2:00				5	21	28:20	K
	40	1:50			2	16	26	46:20	N
	50	1:50			6	24	44	76:20	O
	60	1:50			16	23	56	97:20	Z
	70	1:40		4	19	32	68	125:20	Z
	80	1:40		10	23	41	79	155:20	Z
150	5						0	2:30	C
	10	2:20					1	3:30	E
	15	2:20					3	5:30	G
	20	2:10				2	7	11:30	H
	25	2:10				4	17	23:30	K
	30	2:10				8	24	34:30	L
	40	2:00			5	19	33	59:30	N
	50	2:00			12	23	51	88:30	O
	60	1:50		3	19	26	62	112:30	Z
	70	1:50		11	19	39	75	146:30	Z
	80	1:40	1	17	19	50	84	173:30	Z
160	5						0	2:40	D
	10	2:30					1	3:40	F
	15	2:20				1	4	7:40	H
	20	2:20				3	11	16:40	J
	25	2:20				7	20	29:40	K
	30	2:10			2	11	25	40:40	M
	40	2:10			7	23	39	71:40	N
	50	2:00		2	16	23	55	98:40	Z
	60	2:00		9	19	33	69	132:40	Z
	70	1:50	1	17	22	44	80	166:40	Z
170	5						0	2:50	D
	10	2:40					2	4:50	F
	15	2:30				2	5	9:50	H
	20	2:30				4	15	21:50	J
	25	2:20			2	7	23	34:50	L
	30	2:20			4	13	26	45:50	M
	40	2:10		1	10	23	45	81:50	O
	50	2:10		5	18	23	61	109:50	Z
	60	2:00	2	15	22	37	74	152:50	Z
	70	2:00	8	17	19	51	86	183:50	Z
180	5						0	3:00	D
	10	2:50					3	6:00	F
	15	2:40				3	6	12:00	I
	20	2:30			1	5	17	26:00	K
	25	2:30			3	10	24	40:00	L
	30	2:30			6	17	27	53:00	N
	40	2:20		3	14	23	50	93:00	O
	50	2:10	2	9	19	30	65	128:00	Z
	60	2:10	5	16	19	44	81	168:00	Z
190	5						0	3:10	D
	10	2:50				1	3	7:10	G
	15	2:50				4	7	14:10	I
	20	2:40			2	6	20	31:10	K
	25	2:40			5	11	25	44:10	M
	30	2:30		1	8	19	32	63:10	N
	40	2:30		8	14	23	55	103:10	O
	50	2:20	4	13	22	33	72	147:10	Z
	60	2:20	10	17	19	50	84	183:10	Z

*See Table 1-11 on page 259 for repetitive groups in no-decompression dives.

(FORMERLY TABLE 1–6, 1963 DIVING MANUAL)

TABLE 1–11.—*No-decompression limits and repetitive group designation table for no-decompression air dives*

Depth (feet)	No-decompression limits (min)	Repetitive groups (air dives)														
		A	B	C	D	E	F	G	H	I	J	K	L	M	N	O
10	-----	60	120	210	300	-----	-----	-----	-----	-----	-----	-----	-----	-----	-----	-----
15	-----	35	70	110	160	225	350	-----	-----	-----	-----	-----	-----	-----	-----	-----
20	-----	25	50	75	100	135	180	240	325	-----	-----	-----	-----	-----	-----	-----
25	-----	20	35	55	75	100	125	160	195	245	315	-----	-----	-----	-----	-----
30	-----	15	30	45	60	75	95	120	145	170	205	250	310	-----	-----	-----
35	310	5	15	25	40	50	60	80	100	120	140	160	190	220	270	310
40	200	5	15	25	30	40	50	70	80	100	110	130	150	170	200	-----
50	100	-----	10	15	25	30	40	50	60	70	80	90	100	-----	-----	-----
60	60	-----	10	15	20	25	30	40	50	55	60	-----	-----	-----	-----	-----
70	50	-----	5	10	15	20	30	35	40	45	50	-----	-----	-----	-----	-----
80	40	-----	5	10	15	20	25	30	35	40	-----	-----	-----	-----	-----	-----
90	30	-----	5	10	12	15	20	25	30	-----	-----	-----	-----	-----	-----	-----
100	25	-----	5	7	10	15	20	22	25	-----	-----	-----	-----	-----	-----	-----
110	20	-----	-----	5	10	13	15	20	-----	-----	-----	-----	-----	-----	-----	-----
120	15	-----	-----	5	10	12	15	-----	-----	-----	-----	-----	-----	-----	-----	-----
130	10	-----	-----	5	8	10	-----	-----	-----	-----	-----	-----	-----	-----	-----	-----
140	10	-----	-----	5	7	10	-----	-----	-----	-----	-----	-----	-----	-----	-----	-----
150	5	-----	-----	5	-----	-----	-----	-----	-----	-----	-----	-----	-----	-----	-----	-----
160	5	-----	-----	-----	5	-----	-----	-----	-----	-----	-----	-----	-----	-----	-----	-----
170	5	-----	-----	-----	5	-----	-----	-----	-----	-----	-----	-----	-----	-----	-----	-----
180	5	-----	-----	-----	5	-----	-----	-----	-----	-----	-----	-----	-----	-----	-----	-----
190	5	-----	-----	-----	5	-----	-----	-----	-----	-----	-----	-----	-----	-----	-----	-----

Instructions for Use

I. No-decompression limits:

This column shows at various depths greater than 30 feet the allowable diving times (in minutes) which permit surfacing directly at 60 feet a minute with no decompression stops. Longer exposure times require the use of the Standard Air Decompression Table (table 1–10).

II. Repetitive group designation table:

The tabulated exposure times (or bottom times) are in minutes. The times at the various depths in each vertical column are the maximum exposures during which a diver will remain within the group listed at the head of the column.

To find the repetitive group designation at surfacing for dives involving exposures up to and including the no-decompression limits: Enter the table on the *exact or next greater depth* than that to which exposed and select the listed exposure time *exact or next greater* than the actual exposure time. The repetitive group designation is indicated by the letter at the head of the vertical column where the selected exposure time is listed.

For example: A dive was to 32 feet for 45 minutes. Enter the table along the 35-foot-depth line since it is next greater than 32 feet. The table shows that since group D is left after 40 minutes' exposure and group E after 50 minutes, group E (at the head of the column where the 50-minute exposure is listed) is the proper selection.

Exposure times for depths less than 40 feet are listed only up to approximately 5 hours since this is considered to be beyond field requirements for this table.

1.5.2 U.S. NAVY DIVING MANUAL 1.5.2

(FORMERLY TABLE 1-7, 1963 DIVING MANUAL)

TABLE 1-12.—*Surface Interval Credit Table for air decompression dives*

[Repetitive group at the end of the surface interval (air dive)]

Repetitive group at the beginning of the surface interval from previous dive	Z	O	N	M	L	K	J	I	H	G	F	E	D	C	B	A
Z	0:10 0:22	0:23 0:34	0:35 0:48	0:49 1:02	1:03 1:18	1:19 1:36	1:37 1:55	1:56 2:17	2:18 2:42	2:43 3:10	3:11 3:45	3:46 4:29	4:30 5:27	5:28 6:56	6:57 10:05	10:00 12:00*
O		0:10 0:23	0:24 0:36	0:37 0:51	0:52 1:07	1:08 1:24	1:25 1:43	1:44 2:04	2:05 2:29	2:30 2:59	3:00 3:33	3:34 4:17	4:18 5:16	5:17 6:44	6:45 9:54	9:55 12:00*
N			0:10 0:24	0:25 0:39	0:40 0:54	0:55 1:11	1:12 1:30	1:31 1:53	1:54 2:18	2:19 2:47	2:48 3:22	3:23 4:04	4:05 5:03	5:04 6:32	6:33 9:43	9:44 12:00*
M				0:10 0:25	0:26 0:42	0:43 0:59	1:00 1:18	1:19 1:39	1:40 2:05	2:06 2:34	2:35 3:08	3:09 3:52	3:53 4:49	4:50 6:18	6:19 9:28	9:29 12:00*
L					0:10 0:26	0:27 0:45	0:46 1:04	1:05 1:25	1:26 1:49	1:50 2:19	2:20 2:53	2:54 3:36	3:37 4:35	4:36 6:02	6:03 9:12	9:13 12:00*
K						0:10 0:28	0:29 0:49	0:50 1:11	1:12 1:35	1:36 2:03	2:04 2:38	2:39 3:21	3:22 4:19	4:20 5:48	5:49 8:58	8:59 12:00*
J							0:10 0:31	0:32 0:54	0:55 1:19	1:20 1:47	1:48 2:20	2:21 3:04	3:05 4:02	4:03 5:40	5:41 8:40	8:41 12:00*
I								0:10 0:33	0:34 0:59	1:00 1:29	1:30 2:02	2:03 2:44	2:45 3:43	3:44 5:12	5:13 8:21	8:22 12:00*
H									0:10 0:36	0:37 1:06	1:07 1:41	1:42 2:23	2:24 3:20	3:21 4:49	4:50 7:59	8:00 12:00*
G										0:10 0:40	0:41 1:15	1:16 1:59	2:00 2:58	2:59 4:25	4:26 7:35	7:36 12:00*
F											0:10 0:45	0:46 1:29	1:30 2:28	2:29 3:57	3:58 7:05	7:06 12:00*
E												0:10 0:54	0:55 1:57	1:58 3:22	3:23 6:32	6:33 12:00*
D													0:10 1:09	1:10 2:38	2:39 5:48	5:49 12:00*
C														0:10 1:39	1:40 2:49	2:50 12:00*
B															0:10 2:10	2:11 12:00*
A																0:10 12:00*

Instructions for Use

Surface interval time in the table is in *hours* and *minutes* (7:59 means 7 hours and 59 minutes). The surface interval must be at least 10 minutes.

Find the *repetitive group designation letter* (from the previous dive schedule) on the diagonal slope. Enter the table horizontally to select the surface interval time that is exactly between the actual surface interval times shown. The repetitive group designation for the *end* of the surface interval is at the head of the vertical column where the selected surface interval time is listed. For example, a previous dive was to 110 feet for 30 minutes. The diver remains on the surface 1 hour and 30 minutes and wishes to find the new repetitive group designation: The repetitive group from the last column of the 110/30 schedule in the Standard Air Decompression Tables is "J." Enter the surface interval credit table along the horizontal line labeled "J." The 1-hour-and-30-minute surface interval lies between the times 1:20 and 1:47. Therefore, the diver has lost sufficient inert gas to place him in group "G" (at the head of the vertical column selected).

*NOTE.—Dives following surface intervals of *more* than 12 hours are not considered repetitive dives. *Actual* bottom times in the Standard Air Decompression Tables may be used in computing decompression for such dives.

(FORMERLY TABLE 1-8, 1963 DIVING MANUAL)

TABLE 1-13.—*Repetitive dive timetable for air dives*

Repetitive groups	Repetitive dive depth (ft) (air dives)															
	40	50	60	70	80	90	100	110	120	130	140	150	160	170	180	190
A	7	6	5	4	4	3	3	3	3	3	2	2	2	2	2	2
B	17	13	11	9	8	7	7	6	6	6	5	5	4	4	4	4
C	25	21	17	15	13	11	10	10	9	8	7	7	6	6	6	6
D	37	29	24	20	18	16	14	13	12	11	10	9	9	8	8	8
E	49	38	30	26	23	20	18	16	15	13	12	12	11	10	10	10
F	61	47	36	31	28	24	22	20	18	16	15	14	13	13	12	11
G	73	56	44	37	32	29	26	24	21	19	18	17	16	15	14	13
H	87	66	52	43	38	33	30	27	25	22	20	19	18	17	16	15
I	101	76	61	50	43	38	34	31	28	25	23	22	20	19	18	17
J	116	87	70	57	48	43	38	34	32	28	26	24	23	22	20	19
K	138	99	79	64	54	47	43	38	35	31	29	27	26	24	22	21
L	161	111	88	72	61	53	48	42	39	35	32	30	28	26	25	24
M	187	124	97	80	68	58	52	47	43	38	35	32	31	29	27	26
N	213	142	107	87	73	64	57	51	46	40	38	35	33	31	29	28
O	241	160	117	96	80	70	62	55	50	44	40	38	36	34	31	30
Z	257	169	122	100	84	73	64	57	52	46	42	40	37	35	32	31

Instructions for Use

The bottom times listed in this table are called "residual nitrogen times" and are the times a diver is to consider he has *already* spent on bottom when he *starts* a repetitive dive to a specific depth. They are in minutes.

Enter the table horizontally with the repetitive group designation from the Surface Interval Credit Table. The time in each vertical column is the number of minutes that would be required (at the depth listed at the head of the column) to saturate to the particular group.

For example: The final group designation from the Surface Interval Credit Table, on the basis of a previous dive and surface interval, is "H." To plan a dive to 110 feet, determine the residual nitrogen time for this depth required by the repetitive group designation: Enter this table along the horizontal line labeled "H." The table shows that one must *start* a dive to 110 feet as though he had already been on the bottom for 27 minutes. This information can then be applied to the Standard Air Decompression Table or No-Decompression Table in a number of ways:

(1) Assuming a diver is going to finish a job and take whatever decompression is required, he must add 27 minutes to his actual bottom time and be prepared to take decompression according to the 110-foot schedules for the sum or equivalent single dive time.

(2) Assuming one wishes to make a quick inspection dive for the minimum decompression, he will decompress according to the 110/30 schedule for a dive of 3 minutes or less (27+3=30). For a dive of over 3 minutes but less than 13, he will decompress according to the 110/40 schedule (27+13=40).

(3) Assuming that one does not want to exceed the 110/50 schedule and the amount of decompression it requires, he will have to start ascent before 23 minutes of actual bottom time (50−27=23).

(4) Assuming that a diver has air for approximately 45 minutes bottom time and decompression stops, the possible dives can be computed: A dive of 13 minutes will require 23 minutes of decompression (110/40 schedule), for a total submerged time of 36 minutes. A dive of 13 to 23 minutes will require 34 minutes of decompression (110/50 schedule), for a total submerged time of 47 to 57 minutes. Therefore, to be safe, the diver will have to start ascent before 13 minutes or a standby air source will have to be provided.

FIG. 1–32A. REPETITIVE DIVE WORKSHEET (SAMPLE FOR REPRODUCTION)

REPETITIVE DIVE WORKSHEET

I. PREVIOUS DIVE:

___ minutes } see table 1-5 or 1-6 for repetitive group designation } Group___
____ feet

II. SURFACE INTERVAL:

__hours___minutes on surface } see table 1-7 for new group } Group___
Group___ (from I.)

III. RESIDUAL NITROGEN TIME:

____ feet (depth of repetitive dive) } see table 1-8 } ___minutes
Group___ (from II.)

IV. EQUIVALENT SINGLE DIVE TIME:

___ minutes (residual nitrogen time from III.)

(add) ___ minutes (actual bottom time of repetitive dive)

(sum) ___ minutes

V. DECOMPRESSION FOR REPETITIVE DIVE:

___ minutes (equivalent single dive time from IV.) } see table 1-5 or 1-6
____ feet (depth of repetitive dive)

☐ No decompression required

or

Decompression stops: ____ feet ____ minutes
____ feet ____ minutes
____ feet ____ minutes
____ feet ____ minutes

FIG. 1–32A. —Repetitive dive worksheet (filled in).

REPETITIVE DIVE WORKSHEET

I. PREVIOUS DIVE:

24 minutes } see table 1-5 or 1-6 for
105 feet } repetitive group designation } Group H

II. SURFACE INTERVAL:

2 hours 0 minutes on surface } see table 1-7
Group H (from I.) } for new group } Group E

III. RESIDUAL NITROGEN TIME:

145 feet (depth of repetitive dive) } see table
Group E (from II.) } 1-8 } 12 minutes

IV. EQUIVALENT SINGLE DIVE TIME:

12 minutes (residual nitrogen time from III.)

(add) 15 minutes (actual bottom time of repetitive dive)

(sum) 27 minutes

V. DECOMPRESSION FOR REPETITIVE DIVE:

27 minutes (equivalent single dive time from IV.) } see table
145 feet (depth of repetitive dive) } 1-5 or 1-6

☐ No decompression required

or

Decompression stops: 20 feet 8 minutes
10 feet 24 minutes
____ feet ____ minutes
____ feet ____ minutes

SPECIAL—BRAND-NEW

TREATMENT BY RECOMPRESSION

Patient with Symptoms of Decompression Sickness or Air Embolism[1*]

(Simplified Procedure Using U.S. Navy Tables)

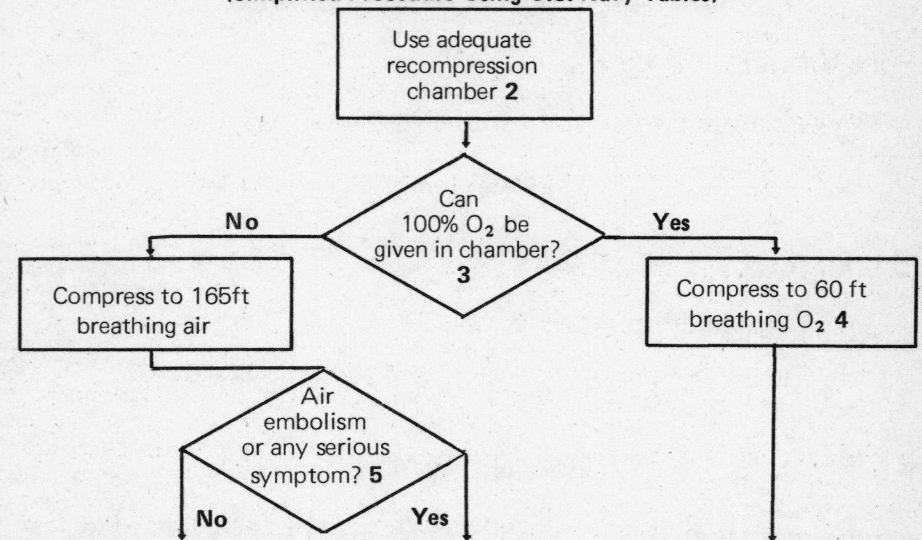

Use adequate recompression chamber **2**
Can 100% O_2 be given in chamber? **3**
No
Yes
Compress to 165ft breathing air
Compress to 60 ft breathing O_2 **4**
Air embolism or any serious symptom? **5**
No
Yes

Equiv. feet **6**	Table 2A	Table 4
165	30 min **7**	30-120 min **8**
140	12	30
120	12	30
100	12	30
80	12	30
60	30	6 hr **9**
50	30	6 hr
40	30	6 hr
30	2 hr	12 hr **10**
20	2 hr	2 hr
10	4 hr	2 hr
To surface	1 min	1 min

Table 6		
Equiv. feet	Min	Gas
60	20	O_2 **11**
	5	air
	20	O_2
	5	air
	20	O_2 **12**
	5	air **13**
60 to 30	30	O_2
30	15	air
	60	O_2
	15	air
	60	O_2 **14**
30 to surface	30	O_2

***Boldface numbers refer to accompanying notes.**

NOTE: This table and the accompanying explanatory material were prepared by E. H. Lanphier, M.D., for the 13th edition (in preparation) of **The Merck Manual,** published by Merck & Co., Inc., Rahway, N.J.

NOTES for Table **Treatment by Recompression**

1. The patient is assumed to have undergone decompression (reduction of surrounding pressure, as in ascent from a dive, exit from a hyperbaric chamber or caisson, or ascent to altitude) within 24 hr preceding onset of signs/symptoms consistent with diagnosis of decompression sickness or air embolism.

2. Adequacy of a treatment chamber implies such characteristics as working pressure equivalent to at least 165 ft (73.4 psi, 6 atm abs), sufficient air supply for operation at such pressure, qualified operators and supervision, and necessary supporting facilities.

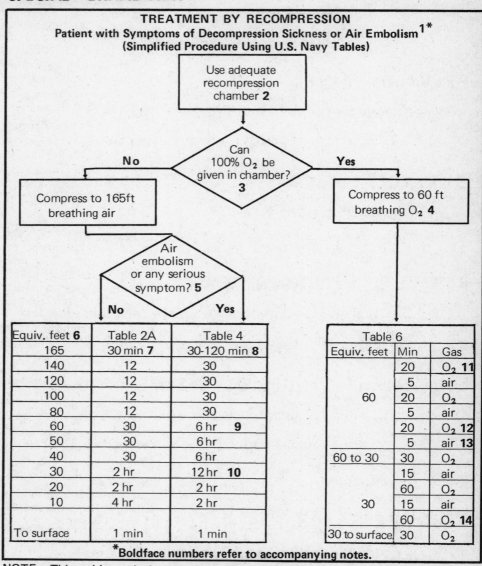

Medical installations in localities of concern should know the location of the nearest adequate chamber, the means of reaching it most rapidly, and the most appropriate source of consultation by telephone.

3. Satisfactory administration of oxygen to patient in chamber requires a good demand-mask or equivalent system assuring delivery of essentially 100 percent oxygen. (The oxygen tables assume and require inspiration of oxygen without significant admixture of air.) Extreme danger of fire requires that chamber-atmosphere oxygen concentration be kept close to that of normal air. A separate exhaust system for exhaled oxygen reduces the necessity for very high rates of continuous chamber ventilation. In patients who report previous episodes of oxygen toxicity (see Note **d**), oxygen tables should be utilized cautiously.

4. U.S. Navy treatment for cases of air embolism in submarine escape training (implying brief exposure to pressure and very prompt treatment) involves these steps according to Table 6A: 1) Take patient directly to 165 ft breathing air. 2) If major relief of symptoms occurs within 30 min (time including descent to 165 ft), ascend to 60 ft (spend 4 min in ascent). 3) Continue treatment following Table 6. (If symptoms persist after 30 min at 165 ft, follow Table 4). (See Note **c**.)

5. If the symptoms and circumstances are suggestive of air embolism, treatment as for serious symptoms is indicated even with prompt and favorable response to recompression. Serious symptoms can be defined as follows: 1) Any sign or symptom with onset while patient was still under pressure during decompression. 2) Any neurological abnormality, including unconsciousness, convulsions, weakness, numbness, inability to use arms or legs, blindness, deafness, dizziness, or loss of speech. 3) Respiratory symptoms suggestive of chokes: shortness of breath, coughing on deep inspiration, tracheal irritation, and/or substernal pain.

6. The pressure equivalent to one foot of sea water is 0.445 pounds per square inch (psi) or 1/33 (0.03) atm.

7. If patient has not shown complete or very substantial relief in 30 min, proceed on Table 4. (See Note **c**.)

8. The time spent at 165 ft depends upon patient's response. He should be examined as thoroughly as possible. If relief appears to be complete in less than 120 min, ascend to 140-ft stop and continue according to Table 4. If relief is incomplete or questionable, remain at 165 ft for full period. Do not overstay 120 min except in acute difficulty and under competent advice. (See Note **c**.)

9. Some authorities believe that Table 4 treatment can be completed successfully by shifting to Table 6 at 60 ft and extending Table 6 as described in Notes **13** and **14**.

10. The final hour of the stops at 30, 20, and 10 feet can be spent on oxygen if a suitable means of administration is available. (See Note **3**.)

11. Examine and observe patient carefully during this period. Worsening, or failure of serious symptoms to improve, may occasionally justify going to 165 ft (breathing air) and following Table 4. (See Note **c**.)

12. Patient breathing oxygen must be observed carefully by a tender within the chamber. (See Note **d**.)

13. If patient's condition is not considered fully satisfactory at conclusion of normal period at 60 ft, or if an additional safeguard is desired for any reason, give an additional cycle of treatment (20 min oxygen, 5 min air) at 60 ft. Observe carefully for any evidence of oxygen toxicity. (See Note **d**.)

14. The period at 30 ft may also be extended by one cycle (15 min air, 60 min oxygen).

GENERAL NOTES ON RECOMPRESSION

a. Examination of patient. Thorough examination is important but takes second place to prompt treatment of serious symptoms. Examination can be conducted under pressure early in treatment if necessary. It is important not to miss serious symptoms that would influence the course of treatment. Before going to a shallower stop, at least have the patient walk the length of the chamber, do a few mild exercises, and read a few lines of print.

b. Tending the patient. A competent individual must be with the patient at all times. The tender will examine and monitor the patient if a physician cannot enter the chamber, will be alert for any changes in signs or symptoms, will watch especially for evidence of oxygen toxicity, and will take care of the patient's general needs.

Tenders who enter and leave must have adequate decompression. Tenders who are with the patient throughout treatment must breathe oxygen during the last 30 min of ascent on some schedules and will gain a safety factor from doing so in any case.

c. Failure to respond, worsening, and recurrence. Table 4 has long been regarded as the treatment of "last resort." This view is still widely held and is reflected in notes above. In general, however, oxygen treatment tables now have a far better success rate than air treatment tables. Some authorities avoid Table 4 entirely when oxygen can be given and in any case limit periods on air at 165 ft to 30 min or less.

Table 6 oxygen treatment can be extended (Notes **13** and **14**). It can also be repeated. Adjunctive medical treatment (Note **e**) should be considered when the response to recompression and oxygen is not prompt and adequate.

A fundamental rule is not to continue ascent if a patient's condition has worsened. This situation is handled as a recurrence during treatment. Detailed rules for dealing with recurrence are provided in the **U.S. Navy Diving Manual.** In general, these call for return to greater depth with ascent on a more conservative table.

The possibility of **late recurrence** dictates keeping the patient close to the chamber for at least 6 hr after treatment and in the vicinity for at least 24 hr.

d. Oxygen toxicity. Convulsive oxygen poisoning can develop in some patients at 60 ft despite air-breathing intervals. Tend carefully, being alert for premonitory signs or symptoms. Common ones include local twitching, nausea, dizziness, restlessness, irritability, and confusion. If necessary, interrupt O_2 for 15 min after reaction subsides and resume schedule at point of interruption. Pulmonary oxygen toxicity is unlikely to develop except possibly on extended Table 6 or in repetition of treatment. Substernal distress and reduction of vital capacity are early manifestations.

e. Medical adjuncts to recompression. A patient who requires recompression may also require first aid or some other medical or surgical procedure. In most instances, both can be accomplished or the priorities are clear. Adequate fluid intake is important.

Medical treatment may form a necessary or desirable supplement to the treatment of bends or air embolism. An obvious example occurs in the presence of decompression shock, where maintenance of normal blood volume by usual methods is clearly indicated. **Low Molecular weight dextran** (Dextran 40, Rheomacrodex) is being used increasingly to combat hematologic changes especially in patients with severe or longstanding symptoms. (The usual maximum is one liter/day for 5 days.)

Steroids are considered a useful adjunct by some, emphatically so in suspected spinal cord edema. A suggested dose is Decadron, 10 mg I.V., followed by 4 mg I.M. every 6 hr. Tapering is not required for use not longer than 72 hr. The possibility of lowering O_2 tolerance suggests withholding steroids until the 30-ft stage of Table 6.

Use of **heparin** remains controversial. It has been advocated in shock and to combat hematologic changes.

Sedatives and narcotics may obscure the symptomatology and entail risk of respiratory insufficiency. They should be avoided or given in minimal effective dosage. **Aspirin** can be given in usual amounts. It is administered routinely in some centers.

Routine precautions in handling medications at pressure include opening ampules and needling the stoppers of vials and I.V. bottles before compression. An inadequately vented I.V. bottle may, for example, implode on descent or deliver its contents (including air) very rapidly on ascent.

B. DECOMPRESSION/REPETITIVE DIVE TABLES *

THE "NU-WAY" REPETITIVE DIVE TABLES

TABLE 1-12 SURFACE INTERVAL CREDIT TABLE (TIMES IN HR:MIN)

NEW GROUP	A	B	C	D	E	F	G	H	I	J	K	L	M	N	O	Z
A	12:00 0:10	12:00 2:11	12:00 2:50	12:00 5:49	12:00 6:33	12:00 7:06	12:00 7:36	12:00 8:00	12:00 8:22	12:00 8:41	12:00 8:59	12:00 9:13	12:00 9:29	12:00 9:44	12:00 9:55	12:00 10:06
B		2:10 0:10	2:49 1:40	5:48 2:39	6:32 3:23	7:05 3:58	7:35 4:26	7:59 4:50	8:21 5:13	8:40 5:41	8:58 5:49	9:12 6:03	9:28 6:19	9:43 6:33	9:54 6:45	10:05 6:57
C			1:39 0:10	2:38 1:10	3:22 1:58	3:57 2:29	4:25 2:59	4:49 3:21	5:12 3:44	5:40 4:03	5:48 4:20	6:02 4:36	6:18 4:50	6:32 5:04	6:44 5:17	6:56 5:28
D				1:09 0:10	1:57 0:55	2:28 1:30	2:58 2:00	3:20 2:24	3:43 2:45	4:02 3:05	4:19 3:22	4:35 3:37	4:49 3:53	5:03 4:05	5:16 4:18	5:27 4:30
E					0:54 0:10	1:29 0:46	1:59 1:16	2:23 1:42	2:44 2:03	3:04 2:21	3:21 2:39	3:36 2:54	3:52 3:09	4:04 3:23	4:17 3:34	4:29 3:46
F						0:45 0:10	1:15 0:41	1:41 1:07	2:02 1:30	2:20 1:48	2:38 2:04	2:53 2:20	3:08 2:35	3:22 2:48	3:33 3:00	3:45 3:11
G							0:40 0:10	1:06 0:37	1:29 1:00	1:47 1:20	2:03 1:36	2:19 1:50	2:34 2:06	2:47 2:19	2:59 2:30	3:10 2:43
H								0:36 0:10	0:59 0:34	1:19 0:55	1:35 1:12	1:49 1:26	2:05 1:40	2:18 1:54	2:29 2:05	2:42 2:18
I									0:33 0:10	0:54 0:32	1:11 0:50	1:25 1:05	1:39 1:19	1:53 1:31	2:04 1:44	2:17 1:56
J										0:31 0:10	0:49 0:29	1:04 0:46	1:18 1:00	1:30 1:12	1:43 1:25	1:55 1:37
K											0:28 0:10	0:45 0:27	0:59 0:43	1:11 0:55	1:24 1:08	1:36 1:19
L												0:26 0:10	0:42 0:26	0:54 0:40	1:07 0:52	1:18 1:03
M													0:25 0:10	0:39 0:25	0:51 0:37	1:02 0:49
N														0:24 0:10	0:36 0:24	0:48 0:35
O															0:23 0:10	0:34 0:23
Z																0:22 0:10

TABLE 1-13 REPETITIVE DIVE TIMETABLE FOR AIR DIVES

RESIDUAL NITROGEN TIMES ABOVE (MINUTES) FOR REPETITIVE DIVE DEPTH BELOW (FT.)

NEW GROUP	40'	50'	60'	70'	80'	90'	100'	110'	120'	130'	140'	150'	160'	170'	180'	190'
A	7	6	5	4	4	3	3	3	3	3	2	2	2	2	2	2
B	17	13	11	9	8	7	7	6	6	6	5	5	4	4	4	4
C	25	21	17	15	13	11	10	10	9	8	7	7	6	6	6	6
D	37	29	24	20	18	16	14	13	12	11	10	9	9	8	8	8
E	49	38	30	26	23	20	18	16	15	13	12	12	11	10	10	10
F	61	47	36	31	28	24	22	20	18	16	15	14	13	13	12	11
G	73	56	44	37	32	29	26	24	21	19	18	17	16	15	14	13
H	87	66	52	43	38	33	30	27	25	22	20	19	18	17	16	15
I	101	76	61	50	43	38	34	31	28	25	23	22	20	19	18	17
J	116	87	70	57	48	43	38	34	32	28	26	24	23	22	20	19
K	138	99	79	64	54	47	43	38	35	31	29	27	26	24	22	21
L	161	111	88	72	61	53	48	42	39	35	32	30	28	26	25	24
M	187	124	97	80	68	58	52	47	43	38	35	32	31	29	27	26
N	213	142	107	87	73	64	57	51	46	40	38	35	33	31	29	28
O	241	160	117	96	80	70	62	55	50	44	40	38	36	34	31	30
Z	257	169	122	100	84	73	64	57	52	46	42	40	37	35	32	31

DEPTH (FEET)	NO DECOMPRESSION LIMITS	BOTTOM TIMES FOR AIR DIVES (MINUTES)														
		A	B	C	D	E	F	G	H	I	J	K	L	M	N	O
10	–	60	120	210	300											
15	–	35	70	110	160	225	350									
20	–	25	50	75	100	135	180	240	325							
25	–	20	35	55	75	100	125	160	195	245	315					
30	–	15	30	45	60	75	95	120	145	170	205	250	310			
35	310	5	15	25	40	50	60	80	100	120	140	160	190	220	270	310
40	200	5	15	25	30	40	50	70	80	100	110	130	150	170	200	
50	100	–	10	15	25	30	40	50	60	70	80	90	100			
60	60	–	10	15	20	25	30	40	50	55	60					
70	50	–	5	10	15	20	30	35	40	45	50					
80	40	–	5	10	15	20	25	30	35	40						
90	30	–	5	10	12	15	20	25	30							
100	25	–	5	7	10	15	20	22	25							
110	20	–	–	5	10	13	15	20								
120	15	–	–	5	10	12	15									
130	10	–	–	5	8	10										
140	10	–	–	5	7	10										
150	5	–	–	5												
160	5	–	–	–	5											
170	5	–	–	–	5											
180	5	–	–	–	5											
190	5	–	–	–	5											

TABLE 1-11 "NO DECOMPRESSION" LIMITS AND REPETITIVE GROUP DESIGNATION TABLE FOR "NO DECOMPRESSION" AIR DIVES

CAUTION:

THESE "RESIDUAL NITROGEN TIMES" ARE THE TIMES A DIVER MUST ASSUME HE HAS ALREADY SPENT ON THE BOTTOM BEFORE HE STARTS A REPETITIVE DIVE TO A SPECIFIC DEPTH.

—— INSTRUCTIONS ——

ALL TABULATED BOTTOM TIMES (MINUTES), AND ALL TABULATED DEPTHS (FEET) HAVE BEEN TAKEN FROM THE U. S. NAVY DIVING MANUAL OF MARCH 1970.

1 TO CALCULATE A REPETITIVE DIVE UPON SURFACING FOR DIVES INVOLVING EXPOSURES UP TO AND INCLUDING THE "NO DECOMPRESSION LIMITS": ENTER TABLE 1-11 ON THE EXACT OR NEXT GREATER DEPTH THAN THAT TO WHICH EXPOSED, AND SELECT THE LISTED EXPOSURE TIME EXACT OR NEXT GREATER THAN THE ACTUAL EXPOSURE TIME. THE REPETITIVE GROUP DESIGNATION IS INDICATED BY THE LETTER AT THE HEAD OF THE VERTICAL COLUMN WHERE THE SELECTED EXPOSURE TIME IS LISTED.

2 CONTINUE THE VERTICAL MOTION ALONG THE STRAIGHT LINES JOINING TABLE 1-11 TO TABLE 1-12. ENTER THE TABLE VERTICALLY TO SELECT THE ELAPSED SURFACE INTERVAL TIME. THE NEW REPETITIVE GROUP DESIGNATION FOR THE SURFACE INTERVAL IS TO THE RIGHT OF THE HORIZONTAL COLUMN WHERE THE ELAPSED SURFACE INTERVAL TIME IS LISTED.

3 CONTINUE THE RIGHTHANDED MOTION TO ENTER 1-13 ON THE HORIZONTAL COLUMN TO THE RIGHT OF THE NEW REPETITIVE GROUP DESIGNATION. THE TIME IN EACH VERTICAL COLUMN IS THE RESIDUAL NITROGEN TIME. IT IS A PENALTY TIME; ie, THE TIME A DIVER MUST ASSUME HE HAS ALREADY SPENT ON THE BOTTOM BEFORE HE STARTS A REPETITIVE DIVE TO THE DEPTH SPECIFIED AT THE BOTTOM OF THE COLUMN.

C. AIR PURITY REQUIREMENTS FOR UNDERWATER BREATHING *

1. The subsequent paragraphs briefly describe the minimum specification requirements for air to be used for sport diving activities. This includes atmospheric air as well as air synthesized by blending oxygen and nitrogen in the proper proportions.

A detailed description of the several grades of air available will be found in CGA Pamphlet G-7.1 which can be ordered from the Compressed Gas Association, Inc., 500 Fifth Avenue, New York, New York 10036. This pamphlet covers specification requirements for all types and grades of air which are commercially available and for which an end usage has been established through combined industrial experience. It does not attempt to recommend or establish end-usage designations for specific types or grades of air, since such decisions must be made by the user. Consideration of this information has caused the Z-86 Committee of American National Standards Institute (ANSI) to designate Grade E as the minimum quality of air to be used for sports diving activities.

A companion Pamphlet G-7, which can be ordered from the same source, discusses precautions that should be taken when air is used for breathing purposes.

2. Limiting characteristics in Grade E breathing air:

a. Oxygen percentage by volume—19 to 23 (balance predominantly nitrogen).

b. The water content of compressed air required may vary with the intended use from *saturated* to *very dry*. If a specific water limit is required, it should be specified as a limiting dewpoint or concentration in parts per million by volume. Dewpoint is normally expressed in temperature °F. at one atmosphere absolute pressure. A conversion table equating °F, °C, and parts per million by volume is shown below:

Dew Point °F.	Dew Point °C.	PPM (V/V)	MG/LIT
—110	—78.9	0.58	0.00045
—105	—76.1	0.94	0.00070
—100	—73.3	1.5	0.0011
—95	—70.5	2.3	0.0017
—90	—67.8	3.2	0.0024
—85	—65.0	5.0	0.0037
—80	—62.2	7.1	0.0055
—75	—59.4	10.6	0.0079
—70	—56.7	16.1	0.012
—65	—53.9	24.2	0.018
—60	—51.1	30.9	0.023
—55	—48.3	43.0	0.032
—50	—45.6	60.5	0.045
—45	—42.8	87.3	0.065

* Promulgated by Z-86 Committee.

Conversion Table—*Continued*

Dew Point °F.	Dew Point °C.	PPM (V/V)	MG/LIT
—40	—40.0	121	0.09
—35	--37.2	161	0.12
—30	—34.4	229	0.17
—25	—31.6	382	0.21
—20	—28.9	403	0.30
—15	—26.1	538	0.40
—10	—23.3	685	0.51
—5	—20.5	900	0.67
—0	—17.8	1,180	0.88

Moisture Conversion Data (all referred to 70° F. and 14.7 psig):

c. Condensed hydrocarbons—5 parts per million by volume

d. Carbon monoxide—10 parts per million by volume

e. Carbon dioxide—500 parts per million by volume

f. Odor is difficult to measure. Breathing air should be free of any pronounced odor.

3. There are several adequate analytical techniques used to determine the content of each constituent of air. These procedures are described in CGA Pamphlet G-7.1 referred to earlier.

A relatively inexpensive way to check the carbon monoxide and carbon dioxide content is with an apparatus employing a comparison tube filled with a color reactive tube. (Two manufacturers of this type of equipment are the Mine Safety Appliances Co. of Pittsburgh, Pa. and Unico Environmental Instruments, Inc. of Fall River, Mass. Undoubtedly there are other manufacturers of whom we are not aware.)

D. AMERICAN NATIONAL STANDARD MINIMUM COURSE CONTENT FOR SAFE SCUBA DIVING INSTRUCTION *

1. Scope and Purpose

This standard provides minimum course content requirements for safe scuba (self-contained underwater breathing apparatus) instructions in sport diving. The requirements set forth herein should, under no conditions, be considered as standards for optimum training in the use of scuba. Instructional programs which extend beyond these dequirements should, in fact, be encouraged.

The requirements of this standard are meant to be comprehensive but general in nature. That is, the standard presents all the subject areas essential for minimum scuba training in sport diving, but it does not give a detailed listing of the skills and information encompassed by each area. For example, these minimum specifications require that a basic skin and scuba course should cover the physical description, operating principles, use, and maintenance of at least fifteen equipment items. These items are simply listed in the standard; it is assumed that detailed course outlines which meet this standard would include specific techniques for the use and maintenance of each item.

Although the information categories outlined herein are given in what may appear to be a logical sequence, the outline should not be reviewed as a lesson plan. That is, the order in which the information is presented in this standard, while important, should not necessarily define the sequence of a class lesson plan. Similarly, the requirements presented in this document do not

*This standard is one of a series of American National Standards on underwater safety. American National Standards Committee Z-86 was initiated on July 13, 1961, under the secretariat of the Compressed Gas Association. On March 25, 1968, the Council for National Cooperation in Aquatics became secretariat of the Z-86 project.

The Z-86.3 Subcommittee on Safe Diving Instruction consists of representatives from each of the major organizations involved in sport diver instruction on a national basis, as well as other individuals with personal expertise in the field. Representatives of localized instructor groups with notable reputations and interest are also consulted. Work sessions were held at regularly scheduled meetings of the Z-86 Standards Committee, at special meetings of the subcommittee, and in connection with a variety of national conventions and conferences which brought together a large number of persons concerned with sport diver instruction. The chairman of the subcommittee also corresponded and met individually with those in a position to contribute to the standard. Late in September of 1971, a major draft review and work session was held with the top management of the four major national instructor organizations. Specific questions raised at that meeting were resolved on an individual basis during the next few months. Early in 1972 the standard was submitted to the Standard Institute for approval. It was approved as an American National Standard on August 31, 1972.

This material is reproduced with permission from American National Standard Minimum Course Content for Safe Scuba Diving Instruction Z-86.3-1972 copyright 1972 by the American National Standards Institute, copies of which may by obtained from the American National Standards Institute, 1430 Broadway, New York, N.Y. 10018.

indicate the emphasis which should be placed upon a particular subject area, or the manner in which these subjects are to be taught. Course outlines, lesson plans, and other training aids prepared by nationally recognized organizations responsible for sport diver training should be used as guidelines for the sequencing and emphasis of course content requirements presented in this standard. Decisions as to sequencing and emphasis should be left to the discretion of the certified instructor and should be made within the context of environmental factors, student characteristics, and other relevant considerations.

For the purposes of this standard, basic scuba (open-circuit air) instruction is defined as that traditionally required for certification by a nationally recognized training organization. This certification, in turn, generally entitles a card holder to procure air, equipment, and other services by diving shops throughout the country. It is assumed that such individuals have received training in the fundamentals of the sport adequate to permit them to engage safely in open-water diving with experienced companions.

2. Eligibility for Certification

2.1 Prerequisites. In order to be certified as a Basic Scuba Diver, an individual shall meet the following minimum prerequisites:

2.1.1 Age. The individual shall be at least 15 years of age; there is no upper age limit.

2.1.2 Physical Condition and Watermanship. The individual shall be able to swim 200 yards continuously without fins in less than 6 minutes, and shall be able to stay afloat or tread water for 10 minutes without accessories.

2.2 Recommendations. In addition to the prerequisites for a basic scuba diving course given in *2.1*, it is also recommended that applicants for training have successfully completed a junior or senior lifesaving course, or otherwise demonstrated the ability and discipline to complete a formal aquatic course involving both classroom and water activities.

It is also strongly recommended that the candidate for training be certified as medically fit for diving by a licensed physician who has been appraised of the physical and medical stresses associated with this sport.

3. Minimum Course Content

3.1 Prerequisite and Introductory Information. To the greatest extent possible the following information should be made available to students prior to the first class meeting, and then reiterated at that time:

- I. Course prerequisites (see *2.1*)
- II. Scope of course
  - A. Content
  - B. Limitations of eventual qualification
- III. Equipment requirements
- IV. Safety regulations and other course procedures

3.2 Equipment. Students to be certified should demonstrate a basic understanding of the physical description, operating principles, maintenance, and competent use of the items listed in *3.2*. The subcategories of information which should be taught about the face mask are presented as an example of recommended course detail in covering physical description, maintenance, and competent use of each equipment item.

- I. Face mask
  - A. Physical description
    1. Lens
    2. Skirt
    3. Band
    4. Strap
    5. Anchor
    6. Equalizer
    7. Purge
    8. Shape
    9. Contour

- B. Maintenance
  1. Inspection
  2. Cleaning
  3. Storage
- C. Use
  1. Donning
  2. Sealing
  3. Pressure equalization
  4. Clearing
  5. Defogging

II. Fins
III. Snorkel
IV. Inflatable flotation vests
V. Exposure suits
VI. Weights and belt
VII. Float and flag
VIII. Knife
IX. Scuba
- A. Tanks
- B. Valves
  1. Spring-loaded reserve
  2. Other
- C. Demand regulators
- D. Submersible pressure gage
- E. Backpacks and quick-release harness

X. Other accessory items. Students to be certified should demonstrate general familiarity with:
- A. Compass
- B. Depth gage
- C. Spear Gun
- D. Decompression meter

3.3 Physics of Diving. Students to be certified should demonstrate a basic understanding of the physical principles of matter and their application to diving activities and hazards.

I. Acoustics
II. Vision
III. Buoyancy
IV. Gas laws–air consumption
V. Heat loss

3.4 Medical Problems Related to Diving. Students to be certified should demonstrate a basic understanding of the cause, symptoms, first aid and treatment, and prevention of the medical problems listed in *3.4.* Discussion of cause, symptoms, first aid and treatment, and prevention should cover those issues described in nationally recognized textbooks.

I. Direct effects of pressure (mechanical)
- A. Descent
  1. Ears
  2. Sinuses
  3. Mask
  4. Lungs
  5. Suit
  6. Teeth
  7. Stomach and intestines
- B. Ascent
  1. Gas expansion (ears, sinuses, lungs, stomach and intestines)
  2. Lung overexpansion (air embolism and related accidents, including mediastinal emphysema, pneumothorax, and subcutaneous emphysema)

II. Indirect effects of pressure (physiological)
- A. Decompression sickness
- B. Nitrogen narcosis
- C. Carbon dioxide toxicity
  1. Breath-holding
  2. Scuba diving
- D. Oxygen toxicity
- E. Anoxia–breath-holding
- F. Carbon monoxide toxicity

III. Other hazards
- A. Fatigue and exhaustion
- B. Exposure
- C. Drowning
- D. Cramps
- E. Injuries due to marine life
  1. Bites
  2. Poisonous seafoods, stings, and punctures
  3. Venom
  4. Mechanical injuries (abrasions, etc.)
- F. Voluntary hyperventilation and shallow-water blackout
- G. Involuntary hyperventilation

3.5 Scuba Water Skills. Students to be certified should demonstrate the ability to competently perform the following skills:

I. Entry
II. Descent and ascent, including pressure equalization
III. Underwater swimming
IV. Mask-clearing
V. Mouthpiece-clearing—snorkel and regulator
VI. Buddy system, including buddy breathing
VII. Underwater and surface vest and buoyancy control
VIII. Underwater problem-solving
IX. Full-gear surface-snorkel swimming
X. Weight-belt ditching
XI. Gear removal and replacement in water
XII. Emergency ascent

3.6 Use of Diving Tables. Students to be certified should demonstrate the ability to determine no-decompression limits and general familiarity with tables used to solve problems regarding:

I. Decompression
II. Repetitive dives

3.7 Diving Environment. Students to be certified should demonstrate knowledge of local and general conditions and their best possible effect on the diver with regard to the following:

I. Water
 A. Temperature
 B. Clarity
 C. Movements (surface action, currents, tides, etc.)
 D. Density
II. Topography
 A. Bottoms
 B. Shorelines
III. Marine and Aquatic Life
 A. Animal
 B. Plant

3.8 General Information and Procedures. Students to be certified should demonstrate a working knowledge of the following:

I. Dive planning
II. Use of equipment accessories
III. Communications, both underwater and on the surface
IV. Surface survival techniques
V. Skin and scuba rescue techniques
VI. Diving-related first aid
VII. Safe shore and boat diving procedures

3.9 Open-Water Training. Students to be certified must demonstrate the ability to comfortably adapt to the diving environment in scuba gear. Skills to be demonstrated should include items I through IX of *3.5,* except for buddy breathing.

E. UNDERWATER ACCIDENT REPORT

UNDERWATER ACCIDENT REPORT

Forward report to:
NATIONAL UNDERWATER ACCIDENT DATA CENTER
P.O. Box 68 — Kingston, R. I. 02881

VICTIM INFORMATION

Name of Victim: ....
Last First Middle

Address: ....

.... State ....

Victim's Sex ..... Age ..... Hgt. ...... Wgt. ......

Marital Status: M .... S .... D .... W ... UNK ...

Occupation ....

Employer ....

LOCATION OF ACCIDENT

Location of Accident (use landmarks, distance from prominent terrain features. Attach Chart or Map if available) .... State ....

CIRCLE LOCATION
(By Code Number)
1. Ocean, Bay, Sea
2. Minor Lake, Pond, Slough
3. Quarry, Pit, Open Mine
3A. Cave
4. River
5. Major Lake, Pond
6. Swimming Pool
7. Great Lakes

TIME AND PLACE OF ACCIDENT

Date and Time of Accident ....
Day Mo. Yr. Use 24-Hr. Clock

Date and Time of Death ....

Date and Time of Recovery ....

Death Occurred in Water? ....
(Yes or No)

Autopsy Performed: ....
(Yes or No)

Cause of Death: ....

Medical Examiner ....
Name

....

....
Address Phone

CODE FOR NON-FATAL INCIDENT
Circle one only (A, B, C, or D) which best describes seriousness of incident. Important: Report all "incidents", however minor. Describe in detail on page 4. Include equipment factors.

A. Incapacitating injury rendering person unable to perform normal activities as walking or diving or to leave scene without assistance.
B. Nonincapacitating evident injury as loss of blood, abrasions, lump on head, etc.
C. Possible injury indicated by complaining of pain, blackout, limping, nausea, etc.
D. Incident with no apparent injury, (near miss, etc.)

DESCRIPTION OF DIVES AND ACTIVITIES

Description of all dives within previous 12 hours including accident dive.

Depth	Time Down	Surface Interval
....	....	....
....	....	....
....	....	....
....	....	....
....	....	....

Type of Diving: (Explain if Necessary)

Scuba ...... Skin ...... Other ..... Unknown .....

Others in accident ....
(Yes or No)

Separate report filed ....
(Yes or No)

At time of incident, Activities engaged in:

Recreational	.....
Commercial	.....
Under instruction	.....
Instructing	.....
Cave diving	.....
Spear fishing	.....
Photography	.....
Night diving	.....

At time of incident, Buddy record:

Diving alone	.....
Diving with buddy	.....
Buddy distance	.....
Diving with more than one	.....
Distance to next nearest diver	.....

Vessels involved ....
(Yes or No)

U.S. Coast Guard aid sought ....
(Yes or No)

(Give Details in "Description of Accident", Name, Captain, Address, Phone, etc.)

WITNESSES

Name	*Address*	*Phone*	*Function/Role*
....	....	....	....
....	....	....	....
....	....	....	....
....	....	....	....

Reported by:
Name ....
Address ....
City .... Phone ....

Other Contacts:
Name ....
Address ....
City .... Phone ....

ENVIRONMENTAL CONDITIONS

Sea: Calm .... Moderate .... Rough ....

Current: Slight .. Moderate .. Strong .. Direction ...

Wave Height: ... Water Depth: ... Type Bottom: ...

Water Temperature: (°F) ....

Weather: Clear .. Cloudy .. Fog .. Snow .. Rain ..

Thunderstorm .. Tornado, Hurricane .. Other ..

Wind Force .... Direction ....

Air Temperature: (°F) ....

VISIBLE INJURIES

Illustrate all visible injuries (cuts, abrasions, fractures, etc.)

....

....

....

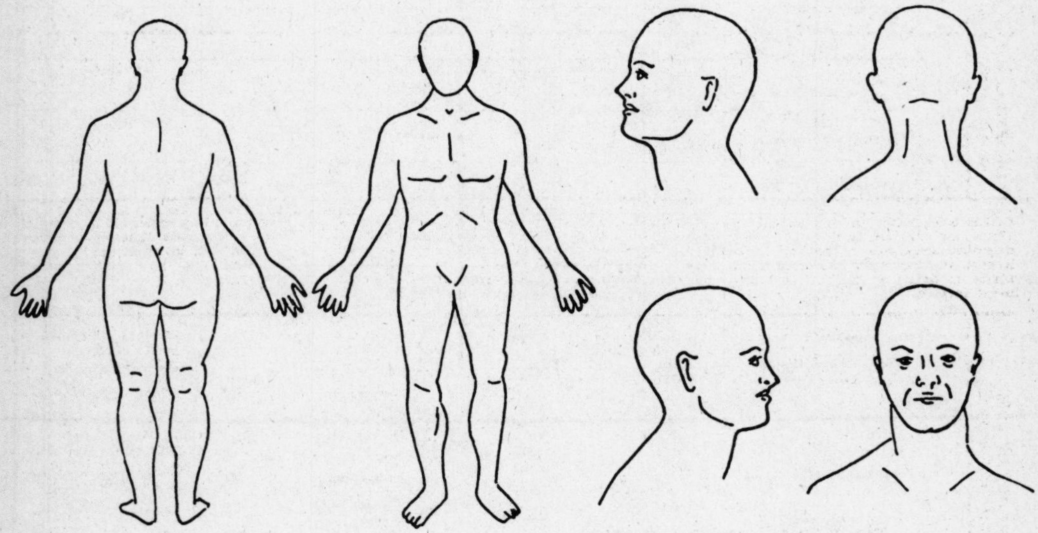

EXPERIENCE DATA

Swimming Experience: Years ......

Skindiving Experience: Years ......

Scuba Experience: Years ......

Courses and Agency

(1) .... Certification Date ....

(2) .... -DO- ....

(3) .... -DO- ....

HUMAN FACTORS

Hours of sleep in past 24 hours ....

Time of last meal .... What and how much? ....

Time of last alcoholic drink .... What and how much? ....

Any known physical ailments, disability or impairment? ....

....

EQUIPMENT DATA

NOTE: *Equipment Brand, Type and Serial Number data need be included only if malfunction or failure was contributory to the incident.*

Equipment Data Date and Time of Inspection	Brand, Type	Present Before Diving (Yes or No)	Present at Time of Recovery (Yes or No)	Condition	Equipment	Brand, Type, Serial No.	Present Before Diving (Yes or No)	Present at Time of Recovery (Yes or No)	Condition
Diving Suit					Knife (Posit.)				
Hood					Ab Iron				
Boots or Socks					Flashlight				
Gloves or Mits					Depth Gauge				
Mask					Spear Gun				
Snorkel					Compass				
Fins					Regulator				
Weight Belt (lbs.)					Tank				
Buckle					Reserve				
Flotation Device					Watch				
Other Equipment									

Flotation Device: Used ....
(Yes or No)

Tested after event? ....
(Yes or No)

Regulator Tested? ....
(Yes or No)

Results ....

Tank: Air Left .... MFG. .... Date ....
(PSIG)

Last Hydro-Test Date ....

Last Visual Inspection Date ....

Internal Condition: Clean ....

Slight Corrosion ....

Extensive Corrosion ....

By: ....
NAME ADDRESS PHONE

Special Comments on Equipment ....

Equipment Inspected by: ....
NAME ADDRESS PHONE

Equipment: Released to/or Held by: ....
NAME ADDRESS PHONE

DETAILED DESCRIPTION OF ACCIDENT

Describe in detail how the accident happened, including what the person was doing, any specific marine life or objects and the action or movement which led to the event. Include details of first aid or resuscitation efforts. Describe any "Decompression" and/or "Recompression-Treatment" in description of accident.

American National Standard Z-86.2 "Underwater Accident Report Form" approved by ANSI, September 27, 1973.

GLOSSARY OF SKIN AND SCUBA DIVING TERMS

"AB"—abbreviation for "Abalone."

ABSOLUTE PRESSURE—total pressure from all sources such as atmosphere and water. Usually referred to in absolute atmospheres (ATA).

ABSORBENT—a substance capable of taking something into itself. Rebreathers contain a chemical absorbent capable of removing CO_2 from expired breath.

ABYSSAL DEPTH—any vast depth. Prior to the invention of the bathysphere and other modern depth-probers, this designation was given to most depths over 300 fathoms.

AIR EMBOLISM—obstruction of blood vessels by gas bubbles. In diving, the term is generally applied to obstruction of a vessel or vessels supplying the brain. In this case, *traumatic arterial gas embolism* is more precise. The word *traumatic* indicates that the condition results from some kind of injury. In diving, the injury generally results from overinflation of the lungs, as may occur in breath-holding during ascent from depth. Gas is forced from the alveoli into the blood vessels of the lungs. The resulting bubbles are then carried through the heart and into the body's arterial blood supply. Death is a common end result of untreated bubble-blockage of brain arteries.

ADRIFT—loose from mooring or not held fast.

ALVEOLAR EXCHANGE—transposition of oxygen to the blood and removal of carbon dioxide in the alveoli of the lungs.

AMBIENT PRESSURE—pressure of water (including air pressure above it) upon objects placed in it (surrounding pressure). It is expressed in terms of Absolute Pressure.

APPARATUS—an assembly of materials or parts designed to perform a specific operation. For example, open-circuit scuba, arbalete, rebreather.

ARTIFICIAL RESPIRATION—any means by which an alternating increase and decrease in chest volume is created, while maintaining an open airway in mouth and nose passages. Mouth-to-mouth or -nose resuscitation is now accepted as the best method.

BACKWASH—often called "undertow" or "runout." Water piled on shore by breaking waves sets up an outward current. This is an advantage when entering from the beach.

BAR—an offshore bank or shoal forming a ridge above the bottom.

BAROTRAUMA—injury due to effects of pressure.

BLUFF BANK—a bank usually located on the convex side of a river's curve which is subject to vertical plunges due to underwater erosion. Hazardous to divers and surface craft.

BORE—a single high wave moving upstream at the mouth of a river. Caused by incoming tide opposing river current. Knowing tide tables will prevent divers from being caught by this phenomenon. Also called "eagre."

BOTTLE—hollow metal vessel "cylinder" used to contain compressed breathing gases equipped with narrow neck opening and retaining valve.

BOYLE'S LAW—the pressure of a given quantity of gas whose temperature remains unchanged varies inversely as its volume.

BREAKERS—waves broken by shore, ledge, or bar.

BREAKWATER—a structure built to break the force of waves.

BREATHING AIR—commercially prepared or machine-compressed air which is free of contaminants that would be injurious to a diver operating under pressure.

BREATHING DEVICE—an apparatus which enables divers to breathe underwater.

BUDDY BREATHING—the sharing by two or more divers of the same tank. An emergency technique used when one person's air supply is exhausted.

BUG—short for "lobster."

BUOYANCY—(1) the upward force exerted upon an immersed or floating body by a fluid; (2) neutral, positive, and negative. *Neutral* allows the diver to remain at a depth without effort. *Positive* will cause the diver to rise toward the surface, and requires effort to remain at depth. *Negative* results in the diver's sinking toward the bottom, and can be dangerous if not controlled.

CALM—a wind of less than one knot or one mile per hour.

CHANNEL—the deeper part of a river, harbor, or strait.

COASTAL CURRENTS—movements of water which generally parallel the shoreline. Such currents may be caused by tide or wind.

COMPRESSED-AIR DEMAND-TYPE UNITS—a breathing device using compressed air that is delivered to the diver through a regulator, as he demands it by inhalation.

CREST—maximum height of a wave.

CURRENT—a horizontal movement of water. Currents can be classified as tidal and nontidal. Tidal currents are caused by forces of the sun and moon and are manifested in the general rise and fall occurring at regular intervals and accompanied by movement in bodies of water. Nontidal currents include the permanent currents in the general circulatory systems of the sea as well as temporary currents arising from weather conditions.

CYCLODIAL WAVES—inshore waves that are short and choppy and forceful when produced by strong winds.

CYLINDER—in diving terminology, means a compressed breathing gas container. (*See* Bottle).

DALTON'S LAW—the partial pressure of a given quantity of gas is the pressure it would exert if it alone occupied the same volume. Also, the total pressure of a mixture of gases is the sum of the partial pressures of the components of the mixture.

DARK WATER—when visibility is reduced to a minimum by material in suspension or by lack of natural light.

DEBRIS—results of destruction or discard, wreckage, junk.

DECOMPRESSION—to release from pressure or compression. In diving, the term is often applied to the process of following a specific decompression table or procedure during ascent.

DECOMPRESSION SICKNESS—illness or injury resulting from formation of gas bubbles in the blood or tissues during or following ascent or decompression. In this case, the bubbles arise from gas that was dissolved in blood or tissues under increased pressure.

DENSITY—the weight (mass) of anything per unit of volume.

DIAPHRAGM—a dividing membrane or thin partition. The thin muscle separating the chest cavity from the abdominal cavity. The rubber (or other material) separating the demand chamber in a regulator from the surrounding water.

DISLOCATION WAVES—inaccurately called "tidal waves." Caused by underwater landslide, earthquake, or volcanic eruption. (Also called "seismic waves.")

EAGRE—*see* Bore.

EBB CURRENT—(1) the movement of tidal current away from shore or down a tidal stream; (2) a tide that is flowing out or causing a lower water level.

EDDY—a circular movement of water—in a comparatively limited area—formed on the side of a main current. May be created at a point where the mainstream passes a projection or meets an opposite current.

EEL GRASS—long, thin, green strands which grow along the coast in rocky areas.

EPICENTER—the term used in oceanography, wave mechanics, and other appropriate fields to denote the focal point of great waves.

ESTUARY—where tide meets river current. A narrow arm of the sea meeting the mouth of a river.

EXHALE—to breathe out.

EXPIRATION—the act of breathing out or emitting air from the lungs.

FETCH—"length of fetch" is the extent of water over which a wind blows and develops waves. The greater the distance the greater the possibility of large waves developing.

FINS—any device attached to the feet to increase area. Experimentation and ability will determine area and design best suited to the individual. Also appendages of fishes.

FLOOD TIDE—the tide at its greatest height.

FLOTATION GEAR—any device employed to support the diver or to add additional emergency buoyancy.

FLOTSAM—wreckage of a ship or its cargo found floating on the sea.

FORCED WAVE—a wave generated and maintained by a continuous force.

FREE WAVE—a wave that continues to exist after the generating force has ceased to act.

FUNGUS—a group of simple plants that contain no chlorophyll and must therefore feed on living or dead plants or animals. The parasitic fungi are most dangerous to man.

GAUGE PRESSURE—indicates the difference between the pressure being measured and the surrounding atmospheric pressure. The zero reading on the average gauge indicates atmospheric pressure.

GROIN—a structure projecting from shore that is designed to break the current and thereby check erosion and build out the shore by causing a deposit of new material.

GROUND SWELL—large, usually smooth-swelling waves.

GUST—a sudden brief outburst of wind.

HALF-TIDE LEVEL—also called "mean tide level." A plane midway between mean high water and mean low water.

HEMORRHAGE—any discharge of blood from blood vessels.

HENRY'S LAW—at a constant temperature, the amount of a gas which dissolves in a liquid, with which it is in contact, is proportional to the partial pressure of that gas.

HIGH WATER—the maximum height reached by a rising tide. The height may be due to periodic tidal forces alone or be augmented by weather conditions.

HOOKAH—a diving apparatus consisting of a demand regulator worn by the diver and hose connected to a compressed air supply at the surface.

HURRICANE—originates over water (as do typhoons) and consists of wind rotating counterclockwise at a tremendous velocity from 75 to 100 mph. Develops in a low-pressure center and is usually accompanied by abnormally high tides. May often travel 60 mph. Diameter may range between 150 and 300 miles. Such a storm will ruin safe diving in areas covered for many days, change shoreline and bottom contours.

INHALATION—the process of permitting air to enter the lungs.

INLET—a narrow strip of water running inland or between two islands.

INSPIRATION—the act of breathing in.

JETTY—a structure, as a pier, extended into a sea, lake, or river, to influence the current or tide in order to protect a harbor.

KELP—various large brown sea weeds (Laminariaceae and Fucaceae).

KNOT—velocity unit of one nautical mile (6,080.20 ft.) per hour. Equivalent to 1.689 ft. per sec. To convert feet per second into knots, multiply by 0.592.

LAND BREEZE—a breeze from the direction of the land.

LANDWARD—in the direction of or being toward the land.

LEE—a sheltered place or side, that side of a ship that is farthest from the point from which the wind blows.

LEEWARD—pertaining to or in direction of, the lee side. Opposed to "windward".

LEEWARD TIDE—a tide running in the same direction in which the wind blows.

LEEWAY—drifting to the leeward caused by wind or tide.

LIGHT BREEZE—a wind of 4 to 6 knots.

LIMITING ORIFICE—a hole or opening, usually of calculated size, through which the passage of a liquid or gas may be restricted within specified limits, as determined by pressure drop across the opening to control the rate of flow.

LONGSHORE CURRENTS—movement of water close to and parallel to the shoreline.

LOW WATER—the minimum level reached by a falling tide. The height may be solely the result of periodic tidal forces or further affected by weather conditions.

MARTINI'S LAW—a humorous "gas law" invented to help explain *nitrogen narcosis.* The "law" states that the mental effect of each 50 feet of descent, breathing air, is approximately equivalent to that of one (American-style) dry martini.

MASK—a skirted glass or plastic window constructed to provide air space between eyes and water and to permit both eyes to see in the same plane. The skirt makes contour contact with the face, preserving air space. Pressure may be equalized by breathing into the mask. The full mask covers eyes, nose, and mouth. The regular mask covers eyes and nose only.

MODERATE BREEZE—a wind of 11 to 16 knots (13 to 18 mph).

MODERATE GALE—a wind of 28 to 33 knots (32 to 38 mph).

NARCOSIS—a reversible condition characterized by stupor or insensibility. In diving, narcosis generally refers to a state of altered mental function ranging from mild impairment of judgment or euphoria (false sense of well-being) to complete loss of consciousness. In many respects it resembles alcoholic intoxication (see Martini's Law). It is produced by exposure to increased partial pressure of nitrogen and certain other gases, but the actual mechanism remains in question.

NAUSEA—any sickness of the stomach creating a desire to vomit.

NAUTICAL MILE—also known as a "geographical mile." A unit of distance designed to equal approximately 1 minute of arc of latitude. According to the National Bureau of Standards, its length is 6,080.20 ft. It is approximately 1.15 times as long as the statute mile of 5,280 ft.

NEAP TIDE—a "nipped tide" or "scanty" tide which occurs near the first and third quarters of the moon; is low because of the sun and moon pulling at right angles to each other.

NONTIDAL CURRENT—current that is due to causes other than tidal forces. Classed as nontidals are the Gulf Stream, the Japan current, Labrador, and equatorial currents which are part of general ocean circulation. Also classed in this category are river discharges and temporary currents set up by winds.

NURSING—*see* BUDDY BREATHING.

PARTIAL PRESSURE—the concentration of oxygen in air is 20.94 per cent. If the ambient pressure is 1.0 atmosphere absolute, the partial pressure of oxygen in dry air is 0.2094 atm.

PHYSICS OF DIVING—the application of physical laws and principles to man's activities underwater.

PHYSIOLOGY OF DIVING—the organic process and phenomena dealing with life and functions of organs of human beings while in water environment.

QUICKSAND—sand that is partly held in suspension by water. Varying in depth, it easily yields to pressure of person or object. Resembles ordinary sand or mud and occurs on flat shores and along rivers having shifting currents.

RECOMPRESSION—returning a diver to increased pressure for treatment of decompression sickness (*q.v.*) or air embolism (*q.v.*). This is properly accomplished in a recompression chamber in accordance with specific rules and tables.

REEF—a ridge or chain of rocks, sand, or coral occurring in or causing shallow areas.

REGULATOR—an automatic device for maintaining or adjusting the flow of air equal to the ambient pressure of the water.

RESPIRATORY MINUTE VOLUME—the amount of air inhaled and exhaled per minute to maintain proper body function. This is variable, depending on exertion and the individual.

RESIDUAL VOLUME—that volume of air which remains in the lungs after the most forceful exhalation.

RIP CURRENT—a strong current of limited area flowing outward from the shore. It may be visible as a band of agitated water with the regular wave pattern altered. This type of current is caused by the escape of water piled between shore and bar or reef by wave action. The rush of escaping water is accentuated by its flow through a gap in the bar or reef. Such currents are dangerous to the uninitiated and are the cause of many drownings at ocean beaches. However, when located by divers (skin and scuba) they are often used to facilitate entry to areas beyond the bar or reef.

RUBBER (OR DIVING) SUIT—partial or complete covering for the diver, primarily to insulate and preserve body heat. Classified as *wet* and *dry*. Wet suits of foam neoprene usually permit a thin layer of water to contact diver's skin. Dry suits (rubber sheet) prevent contact with water but require the additional insulation afforded by cloth underclothing (or wet suit).

RUNOUT—same as RIP CURRENT.

RUPTURE—breaking apart, bursting, as an ear drum under unequalized pressure.

SAFETY HITCH OR BUCKLE—any fastening device that may be operated to release with one hand, easily and quickly—a must.

SAND BAR—a body of sand built up by action of waves or currents.

SCUBA—*s*elf-*c*ontained *u*nderwater *b*reathing *a*pparatus. Any free diving unit containing necessary elements to support life under water.

SEA ANCHOR—a drag thrown overside to keep a craft headed into the wind.

SEA BOTTOM SLIDE—a landslide under water usually causing a tsunami, or dislocation wave.

SEA BREEZE—a breeze blowing over land from the sea.

SEA NEWS—rip current.

SEA PUSSES—rip current.

SEAWARD—away from land toward the open sea.

SEAWAY—one of the sea traffic lanes or routes; a vessel's headway; an area where a moderate or rough sea is running.

SEAWORTHY—fit for aquatic hazards; able to withstand usual sea conditions.

SEICHES—a geological term for "dislocation wave." *See* SEA BOTTOM SLIDE.

SHOAL—a place where a sea, river, etc., is shallow because of bank or bar.

SINGLE-HOSE UNIT—open-circuit scuba having a single intermediate pressure hose with first-stage pressure reduction at the yoke (tank attachment), second or ambient reduction at the mouthpiece. The exhaust is at the mouthpiece.

SINUS SQUEEZE—damage of tissue lining of air sinuses in the head due to failure of pressure in sinus to equalize with ambient pressure. Pain in sinuses is the signal to stop descent; rise several feet (pain diminishes). Try again cautiously. If pain persists, don't dive.

SKIN DIVING—diving without the use of scuba.

SLACK WATER—the state of a tidal current when its velocity is near zero, especially the moment when a reversing current changes direction and its velocity is zero. Occurs at high and low tide.

SNORKEL—a J-shaped tube, the short end of which is held in the mouth, the long end protruding above the surface, permitting breathing without raising the nose out of the water when swimming face down on the surface.

SPEAR GUN—any device which propels a spear from a gunlike frame. Usually rubber, spring, or gas powered.

SPECIFIC GRAVITY—the ratio of the density of a substance to water.

SPINDRIFT—sea spray sometimes called spoondrift; the spray and water driven from the tops of waves by wind.

SPORT DIVER—one who dives with or without scuba for game, photography, exploring, or love of the medium.

SPRING TIDES—the highest and the lowest course of tides occurring every new and full moon.

SPUME—frothy matter, foam, or scum usually collected at water line.

SQUALL—a gust of wind generally accompanied by rain or snow with nimbus clouds. Intense and of short duration.

STANDARD ATMOSPHERIC PRESSURE—the unit of pressure used in underwater practice and called one atmosphere.

STORM—winds of 56 to 65 knots (64 to 75 mph). Between gale and hurricane.

STRONG BREEZE—a wind of 22 to 27 knots (25 to 31 mph).

STRONG GALE—a wind of 41 to 47 knots (47 to 54 mph).

SUIT—*see* RUBBER.

SURF—waves breaking upon a shore.

SURGE—a great rolling swell of water, a violent rising and falling.

SWELL—a large and more or less smooth wave.

SYMPTOMS—perceptible changes in body state or function that may be indicative of disease or injury. Strictly, the word applies to changes perceptible to the individual himself, but it is often used to include *signs,* which are abnormalities that can be detected by an observer or examiner. Making this distinction is often useful.

TANKS—a term also used to denote containers of compressed gases. (*See* Bottle.)

THERMOCLINE—a temperature gradient. Especially one making a sharp change. A layer of water in a thermally stratified body of water separating an upper warmer, lighter, oxygen-rich zone from a lower colder, heavier, oxygen-poor zone. A stratum in which temperature declines at least one degree centigrade with each meter increase in depth.

TIDAL VOLUME—the volume of air passing in and out of the lungs with each natural inspiration and expiration.

TIDE—the periodic rise and fall of water level due to the gravitational attraction of the moon and sun acting on the earth's rotating surface.

TIDE RIP—wave and eddies in shoal water caused by tide.

TIDE WAVE—a long-period wave that has its origin in the tide-producing force and which displays itself in the rising and falling of the tide.

TOXIC—poisonous.

TROCHOIDAL WAVES—deep-water trains of waves that have great distance between crests with gentle slopes. They are the result of wind pressure, local or distant.

TROUGH—the hollow or low area between crests of waves.

TYPHOON—originates over water and consists of winds rotating in counterclockwise motion at tremendous velocity (75 to 150 mph). Develops in a low-pressure center and is accompanied by high tides. Seldom travels faster than 12 mph. Diameter may range from 150 to 300 miles.

UNDERTOW—a seaward current near the bottom of a sloping beach. It is caused by the return, under the action of gravity, of the water carried up to the shore by wave action. (*See* Backwash.)

VALVE—a device that starts, stops, or regulates the flow of gas or air in diving equipment.

VEST—a basic diving equipment essential. The majority of vests available are designed to provide positive buoyancy at the surface when desired and to afford buoyancy control by means of diver-initiated volume variation. Buoyancy control below the surface is maintained either by oral inflation or by valve-controlled gas supply. Few are so equipped as to provide adequate "emergency" inflation by gas cartridge at average diving depths.

VITAL CAPACITY—the maximum volume of air that can be expired after a maximum inspiration.

VOLUME—space measured by cubic units.

WAVE—an oscillatory movement in a body of water which results in an alternate rise and fall of the surface. These motions are the result of wind, water displacement (earthquake, landslide), and the gravitational pull of sun and moon (tides). Maximum height is called the crest or high-water phase. The minimum height is called the trough or low-water phase. The period of a wave is the interval of time between the occurrence of successive crests at any given place. The length of a wave is the distance between two successive crests.

WAVE HEIGHT—the vertical distance from preceding trough to crest.

WHOLE GALE—wind of 48 to 55 knots (55 to 63 mph).

WINDWARD—the point or side from which the wind blows; toward the wind; in the direction from which the wind blows. Opposed to *leeward.*

YOKE—a device for attaching regulators to cylinders so as to make a leak-proof seal. No more than finger pressure should be used to attach.

INDEX